COMPUTER SCIENCE, TECHNOLOGY AND APPLICATIONS

RECENT ADVANCES IN PROVIDING QOS AND RELIABILITY IN THE FUTURE INTERNET BACKBONE

COMPUTER SCIENCE, TECHNOLOGY AND APPLICATIONS

Additional books in this series can be found on Nova's website under the Series tab.

Additional E-books in this series can be found on Nova's website under the E-book tab.

COMPUTER SCIENCE, TECHNOLOGY AND APPLICATIONS

RECENT ADVANCES IN PROVIDING QOS AND RELIABILITY IN THE FUTURE INTERNET BACKBONE

NING WANG
GEORGE PAVLOU
AND
MOHAMED BOUCADAIR
EDITORS

Nova Science Publishers, Inc.
New York

For permission to use material from this book please contact us:
Telephone 631-231-7269; Fax 631-231-8175
Web Site: http://www.novapublishers.com

LIBRARY OF CONGRESS CATALOGING-IN-PUBLICATION DATA

Recent advances in providing QoS and reliability in the future Internet
backbone / editor, Ning Wang.
p. cm.
Includes index.
ISBN 978-1-61761-858-1 (hardcover)
1. Internet--Quality control. 2. Computer networks--Quality control. I.
Wang, Ning, 1974-
TK5105.875.I57R41683 2010
004.67'8--dc22
2010036157

Published by Nova Science Publishers, Inc. † New York

CONTENTS

PREFACE

Ning Wang, George Pavlou and Mohamed Boucadair

INTRODUCTION

With the advent of various emerging network services in recent years, mainly multimedia-based ones such as IP telephony, IP Television, live video streaming, online gaming, etc., the current best-effort based Internet infrastructure has become more and more struggling in providing comprehensive support for these applications.

Despite the QoS (*Quality of Services*) frameworks proposed in the 1990's, such as Integrated Services (IntServ) and Differentiated Services (DiffServ), large-scale deployments have not been seen across the global Internet till now, and this slow progress has significantly hindered the development of the relevant services. In addition, network resilience to failures has become another major concern by today's ISPs (Internet Service Providers), as QoS *assurance* to end-users may be severely impacted by various failures which are very common in operational networks today.

In recent years numerous proposals have been made towards the design of the future Internet that aims to offer guaranteed QoS, reliability and availability to end-users/customers, but without completely relying on the legacy transport platforms. Accompanied with this trend, new architectures, mechanisms and protocols on QoS, reliability and robustness have been proposed in the research community that can be deployed under such an environment.

Before introducing individual contributions of this book, the following section aims to provide a holistic overview on the *service delivery chain* in which QoS assurance are key components. The contribution of QoS and reliability mechanisms are essential for the delivery of services with satisfactory quality levels. Note that QoS is not a goal per se but a means to achieve service objectives expressed as pertinent KPIs (*Key Parameter Indicators*) which can be service-specific (e.g., IP TV, VoIP, Internet, Mobile, etc.).

SERVICE ASSURANCE: A KEY COMPONENT IN THE SERVICE DELIVERY

Now, the authors illustrate a typical tier-1 ISP's view on delivering service assurances to customers in the Internet business marketplace. First of all, two categories of customers can be considered: *Mass-market* and *Corporate*. Each type of customer has dedicated requirements with regard to the delivered services, especially in terms of QoS / QoE (*Quality of Experience*) and service availability. For corporate customers, these requirements are "hard" ones (and not "loose" ones as may be the normal case for "Mass-Market" customers). Pertinent indicators to let the customer assess the level of the delivered services should be provided by the ISP owing to the implementation of suitable service assurance functions. This practice is already implemented for some services such as IP Interconnection Agreements where indicators such as MTBF (*Mean Time Between Failures*), MTBR (*Mean Time Between Repairs*), MTTR (*Mean Time To Restore*) and OWD (*One-Way Delay*) are agreed between the Customer and its ISP. In order to meet these objectives (i.e., technical clauses included in SLAs (*Service Level Agreements*)), numerous resource engineering operations are enforced and associated means (e.g., tools, protocols, architectures, etc.) deployed to monitor and measure the outcome of engineered services. In addition, a NOC (*Network Operations Center*) is designated to intervene and to solve the experienced degradation or the unavailability of a service.

QoE assurance, and service supervision in particular, is a critical component in the service management environment and therefore in the value creation chain. Within ISP organisations, dedicated organisational and functional structures should be implemented to efficiently monitor and assess the grade of deployed services and also the grade of perceived delivered services by end-users. Appropriate actions are consequently enforced to solve encountered problems and put any disrupted service back to normal. Various tools (e.g., probes, reporting tools, etc.) are to be deployed to continuously provide feedback on the status of running services and potential operational issues. Enhancements to the current practices should be proposed in order to enhance the QoE as perceived by end-users and also to speed up the process of network/service anomaly detection and repair. In this context, automation is expected to be a possible feature to improve the supervision system and its methods. The introduction of automation does not mean zero-fault, but contributes to optimise communication between involved actors (in the service anomaly detect and repair chain), to interconnect all deployed supervision tools and to aggregate reported data, etc."

For its own operations, a given ISP should implement "Service Fulfilment" functions which are responsible for checking if the services delivered to the subscribed users are consistent with what has been subscribed by them. These functions may also be used as inputs to "Service Assurance"-related functions. Besides these "business"-sensitive functions, the ISP should be able to continuously, and preferably in real-time, control the level of its engineered/offered services. Indeed, network anomalies such as nodes outage, link failures, degradation of the QoS of voice streams, routing disruption, should be reported to appropriate desks. Ideally, the problem should be solved (or at least detected and handled) before receiving the complaints from customers.

Figure 1 illustrates the main ISP views to be considered when deploying network services. Each of these views represents a particular view in the life cycle of a service. The challenge for an ISP is that the delivered service (which corresponds to the "*Measured Service*") should be close to the "*Offered Service*" as agreed in an SLA. "*Measured Service*" helps to verify if the "*Engineered Service*" is aligned with the guidelines elaborated at the stage of "*Designed Service*" in order to deploy the "*Targeted Service*".

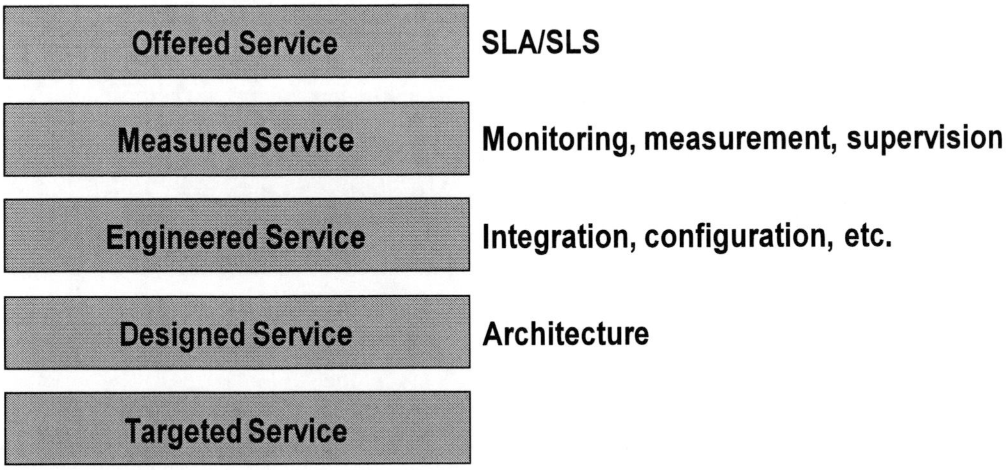

Figure 1. Service views.

The lifecycle of a service involves several actors with distinct operations and techniques. Each of these actors is involved in a time-phased manner. The "*Targeted Service*" is technology-agnostic and it is described as a set of service requirements and objectives. These requirements are then translated and accommodated to an architectural and technological view during the "*Designed Service*" phase. Once accomplished, appropriate engineering rules are drawn and required configurations are enforced. This phase refers to the "*Engineered Service*" stage.

Figure 2 identifies the scope of supervision and its role. In relation to Figure 2, supervision is the operation which ensures that the "*Measured Service*" is in conformance with the "*Targeted Service*". This assumes prior control operations have been achieved by a given ISP. Particularly, the "*Designed Service*" must be in conformance with the "*Targeted Service*" and the "*Engineered Service*" must be aligned with the recommendations issued during "*Designed Service*" phase. These control operations can be done by the network administrator or by using appropriate tools. Moreover, the enforced configuration should be evaluated and its sanity is checked. As an example, it is not acceptable that a mis-configuration is not detected before it has an impact on the offered services. In addition to this sanity check, validation activities should be undertaken to evaluate the overall behaviour of integrated systems.

Supervision is achieved thanks to different techniques such as measurement probes and local agents, which are distributed across the operated infrastructure. In such a scenario, information might be collected through both "push" and/or "pull" systems and also by conducting concrete testing activities according to pre-defined or new scenarios.

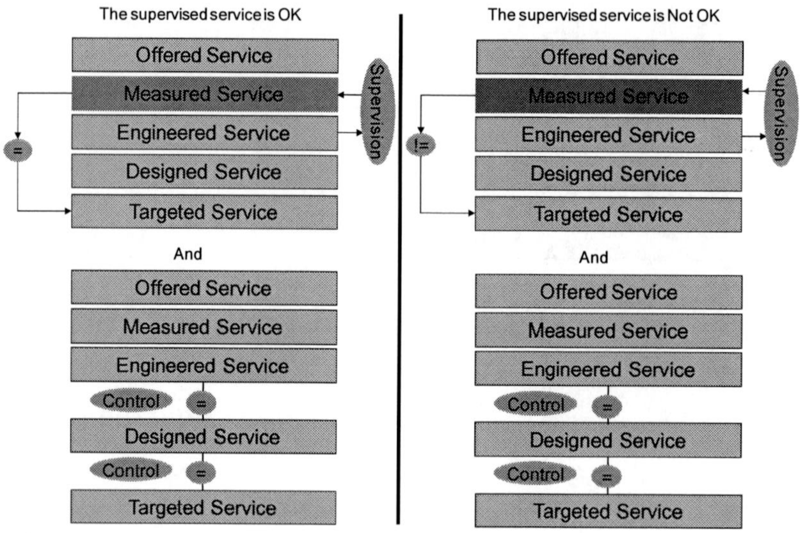

Figure 2. Supervision Role.

However, supervision is not reduced to the simple collection of data. Different treatments (e.g., data correlation) might be applied to this information and appropriate policies can be defined to handle it (e.g., classification, prioritization, etc.). Supervision is to be considered a (near-) real time function, as it must rely on the most up-to-date status of the network/service, in order to detect as soon as possible any anomaly occurrence. Therefore, upon the detection of an anomaly, supervision is to provide necessary information to qualify it and provide reports destined to the teams in charge of its resolution. An efficient supervision function should ensure or at least ease the following:

- Identification of impacted nodes and other deployed resources;
- Identification of impacted services and evaluation of the impact;
- Identification of the impacted geographic zone;
- Propose candidate actions;
- A highly automated process to issue tickets and notify privileged contact points (which may be applications, responsible for enforcing the configuration on operated resources).
- The supervision should be proactive: This needs that the appropriate probes, indicators, decision-making process have been put in place to detect any service alteration and then notify hot-line operators before receiving customer claims.

Some of delivered services may not be exclusive to customers located in a single country (e.g., limited to the geographical frontiers of UK or France) but can be delivered to subscribers located in other countries. Indeed, these services may rely on dedicated infrastructures deployed locally (e.g., ATM access infrastructure) or rely on some "portions" of service platforms located in another country (therefore with some limitations due to the location of these portions of the service delivery chain).

QoS and Reliability: Challenges to Meet Business Objectives

As indicated above, QoS and reliability techniques are key techniques in the delivery of highly available services with expected service levels as expressed in SLAs. Existing paradigms may not be sufficient to meet all service objectives (e.g., ability to ensure guaranteed QoS among a set of AS (*Autonomous Systems*), inter-domain monitoring systems spanning over several administrative domains, etc.), therefore new approaches are to be elaborated and proposed so as a complete solution for ISPs. Concretely, the design of new paradigms in supporting QoS and reliability in the Future Internet may follow either incremental or more "disruptive" approaches. On one hand, various resource management and control functions can be built on top of existing QoS-aware network platforms such as DiffServ (*Differentiated Services*). The ultimate goal is to provision network resources in an optimised manner in order to support specific QoS requirements specified in SLAs with customers. Currently two distinct research challenges have been envisioned as far as QoS provisioning is concerned:

- *End-to-end QoS across several ISP networks.* Compared with the scenario of resource provisioning within one single autonomous domain where the ISP has full view and control over its own resources, how to enable end-to-end QoS across multiple networks is a much more difficult issue to be tackled. The difficulties come from the following facts. First of all, each single ISP is not able to capture relevant information (e.g., topology, resource availability) outside its own network in order to perform inter-domain QoS provisioning independently. Secondly, individual ISPs may have their own policies in resource configuration according to specific service targets (e.g. with different types of considered QoS metrics), and hence it is difficult to simply "concatenate" QoS capabilities in order to achieve end-to-end requirements. Fundamentally, the key challenge is how to allow ISPs to "colla-borate" with each other in heterogeneous environments in order to provide end-to-end QoS with maximum mutual benefits/profits in the Internet business marketplace.
- *QoS assurance against network and traffic dynamics.* Most proposed QoS solutions in the literature follow offline approaches in the sense that network resources are pre-configured according to the forecasted traffic demand and QoS requirements (through SLAs). Such configurations will remain static during the operation time and hence it is not difficult to imagine how to achieve QoS assurance against adverse network and traffic dynamics (e.g., failures and congestions) will become a key issue. To accomplish this, two distinct tasks can be conceived. First of all, the network needs to accurately capture the current network states and conditions in an efficient way, based on which the appropriate control functions can be applied to change the network behaviour accordingly. Secondly, efficient online or adaptive QoS mechanisms should be employed for accommodating various types of dynamics in order to offer sustainable QoS assurances.

CONTRIBUTIONS FROM THIS BOOK

Individual chapters included in this book offer recently proposed QoS solutions in multiple and complimentary dimensions of the overall QoS puzzle as described above. These include not only inter-domain routing schemes for end-to-end QoS requirements, but also novel techniques that can be used for adaptive QoS control solutions in dynamic environments. In addition, other contributions include practical evaluation and analysis on QoS issues in real operational network environments as well as distinct use cases with specific applications.

On the other hand, network reliability is another important feature that needs to be considered in the design of future Internet. Nowadays, it has been widely accepted that network protection operation against various types of failures plays a vital role in offering seamless QoS assurances to customers. Broadly speaking, the following two requirements can be envisaged: First of all, the provisioning of protection solutions should also satisfy the original end-to-end QoS requirements such that customer traffic will not suffer from QoS deterioration both during and after network recovery operations. Secondly, relevant solutions should follow the "make-before-break" strategy in the sense that all backup solutions (e.g. protection paths) should be pre-provisioned a priori before the actual failure occurs. In this case customer traffic can be seamlessly diverted around the failure without causing any perceived service disruptions to end users. As far as future Internet is concerned, a new requirement is that the network should be sufficiently intelligent in *self-provisioning* of protection solutions rather than relying on manual configurations by network administrators. How this feature can be achieved will also be described in one of the chapters in this book.

HOW THIS BOOK IS STRUCTURED?

The authors aim to provide in this book an overview of the specific research issues and proposed solutions dealing with Internet QoS and reliability. Indeed, enclosed chapters cover a wide variety of areas, including: terminology, reliability and robustness, resource management, admission control, inter-domain QoS models, inter-domain QoS monitoring, QoS and TE (*Traffic Engineering*), performance measurements and finally operational lessons from real QoS deployment.

Hereafter, the authors provide a brief summary on each chapter that has been included in this book:

- The chapter *QoS Beyond Myth* aims to offer a comprehensive analysis on the fundamental concept of QoS from the viewpoint of a typical tier-1 ISP. This chapter defines the notion and the scope of the network QoS. Furthermore, it identifies specific issues that QoS paradigms are able to solve and those they cannot. This chapter provides also a list of the encountered practical concerns in operational deployments when enforcing QoS policies in operational ISP networks.
- The chapter *Differentiated Queueing Service (DQS) for End-to-End QoS Provisioning: An Evaluation from Per-flow, Per-class to Per-packet* presents an in-depth study on a variety of QoS mechanisms, including per-flow (IntServ), per-class

(DiffServ), and the newly proposed per-packet based paradigm, which is also known as Differentiated Queueing Service (DQS). Such a technique, being applicable in both backbone and wireless network environments, aims to offer granular QoS to different applications according to their end-to-end QoS requirements and path conditions with a scalable structure.

- The chapter *Admission Control and Network Capacity Management for Future IP Quality of Service* focuses on an important topic: Admission control techniques. This chapter identifies technical issues related to network capacity management, especially from the perspective of bandwidth allocation and the support of admission control for real-time traffic in IP DiffServ-enabled domains. This chapter concludes that the performance of the deployed tools depends on the topological placement of the employed bandwidth allocation and admission control functions. Furthermore, a new candidate algorithm is investigated for enabling admission control to achieve various objectives such as performing traffic load conditions without requiring frequent reconfigurations.
- The chapter *Performance Measurement and Optimization for Relative QoS of Multiparty Communications* focuses on multiparty communications (i.e., 1-to-N) in the Internet. The concept of multiparty communication is introduced together with a set of metrics to assess the perceived quality in such communication services. This chapter also specifies a QoS optimization algorithm for online gaming applications in the context of DiffServ-based networks. This algorithm is responsible for monitoring the delay experienced by all clients in a client-server based topology, and also manipulating the priority of each client's traffic corresponding to the network situation.
- The chapter *QoS Deployment and Operation on Super-JANET* offers useful experiences and lessons learned from the practical deployment of QoS in an operational network (the UK JANET) which is a QoS development project conducted from 2002 to 2007. This project enables the opportunity for academics together with JANET (UK) to assess the validity of QoS production on the SuperJANET network. Multiple phases have been taken into account: deployment, configuration, performance, operations and management, and the impact on services. This chapter indicates that while DiffServ-based QoS can be deployed on an end-to-end basis in large-scale networks, the required operational overhead could be significant.
- Four chapters in this book particularly focus on QoS provisioning and control from the Inter-domain perspective:

    - The chapter *An Architectural Framework for Inter-domain Quality of Service Monitoring to Support Service Assurance and Resource Management* focuses on how to deploy inter-domain monitoring system across multiple ISP networks. It defines a framework for inter-domain QoS monitoring in three domain interconnection schemes: the source-based, the cascaded and the bilateral models. The results presented in this chapter has suggested that in the source-based model it would be difficult to manage in terms of establishing inter-domain SLS contracts between adjacent ISPs, and hence to further perform end-to-end QoS monitoring and resource management. While, the cascaded and bilateral models make it possible to build IP QoS services on a global basis by maintaining contractual relationships with adjacent ISPs.

- The chapter *Interconnection Models for QoS-Based IP Service Offering* proposes and evaluates QoS interconnection models between neighbouring ISPs. New concepts required to understand and to establish inter-domain QoS interconnection models are defined and elaborated. In particular, both source-based and the cascaded models are discussed. The authors claim that the use of the source-based model for a large number of domains would be increasingly difficult to manage, and therefore recommend the implementation of the cascaded model which is more scalable. This chapter also describes a proposal to convey QoS-related information in BGP (Border Gateway Protocol) so as to assist the inter-domain routing decision-making process in order to select optimised inter-domain paths that satisfy specific QoS service requirements.
- The chapter *Inter-Domain Path Computation with Multiple QoS Constraints* studies a scenario where enhanced QoS can be ensured owing to the introduction of MPLS and PCE (Path Computation Element) techniques. This chapter describes two efficient algorithmic approaches for implementing multi-constrained inter-domain paths relying on the collaboration of individual PCEs located in several ISP domains. This chapter assumes that BGP paths are pre-provisioned, based on which the PCE machinery is enforced. Efficient heuristics are described based on an online computation approach, accompanied with methods to integrate the proposed procedures with existing protocols.
- The chapter *Combining Intelligent Route Control with Backbone Traffic Engineering to Deliver Global QoS-enabled Services* proposes a dynamic inter-domain route control (IRC) system for enhancing end-to-end QoS across the Internet. Typically, multi-homed (stub) domains may apply such a paradigm, assisted with path monitoring techniques, in order to achieve better QoS and TE performances. The novelty of this piece of work is a promising solution towards loose, or in other words, "better-than-best-effort" QoS through intelligent inter-domain route control and traffic engineering performed by "edge" networks in the Internet. Such an approach can be regarded as a complementary solution to the (domain-level) hop-by-hop PCE-based paradigms that aim potentially at hard QoS guarantees across multiple autonomous domains.

- Two other chapters are dedicated to network reliability design:

  - The chapter *Self-Protecting Multipaths (SPM): Efficient Resilience for Transport Networks* describes a simple but efficient protection switching mechanism that can be used in connection-oriented packet switched networks such as MPLS environments. The basic idea is to establish multiple disjoint paths between node pairs and apply optimized load balancing functions across them in various network failure scenarios. Such an approach is able to achieve sustainable backup network capacity against both node and link failures. According to the extensive simulation results, the protection efficiency of the proposed SPM paradigm outperforms a wide variety of existing network protection approaches.

- The chapter *Reliability Analysis of Protection Methods for the Future Internet Backbone* offers in-depth theoretical modelling and analysis for accurate prediction of relevant network protection metric values in backbone Internet infrastructure, typically optical networks. This modelling is supported by several distinct scenarios illustrated in the chapter, such as unprotected connections, unidirectional/bidirectional path-switching ring as well as shared protections. This piece of work will provide a potential tool of modelling generic network reliability control, in particular protection paradigms to be applied in the future Internet backbone.

While there is no doubt that this book is not able to cover all the emerging paradigms towards future Internet QoS and reliability, the authors do hope it is able to offer readers some flavour in relevant research and development progress in the recent years.

Enjoy reading this book!

Ning Wang, George Pavlou and Mohamed Boucadair

In: Recent Advances in Providing QoS and Reliability... ISBN 978-1-61761-858-1
Editors: N. Wang, G. Pavlou and M. Boucadair

Chapter 1

QoS Beyond Myth

P. Lévis
Orange Labs, 42, Rue des Coutures, Caen, France

Abstract

The main objective of this chapter is to clearly and unambiguously state what network QoS is, and what it is not, what problems it can solve, what problems it cannot solve, and to point out what difficulties are encountered for operational deployments. First, a double definition of network QoS is provided, then, the main QoS parameters characterising a network service are described; a special emphasis is then put on the notion of network congestion which is central to the QoS issue, a brief overview of the QoS mechanisms is then given (including DiffServ mechanisms), followed by some deployment issues, and finally, the last section gives some rules learnt from the attempts to make QoS an operational reality.

1. Introduction

QoS was a very hot topic some years ago with the work endorsed at the IETF, first in the IntServ (Integrated Services) Working Group (WG) [1], and then and foremost, in the Diffserv WG (Differentiated Services Working Group) [2]. Then, after the abandon of some ambitious efforts that should have led to QoS deployment in a large scale, like Qbone Internet2 initiative [3], the interest significantly decreased, making room for disappointment, and lack of interest. Many people even no more believed in the feasibility of QoS. To date however, little by little, QoS makes its way in ISPs' networks, but not in how it was previously imagined; rather in a more cautious and efficient way. It seams network administrators begin to understand and integrate the lessons learnt from the past attempts on QoS.

2. Two Definitions for Network QoS

Fundamentally, we can provide two definitions, from two complementary viewpoints, of the QoS notion.

The first definition focuses on performance parameters:

- The QoS is the set of values taken by the network performance parameters: one-way delay [4], one-way delay variation (a.k.a. jitter) [5], error rate [6], bandwidth or capacity [7], during the transmission of packets. We can:
    - Measure QoS;
    - Guarantee a certain QoS level.

The second definition focuses on specific mechanisms that aim to control the level of delivered performance:

- QoS is the set of mechanisms that can be added to a best-effort (BE) network, in order to guarantee a certain level of QoS (from the meaning of the first definition), for a targeted set of packets, and at the detriment of other packets.

The QoS mechanisms we are talking about are mainly those to be used in case there is not sufficient bandwidth and hence congestions are liable to happen.

We should not see as compulsory the activation of specific QoS mechanisms, according to the second definition, to be able to guarantee the users a level of QoS, according to the first definition. We can guarantee performance values in a purely best-effort network, to the extent that this network is sufficiently dimensioned regarding the volume of flows that crosses it, and correctly engineered.

3. QoS Service Parameters

We split the service contract (also denoted as SLA for Service Level Agreement), agreed between a customer and a service provider, in a set of elementary agreements. By definition, we will say that each elementary agreement or SLA (translated into Service Level Specification (SLS)) deals with a single one-way flow. A SLS is the technical description of the QoS given to a particular flow, during its transfer through a given network.

A flow can be defined as a set of packets that altogether build up a meaningful unit for a network manager. More precisely, see [8], a flow is defined as a set of packets passing an observation point in the network, during a certain time interval. All packets belonging to a particular flow have a set of common properties. A packet is defined as belonging to a flow if it completely satisfies all the defined properties of the flow, such as a set of protocol parameter values (e.g. the source IP address belonging to a given subnet). A flow can be the concatenation of several application sessions that have not necessarily the same emitting and receiving endpoints. For example: "the set of packets that carry FTP (File Transfer Protocol) or HTTP (Hyper Text Transport Protocol) data from a site A, to a site B, of a given enterprise" can constitute the flow of an SLS if the same QoS level has been negotiated for this whole set of communications.

The purpose of an SLS is to provide the customers with a framework where they can express all their QoS requirements, and from which the service provider can configure its network resources in order to satisfy its customers' requests. From a client standpoint, the SLS provides a technical description concerning the connectivity service that has been subscribed, but say nothing on how the QoS is enforced in the service provider network side.

There is a real independence, theoretically even a total independence, between the level of QoS actually delivered by the network, and the level of QoS guaranteed to the customers by the SLSs. The difference reflects a risk factor to take into account to optimise the ratio Cost/Benefits [9]. Trying to systematically engineer the network to get zero loss during 100% of the time, is likely to cost too much compared with the expected benefit.

To date, there is no standard definition for SLS parameters. Basically, in a SLS, the QoS Guarantees are related to:

- one-way transit delay;
- packet delay variation or jitter;
- packet loss.

The value of these three parameters are guaranteed for a given throughput level (or capacity).

4. Network Congestion

Congestion plays a major role in the quality of a network. When a flow traverses a router, the router can be in one of the three following states:

- "Empty" state, where the flow meets empty queues;
- "Loaded" state, where the flow meets loaded, but not saturated, queues (at least on packet), mainly due to the absorption of a transient burst;
- "Congestion" state, where the flow meets overloaded queues yielding packet losses.

If, and only if, we consider that the degradations brought by congestion phenomena are likely to be incompatible with the QoS level we want to achieve, we add in the network some relevant QoS mechanisms (according to the second definition) in order to reduce, control, and/or get rid of these congestion phenomena. When the network nodes are not subject to congestion, or are not close to congestion, the QoS mechanisms are not activated.

The activation of QoS mechanisms always benefit to some flows at the detriment of the others (if a shared infrastructure is used). Some flows will perceive the network as lightly or not at all congested (the ones which are protected by the QoS mechanisms), whereas some flows will perceive the network as heavily congested. This idea has been stated, in a very relevant way, by Van Jacobson particularly in [10]: *Give "better" service to some (at the expense of giving worse service to others - despite QoS fantasies to the contrary, it's a zero-sum game).*

These QoS mechanisms are efficient in case of congestions, but are completely powerless in case of other network perturbations like breakdowns.

5. Some Typical QoS Mechanisms to Overcome Network Congestion

5.1. Schedulers

Within a given node, the forwarding process consists in conveying packets from their incoming interfaces, towards their outgoing interfaces. Resources used by this process are:

- Internal memory (queues);
- Bandwidth on the outgoing link.

A scheduler is part of the forwarding process. It allows the allocation of resources in a flow-based way, mainly in terms of bandwidth reservation. Owing to Diffserv influence, when people speak of QoS, they often refer to this kind of mechanisms.

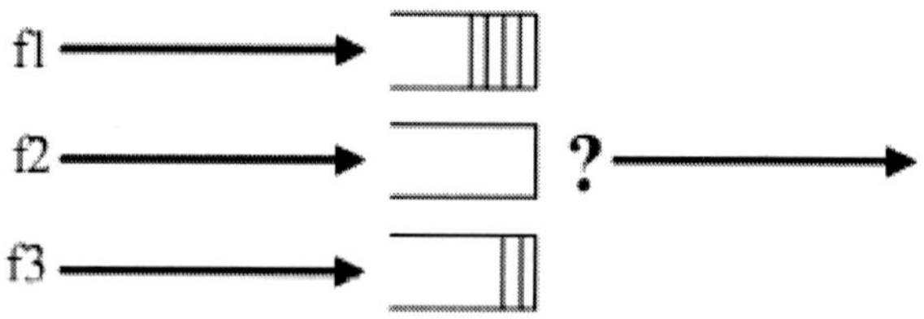

Figure 1. Scheduler.

Let's have three different queues, each queue is filled with packets that must use the same outgoing link. These packets can come from different incoming interfaces; they have been put in the relevant queue after a classification and filtering process, based on one or several well indentified protocol field values, in particular the IP Differentiated Services Code Point defined by Diffserv (DSCP) [11]. The level of flow granularity in a queue can range from a single application session, for instance in the IntServ approach), to a big aggregate (for instance in the DiffServ approach). At time "t", the scheduling algorithm will determine which queue must be emptied, and for how long. In other words, the scheduling algorithm will determine what bandwidth is to be allocated to the queue.

One main encountered difficulty is how to set-up and configure these mechanisms in an operational network. On one hand the QoS to be guaranteed is expressed in terms of delay, jitter, and loss; and on the other hand, none of these parameters is directly accessible when you configure a network node. In fact, a network administrator has access to the following parameters:

- The type of scheduling algorithm (e.g., Priority Queueing, Weighted Fair Queuing);
- The number of queues and their lengths;
- The bandwidth (BW) allocated to the flow of each queue.

An administrator never directly tunes in his routers the values of delay, jitter, or packet loss. The end-to-end parameters will of course depend on the routers configuration, but by no means, through explicit laws and equations. Actually, these values will be essentially known by network measurement.

Another source of problems is that the network handles aggregates (at least in DiffServ), the configuration is made on aggregates, whereas, what interests end users is how their flows behave, and not the aggregate that contains their flows.

5.2. Schedulers and Bandwidth Allocation

We propose a classification of different bandwidth allocation types to a flow, dedicated to a particular queue, in a scheduler located in a router. Let's consider the router placed at the entrance of a transmission link, a set of "n" flows, put in "n" queues, which want to access the transmission link.

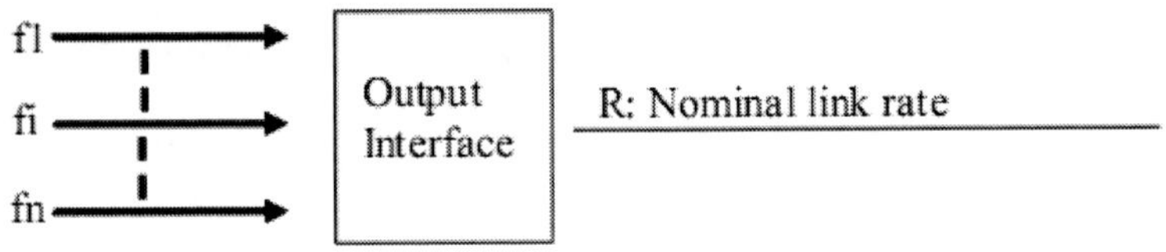

Figure 2. Contention between flows for sharing R.

"R" is the physical bandwidth limit (capacity) of the link. Let's consider a particular flow "fi". Figure 3 illustrates all possible bandwidth allocation patterns for this flow. Three allocation zones are defined: Absolute, Relative, and Prohibited. The points in the figure symbolise the value of the bandwidth used by the flow "fi" at time "t". If we make the size of the three zones in Figure 3 vary from zero to "R", we can graphically represent all possible strategies of bandwidth allocation.

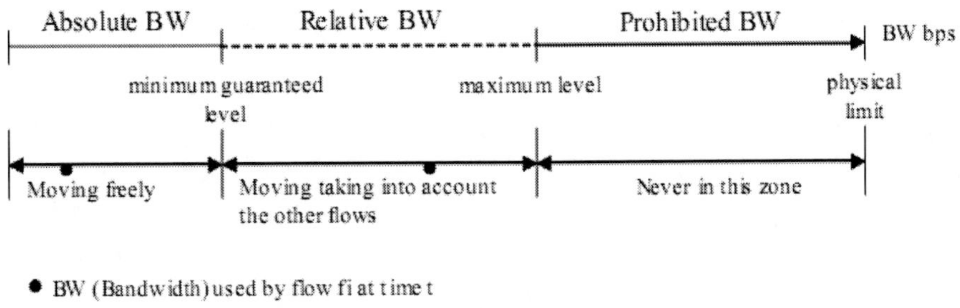

Figure 3. Bandwidth allocation types.

The "Absolute BW" zone defines always-available bandwidth for "fi", with a limit which is a minimum guaranteed level of bandwidth, no matter the current level (i.e. number of packets per second) of the other active flows is. The scheduler configuration of the minimum for all the flows, must conform to the following rule: Sum (minimal BW) $\leq$ physical limit.

The "Relative BW" zone defines a level of bandwidth exceeding the absolute minimum guaranteed. The current level of bandwidth availability depends on the current level of activity of the other flows. There are several possible allocation scenarios for relative bandwidth:

- No specific sharing rules are defined. The concurrent flows share the exceeding bandwidth BW in the spirit of the best-effort.
- A weight "pi" is assigned to each flow. In case of congestion, "fi" receives a level of BW according to the ratio of its own weight to the sum of the other current flows in activity.
- Sub-case of the previous bullet, each "pi" is in proportion to the minimum guaranteed BW. This is how the so-called Weighted Fair Queuing (WFQ) algorithm [12] works.
- Each flow is assigned a level of priority. At time "t", a given queue can be emptied if, and only if, there is no packet left in any queue with a higher priority. Actually, only the flow with the highest priority has an absolute BW, often restricted by the configuration of a maximum value.
- A level of probability of destruction is dynamically attributed to each flow. Typically, this level depends on the level of activity of the flow: the more active the flow is, the higher this probability is. The flows with highest priorities see their packets deleted first. This is how the so-called Random Early detection (RED) algorithm [13] works.

The "Prohibited BW" defines the maximum bandwidth a flow can be allocated. This value cannot be exceeded in any case.

It is important to note that, except for the maximum limitation, these scheduling mechanisms will modify the natural repartition of the current flows if, and only if, there is a congestion incurred by a contention between the flows. For instance, let "f1" and "f2 be" two flows of 3Mbps each, which arrive at two incoming interfaces of the router, and exit by the same outgoing interface, whose nominal rate is higher than 6Mbps. Suppose a minimum guaranteed bandwidth of 5Mbps has been allocated to "f1", and of 1Mbps to "f2". To the extent the router can forward 6 Mbps with no loss, the two flows will exit as they entered, with a rate of 3 Mbps each.

5.3. Diffserv Approach: PHB and PDB

A scheduler (enabled in a node) enforces a given behaviour with regard to packets traversing that node. More generally, this behaviour is called a PHB (Per-Hop Beahvior) [14]. The two most popular PHBs defined at the IETF in the scope of Diffserv are: AF (Assured Forwarding) [15] and EF (Expedited Forwarding) [16]. A PHB is supposed to be a description of the process of commutation, independent of the mechanisms and algorithms really implemented. However, the limit is not always very clear between what a behaviour is, and what an implementation of a mechanism related to a particular algorithm is. For example, from the Diffserv perspective, the RED algorithm can be quoted as a component of the AF PHB, i.e. as a descriptive element, because it is a public algorithm and not a particular implementation (as opposed, for example, to the Cisco implementation of the RED algorithm).The same PHB can be achieved by various mechanisms and algorithms. The PHB the router will apply to a received packet is selected according to the value of the DSCP carried in the IP header. Different values of DSCP can be mapped onto the same PHB.

A PHB is a minimum unit of component for provisioning services across a network To set up a service, it is necessary to deploy not only a particular PHB in the network nodes, but also other mechanisms and protocols, such as: an admission policy at the entrance of the network, the provisioning of a whole set of resources in the network, in a coherent way in order to deliver the proper service to the users. Two operators can thus offer two different services, if they for example apply two different access control policies, whereas they have deployed the same PHB in each of their network, because each PHB, in each network, will handle different traffic patterns.

A given PHB should not be closely linked to a single type of service. However, the definition of a PHB is often accompanied by the outline of a particular service which could rest on this PHB. That means, people who devised PHBs (mainly AF and EF) had indeed, a particular type of service in mind. In the same way, the EF PHB, in its strict definition, mentions only operations at the network nodes; it however loses any legitimacy if it is not associated with a tight admission control, at the border of the network. This does not prevent from assembling any type of service with any type of PHB, if it is considered to be relevant and feasible, even if at the beginning, the service suggested with this PHB was different.

The Per-Domain Behavior (PDB) notion [17] has been introduced in DiffServ, in order to capture the behaviour of a whole network (called also a "domain") in complement to the PHB notion that captures the behaviour of a single node. This information is of primary importance, because it is not the performance of crossing one node that matters, but indeed the performance of crossing all the nodes of a network. Unfortunately, this effort only started at the end of the DiffServ Working Group lifetime, and surprisingly, did not spark much interest and debate. Most of the people stuck to the notion of PHB, and never really integrated the notion of PDB. One reason is surely the one already stated in Section 5.1, the lack of explicit rules and equations that can bind a PHB deployed in the nodes of a network, with the PDB associated to this network.

6. Some Issues about QoS Deployment

6.1. Who Needs to Adapt: Networks or Applications?

Performance objectives can be achieved according to two different tracks: enhance the network, or enhance the application. Being a little simplistic, the first approach has been endorsed by people with network connection oriented (namely ATM) backgrounds, whereas the second approach has been advocated by pro IP people. The first approach considers the applications have strong requirements, historically coming from the telephone service, and considers that the network has no choice but to provide a tight QoS, unless the service cannot be delivered at all. A too stiff attitude in this position made, for example, that early tests that proved the feasibility of VoIP over the Internet, were completely denied by many ISPs. The second approach considers the best-effort service as the generic network service available to all applications, and considers that it can be enhanced to a certain extent and in a limited scope (DiffServ in some nodes). This approach strongly relies on Layer-4 mechanisms (such as in TCP) and Layer-7 mechanisms (such as error detection and correction codes, handled at the application level). This later approach has proven its efficiency in the current Internet, but also its limitation in case tight and sustained quality is the target. For the first approach, QoS in the network according to its second definition (see Section 2.), is the norm; for the second approach, QoS in the network is the exception (the norm being best-effort).

6.2. Where to Put QoS Mechanisms?

Typically, QoS mechanisms can be applied in three different areas: Customer, Access Link, and Backbone.

To each area, correspond one or several solutions.

- Customer Area. Solutions vary according to the nature of the customers: residential customers and enterprise customers. They are based, for instance, on switches with 802.1D QoS mechanisms, PCs with different priorities in the OS processing, traffic shaper on PC output interface;
- Access Link Area. Solutions are based on traffic shaper mechanisms;
- Backbone Area. Solutions are based on Diffserv,: DiffServ, traffic engineering.

The most sensitive area is often the Access Link. For instance, for enterprise VPN (Virtual Private Network), the flows inside the premises commonly reach 100 Mbps, whereas the Access Link rate could be much lower. A traffic shaper (based on a scheduler), can be put at the exit point of the enterprise's network, to allocate a different level of bandwidth to the different flows, according to the enterprise policy.

6.3. QoS Vs. over-Provisioning

QoS mechanisms allow, in case of congestion, to forward with a guaranteed level of performance, some particular and well identified flows (for example further to some SLSs negotiation). We can envisage a "reasonably provisioned" network with some mechanisms to isolate flows with the lowest priority, from flows with the highest priority (each gets its own demanded resources). The rationale is: many flows are not predictable and peaks can create some degradation, QoS mechanisms will carry these degradations forward, to the flows with the lowest priority.

Hence, QoS mechanisms would avoid over-provisioning a network. However, this statement should be somehow reconsidered. Some bandwidth must be reserved for QoS guaranteed flows, therefore, the higher the volume of guaranteed flows is, the more bandwidth is reserved. If a large percentage of QoS guaranteed flows is requested, then over-provisioning cannot be avoided; and more particularly, when the target is tight QoS, the reservations must be made at the level of peak values. The conclusion is that: QoS should only concern a little percentage of the total traffic.

6.4. QoS and Device Performance

QoS mechanisms like schedulers in routers, are only active when congestion occurs. If we consider router switching performance, typically the throughput, we can distinguish two router states:

- The router has no risk to act close to its maximum switching capability. For instance, consider 5 Ethernet input interfaces at 10Mbps, each interface is loaded with a 1Mbps traffic, all these flows exit in a single outgoing interface of a nominal rate of 2Mbps. The router is in a congested state but quite far from its switching capability. In this case, the activation of QoS mechanisms should provide the performance and the behavior expected.
- The router is likely to be close or over its maximum switching capability. For instance, let's consider the same physical configuration, with an 8Mbps flow on each input. The router may be over its performance limit for two reasons: the incoming interface cannot stand an 8Mbps rate (it is a bottom-of-the-range card and packets are small), the router overall switching capacity is lower than 40Mbps. In this case, the activation of QoS mechanisms in bringing even higher load on the processors, can only decrease the level of performance of the router. The activation of the QoS mechanisms cannot bring, in this context, the expected behavior, and the router can completely mislead and choose to delete the wrong packets.

Network administrators should not be in the (false) logic that QoS will avoid updating the network resources. To achieve an efficient QoS service, the routers must evolve in their hardware and software performance, in order to always remain under their switching capability. The consequence is that: the configuration of QoS mechanisms in routers is likely to go along with an upgrade of the router and interfaces capacity, which can imply a significant cost.

6.5. QoS and Security

The activation of QoS mechanisms in a core ISP network brings serious security issues. It is compulsory to enforce the exact QoS policy, to ensure that only the authorized users, the ones who have paid for the service, can benefit from the privilege treatments. It is also compulsory to control who, and how, is accessing the privilege treatments in order not to congest the resources and to avoid Denial of Service attacks. For instance, if the selection is based on DiffServ DSCP in order to differentiate the treatment, control policies must be activated in every ingress node of the ISP backbone network, especially in the access links where no SLS have been negotiated, and all DSCPs must be forced to zero.

7. What We Have Learnt from Experience in Operational QoS Deployment

Here is a list of issues that should be considered prior to any QoS deployment:

- There are maybe (certainly?) some more urgent decisions to take, than to decide to put QoS mechanisms to improve the quality of a network.
- Have a complete and thorough study of the reasons that motivate the deployment of QoS mechanisms in a network. Go one step further beyond some simple assumptions, such as: "QoS is what users want, users are ready to pay for QoS, QoS will bring extra revenues".
- Do not justify QoS mechanisms, with regard to over-provisioning, for economic reasons. Money spent to manage congestions in a network can be used to build bigger pipes. It is now commonly recognized that the introduction of QoS in a network is complex and expensive. It is, in no ways, a straightforward process.
- Make sure your network does need QoS mechanisms. There is a reasoning, which was for a long time the mainstream thinking, that says a network can correctly behave, meaning deliver a satisfactory service to the users, only, and only if, it is tightly controlled. It is why a mechanism such as CSMA/CD (Ethernet) was sometimes deemed as performing too poorly to be a long lasting professional solution, compared to Token Ring or FDDI (Fiber Distributed Data Interface), or other 100VG AnyLAN! So, be sure, if you add QoS mechanisms, that they will actually improve your network services.
- Keep it Simple: whatever you can be told, QoS at large scale is still an exploratory subject.
- Have a deep knowledge of how your network performs without any specific QoS mechanisms. This network assessment requires advanced measurement capabilities. It is the first compulsory step towards QoS deployment. Measurement will still be required, even when QoS has been enabled, in order to control the network performance parameters.
- Do not exactly match QoS service offering with network capacity. Actual performance of the network, meaning accessible from measurement, is one thing; the definition of QoS services proposed to the users is another one. A specific set of mechanisms should not systematically correspond to a specific QoS service flavour. There must be a coherency between the two, but not necessarily a complete similarity. To a certain extent, we could imagine a network largely dimensioned, which makes no difference between the treatment of the different flows, and on top of which a commercial offer is built with two different offers: ordinary service, and premium service. Two different commercial services will then be mapped to the same network mechanisms. This would be very similar to the fact that some clothes, which are cheap when they only have a generic brand, are expensive when they are sold in a luxurious shop, under a famous brand.
- QoS mechanisms are not mandatory all along the end-to-end path to guarantee a service. To ensure a guaranteed service through several networks, it is not always necessary to populate all network devices within each network (refer to the three

areas depicted in Section 6.2) with QoS mechanisms. A rather largely over-provisioned backbone, for example, can suit because the number of congestions expected is close to zero. Typically, the need for QoS mechanisms appears at the Acces Link. The lack of QoS mechanisms does not assume the lack of contractual agreement.

- Always reserve a large part of the resources to best-effort. The best-effort model allows any user to communicate with any other user across the global Internet. The best-effort model allows anybody to provide services accessible from almost anywhere in the world (anywhere where Internet is present of course). Lastly, the best-effort model allows anybody to access any global service. The QoS model, due to its difficulty in extending to multiple domains, is inevitably a restriction of this opening. To maintain services such as the Web, it is essential that QoS does not develop at the detriment of the best-effort service. Moreover, in terms of being attractive to the users, the choice of an operator can be done as well on the quality of its best-effort as on its services of higher quality. QoS should only concern one tiny proportion of the overall Internet traffic.
- Do not be too application-specific in the implementation of QoS mechanisms. The more QoS services to be optimized for particular applications, the more it will be difficult to make the network evolve to face the emergence of new applications, and the more it will be difficult to correctly stick to the requests from customers. For instance, the POTS (Plain Old Telephony Service), was devised and optimised to make phone calls, its adaptation to data communications has rapidly shown its limits.

Conclusion

QoS is a complex subject, especially as far as operational deployments are concerned. To date, it is mainly deployed close to the access, but not in the core networks. There are, at least, two major reasons. First, best-effort has proven to be an efficient service even for applications flows that require rather tight network performance parameters. Second, there is no magic math that makes it possible to tune each node in each network, in order to achieve exact predefined end-to-end values for QoS, such as: throughput, loss, delay and jitter. Lastly, the cost of over-provisioning is not necessarily bigger than introducing sophisticated protocols/algorithms/tools to set and configure QoS classes, PHB, and so forth.

References

[1] J. Wroclawski, The Use of RSVP with IETF Integrated Services, RFC2210, September 1997.

[2] S. Blake, D. Black, M. Carlson, E. Davies, Z. Wang, W. Weiss, An Architecture for Differentiated Service, RFC 2475, December 1998.

[3] QBone Premium Service, http://qbone.internet2.edu/premium/.

[4] G. Almes, S. Kalidindi, M. Zekauskas, A One-way Delay Metric for IPPM, RFC2679, September 1999.

[5] C. Demichelis, P. Chimento, IP Packet Delay Variation Metric for IP Performance Metrics (IPPM), RFC3393, November 2002.

[6] G. Almes, S. Kalidindi, M. Zekauskas, A One-way Packet Loss Metric for IPPM, RFC2680, September 1999.

[7] P. Chimento, J. Ishac, Defining Network Capacity, RFC5136, February 2008.

[8] B. Claise, Specification of the IP Flow Information Export (IPFIX) Protocol for the Exchange of IP Traffic Flow Information, RFC 5101, January 2008.

[9] B. Teitelbaum, S. Shalunov, What QoS research hasn't understood about risk, Proceedings of the *ACM SIGCOMM workshop on Revisiting IP QoS*, Pages: 148 – 150, 2003.

[10] V. Jacobson, Towards Differentiated Services for the Internet, Bay Networks Architecture Lab Boston, MA, November 25, 1997.

[11] K. Nichols, S. Blake, F. Baker, D. Black, Definition of the Differentiated Services Field, RFC 2474, December 1998.

[12] D. Stiliadis, A. Varma, Latency-rate servers: a general model for analysis of traffic scheduling algorithms, *IEEE/ACM Transactions on Volume 6*, Issue 5, Page(s):611 – 624, Oct. 1998.

[13] S. Floyd, V. Jacobson, Random Early Detection gateways for Congestion Avoidance, IEEE/ACM *Transactions on Networking*, V.1 N.4, p. 397-413, August 1993,

[14] S. Blake, D. Black, M. Carlson, E. Davies, Z. Wang, W. Weiss, An Architecture for Differentiated Services, RFC 2475, December 1998.

[15] J. Heinanen, F. Baker, W. Weiss, J.Wroclawski, Assured Forwarding PHB Group, RFC 2597, June 1999.

[16] B. Davie, A. Charny, J.C.R. Bennett, K. Benson, J.Y. Le Boudec, W. Courtney, S. Davari, V. Firoiu, D. Stiliadis, An Expedited Forwarding PHB (Per-Hop Behavior), RFC 3246, March 2002.

[17] K. Nichols, B. Carpenter, Definition of Differentiated Services Per Domain Behaviors and Rules for their Specification, RFC 3086, April 2001.

In: Recent Advances in Providing QoS and Reliability... ISBN 978-1-61761-858-1
Editors: N. Wang, G. Pavlou and M. Boucadair

Chapter 2

DIFFERENTIATED QUEUEING SERVICE (DQS) FOR END-TO-END QOS PROVISIONING: AN EVALUATION FROM PER-FLOW, PER-CLASS TO PER-PACKET

***Shengming Jiang*[1]**
School of Electronic and Information Engineering
South China University of Technology, China

ABSTRACT

The future Internet is expected to provide granular end-to-end (e2e) QoS to various applications in different path situations (e.g., path lengths). Many proposals aiming at providing granular and scalable QoS in the literature, such as per-flow IntServ and per-class DiffServ, rely on sophisticated output schedulers, which often require hardware implementation for high-speed packet forwarding. This may cause a scalability problem in increasing QoS granularity since the more granular QoS, the more complex schedulers should be. Therefore, a per-packet QoS provision approach, Differentiated Queueing Services (DQS), was proposed to provide granular QoS to different applications according to their e2e QoS requirements and path situations with a scalable structure. Instead of using sophisticated output schedulers, DQS relies on buffer admission control (BAC) for QoS provisioning. Different from output schedulers, BAC queues packets according to their e2e delay requirements to bind various delays upon their arrival so that service decision will not be made at the moment while the server is released. This chapter gives a brief evaluation on these three QoS provisioning approaches in terms of e2e QoS provisioning and implementation issues.

1. INTRODUCTION

Quality of Service (QoS) has been studied for more than two decades especially for ATM and IP networks. But this issue has not been well resolved particularly for IP since by nature IP can only provide best-effort services at packet level. The major packet-level QoS

---

[1] Email: shmjiang@scut.edu.cn.

mechanisms include scheduling and buffering [Guerin99]. Typical QoS schemes proposed for IP include per-flow IntServ and per-class DiffServ. IntServ provides granular QoS at flow level. However, such per-flow treatment needs to store voluminous information in routers, which is one of the major contributors to the so-called scalability problem especially in core networks. To overcome this problem, per-class DiffServ was proposed, which suggests aggregating flows with the same type of QoS requirements so that a router only needs to handle classified and aggregated flows instead of individual flows for QoS provisioning. The major disadvantages of DiffServ over IntServ include (i) lack of QoS granularity and (ii) possible QoS over-provisioning.

There is also lots of work to address the scalability problem of IntServ and improve the QoS granularity of DiffServ such as "stateless per-flow QoS guarantee", which provides per-flow QoS guarantee with less scalability problem [Stoica99, Zhang00, Jiang04b]. The basic ideas of those schemes include (i) allowing packets to carry flow state information to avoid per-flow information storage and per-flow call admission control (CAC) in core networks and (ii) properly re-aggregating aggregated flows of the same class from different links in a router using class-based schedulers. To trade off between QoS granularity and implementation complexity, a combination of IntServ and DiffServ has also been studied. However, these proposals still depend on sophisticated output schedulers for QoS provisioning. The major drawback of doing so is that implementation complexity will increase with QoS granularity so that a scheduler may become a bottleneck for high-speed links since it needs to make a decision on-the-fly for every packet.

In order to provide a scalable and integral solution for granular end-to-end QoS, a new QoS provisioning structure, Differentiated Queueing Services (DQS), was initially proposed to support end-to-end QoS in wired networks in [Jiang04a, Jiang05], and later was applied in wireless networks in [Teng08]. DQS tries to radically change the situation of packet-level QoS provisioning. Different from per-flow IntServ and per-class DiffServ, DQS is a per-packet QoS mechanism, by which, QoS requirement is clearly defined for each packet. By slightly increasing packet overhead, DQS can provide a scalable and integral solution for granular end-to-end QoS provisioning without using sophisticated schedulers.

This chapter will provide a qualitative study on per-packet DQS in comparison with per-flow IntServ and per-class DiffServ. The remainder of this chapter is organized as follows. Section II introduces DQS. The principle of e2e QoS provisioning of each approach is evaluated in terms of per-hop QoS services, QoS granularity and e2e QoS solution in Section III. Their major implementation issues are discussed in terms of output schedulers, queueing structure, BAC and CAC in Section IV. Some author's pre-mature opinions on QoS mechanism design are summarized in Section V. Finally this chapter is concluded in Section VI.

2. Overview of Differentiated Queueing Services (DQS)

Instead of using per-flow or per-class QoS approaches, DQS proposes a per-packet QoS approach, which is enforced through per-hop service. A per-hop service to a packet is determined by a node according to the QoS requirement of this packet over its remaining journey and the situation of its remaining path. An e2e QoS is just one of the combinations of per-hop services provided by each node of the path, which can be numerous to meet different e2e QoS requirements. A granular packet-level QoS (particularly delay) is provided by queueing packets properly in the buffer according to its e2e delay through buffer admission control (BAC). BAC is traditionally used for congestion control (e.g., RED [Lin97]) rather than QoS provisioning. Similar to the dynamic packet state approach [Stoica99, Firoiu02], DQS also lets each packet carry its e2e QoS requirement. In this case, whether the delay of an arriving packet can be bound is able to be perceived upon its arrival at a router. Thus, the router can drop early the packets which are perceived to surely fail in their delay guarantee in order to reduce resource wastage. For those perceived to probably fail, their service qualities are downgraded instead of dropping them immediately to reduce dropping ratio. Consequently, e2e delay guarantee becomes an issue on packet dropping ratio guarantee since each received packet is surely guaranteed in terms of its e2e delay and those that cannot be guaranteed are dropped as mentioned above. For jitter, it is supposed to be handled at the end-points of a network to simplify the implementation and operation of intermediate network units.

With DQS, a packet's initial priority (q_0) to be referred by a router is determined by its latest departure time (e), which can be approximated by its arrival time (a) and its delay bound (d) at this node as follows: $q_0 = e^{-1} \approx a + d$, which can be determined only upon its arrival. Here, the priority just determines the order that each packet will be severed. The priority function of a queued packet against time (t) is given by $q(t) = 1/(e - t)$, which means, when $t \rightarrow$ e, the packet must be served in order to bind its delay. If a packet has not been served after e, its priority becomes negative, which means that it should be either dropped or marked as a non-guaranteed packet. In the latter case, this packet can be queued in an FIFO buffer. This decision is made by BAC upon a packet's arrival to decide whether admitting it, downgrading its service quality or dropping it. Note that, d for a packet can be estimated by its remaining lifetime (R) and the potential delay over its remaining journey (r) to its destination, i.e., $d = R - r$.

In fact, DQS is similar to the earliest-deadline-first (EDF) scheduler [Liu01, Zhang01] in terms of ways differentiating service order. However, they are different significantly as discussed below. (i) Different from DQS, with EDF, a packet's priority always increases with its dwelling time in the queue. (ii) Like other schemes, EDF aims at a common delay bound for all packets using the same service. As mentioned in [Georgiadis96, Guerin99], EDF by itself cannot provide efficient e2e delay guarantee. With DQS, delay guarantee for both newly arriving and existing packets are the condition for a packet to be admitted to the buffer. (iii) EDF uses sophisticated output schedulers while DQS mainly relies on BAC for QoS provisioning.

3. End-to-End QoS Provisioning

This section compares IntServ, DiffServ and DQS in terms of packet-level QoS provisioning with focus on per-hop service, QoS granularity and end-to-end QoS solutions. Figure 7 summarises this comparison in its upper half part and details are discussed below.

3.1. Per-Hop Service (PHS)

A PHS refers to actions to be taken by a router in order to provide corresponding QoS to an arriving packet. For IntServ, a router will treat each arriving packet according to the QoS requirement of the flow that the packet belongs to. Hence a router can only provide flow-level QoS, which means that every packet belonging to the same flow will be treated identically by the same router. In other words, IntServ cannot efficiently handle packets with different QoS requirements from the same flow. However, IntServ allows different routers to offer different PHSs since a router can determine its PHS according to the availability of its resource subject to the QoS requirement of a flow.

To avoid the scalability problem of IntServ for implementation (which is discussed in Section IV.1), DiffServ adopts per-class QoS instead of per-flow QoS. With DiffServ, a PHS is defined according to the collective QoS requirements of particular types of application (e.g., voice, video and data) rather than the QoS requirement of an individual flow. Thus, QoS services are classified for different types of applications. A router treats each packet according to its class-tag and the packets tagged with the same class will be treated identically by every router. Furthermore, DiffServ suggests aggregating individual flows with the same type of QoS requirements into one. In this case, an aggregated flow should be served such that the most stringent QoS requirement of an individual flow can be satisfied. Consequently, each individual flow should be treated equally with the most stringent QoS by every router. This will lead to QoS over-provisioning to some flows. Similar to IntServ, since each packet from the same flow will be marked with the same class, DiffServ cannot handle packets with different QoS requirements within the same flow.

DQS is quite similar to IntServ in terms of its PHS, i.e., treating each flow differently according to its e2e QoS requirement. However, they are still different from each other as discussed below. With DQS, a router can further treat packets belonging to the same flow differently to further optimize network resource utilization according to (i) their different QoS requirements; (ii) their remaining lifetimes subject to their e2e delay bounds and (iii) the situation of the remaining journey such as packet's travel latency. This is thanks to that the QoS requirement over the remaining journey of a packet can be explicitly carried by the packet itself. However, for both IntServ and DiffServ, a router cannot adjust its PHS to a packet according to the above items (i) - (iii) since no information is available to routers for such adjustment.

3.2. QoS Granularity

Although the e2e QoS requirements of the same type of applications are identical, the difficulty in providing a PHS still depends on and varies with path situations, particularly the number of hops that a path consists of. In general, the less hops a path has, the easier for a router to support the same e2e QoS. As demonstrated in Figure 1(a), given an e2e delay bound of 250 ms, per-hop delay bound for a path consisting of 8 hops is only 31.25 ms while that for a path consisting of 4 hops can be 62.5 ms as shown in Figure 1(b). It should be much easier to provide a PHS of 62.5 ms than that of 31.25 ms. Given an e2e-delay bound of 250 ms, every node along the path can provide an identical PHS as illustrated in Figure 1(c) with 60 ms or provides various PHSs so long the e2e delay can be bounded as illustrated in Figure

1(d). The former is often adopted by per-class based schemes since, once the service class of a flow is determined, it is usually unchanged across the network. The latter can be realized by per-flow and per-packet based schemes, which can decide PHSs according to the availability of local resource with subject to QoS requirements. Such kind of per-hop QoS treatment can leverage the utilization of various amounts of network resources available at different routers.

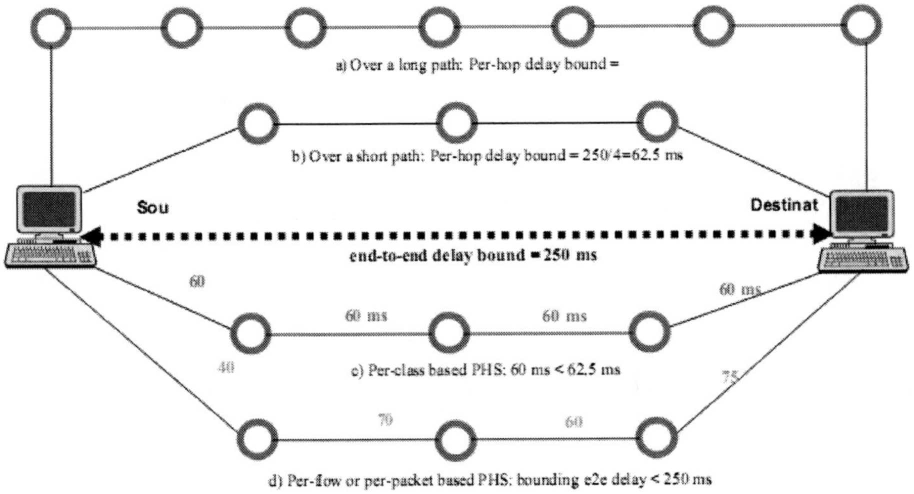

Figure 1. PHSs versus path situations.

With IntServ, a resource reservation is carried out for every flow by using the RSVP signalling protocol [Braden97]. This can allow different routers in a path to allocate different amounts of network resources to provide QoS for the same flow, hence different PHSs. Therefore, the PHS provided by IntServ can adapt to path situations but at call-level only since the PHS is pre-determined during the resource reservation process and will not be changed at packet-level. However, DQS can enable PHSs to adapt to path situations as discussed in Section II. For both IntServ and DQS, due to their flexible PHSs, the number of e2e QoS services is not limited since combinations of PHSs provided by all nodes of a path can be numerous.

Since DiffServ is class-based, it cannot provide e2e QoS granularity similar to those provided by IntServ and DiffServ. This is because a class is determined according to the nature of application types and the same class will be treated identically by different routers in a path. Therefore, a flow over a short path is classified into the same class as others over a long path if they belong to the same type of applications (e.g., voice). Thus, a flow may not be able to find an e2e QoS service that can well meet its e2e QoS requirements according to its current path situation. Furthermore, DiffServ also aggregates multiple individual flows of one type into a big flow. This makes each individual flow in an aggregated one to be treated equally with the most stringent QoS by every router. Both above treatments may lead to QoS over-provisioning to some flows. Furthermore, since the same class of a flow will be used by every router in a path, the number of e2e QoS services that DiffServ can provide is limited to the number of its PHSs. With the currently defined per-hop-behaviours (PHBs), DiffServ can provide only two types of end-to-end QoS, i.e., Premium Service (PS) and Assured Service (AS).

3.3. End-to-End QoS Solutions

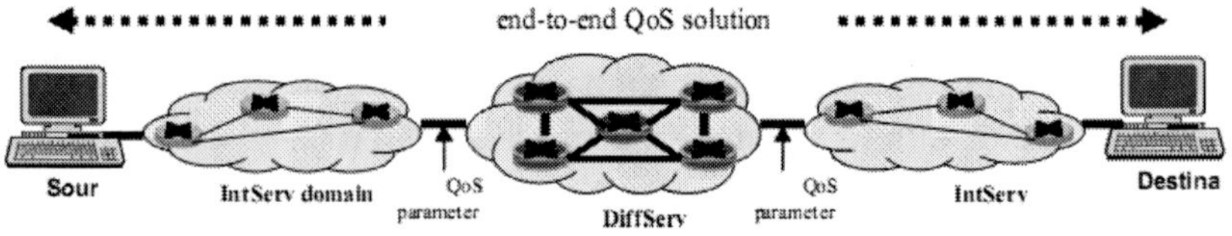

Figure 2. End-to-end QoS solution with IntServ plus DiffServ.

Since IntServ is not scalable especially in core networks while DiffServ cannot provide granular e2e QoS as discussed earlier, their combination with IntServ being used in edge networks while DiffServ in core networks is proposed to provide more granular e2e QoS than DiffServ with a more scalable solution than IntServ as illustrated in Figure 2. In this case, a conversion between QoS parameters used by IntServ and DiffServ is required in the interface between these two types of networks. This conversion not only increases network complexity but also introduces extra delay and loss, resulting in a new scalability problem, since this operation needs to be carried out for each packet. However, one consensus for next generation network design is to convert different types of networks into one such as the ***All-IP*** approach. Therefore, an integral e2e QoS solution across the global network is more desirable than a combination of different QoS support technologies.

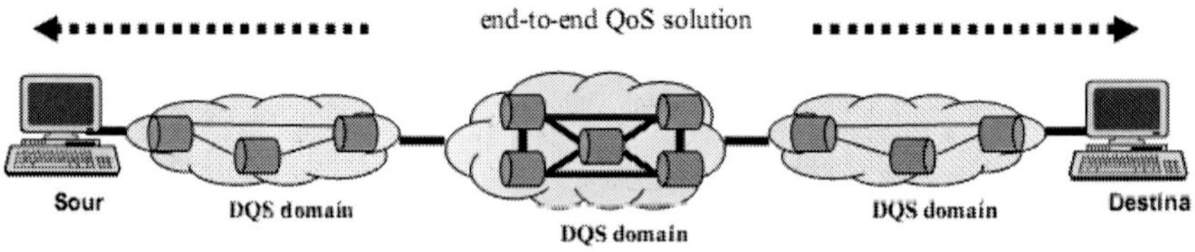

Figure 3. End-to-end QoS solution with DQS.

With DQS, the information on e2e QoS is carried by every packet so that each router that a packet visits will treat this packet in the same way by BAC although PHSs to be provided by different routers may vary. This processing method also avoids the scalability problem of IntServ caused by per-flow information storage and can be used in both edge and core networks. Here, a main concern is that whether BAC is scalable to the number of packets queued in a buffer for queuing operation especially in a core router since a large number of packets may be present therein. As discussed in Section IV.3, with a proper queueing algorithm, the performance of packet forwarding will not be affected by queuing operation. Therefore, the end-to-end QoS solution provided by DQS can be seamless across the whole network without QoS parameters conversion used in the interface between IntServ and DiffServ networks as illustrated in Figure 3. Therefore, an integral scalable and granular e2e QoS solution can be realized with DQS.

3.4. Issues on Interoperability between DQS, IntServ and DiffServ

An e2e network connection may span over multiple QoS domains, namely, IntServ, DiffServ and DQS, hence there is an interoperability issue between these domains when they co-exist. Since such issue between IntServ and DiffServ has been discussed extensively in the literature, this section only briefly discusses the interoperability between DQS and IntServ as well as DiffServ.

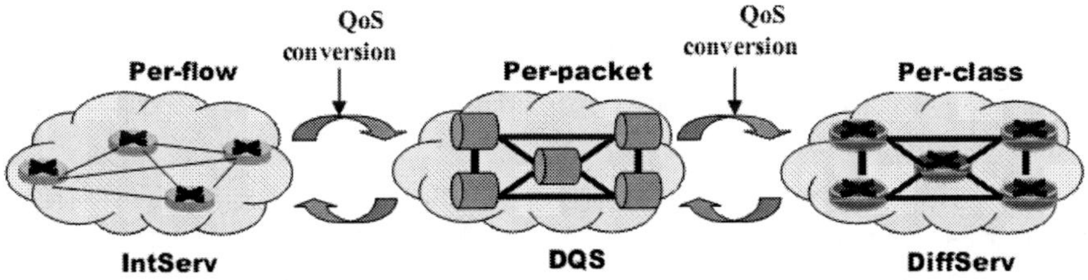

Figure 4. Interconnection between DQS and IntServ as well as DiffServ domains.

Similar to the interoperability between IntServ and DiffServ domains, when a DQS domain is linked with an IntServ domain, some QoS parameter or information conversion needs to be carried out for every packet travelling from one domain to another as illustrated in the left part of Figure 4. Since IntServ is per-flow based while DQS is per-packet based for QoS provisioning, when a packet is from a DQS domain heads to an IntServ domain, its per-packet QoS parameters need to be converted into per-flow QoS parameters, and vice versa. Particularly from IntServ to DQS, no e2e QoS information is carried by an arriving packet, and this information should be available at the edge of the IntServ domain for each flow so that it can be used for the QoS parameter conversion. It is relatively easy for a packet from a DQS domain going to an IntServ domain since the e2e QoS information is carried by every packet.

As illustrated in the right part of Figure 4, between DQS and DiffServ, the major difficulty stems from converting the QoS information of packets from the DiffServ domain going to the DQS domain because the information carried by such a packet is not for e2e QoS but for per hop behaviour (PHB) as defined by the class tag. To form the e2e QoS information, the number of hops that the packet is going to visit in its remaining journey should be known. This number is also useful to partition the e2e QoS task for a packet from a DQS domain into PHBs to be used by the DiffServ domain. Alternatively, another solution to avoid the above conversion between e2e QoS information and packet class is to allow a DQS-packet to carry class-like QoS information too in addition to e2e QoS information.

The interoperability issue may also exist between different DQS domains if they apply various e2e QoS definitions. This is because the e2e QoS information should be understood in the same way by every node that a packet is going to visit; otherwise, e2e QoS provisioning cannot be assured. A straightforward solution to this problem is to define a common e2e QoS expression format, which can be negotiated by the relevant domains.

4. Implementation Issues

This section discusses some implementation issues of IntServ, DiffServ and DQS as well as their effects to scalability. The QoS components discussed here include output schedulers, queue structure, buffer admission control (BAC) and call admission control (CAC). Figure 7 summarizes this comparison in its low half and more discussions are provided below.

4.1. Output Scheduler

An output scheduler needs to decide on-the-fly which packet should be transmitted first in the presence of multiple packets contending for transmission service when the transmitter becomes free. By being 'on-the-fly', it means that the decision needs to be made almost at the same time while the server is released. Therefore, the difficulty in implementing an output scheduler depends on how many competing packets and how much information need to be considered in making such a decision.

For IntServ, the number of competing packets increases with the number of on-going flows and with that of classes for DiffServ. The most important information to be considered at this stage is delay bound of every ongoing flow for IntServ and each class for DiffServ while packet dropping priority may be also taken into account simultaneously. This QoS information is usually stored in routers in a path that a flow travels for IntServ since such information is necessary for output schedulers to treat packets accordingly. Obviously, it is difficult for a router to treat a large number of flows since this information will be voluminous in this case. IntServ is not scalable further due to its reliance on output schedulers for differentiating services of packets belonging to different flows. The complexity of output schedulers is increased with the number of flows to be handled.

With DiffServ, QoS requirements are usually projected into classes to be carried by packets. A class here is determined according to collective QoS requirement of a particular type of applications rather than those of an individual flow. Therefore, the number of classes to be treated by a router is much less than that of on-going flows. Currently, the major services provided by DiffServ include premium service (PS) and assured service (AS). PS provides a low loss, low latency and low jitter service with assured bandwidth mainly for delay-sensitive applications with virtual leased-line services such as voice applications. AS differentiates services with relative QoS assurance by using active buffer management (ABM) [Braden98] to emphasize expected throughput. More sub-classes of services have been defined for various packet drop precedence [Heinanen99]. Therefore, the scalability problem is not an issue for DiffServ. However, with a large number of classes, DiffServ may still face the similar problem.

For DQS, e2e QoS information is carried by every packet so that it avoids the necessity of QoS information storage required by IntServ. If the e2e QoS requirements of all traffic in a network can be explicitly defined, the service order of every packet can be simply determined by its queueing position in the buffer. In this case, the function of an output scheduler is much simplified by avoiding making on-the-fly service decisions. Instead, a service decision is made by Buffer Admission Control (BAC) upon the arrival of a packet rather than by an output scheduler when the server is released. Therefore, the transmitter does not need to wait for a queuing decision to be made for an arriving packet. However in reality, some traffic has no explicit QoS requirement but needs privileged service such as control traffic. On the other hand, some traffic requires assured QoS while some may only need unsure QoS. To handle the above situations, the output scheduler for DQS needs to be able to prioritize services for these three types of traffic by assuring privileged packets to be served first, then those requiring assured QoS and finally those with unsure QoS. To this end, we can separate these types of traffic with three service priorities, which are discussed in details in Section IV.2. Then, the maximum number of competing packets to be considered is three (i.e., privileged, assured and unsure QoS packets) while the decision-making here is only to check the availability of three types of packets. However, the complexity of the scheduler is not increased with the number of e2e QoS services to be provided by a network.

4.2. Queue Structures

Both IntServ and DiffServ adopt multiple queues linking with one output scheduler. Differently, for IntServ, per-flow sub-queue structure may be used to provide granular QoS to each flow as illustrated in Figure 5(a) while DiffServ adopts per-class queue for every aggregated flow as shown in Figure 5(b). These multiple queues can be either physical (i.e., each sub-queue is allocated with a physical buffer) or logical (i.e., a physical buffer is divided into sub-buffers each corresponding to one sub-queue). The complexity of such type of queue structure increases with the number of on-going flows for IntServ and with that of overall traffic classes for DiffServ.

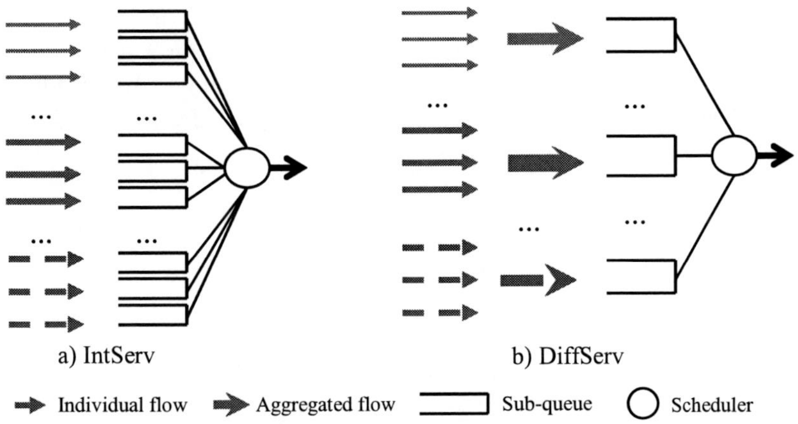

Figure 5. Queue structures for IntServ and DiffServ.

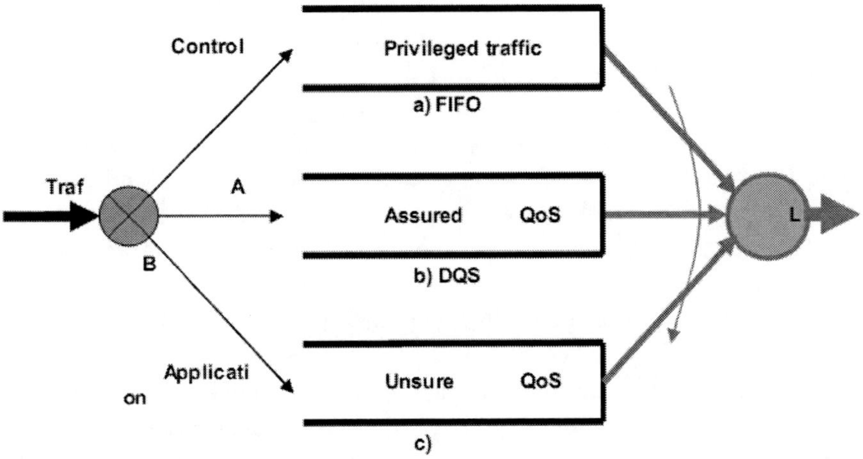

Figure 6. A DQS queue structure for most complex scenario.

Theoretically, DQS can adopt a single queue to support different applications with various QoS requirements. The condition for using a single queue structure is that the e2e QoS requirements of all kinds of traffic in the network can be explicitly quantified (e.g., e2e delay bound). However, in reality, this condition may be compromised in the following cases. There may be different requirements in QoS guarantee degrees required by different applications and even by the same type of applications run by different users. For example, some users emphasize QoS without caring about cost while others try to find better tradeoff between QoS and cost. To satisfy these various requirements, QoS guarantee can be further classified into assured QoS and unsure QoS. With assured QoS, QoS enforcement cannot be compromised. However with unsure QoS, the user can trade off between QoS and cost. Unsure QoS can also be used to treat those packets perceived to probably fail in their e2e QoS guarantee by providing another change rather than dropping them directly due to the dynamic nature of traffic loads. On the other hand, some traffic such as control traffic often needs a privileged service since it is important to network operation but usually has no explicit QoS requirements. To handle the above different types of traffic, a 3-queue structure illustrated in Figure 6 can be used instead of a single queue. In this case, the link service will always be given to the privileged traffic queue first, then to the assured QoS queue and finally the unsure QoS queue. However, the queue structure of DQS will not be affected by the number of e2e QoS services provided by the network. This is different from multi-queue structures used in IntServ and DiffServ.

4.3. Buffer Admission Control (BAC)

In IntServ and DiffServ, BAC may also be used but in a simple form. It can be used to mainly decide whether an arriving packet should be dropped in the case of congestion or tagged if the packet will consume more resource than the pre-reserved one for QoS guarantee. With DQS, BAC needs to decide whether an arriving packet is allowed to enter the queue subject to its QoS requirement and local resource availability; and queues it properly if it is admitted. BAC is usually located at the entrance of a queue, and multiple sub-queues can share a BAC unit as illustrated in Figure 6. Since each admitted packet is queued according to its e2e delay bound that exactly defines the forwarding order, here packet scheduling and forwarding operation become simple.

The crucial part of BAC for DQS is queuing arriving packets, of which, the key operation is packet insertion according to its latest departure time. This is because these operations need to be carried out upon the arrival of every packet. How fast a packet can be inserted into a queue depends on algorithms and data structures adopted for the implementation (e.g., binary search tree [Weiss92]). Although deciding the queuing position of an arriving packet for insertion operation takes time, this decision making will not cause the link transmitter to wait for this queuing decision as discussed below, but this happens when a sophisticated scheduler is used.

Since all packets in the queue are positioned from the head of line (HOL) according to its latest departure time in an ascending order, if an arriving packet should be queued in the HOL, this can be done easily and quickly. In other cases, suppose there are k queued packets that need to be served earlier than an arriving packet, the time for serving these k packets is just the time that can be allowed for queuing this arriving packet. This time is also proportional to the number of queued packets on average. Therefore, the forwarding server does not need to wait for a queuing decision to be made for an arriving packet. An extreme case is that no packet is queued when a packet arrives, then it can be queued immediately in the HOL or passed to an idle sever directly.

To prevent the transmitter from waiting for queueing decision for an arriving packet, alternatively, we can further judge that a packet insertion is necessary only when the buffer occupancy reaches a certain level upon the arrival of a new packet. For example, if the queue length is so small that FIFO is sufficient to guarantee e2e QoS, packet insertion can be avoided to prevent BAC from being a bottleneck. In this case, the transmitter will not wait for a queueing decision for each arriving packet, resulting in high bandwidth utilization. Furthermore, due to some similarity between DQS and EDF as mentioned in Section II, some implementation approaches for EDF schedulers (e.g., [Liebeherr94]) can be borrowed for implementing DQS.

4.4. Call Admission Control (CAC)

CAC is a call-level QoS mechanism aiming at controlling overall new call admissions with respect to the total amount of network resource available in order to provide QoS to all admitted calls. It is a key element to decide statistic QoS metrics such as packet loss rate and average delay. It can also be used jointly to consider packet-level issues to optimize resource allocation for QoS guarantee [Beshai94, Cheung00].

Since IntServ was proposed when ATM was a hot topic, it follows ATM largely to enable IP to provide QoS. Thus, per-flow CAC was suggested, which is similar to per-connection CAC proposed for ATM. However, it is found that this approach also contributes significantly to the scalability problem especially in core networks because of large signalling traffic and processing burden imposed by per-flow CAC to core networks. Therefore, when DiffSevr was proposed to overcome this problem, initially it excluded the use of CAC especially in core networks while resource over-provisioning approach is adopted to support QoS. But later many CAC schemes had been proposed to enable DiffServ to guarantee QoS (e.g., [Marsana07]), particularly those not requiring core routers but edge routers to be involved in CAC operations such as [Chhabra02, Georgoulas05]. For both IntServ and DiffSevr, CAC is used to determine statistic QoS metrics, which mainly include packet loss rate and average delay.

Note that CAC for DQS requires more studies. Here we only discuss some similarities and differences between CAC requirements for IntServ, DiffServ and DQS. CAC for DQS is also used to determine statistic QoS metrics. As discussed earlier, those packets may not be guaranteed will be dropped or their service quality will be downgraded with DQS. A packet may also be lost due to congestion. Similar to packet loss caused by congestion, packet dropping can also be analyzed by CAC. Therefore, in this sense, DQS somewhat converts packet-level delay guarantee into call-level packet dropping ratio guarantee, which can simplify packet-level operation. Note that it is usually more difficult to implement packet-level schemes than call-level ones since the former often requires on-the-fly operation for every packet while the latter does not.

Therefore, a CAC is required for DQS to estimate packet failure (i.e., packet loss plus packet dropping) ratio and to make admission control subject to QoS requirement of the flows under consideration. A CAC able to consider both packet dropping and loss should be able to reduce overall system complexity. Due to similarities between EDF and DQS as discussed in Section II, some work on EDF schedulable conditions in terms of delay bound such as [Firoiu97] can be referred to designing CAC for DQS. It is also possible to use the capacity over-provisioning approach [Menth06], measurement-based CAC [Grossglauser99, Grossglauser03] and end-point based approaches [Bianchi02] to simplify CAC design for DQS.

5. REMARKS

Figure 7 summaries the comparison between the three QoS approaches discussed in Sections III and IV. Here some pre-mature opinions on QoS mechanism designs are summarized.

Compared items	IntServ	DiffServ	DQS
QoS treatment level	*Per-flow*	*Per-class*	*Per-packet*
QoS granularity	*Fine*	*Coarse*	*Fine*
QoS over-provisioning	*Unlikely*	*Likely*	*Unlikely*
Key element for packet-level QoS	*Output scheduler*	*Output scheduler*	*Buffer admission control*
Adaptive packet QoS treatment against path situation	*Not supported*	*Not supported*	*Supported*
Packet-level QoS efforts	*More*	*More*	*Less*
Call-level QoS efforts	*Less*	*Less*	*More*
PHSs from various routers for one flow	*Different*	*Identical*	*Different*
Different packet's QoS within one flow	*Not supported*	*Not supported*	*Supported*
Flow aggregation	*Not required*	*Required*	*Not required*
Packet header re-writing	*Not required*	*Not required*	*Required*
Number of e2e QoS services	*Unlimited*	*Limited*	*Unlimited*
Scalable and integral e2e QoS solution	*No*	*No*	*Yes*
Complexity of scheduler	*Most*	*Simpler*	*Simplest*
On-the-fly scheduling decision	*Hardest*	*Easier*	*Easiest*
Complexity of queue structure	*Most*	*Simpler*	*Simplest*
Buffer admission control	*Simple*	*Simple*	*Complex*
Packet insertion operation	*No*	*No*	*Yes*
QoS metrics considered by call admission control (CAC)	*Packet loss, average delay*	*Packet loss, average delay*	*Packet loss, dropping, average delay*
QoS information treatment	*Stored at routers*	*Carried by packets*	*Carried by packets*
Protocol overhead for QoS	*Short*	*Shorter*	*Longest*
Scalability to the number of flows	*Worst*	*Best*	*Better*

Figure 7. Comparison Between IntServ, DiffServ and DQS.

To enable the original best-effort IP to fully support QoS, per-flow IntServ was initially proposed with emphasis on QoS granularity at flow-level, which is quite similar to ATM's per-connection QoS support. However, IntServ faced more challenges than the connection-oriented ATM in implementation due to its scalability problem mentioned earlier. However, this problem is not just caused by per-flow information storage and processing, but also due to the connectionless nature of IP, with which routing may change paths between a pair of source and destination frequently at packet-level. Such frequent changes in paths make it impossible to maintain a stable resource reservation for a flow to support its QoS during its lifetime, resulting in more operation and traffic overhead caused by redoing resource reservation for path changes. This is also one of the reasons behind 'soft-state' resource reservation adopted by RSVP for IP QoS support.

It seems that DiffServ somewhat goes to another extreme to overcome the scalability problem of IntServ by adopting per-class approach with flow aggregation and jointly using 'bandwidth over-provisioning' philosophy. There is no doubt that DiffServ can rapidly improve the QoS capability of the best-effort IP with a much simpler implementation than IntServ. However, it does not successfully address end-to-end QoS issues over IP especially in terms of its capability and granularity of e2e QoS support as discussed in Sections III and IV.

Today, good e2e QoS support to different applications is one of the user's upmost expectations from network service providers and should be the ultimate target of QoS mechanism designs. If the cost of e2e QoS provisioning is a great concern while more network applications are expected to appear in the future, the 'bandwidth over-provisioning' approach may not be a long-term and economic solution for QoS support. Particularly from the user's point of view, it is unfair and sometime even unacceptable to ask the user to pay for over-provisioned QoS services. Therefore, e2e QoS granularity should be taken into account by QoS designers in addition to the common standardized QoS metrics.

From the network point of view, an application should provide the explicit information on its e2e QoS requirements so that the network can treat it accordingly for QoS granularity. Since the fundamental data unit to be processed by the network layer is the packet, provisioning of per-packet QoS requirement should be helpful for packet-level QoS treatment, and letting each packet carry its QoS requirement should be a reasonable option but at the expense of some extra protocol overhead. On the other hand, packet-level QoS treatment is largely affected by dynamic traffic loads so that it should be designed able to adapt to such dynamic loads instantly in e2e QoS provisioning. These features are missing from both IntServ and DiffServ but supported by DQS as discussed earlier.

For both IntServ and DiffServ (and even other networks such as ATM), output schedulers have been too emphasized while buffer admission control (BAC) has been somewhat ignored in packet-level QoS provisioning. Since scheduling decisions need to be made almost at the same time as the server is released, this imposes great challenges in designing a sophisticated scheduler that can handle a large number of packets with various QoS requirements. In this case, the transmitter may need to wait for scheduling decisions, which is undesirable for high bandwidth utilization. However, BAC can make a queuing decision which is similar to a scheduling decision that can affect QoS support. But BAC allows more time to make such a decision since queuing a packet is done upon its arrival rather than when the server becomes free.

Usually, it is more difficult to implement packet-level QoS mechanisms than call-level ones since the former requires processing of every packet at packet-time scale while the latter does not. This suggests shifting packet-level efforts to call-level ones as much as possible to simplify overall implementation if e2e QoS support is not impacted by such shifting. DQS's effort toward this direction is to convert packet-level delay guarantee into call-level packet dropping ratio guarantee by dropping early the packets which are perceived to surely fail in their delay guarantee as mentioned earlier. Similar to packet loss caused by congestion, packet dropping ratio should also be analyzed by a CAC scheme which is able to consider both packet dropping and packet loss. In this sense, the role of CAC in QoS provisioning should be more emphasized rather than being played down as originally suggested for DiffServ.

6. Conclusion

This chapter gives a brief qualitative evaluation on QoS provisioning approaches from per-flow IntServ, per-class DiffServ to per-packet DQS. We can find that per-packet QoS approach somewhat shifts packet-level QoS efforts from heavy reliance on output schedulers used by both IntServ and DiffServ to exploiting buffer admission control (BAC) as used by DQS. This change is expected to reduce implementation pressure from per-packet on-the-fly scheduling required by output schedulers. On the other hand, per-packet DQS tries to make packet-level QoS services to be unaware of traffic characteristics as much as possible by converting packet delay guarantee into packet dropping ratio guarantee. This somewhat can avoid changes in the implemented network caused by new applications. To this end, both packet loss ratio duc to congestion and packet dropping due to lifetime overdue will be considered by call admission control (CAC). Therefore, CAC for DQS should play more roles than those suggested for IntServ and DiffServ.

However, per-packet DQS is still in its primary stage with a lot of studies required for many challenging issued such as CAC and BAC. An ideal CAC should be able to satisfy various packet failure metrics with less packet-level intervention and less over-provisioned bandwidth to guarantee QoS. A feasible fast packet insertion algorithm is required for BAC so that an arriving packet can be queued quickly according to its e2e delay bound even in the presence of a large number of arriving packets. Furthermore, a joint consideration of congestion control in BAC design can further reduce overall implementation complexity.

Acknowledgment

The author would like to take this opportunity to sincerely thank Editors Dr. Ning Wang, Prof. George Pavlou and Prof. Mohamed Boucadair and also the anonymous reviewers for their valuable comments and suggestions.

REFERENCES

[Beshai94] M. Beshai, R. Kositpaiboon, J. Yan. (1994). Interaction of call blocking and cell loss in an ATM network. *IEEE J. Selected Areas Commun.*, vol. 12, no. 6, pp. 1051-1058.

[Bianchi02] G. Bianchi, F. Borgonovo, A. Capone, L. Fratta, C. Petrioli. (2002). Endpoint admission control with delay variation measurements for qos in ip networks. *ACM SIGCOMM Comp. Commun. Reivew (CCR),* vol. 32, no. 2, pp. 61-69.

[Braden97] R. Braden, L. Zhang, S. Berson. (1997). Resource reservation protocol (RSVP), version 1 functional specification. *Internet Engineering Task Force*, RFC 2205, [Online] Available: http://www.rfc-editor.org/rfc/rfc2205.txt.

[Braden98] B. Braden, D. Clark, J. Crowcroft, B. Davie, S. Deering, D. Estrin, S. Floyd, V. Jacobson, G. Minshall, C. Partridge, L. Peterson, K. Ramakrishnan, S. Shenker, J. Wroclawski, L. Zhang. (1998). Recommendations on queue management and congestion avoidance in the internet. *IETF RFC 2309.*

[Cheung00] M. Cheung, J. Mark. (2000). Resource allocation in wireless networks based on joint packet/call level qos constraints. *Proc. IEEE Global Tele. Conf. (GLOBOCOM)*, vol. 1, San Francisco, USA, pp. 271-275.

[Chhabra02] C. Chhabra, T. Erlebach, B. Stiller, D. Vukadinovic. (2002). Price-based call admission control in a single diffserv domain. *Swiss Federal Institute of Technology*, Tech. Rep. 135.

[Firoiu02] V. Firoiu, J.Y. L. Boudec, D. Towsley, Z. Zhang. (2002). Theories and models for internet quality of service. *Proc. The IEEE*, vol. 90, no. 9, pp. 1565-1591.

[Firoiu97] V. Firoiu, J. Kurose, D. Towsley. (1997). Efficient admission control for edf schedulers. *Proc. IEEE INFOCOM*, Kobe, Japan, pp. 310--317.

[Georgiadis96] L. Georgiadis, R. Guérin, V. Peris, K. Sivarajan. (1996). Efficient network qos provisioning based on per node traffic shaping. *ACM/IEEE Trans. Networking*, vol. 4, no. 4, pp. 482-501.

[Georgoulas05] S. Georgoulas, P. Trimintzios, G. Pavlou, K. Ho. (2005). Heterogeneous real-time traffic admission control in differentiated services domains. *Proc. IEEE Global Tele. Conf. (GLOBOCOM)*, vol. 1, Missouri, USA.

[Grossglauser99] M. Grossglauser, D. Tse. (1999). A frame work for robust measurement-based admission control. *ACM/IEEE Trans. Networking*, vol. 7, no. 3, pp. 293-309.

[Grossglauser03] M. Grossglauser, D. Tse. (2003). A time-scale decomposition approach to measurement-based admission control. *ACM/IEEE Trans. Networking*, vol. 11, no. 4, pp. 550-563.

[Guerin99] R. Guérin, V. Peris. (1999). Quality-of-service in packet networks: basic mechanisms and directions. *Computer Net.*, vol. 31, no. 3, pp. 169-189.

[Heinanen99] J. Heinanen, F. Baker, W. Weiss, J. Wroclawaski. (1999). Assured forwarding phb group. *IETF RFC 2597.*

[Jiang04a] S. M. Jiang. (2004). Granular differentiated queueing services and cost model for end-to-end qos: Principle. *Proc. IEEE Int. Conf. Networks (ICON)*, Singapore, pp. 369-374.

[Jiang04b] Y.M. Jiang, (2004). Lbfa: a stateless approach to scalable support of end-to-ed per-flow service guarantees. *Proc. IFIP Networking Conf.*, Athens, Greece.

[Jiang05] S. M. Jiang. (2005). Granular differentiated queueing services for qos: structure and cost model. *ACM SIGCOMM Comp. Commun. Reivew (CCR)*, vol. 35, no. 2, pp. 13-22.

[Liebeherr94] J. Liebeherr , D. Wrege. (1994). Design and analysis of a high-performance packet multiplexer for multiservice networks with delay guarantees. *University of Virginia*, Tech. Rep. CS-94-29.

[Lin97] D. Lin, R. Morris. (1997). Dynamics of random early detection. *Proc. ACM SIGCOMM*, Cannes, French Riviera,France, pp. 127-137.

[Liu01] Y.E. Liu, W. Wong. (2001). Deadline based channel scheduling. *Proc. IEEE Global Tele. Conf. (GLOBOCOM)*, vol. 4, San Antonio TX, USA, pp. 2358-2362.

[Marsana07] M. Marsana, C. Casettia, G. Mardentea, M. Mellia. (2007). A framework for admission control and path allocation in diffserv networks. *Computer Net.*, vol. 51, no. 10, pp. 2738-2752.

[Menth06] M. Menth, R. Martin, J. Charzinski. (2006). Capacity over provisioning for networks with resilience requirements. *Proc. ACM SIGCOMM*, Pisa, Italy.

[Stoica99] I. Stoica, H. Zhang. (1999). Providing guarantee services without per flow management. *Proc. ACM SIGCOMM*, Cambridge MA, USA.

[Teng08] X. F. Teng, S. M. Jiang, G. Wei, G. Liu. (2008). A cross-layer implementation of differentiated queueing service (dqs) for wireless mesh networks. *Proc. IEEE Veh. Tech. Conf. (VTC)* - Spring, Singapore.

[Weiss92] M. Weiss (1992). Data Structures and Algorithm Analysis in C. *The Benjamin / Cummings Publishing Company, Inc.*

[Zhang00] Z. Zhang, Z. Duan, L. Gao, Y.T. Hou. (2000). Decoupling qos control from core routers: a novel bandwidth broker architecture for scalable support of guaranteed services. *Proc. ACM SIGCOMM*, Stockholm, Sweden.

[Zhang01] Z. Zhang, Z. Duan, Y.T. Hou. (2001). Fundamental trade-offs in aggregate scheduling. *Proc. IEEE Int. Conf. Net. Protocols (ICNP),* vol. 4, University of Minnesota, USA, pp. 129-137.

Shengming Jiang (IEEE membership: A'96-M'00-S'07) received his BEng degree in Shanghai Maritime Institute, China, in 1988, DEA and Dr. degrees in University of Paris VI and University of Versailles Saint-Quentin-En-Yvelines, France, in 1992 and 1995, respectively. From 1988 to 1990, he worked in the Nanjing Petrol Transportation Company, China. He was a research associate in the Department of Electrical and Electronic Engineering and the Computer Science Department, The Hong Kong University of Science and Technology, from February 1995 and August 1997. He was a member of technical staff in Centre for Wireless Communications, National University of Singapore, between September 1997 and July 2000, and a senior member of technical staff and the leader of the network strategic group from July 2001 to March 2003. He was an associate lead scientist and the leader of End-to-End QoS Laboratory in the Institute for Infocomm Research, Singapore, from October 2003 to September 2004. He was with the Faculty of Advanced Technology, University of Glamorgan, the UK, as a principal lecture between July 2007 and August 2009. Currently he is a professor of the School of Electronic and Information Engineering, South China University of Technology. His research interest includes networking issues in both wired and wireless networks as well as mobile computing and applications.

In: Recent Advances in Providing QoS and Reliability... ISBN 978-1-61761-858-1
Editors: N. Wang, G. Pavlou and M. Boucadair

Chapter 3

ADMISSION CONTROL AND NETWORK CAPACITY MANAGEMENT FOR FUTURE IP QUALITY OF SERVICE

Stylianos Georgoulas[a*], Panos Trimintzios[b*] and George Pavlou[*c]

[a] Centre for Communication Systems Research, Faculty of Engineering and Physical Sciences, University of Surrey, Guilford, Surrey, United Kingdom
[b] ENISA (European Network and Information Security Agency), Heraklion, Crete, Greece
[c] Department of Electrical and Electronic Engineering, University College London (UCL) Torrington Place, London, United Kingdom

ABSTRACT

The scope of this chapter is twofold; first we pinpoint certain network capacity management issues related to the provisioning of resources for the support of Quality of Service (QoS) in Future IP networks and we propose practical traffic engineering solutions for dealing with these issues. These practical solutions can assist in coping with the unexpected and unaccounted for QoS deterioration that these issues can cause if they are not taken into account during the network design and configuration phase. Then, taking these issues and solutions into account, we propose efficient and lightweight admission control schemes as means of QoS control in such environments.

1. INTRODUCTION

It is widely accepted that the current Internet is not able to support in a satisfactory fashion emerging services and market demands, such as Voice over IP (VoIP) and real-time

* Email: s.georgoulas@surrey.ac.uk.
* Email: panagiotis.trimintzios@enisa.europa.eu.
* Email: g.pavlou@ee.ucl.ac.uk.

traffic in general. The latter has QoS requirements that the current best effort Internet cannot provide in a resource and cost efficient manner, e.g. without massive bandwidth overprovisioning. Differentiated Services (DiffServ) are seen as the emerging technology to support QoS in IP networks without the inherent scalability problems of Integrated services (IntServ), however, by simply providing forwarding differentiation, DiffServ does not fundamentally solve the problem of controlling congestion.

In this chapter we begin by investigating certain network capacity management related issues with respect to bandwidth allocation and admission control for the support of real-time traffic in DiffServ networks. We validate our study using simulations with the publicly available ns-2 simulator [1]. Taking into account the implications of our network capacity management study we then proceed to present our approach towards admission control for real-time traffic in DiffServ networks. By means of ns-2 simulations we show that our proposed schemes perform well and that they compare favourably against other schemes found in the literature.

2. QoS Requirements of Real-Time Traffic

We assume that real-time traffic applications have strict *delay* and *jitter* requirements, while the *packet loss rate* (PLR) should be bounded. It is very likely that both low delay and jitter requirements will be met in a high-speed network core [2]. Furthermore, a bounded delay requirement can be met by: a) configuring routers to have small queues for the real-time traffic in order to keep the per-hop delay small, and b) having QoS routing processes that choose paths with a low number of hops. Shaping the real-time traffic flows to their peak rate at the network ingress is also advantageous for controlling jitter [3]. It is clear that delay and jitter can be controlled with engineering approaches similar to the ones described above; therefore, in this chapter we consider the Packet Loss Rate (PLR) as the key QoS metric for real-time traffic that needs to be controlled through appropriate bandwidth allocation and admission control functions.

3. Admission Control Schemes for Real-Time Traffic

The various admission control schemes in the literature can be classified into the following three categories according to the method they use to identify the available resources for a new service request: a) Endpoint Admission Control (EAC), b) Traffic Descriptor-based Admission Control (TDAC), and c) Measurement-Based Admission Control (MBAC).

EAC is based on probe packets sent along the transmission path before the flow is established [4]. In this approach and for reasonable setup delays, the metrics do not depict stationary network states and this can result in an unrealistic picture of network congestion. In addition, simultaneous probing by many sources can lead to a situation known as thrashing [4]. That is, even though the number of admitted flows is small, the cumulative level of probe packets prevents further admissions.

TDAC is based on the assumption that traffic descriptors are provided for each flow prior to its establishment. This approach achieves high utilization when the traffic descriptors used are appropriate. Nevertheless, in practice it suffers from several problems [5], the most notable one being the inability to actually come up with appropriate traffic descriptors.

MBAC shifts the task of traffic characterization from the user to the network [5]. This means that the network attempts to "learn" the characteristics of flows through real-time measurements. This approach offers certain advantages. First, the specified traffic descriptors can be very simple, e.g. peak rate only. Second, a conservative specification does not result in overallocation of resources for the entire duration of the service session. Third, when traffic from different flows is multiplexed, the QoS experienced depends on their aggregate behavior, the statistics of which are easier to estimate. However, relying on measured quantities raises certain issues, such as measurement errors [5].

The various admission control schemes can also be classified according to the location where the admission control decision is made. Schemes can be: a) *centralized*, residing at a server, and b) *distributed*, residing typically at ingress/egress nodes.

Centralized schemes require a signaling protocol, with messages exchanged between the sender application and the centralized admission control entity. Also signaling messages are required between the centralized entity and network routers. These messages include the service requirements of the flow and the resource state at each router, therefore admission control is performed by an entity that has complete and up-to-date knowledge of the network topology and resources, which is an ideal situation. However, in practice, centralized schemes have disadvantages. A key issue is the scalability problems of a centralized scheme [6]. Another issue is that a centralized entity constitutes a single point of failure and needs to be replicated for high availability and resilience.

Distributed schemes avoid these problems, but the existence of multiple admission control points means that concurrent admission control decisions may be made by distinct decision points for flows competing for the same downstream resources. This will typically not take into account the effect that simultaneous admissions of flows can have on the state of downstream resources and can potentially lead to unexpected QoS violations. In order to deal with this issue there exist some proposals in the literature [7], such as employing some safety margins to absorb the negative effects of concurrency or involving cooperation between ingress nodes in order to update and 'share' among them the state of the shared resources.

The various admission control schemes can also be classified based on the topological scope of the traffic flows they are targeted to; that is on whether the traffic is intra-domain - i.e. it originates and terminates within the same domain- or inter-domain, in which case the traffic needs to traverse a sequence of transit domains.

For example, the scheme in [8] is distributed measurement-based for intra-domain traffic that passively monitors traffic characteristics (one-way delay) on a per ingress-egress basis at egress nodes. The scheme in [9] is distributed measurement-based applicable to both intra- and inter-domain traffic. The inter-domain traffic case is handled as a repetitive process of per-flow admission control at each domain end-to-end.

A notable approach that has received significant research interest within the Internet Engineering Task Force (IETF) in recent years is the Pre-Congestion Notification (PCN) approach [10]. In this approach, which is a distributed measurement-based one, egress nodes passively measure on a per ingress-egress basis the markings on packets that interior nodes have set depending on the congestion status of the backbone links; appropriate feedback is subsequently sent to the ingress nodes that derive the admission control decision. The PCN approach currently focuses on solutions for intra-domain traffic. For inter-domain traffic,

PCN uses the Integrated Services (IntServ) over DiffServ framework [11] and sees the end-to-end case as a repetitive process of per-flow admission control in each domain; the Resource Reservation Protocol (RSVP) is used as the signaling protocol while PCN operates independently in each domain.

4. Network Capacity Management

In the first part of this chapter we aim to highlight several issues with respect to bandwidth allocation and admission control for the support of real-time traffic in IP DiffServ networks. Due to space limitations we will not describe in detail the simulation setup and simulation results but we will rather concentrate on the implications of our simulation analysis. For more details regarding the simulation setup, the characteristics of the traffic sources and simulation results themselves the interested reader can refer to [12].

The simulation analysis performed for the needs of this part of our work initially focused on examining whether the traffic descriptors of real-time traffic sources remain reliable after the first point of aggregation of the sources. That is whether the original traffic descriptors of real-time traffic sources can be applied in statistical multiplexing formulas in order to derive the required capacity values at various points in a DiffServ network for given target PLR values at these points. The simulation results showed that even though the original traffic descriptors are valid for bandwidth allocation at the first points of aggregation they may not be valid in transit nodes further downstream. This is because sources become correlated and their characteristics are altered as they traverse links and multiplexers. Therefore, translating the PLR constraint to a hop-count constraint (for low values of PLR it can be easily shown that PLR parameters are additive) and using the original traffic descriptors in transit nodes can lead to erroneous bandwidth allocation decisions.

The second part of our network capacity management study was to try to quantify the effects of this 'traffic profile deformation'. As our simulation results showed, in general, traffic profile deformation works against us and using the original traffic descriptors for bandwidth allocation can lead to lead to severe and unpredictable QoS violations in transit nodes.

In the rest of this section we will elaborate on the implications of our network capacity management study and we will present some possible practical traffic engineering solutions for dealing with the raised issues.

4.1. Implication for Bandwidth Allocation and Admission Control

Regarding bandwidth allocation, the results suggest that if, during the network provisioning, the packet loss requirement is translated in a hop count constraint and the bandwidth allocation strategy in core nodes is based on a statistical multiplexing (effective bandwidth) formula, the consequences may be detrimental.

Regarding admission control, the results have certain implications on the effectiveness of an admission control scheme deployed in core nodes of an IP DiffServ network. If a TDAC scheme is deployed in a core node, it may fail if it is based on the original traffic descriptors of the traffic sources. An MBAC scheme is less likely to fail compared to the TDAC scheme, because it relies on real-time measurements of the aggregate traffic and uses only the traffic descriptors of the source requesting admission. However, the original traffic descriptors declared by this one source requesting admission may not depict its behavior in core nodes.

A similar problem for TDAC and MBAC schemes arises when performing admission control for inter-domain traffic. In this case, if an upstream domain submits the original traffic descriptors of the sources to a downstream domain (without taking into account the traffic profile deformation for the sources within this upstream domain) and the downstream domain performs admission control based on those traffic descriptors, this may lead to QoS violations.

In order for any admission control scheme that uses some kind of traffic descriptors to be reliable, when used in nodes other than the first multiplexing point, it should appropriately modify the traffic descriptors to depict the behavior of the sources at that specific multiplexing point. However, this is not trivial, since it requires the estimation of delay variation and induces per flow states [13].

4.2. Practical Traffic Engineering Solutions

A unified approach for bandwidth allocation and admission control that can be used in order to overcome the aforementioned problems is to apply per-flow admission control only at the network ingress and further downstream treat the real-time traffic aggregates in a peak rate manner. This simplifies the network dimensioning process (since it removes the packet loss related hop count constraint in core nodes) and is feasible since, as stated in [14], the edge links are currently considered as the most probable congestion points of a domain, whereas backbone links are overprovisioned. This approach does not induce any additional states in the core network and does not require core routers to be aware of any signaling, which is desired for scalability and resilience reasons, and it is also proven to be very resource-efficient if resilience against network failures is required [15].

5. ADMISSION CONTROL

In this section we will present our approaches towards admission control covering both the cases where the traffic is intra- and inter-domain.

5.1. Admission Control for Intra-Domain Traffic

Our MBAC scheme, which we will present in this section, is based on the unified approach presented in the previous section and makes use of the aforementioned assumptions, being therefore suitable for use in DiffServ networks where per-flow state in the core nodes cannot be kept.

It is worth noting that since in our approach, ingress nodes do not compete for resources at the network core, the scheme can be completely distributed, with an instance of it running at each ingress node without, however, requiring any cooperation or coordination between the ingress nodes.

5.1.1. Admission Control Logic

Our scheme is applicable to real-time sources that are able to provide only even the simplest single traffic descriptor, which is their peak rate and employs the normal distribution based bufferless statistical multiplexing approach given by equation (1)

$$C \approx m + a'\sigma \quad \text{with} \quad a' = \sqrt{-2\ln(\varepsilon) - \ln(2\pi)} \tag{1}$$

where m is the mean aggregate bit rate, σ is the standard deviation of the aggregate bit rate and ε is the upper bound on allowed loss probability. The mean aggregate bit rate and the standard deviation of the aggregate bit rate are derived based on run-time measurements.

In a DiffServ domain we assume that the real-time traffic aggregate is provisioned and engineered in such a way that at least C_{total} bandwidth is available edge-to-edge and every very time a source wants to establish a service instance, it signals this to the ingress node through some "RSVP-like" signaling protocol.

When a new service request arrives we need to calculate an appropriate time period, the *measurement window*, within which we need to take and use measurements for bandwidth estimations (for more details regarding the estimation of the measurement window the interested reader can refer to [16]). The measured parameters are the mean rate of the offered load, $M_{measured}$, and the variance of the offered load, $\sigma^2_{measured}$, at the output queue of the ingress node. Having the measurements and the peak rate p_{new} of the new source, and by making the worst case assumption that the new source will be transmitting at its peak rate, we compute the estimated bandwidth C_{est} as follows:

$$C_{est} = M_{measured} + p_{new} + a'_{PLR}\sqrt{\sigma^2_{measured}} \tag{2}$$

where a'_{PLR} is computed as in equation (1), based on the target PLR bound of the real-time traffic aggregate (since no losses are incurred at the network core the PLR bound at the ingress node can be set equal to the overall PLR bound of the real-time traffic aggregate).

Given that the allocated bandwidth for the real-time traffic aggregate from edge-to-edge is C_{total}, and having computed the estimated bandwidth C_{est}, the admission control criterion in our scheme becomes:

$$\begin{aligned} &\mathit{If} \quad (C_{est} \times APF) \leq C_{total,} \quad \mathit{admit} \\ &\mathit{If} \quad (C_{est} \times APF) > C_{total,} \quad \mathit{reject} \end{aligned} \tag{3}$$

where *APF* is an Admission Policy Factor we involve in the admission control criterion. The use of *APF* reflects the provider's policy on how strict the admission control should be. The decisions for setting the *APF* can be based on simple heuristics or ad hoc engineering methods. In our approach for setting *APF*, we take into account two issues that challenge the effectiveness of any MBAC scheme: (a) the traffic source heterogeneity, and (b) the effects of measurement errors. For more details regarding the setting of *APF* the interested reader can refer to [16].

5.1.2. Performance Evaluation

In order to evaluate the performance of our admission control scheme, we run simulations using the network simulator *ns-2*, with the dumbbell topology of Figure 1.

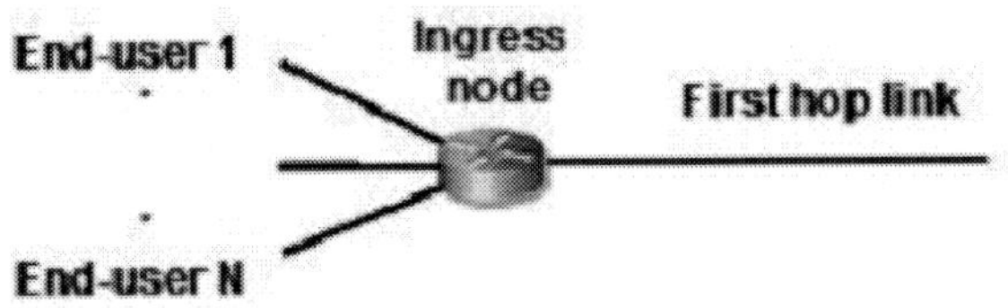

Figure 1. Simulation topology.

We use scenarios with the target bound on packet loss rate for the aggregate real-time traffic is equal to 0.01 and 0.001.These bounds represent typically acceptable PLR values for the VoIP service and for real-time applications in general, according to [17]. We set the output link capacity allocated to real-time traffic equal to 3.33Mbps for the target PLR 0.01 case and equal to 3.56Mbps for the target PLR 0.001 case.

In order to test the *robustness* of the scheme with respect to traffic *heterogeneity* and *long-range dependency*, we use both VoIP and Videoconference traffic sources. In order to test the *robustness* of the scheme with respect to *offered load*, we test varying load conditions ranging from 0.5 to 5, where the value 1 (*reference load)* corresponds to the average load that would be incurred by a source activation rate equal to 1000 VoIP sources/hour.

In order to compare the performance of our scheme, which we call intra-MBAC, against other existing proposals, we implement three other algorithms. The first algorithm is an MBAC scheme described by Zukerman et al in [18] as Rate Envelope Multiplexing (REM), with adaptive weight factor and no histogram update. The reasons for the selection of the specific MBAC scheme (we call it MBAC-ZUK) for comparison with our scheme are that: (a) REM also makes the zero buffer approximation with respect to statistical multiplexing and (b) implementation-wise, in a similar fashion to our scheme, it requires only aggregate bandwidth measurements and the peak rate of the sources requesting admission in order to derive the admission control decision.

The second algorithm is an EAC scheme described by Karlsson et al in [19]. As in [19], we set the probing rate equal to the peak rate of the source requesting admission, we consider probe durations of 0.5sec up to 5sec, and we also assume that there is no latency involved between the probing phase completion and the admission control decision.

The third algorithm is a simple TDAC Peak Rate Allocation scheme (we call it TDAC-PRA) that only admits a new source if the following condition is satisfied:

$$e \ p_i + p_{new} \ J \ C_{total} \tag{4}$$

where $\sum p_i$ is the sum of peak rates of the already established sources. With this scheme, there are no losses, since it does not account for any statistical multiplexing.

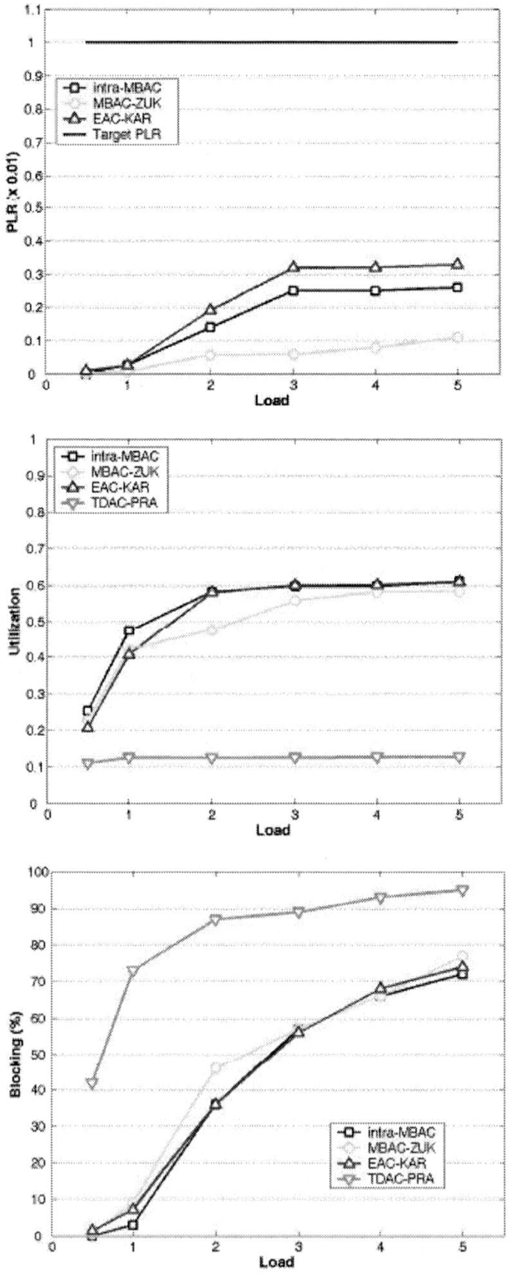

Figure 2. Incurred PLR (top), utilization (middle), and blocking rate (bottom) for Videoconference sources and target PLR 0.01.

As stated in [20], any admission control scheme must address the trade-off between *packet loss* and *utilization*. Therefore for performance evaluation we use these two metrics, together with the average admission rejection rate.

In our simulations we consider three cases for the mixture of traffic sources that request admission: (a) Videoconference sources only, (b) VoIP sources only and (c) Mixed VoIP and Videoconference sources. For TDAC-PRA we do not show PLR results because it is constantly zero. For EAC-KAR, the results shown each time are for the probe duration which gives the best trade-off between packet loss and utilization.

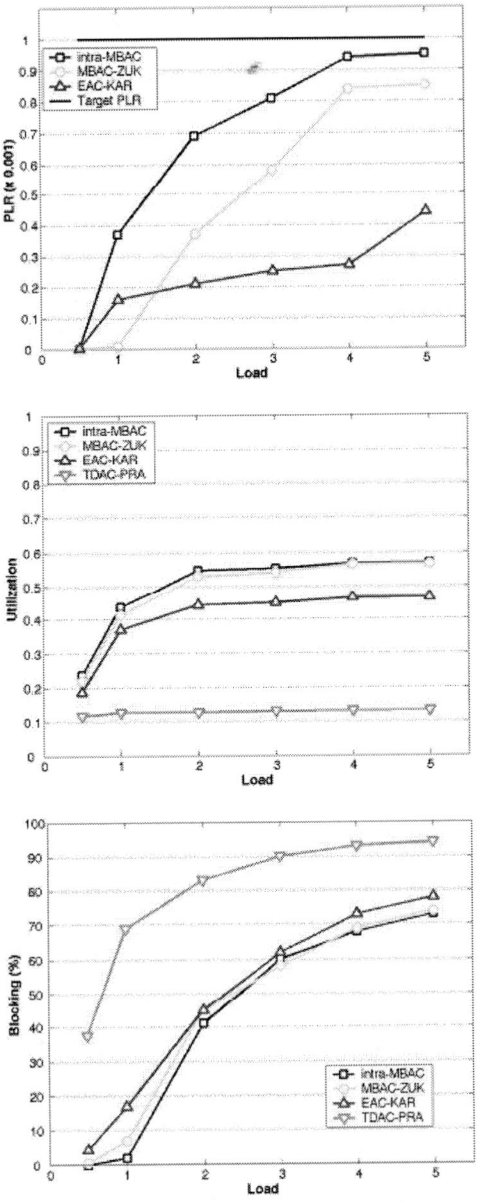

Figure 3. Incurred PLR (top), utilization (middle), and blocking rate (bottom) for Videoconference sources and target PLR 0.001.

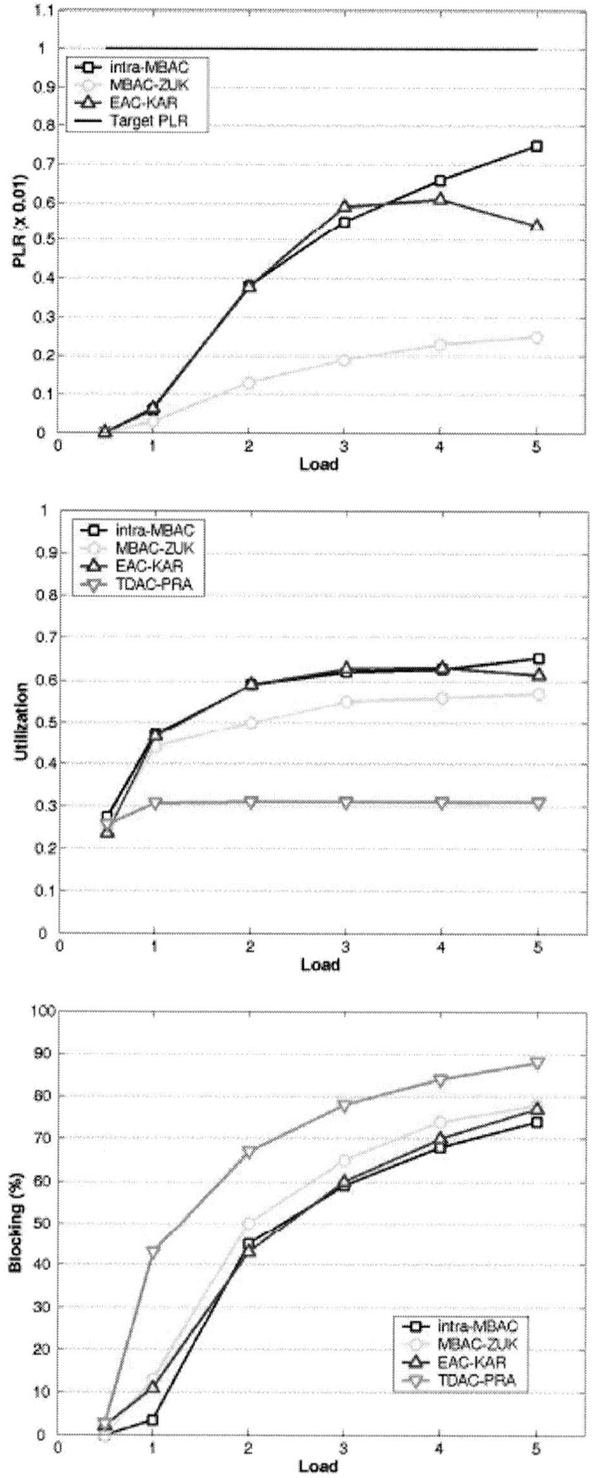

Figure 4. Incurred PLR (top), utilization (middle), and blocking rate (bottom) for VoIP sources and target PLR 0.01.

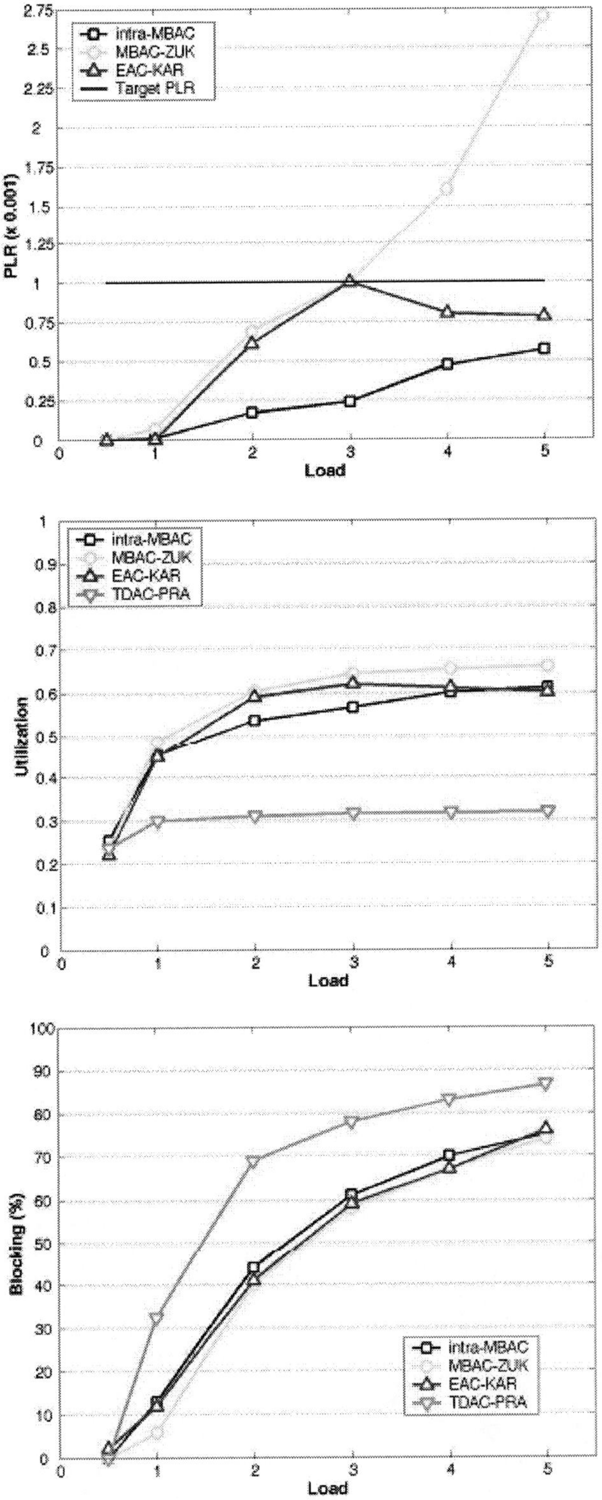

Figure 5. Incurred PLR (top), utilization (middle), and blocking rate (bottom) for VoIP sources and target PLR 0.001.

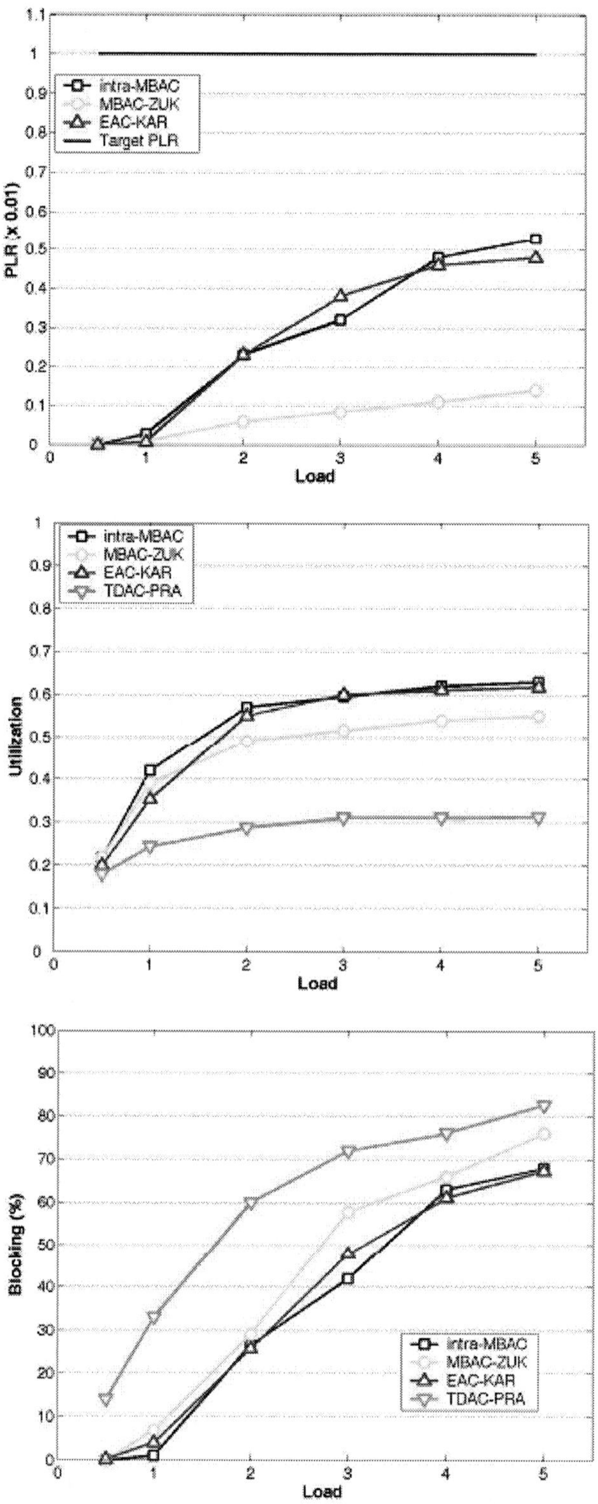

Figure 6. Incurred PLR (top), utilization (middle), and blocking rate (bottom) for mixed sources and target PLR 0.01.

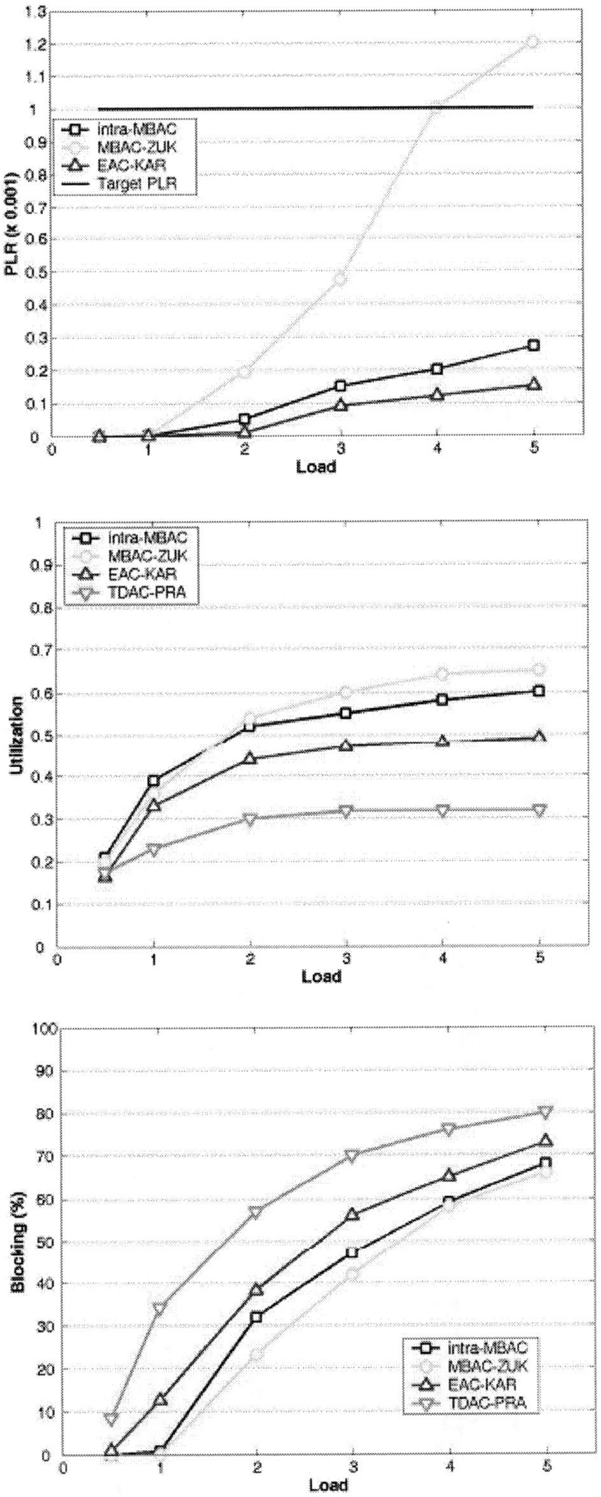

Figure 7. Incurred PLR (top), utilization (middle), and blocking rate (bottom) for mixed sources and target PLR 0.001.

5.1.3. Discussion of the Simulation Results

The simulation results show that intra-MBAC can satisfy the target PLR in all cases (which is the primary objective) without requiring any further reconfiguration of its parameters for individual traffic scenarios and loading conditions and despite the effects of measurement errors. As we show, it is possible without any reconfiguration of its tuning parameters to achieve reasonably good performance regarding utilization and blocking (which is the secondary objective) for a variety of traffic scenarios and loading conditions.

MBAC-ZUK satisfies the target PLR for the target PLR 0.01 case without requiring reconfiguration of its tuning parameters, it fails, however, to satisfy the target PLR 0.001 value for VoIP sources and mixed VoIP and Videoconference traffic scenarios. For these cases new values for its tuning parameters should be sought in a trial-and-error fashion.

EAC-KAR satisfies the target PLR for all simulated cases by appropriately reconfiguring its tuning parameter, following the guidelines in [19]. However, for the VoIP sources only case for both target PLR values and for high loading conditions, this is achieved while entering the thrashing region, which is a region an EAC scheme should avoid entering, which means that the target PLR is not actually satisfied because of the ability of the EAC scheme to adapt to the traffic conditions.

In the following figure the averages of link utilization and blocking rate for all simulated cases and loading conditions for all four schemes, including the scenarios and loading conditions where MBAC-ZUK violates the target PLR, are shown.

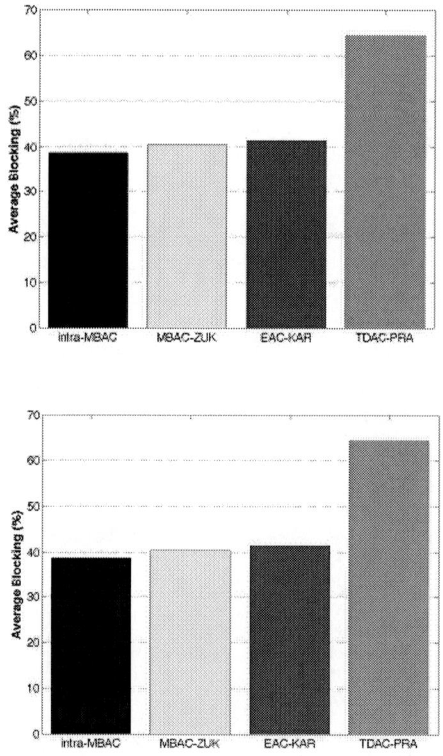

Figure 8. Average utilization (top) and blocking rate (bottom).

As it can be seen, intra-MBAC achieves, on average, the highest utilization and incurs the lowest blocking rate among all schemes, while satisfying the target PLR in all cases and without requiring any reconfiguration of its parameters.

5.1.4. Conclusions

In this section we presented a measurement-based admission control scheme for intra-domain real-time traffic for DiffServ domains. The main advantage of our scheme compared to EAC-KAR and MBAC-ZUK is the fact that it can perform well and consistently for a variety of traffic scenarios without requiring reconfiguration of the involved parameters. Contrary to our scheme and as the simulations showed, both MBAC-ZUK and EAC-KAR fail to meet the QoS objectives and achieve at the same time satisfactory utilization and reasonable blocking rate for a unique setting of the involved parameters.

5.2. Admission Control for Inter-Domain Traffic

In this part of this chapter we will present a distributed measurement-based admission control scheme for inter-domain real-time traffic originating from DiffServ domains, which tries to assure the target QoS levels end-to-end in a multi-domain scenario.

We assume that in each domain where the admission control scheme is applied, there exist two main bottleneck points: a) *ingress nodes* multiplexing traffic from many end-users of the same or upstream domains, and b) *egress nodes* connecting the given domain to another domain through inter-domain links. These assumptions are common in the literature [14] and also allow us to develop solutions inline with the findings of our network capacity management related study.

5.2.1. End-to-End QoS Model

Our admission control scheme is generic and can be used both in traditional QoS-enabled environments, such as the IntServ over DiffServ [11] one, but also in emerging SLA-based QoS-enabled environments, such as the one proposed by the European-funded research project MESCAL [21].

5.2.1.1. Deployment in an Intserv over Diffserv Environment

In an IntServ over DiffServ environment, each domain/autonomous system (AS) between the source and the destination performs admission control on a per-flow basis. The flow characteristics and overall QoS requirements of the real-time traffic flow are included in the PATH message propagated in the forward direction. One should also take into account following our discussion in section 4, that the flow characteristics will have to be reconstructed prior to being submitted to the downstream domains.

In the reverse direction, the ingress routers of each domain perform admission control and propagate upstream, upon successful admission control decision, the RESV message that includes in the Flowspec field, information about the QoS received so far in downstream domains. This will help upstream domains to derive the QoS targets that need to be enforced locally within each domain for the specific flow request.

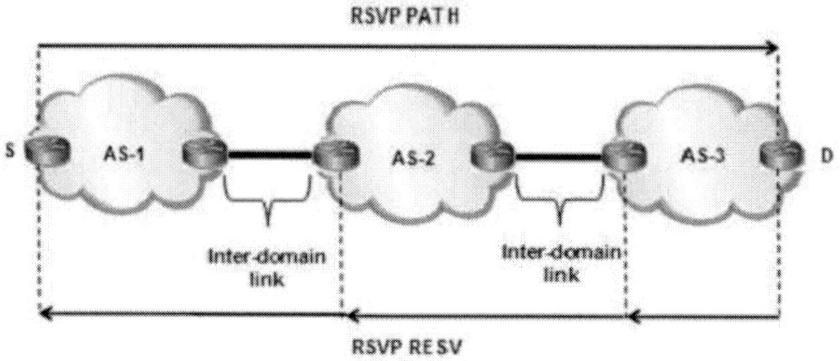

Figure 9. Operations of our scheme in an IntServ over DiffServ environment.

5.2.1.2. Deployment in the Context of a Cascaded QoS Model

In the cascaded QoS model each provider negotiates QoS IP services with other providers. As a result each domain establishes provider-level Service Level Agreements (pSLAs) with the directly connected providers; that is the QoS agreements are between adjacent neighbors and not between providers more than one hop away. This type of agreement is used to provide QoS connectivity from a customer to destinations that may be several domains away. Figure 10 gives an overview of the concepts in this cascaded model.

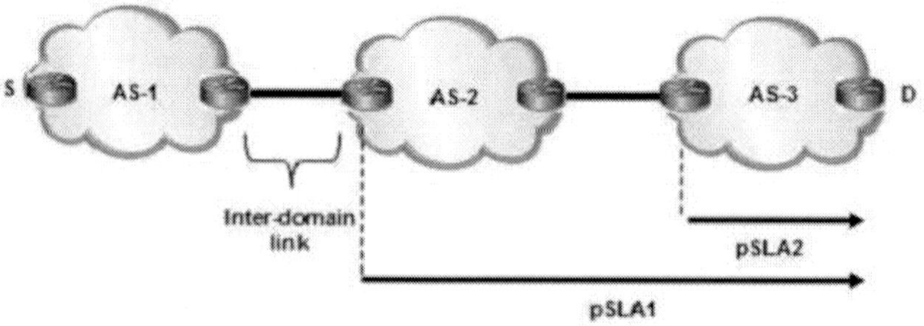

Figure 10. The cascaded QoS model.

In this model, AS-2 negotiates and establishes an agreement with AS-3 ($pSLA_2$) that will allow customers of AS-2 to reach destinations in AS-3 with specific QoS guarantees as long as the total aggregate demand from AS-2 does not exceed the negotiated and agreed bandwidth value in $pSLA_2$. AS-1, in turn, can negotiate with AS-2 an agreement ($pSLA_1$) which defines the QoS guarantees that the traffic exiting AS-1 will receive from the ingress nodes of AS-2 until the end-customers connected to AS-3 as long as the aggregate traffic demand from AS-1 towards the end-customers connected to AS-3 does not exceed the negotiated and agreed bandwidth value in $pSLA_1$. These guarantees are derived by combining the guarantees specified in $pSLA_2$ and the local QoS capabilities of AS-2. As easily proven, delay and jitter parameters are additive and loss parameters for low values are also additive. Therefore, it is straightforward to perform the combination of QoS capabilities and derive the overall QoS guarantees.

Since pSLAs are established for aggregated traffic demands, each network provider typically only needs to manage a limited number of pSLAs. By making the assumption that a cascaded QoS model exists and relevant pSLAs are already negotiated and established, the DiffServ domain AS-1 does not need to signal any of the downstream domains on a per-flow basis for traffic destined to remote destinations. Per-flow signaling is needed only up to the ingress node of the DiffServ domain where the end-user is connected to (AS-1 in Figure 10), which makes it more scalable than the IntServ over DiffServ approach from a signaling overhead point of view. The domain only needs to ensure that its inter-domain traffic does not exceed the negotiated bandwidth value in the corresponding pSLAs and that the QoS received by this traffic within AS-1, when combined with the QoS values specified in the pSLAs, is adequate to guarantee the end-to-end QoS.

5.2.2. Admission Control Logic

The admission control functionality of our scheme is distributed to the edge nodes of a domain. It does not require any cooperation between ingress nodes or any other per ingress-egress operations. The admission control logic tries to ensure that the domain PLR requirement for the inter-domain real-time traffic is met at all times by regulating the admission of new flows but it does not penalize nor terminates existing flows.

In Figure 11 we show the operations of our feedback-based admission control scheme. For simplicity we show only one pair of ingress-egress nodes and the numbers in brackets indicate the sequence of actions/operations in our scheme.

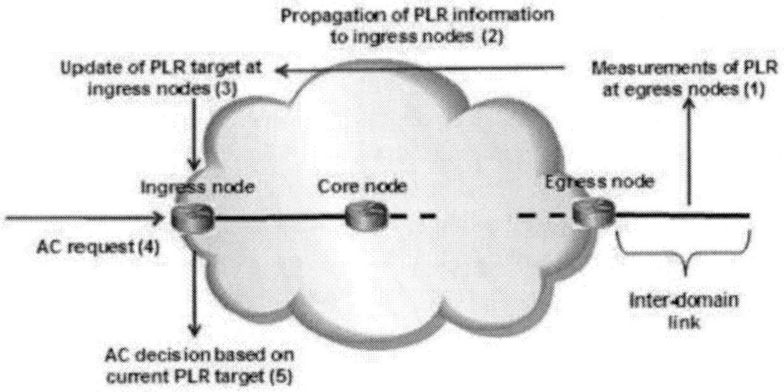

Figure 11. Overview of scheme's operations.

The PLR at the inter-domain links is measured continuously (action 1). Depending on the congestion status, if needed, the measured PLR is propagated back to the ingress nodes (action 2). Based on this information the ingress nodes adjust their PLR target which is used for the admission of new flows (action 3). Therefore, upon a signaled admission request for a flow (action 4), the ingress nodes use the most up-to-date PLR target in order to make an admission decision.

Our admission control logic consists of two functionally different collaborating modules, one operating at each *ingress* node and another operating at each *egress* node. At each egress node the admission control module continuously and passively monitors the state (PLR) of the egress output interfaces. Based on the observed status, i.e. the PLR incurred at intervals of duration T, if needed it communicates the PLR information back to the ingress nodes that use this egress output interface as exit point for their inter-domain real-time traffic. The communicated information relates to the PLR of the overall aggregate traffic that uses a specific egress output interface and not to the PLR of traffic originating from each of the distinct ingresses towards that egress node. This means that the egress nodes do not need to keep any per-ingress state or perform any ingress-specific operations. This PLR information is, in turn, used by the ingress node modules to calculate new target values for PLR to be used for the admission of new flows. In principle our scheme tries to balance the PLR incurred at ingress and egress nodes so that at all times its sum is less than the domain PLR requirement of the real-time traffic.

The functionality of the ingress node module is similar to the one in the case of intra-domain traffic with the difference that the target PLR at ingress nodes can vary based on the feedback information.

The desired functionality of the egress node module is to provide feedback to the ingress nodes modules to regulate the admission of new flows in a smooth and timely manner. In order to achieve this smooth but timely operation, the egress node module when first senses a possible congestion situation, first it tries to correct it by applying a set of 'mild' actions (tries to overcome the congestion situation by setting a more stringent PLR target at the ingress node modules) and if this situation is not resolved, it then adopts more drastic 'emergency' measures (that is block all admission requests until the congestion situation is resolved). The egress node module therefore performs three major functions: a) PLR estimation, by continuously monitoring each of the output links, b) threshold-based alarming, and c) periodic feedback of PLR information to ingress nodes.

Our scheme shares similarities with the PCN approach [10] in the sense that both schemes employ congestion thresholds and are feedback-based; there exist though some distinct differences. Contrary to the PCN approach, in our scheme the core routers do not perform any marking since we assume that the network core is well provisioned. Also, the feedback information is different from the PCN approach; in our scheme it is packet loss related and at the granularity of egress output interfaces rather than based on markings and at the granularity of ingress-egress output interfaces pairs. Furthermore, in our approach the congestion status is fed back to the ingress nodes periodically, whereas in the PCN approach the feedback information is sent upon each flow admission request. Another difference is that in the PCN approach two threshold values need to be set for each link, which means that the number of tuning parameters involved in the admission control process for each ingress-egress path grows linearly with the number of hops in the path. In our approach, regardless of the number of hops between ingress-egress pairs, the number of tuning parameters is constant.

However, if the core network is not well engineered and provisioned, then additional operations -similar to the ones of the PCN approach- in core nodes would be needed to complement our scheme in order to infer the congestion status of the backbone links. In such cases our approach and the PCN approach could operate in a complementary manner. For more details regarding the operations of our scheme the interested reader can refer to [22].

5.2.3. Performance Evaluation

The performance evaluation of our scheme in an IntServ over DiffServ environment is left for future work. Here we will present the performance evaluation of our scheme in a cascaded QoS environment. We do not compare against other MBAC or TDAC schemes, since following the discussion in section 4, in order to do so we would have to appropriately modify these schemes to be applicable in practice; that is find a way to reconstruct the correct traffic descriptors of flows at all nodes where the schemes are indented to be applied (e.g. at all links for the case of most MBAC/TDAC schemes).

Contrary to MBAC and TDAC schemes, the operation of EAC schemes is the same regardless of whether the traffic is for an end-to-end path or for a single link. This behavior is directly comparable with our scheme when applied in the cascaded QoS environment (we call our scheme inter-MBAC). Therefore, we are able to compare our scheme is a pSLA-based environment against one of the existing representative EAC schemes (EAC-KAR of [19]).

We use the topology shown in Figure 12. This topology, although simple, incorporates all the assumptions made by our scheme when applied in the cascaded QoS environment regarding bottleneck points and provider agreements and allows for the operations of both ingress and egress modules to be evaluated.

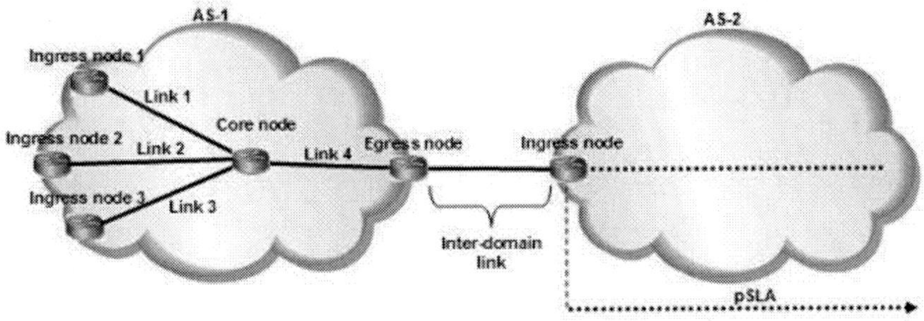

Figure 12. Simulation topology.

We use two cases for the target domain bound on packet loss rate for the aggregate inter-domain real-time traffic; equal to 0.01 (case A) and 0.001 (case B), respectively. In order to keep the end-to-end PLR below the upper end-to-end value of 0.01, in the first case, with domain PLR equal to 0.01, the pSLA in place with AS-2 has to provide almost zero loss guarantees. In the second case, with domain PLR equal to 0.001, the pSLA has to provide low but not zero loss guarantees. We set the capacities allocated at links 1-3 for the inter-domain real-time traffic to 3.33Mbps for case A and to 3.56Mbps for case B. Since we assume that real-time traffic aggregates from different ingress nodes are treated in a peak rate manner at the network core, this means that the capacity allocated for the inter-domain real-time traffic at link 4 is 9.99Mbps and 10.68Mbps respectively. For both cases, we assume that the egress link is underprovisioned by a factor of 0.8. This means that the capacity allocated at the inter-domain link is 7.99Mbps and 8.544Mbps respectively.

In order to test the robustness of the scheme with respect to traffic heterogeneity and long-range dependency, similar to the intra-domain traffic case, we use three traffic scenarios: a) Videoconference traffic only, b) VoIP traffic only, and c) mixed VoIP and Videoconference traffic. The characteristics of the sources are the same as in the case of intra-domain traffic (more details regarding the simulation setup can be found in [22]).

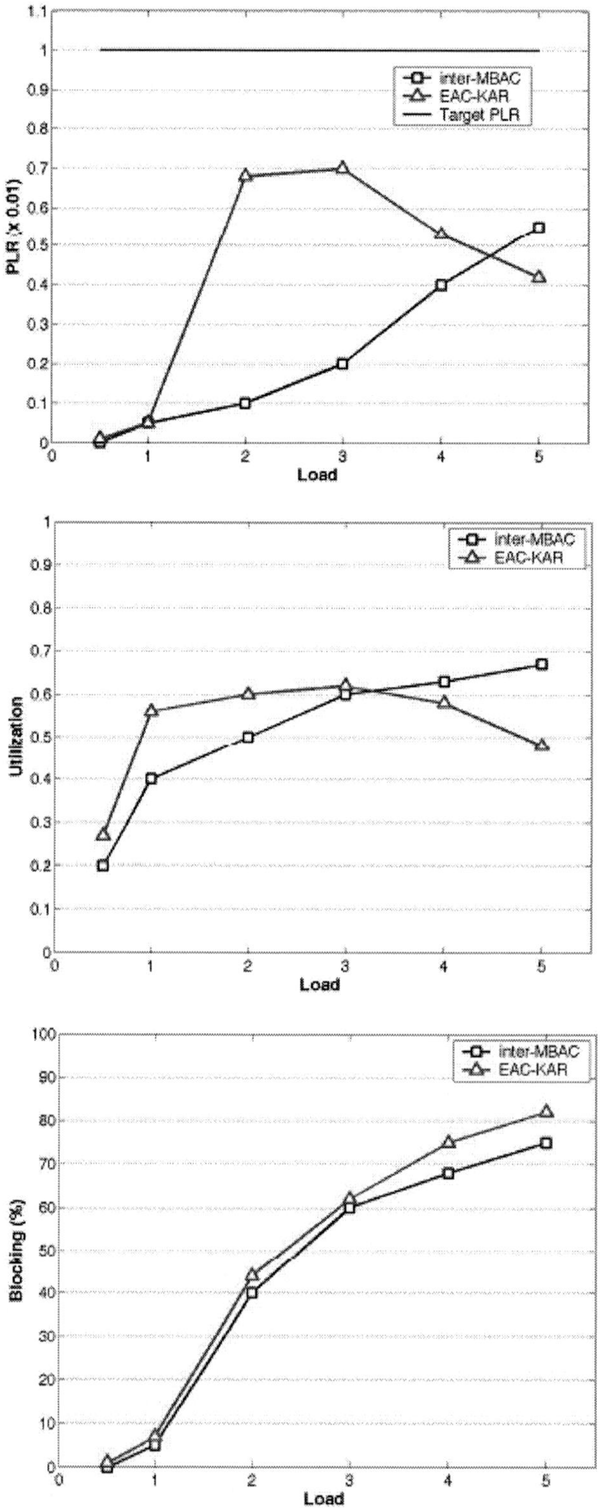

Figure 13. Incurred PLR (top), utilization (middle), and blocking rate (bottom) for Videoconference sources and target PLR 0.01.

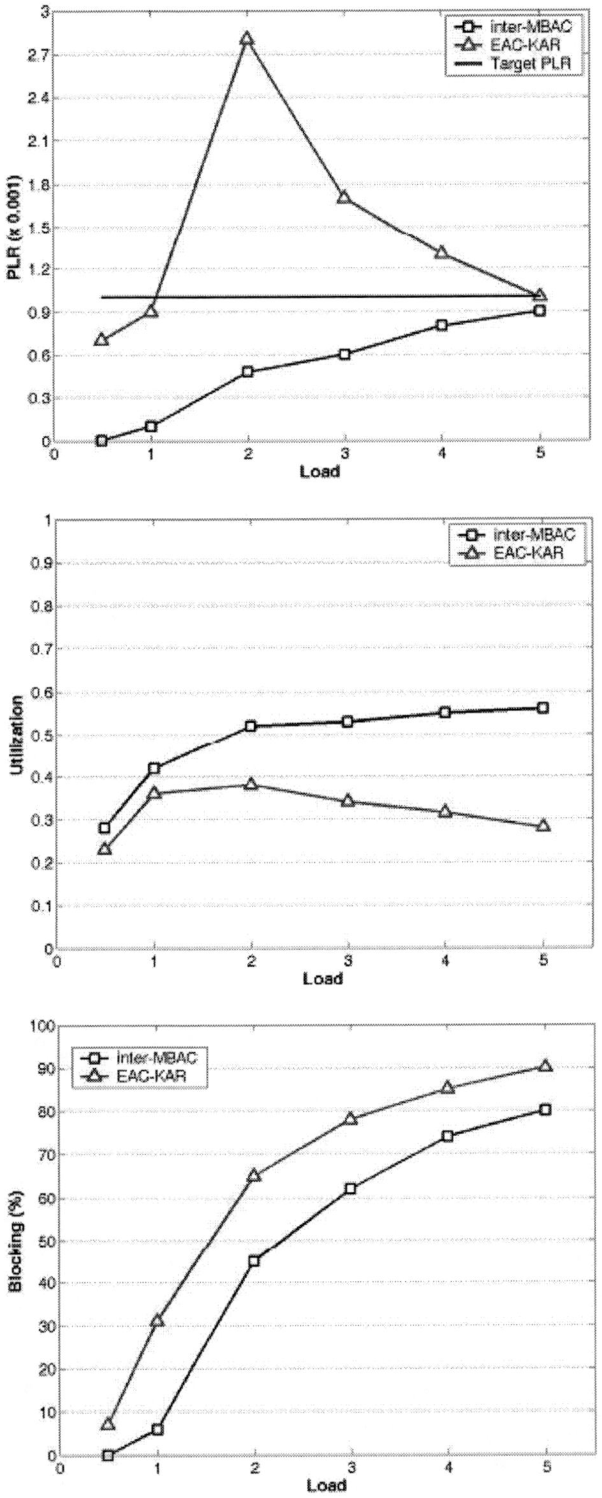

Figure 14. Incurred PLR (top), utilization (middle), and blocking rate (bottom) for Videoconference sources and target PLR 0.001.

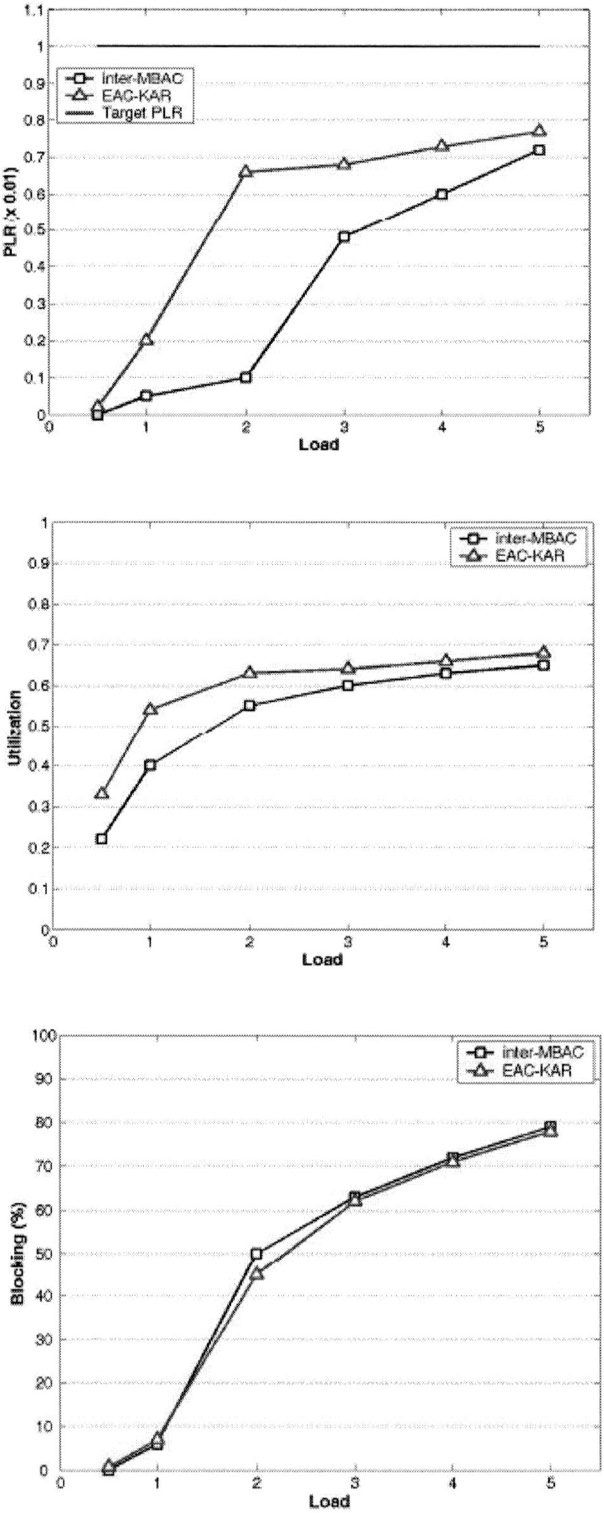

Figure 15. Incurred PLR (top), utilization (middle), and blocking rate (bottom) for VoIP sources and target PLR 0.01.

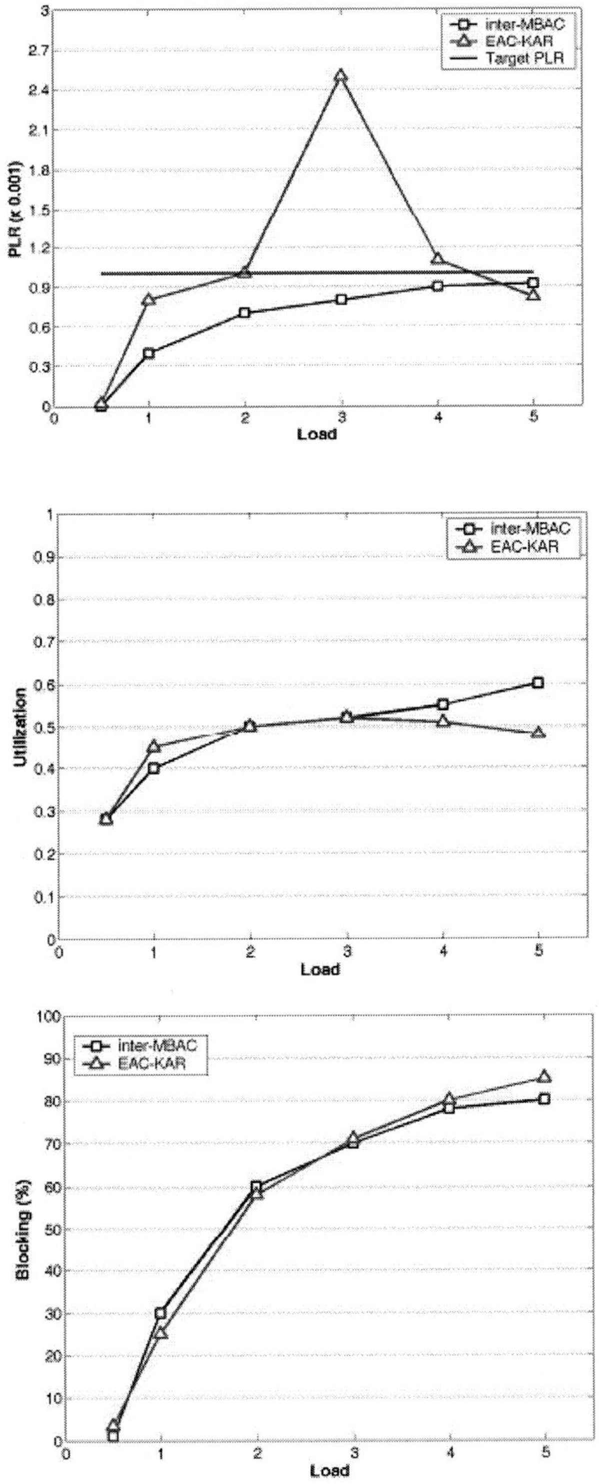

Figure 16. Incurred PLR (top), utilization (middle), and blocking rate (bottom) for VoIP sources and target PLR 0.001.

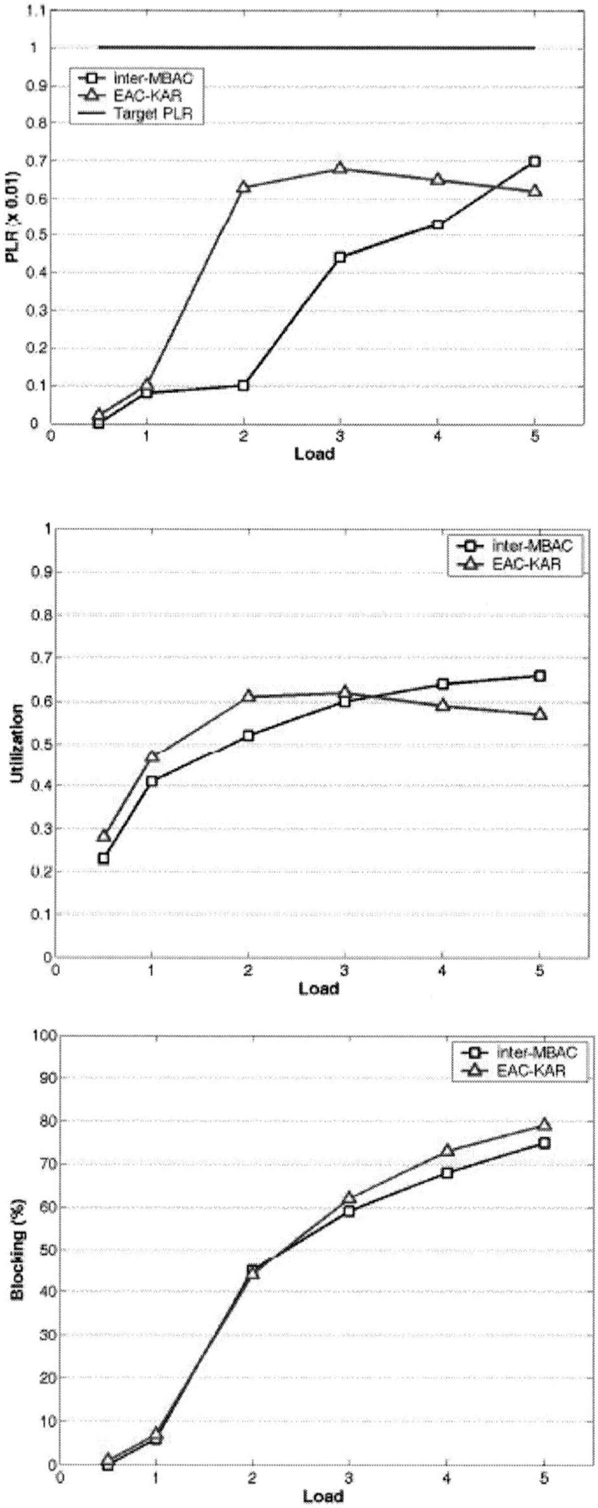

Figure 17. Incurred PLR (top), utilization (middle), and blocking rate (bottom) for mixed sources and target PLR 0.01.

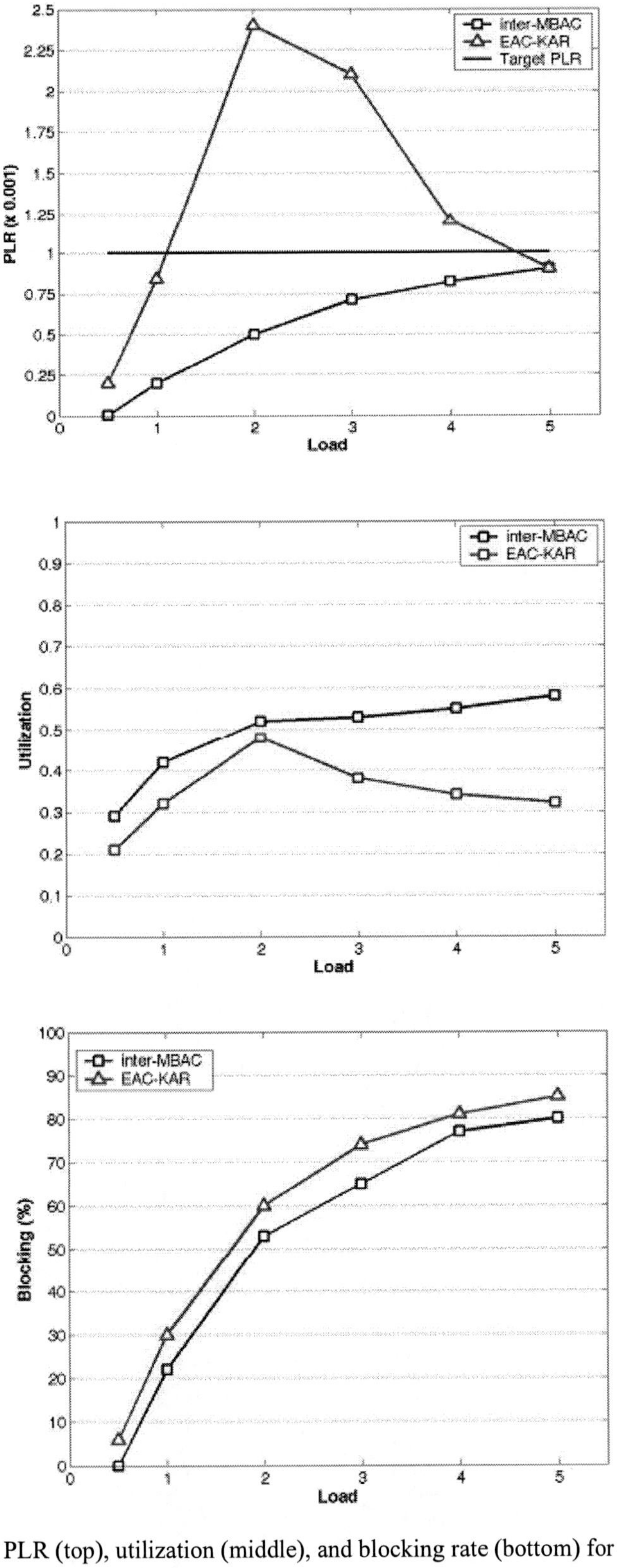

Figure 18. Incurred PLR (top), utilization (middle), and blocking rate (bottom) for mixed sources and target PLR 0.001.

5.2.4. Discussion

The simulation results show that inter-MBAC can satisfy the target PLR in all cases without requiring any further reconfiguration of its parameters for individual traffic scenarios and loading conditions. As we show, it is possible with the same set of values for its tuning parameters to achieve reasonably good performance regarding utilization and blocking for a variety of traffic scenarios and loading conditions.

EAC-KAR satisfies the local target PLR for the target 0.01 case with appropriate setting of its tuning parameter (probing duration), even though for the Videoconference sources only and for the mixed VoIP and Videoconference sources traffic scenarios and for increasing loading conditions this is achieved while the scheme has entered the thrashing region, which translates in reduced utilization and increased blocking rate. For the stringent local target PLR 0.001 case, EAC-KAR fails to satisfy the local target PLR for most loading conditions despite reconfiguring its tuning parameter. Also for the latter case, the target PLR for high loading conditions is satisfied in some scenarios but this is actually due to the thrashing effect.

Regarding the control overhead, since for EAC-KAR the control overhead is dependent on the number of flows, whereas for inter-MBAC the control overhead is dependent not on the number of flows but on the number of edge nodes the control overhead of inter-MBAC is expected to be less than that of EAC-KAR in real network situations.

In the following figure the averages of inter-domain link utilization and blocking rate for all simulated cases and loading conditions for the two schemes, including the scenarios and loading conditions where EAC-KAR violates the local target PLR, are shown.

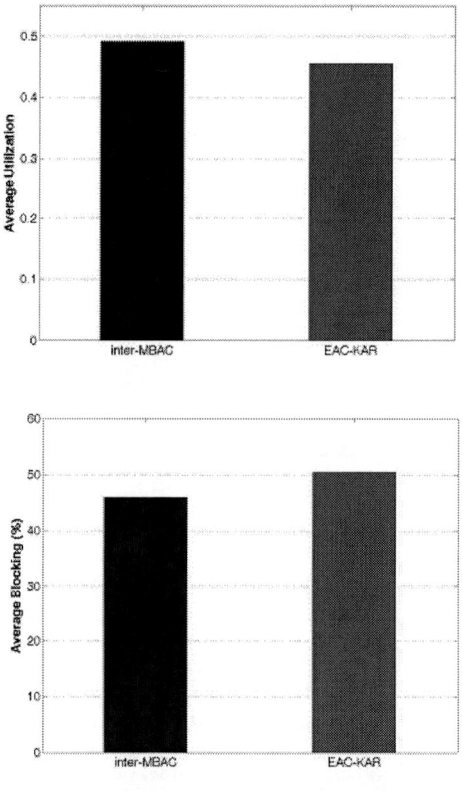

Figure 19. Average utilization (top) and blocking rate (bottom).

As it can be seen, inter-MBAC achieves on average higher utilization and incurs lower blocking compared to EAC-KAR, while at the same time, contrary to EAC-KAR, satisfying the local target PLR value.

5.2.5. Conclusions

In this section we presented a distributed measurement-based admission control scheme for inter-domain real-time traffic originating from DiffServ domains. The scheme is generic enough and can be used both in traditional end-to-end QoS-enabled environments, such as the IntServ over DiffServ one, but also in emerging SLA-based QoS-enabled environments that are based on QoS agreements between network providers. In the future we plan to undertake a more extended evaluation of the performance of our scheme when applied to IntServ over DiffServ environments and compare it to modified MBAC and TDAC schemes in order to fully assert its performance benefits and its scalability.

6. CONCLUSION

In this chapter we initially performed a network capacity management study in order to highlight several issues with respect to bandwidth allocation and admission control for the support of real-time traffic in IP DiffServ network domains. We discussed the implications of topological placement, that is the location of the employed bandwidth allocation and admission control schemes with respect to the end-users requesting the services and the various network boundaries and we showed that their performance depends on it; that is their performance at different points in a DiffServ network domain and for the same traffic load can be quite different and can deviate significantly from the expected targets. We then proposed some practical traffic engineering solutions to address these issues.

Taking into account the implications of our network capacity management study we then proposed admission control schemes for both intra- and inter-domain real-time traffic. The key achievement of this work regarding the approaches towards admission control were the development of admission control functions that: a) are relatively simple and therefore suit the online nature of admission control, b) perform well for a variety of traffic load conditions without requiring frequent reconfiguration of any involved parameters, c) do not require substantial functionality from the DiffServ network side, which is outside the scope of the original DiffServ specification, and d) are generic enough to be used both in traditional QoS-enabled environments, such as the IntServ over DiffServ one, but also in emerging SLA-based QoS-enabled environments.

REFERENCES

[1] Fall, K.; Varadhan, K. "The *ns* manual" (www.isi.edu/nsnam/ns/ns_doc.pdf).
[2] Schollmeier, G.; Winkler, C. "Providing Sustainable QoS in Next-Generation Networks," *IEEE Com. Mag.* 2004, 42, 102-107.
[3] Bonald, T.; Proutiere, A.; Roberts, J. (2001). "Statistical Performance Guarantees for Streaming Flows using Expedited Forwarding," Proceedings of IEEE INFOCOM.

[4] Breslau, L.; Knightly, E.; Shenker, S.; Stoica, I.; Zhang, Z. (2000). "Endpoint Admission Control: Architectural Issues and Performance," Proceedings of ACM SIGCOMM.

[5] Grossglauser, M.; Tse, D. "A Framework for Robust Measurement-Based Admission Control," *IEEE/ACM Trans. Net.* 1999, 27, 237-248.

[6] Chuah, C.; Subramarian, L.; Katz, R.; Joseph, A. (2000). "Resource Provisioning using a Clearing House Architecture," Proceedings of IEEE IWQoS.

[7] Lima, S.; Carvalho, P.; Freitas, V. "Distributed Admission Control in Multiservice IP Networks: Concurrency issues," *J. Com.* 2006, 1, 1-9.

[8] Cetinkaya, C.; Knightly, E. "Scalable Services via Egress Admission Control," *IEEE Trans. Mult.* 2001, 3, 69-81.

[9] Lima, S.; Carvalho, P.; Freitas, V. "Distributed Admission Control for QoS and SLS Management," *J. Net. Sys. Man.* 2004, 12, 397-426.

[10] Eardley, P. (Editor) (2009) "Pre-Congestion Notification Architecture," Internet RFC 5559.

[11] Bernet, Y.; Yavatkar, R.; Baker, F.; Zhang, L.; Speer, M.; Braden, R.; Davie, B.; Wroclawski, J.; Felstain, E. (2000). "A Framework for Integrated Services Operations over DiffServ Networks," Internet RFC 2998.

[12] Georgoulas, S.; Trimintzios, P.; Pavlou, G.; Ho, K. (2006). "On the Location-awareness of Bandwidth Allocation and Admission Control for the Support of Real-time Traffic in Class-based IP Networks," Proceedings of IEEE/IFIP MMNS.

[13] Shiomoto, K.; Yamanaka, N.; Takahashi, T. "Overview of Measurement-based Connection Admission Control Methods in ATM Networks," *IEEE Com. Surv.* 1999, 2, 2-13.

[14] Padmanabhan, V. N.; Qiu, L.; Wang, H. J. (2003). "Server-based inference of Internet Link Lossiness," Proceedings of IEEE INFOCOM.

[15] Menth, M. (2004). "Efficient Admission Control and Routing for Resilient Communication Networks," PhD Thesis, Univ. of Wurzburg.

[16] Georgoulas, S.; Trimintzios, P.; Pavlou, G.; Ho, K. (2005). "Heterogeneous Real-time Traffic Admission Control in Differentiated Services Domains," Proceedings of IEEE GLOBECOM.

[17] Chaded, T. (2000). "IP QoS Parameters", TF-NGN.

[18] Lee, T.; Zukerman, M. (2001). "Admission Control for Bursty Multimedia Traffic," Proceedings of IEEE INFOCOM.

[19] Elek, V.; Karlsson, G.; Ronngren, R. (2000) "Admission Control based on End-to End Measurements," Proceedings of IEEE INFOCOM.

[20] Gibbens, R.; Kelly, F. (1997). "Measurement-based connection admission control," Proceedings of 15th International Teletraffic Congress.

[21] Howarth, M.; Flegkas, P.; Pavlou, G.; Wang, N.; Trimintzios, P.; Griffin, D.; Griem, J.; Boucadair, M.; Morand, P.; Asgari, H.; Georgatsos, P. "Provisioning for Inter-domain Quality of Service: the MESCAL Approach," *IEEE Com. Mag.* 2005, 43, 129-137.

[22] Georgoulas, S.; Pavlou, G.; Trimintzios, P.; Ho, K. (2007). "Admission Control for Inter-domain Real-time Traffic Originating from Differentiated Services Stub Domains", Proceedings of WWIC.

In: Recent Advances in Providing QoS and Reliability... ISBN 978-1-61761-858-1
Editors: N. Wang, G. Pavlou and M. Boucadair

Chapter 4

PERFORMANCE MEASUREMENT AND OPTIMIZATION FOR RELATIVE QOS OF MULTIPARTY COMMUNICATIONS

Lei Liang and Zhili Sun
University of Surrey, Guildford, Surrey, United Kingdom

ABSTRACT

The next generation Internet will provide various services over a heterogeneous network infrastructure including the existing Internet, mobile networks, satellite networks, sensor networks and so on. Many research efforts have been put towards providing satisfied Quality of Service (QoS) over such a network for different services. Multiparty communications is one of these services that will play a very important role. This service introduced some unique QoS requirements in which the relative QoS requirement need be defined and optimized. How to measurement and judge if these QoS requirements have been satisfied by the network will be described here and using the measured results an relative QoS optimization algorithm will be introduced and analyzed

1. INTRODUCTION

Multiparty communications as new network services will play very important roles in the next generation internet. These services are designed to enable more than two people to communicate with each others using the next generation networks, e.g., IP conferencing, online gaming, online stock market and so on. Multiparty communications attend to use multicast routing protocols to make it feasible at network level. However, there is another key aspect we should mention here, the QoS. These services will not win their final success in the fighting with the traditional telephony services without an acceptable QoS. It will be necessary to carry measurements in those multiparty communication systems to provide solid inputs to evaluate the QoS performance as well as appropriately present those results in terms of some well defined parameters.

To determine what parameters are needed to measure is the most important factor before one launch his measurement. It is the key to decide measurement tools, methodologies and accuracy. The Internet Engineering Task Force (IETF) IP Performance Metrics (IPPM) working group developed a set of standard metrics that can be applied to the quality, performance, and reliability of Internet data delivery services. Another working group named Benchmarking Methodology (BMWG) made a series of recommendations concerning the measurement of the performance characteristics of various internetworking technologies, which includes terminology, identifying a set of metrics that aid in the description of traffic characteristics, and methodology, required to collect said metrics. Additionally, the ITU-T Working Group T1A1.3 made similar network performance parameter definition [4].

The IPPM developed a set of measurement parameters as well as the correspondent measurement methodologies with the cooperation with other relative working group such as BMWG, TEWG, ITU-T SG 12 and SG 13. Those parameters and their corresponding metrics include:

- Connectivity: If a packet transmitted from source A to destination B at time T can arrive B, it is said that A has the connectivity to B at time T.
- One-way delay: The difference between the time when the source sends out the first bit of the packet and the time when the destination receives the last bit of the packet
- One-way loss: If a packet transmitted from source A to destination B cannot arrive B in a certain time threshold, it is said that this packet is lost
- Round-trip delay: The sum of the times needed for a test packet travel from source A to destination B and from B back to A.
- One-way delay variation: The difference of the one-way delays of a selected pair of packets in the stream going from source A to destination B.
- Loss patterns: The packet loss distribution.
- Bulk transport capacity: The expected long term average data rate (bits per second) of a single ideal TCP implementation over the path in question.

These traffic parameters and their measurement methodologies were defined by IETF for the purpose of network performance and reliability analysis. They are vital for the network evaluation, especially QoS evaluation. To adopt these measurement technologies from the one-to-one communications to multiparty communications, we will need to identify any different QoS requirements between them. The multiparty communications have additional QoS requirements to one-to-one communications. The latter only have requirements on the absolute QoS while the former one needs additional relative QoS support [1]. The relative QoS requirements come from the nature of the group communications. It means the difference of absolute QoS between all users in a group. If some of users suffer worst absolute QoS than the rest, and if the difference between these two QoS levels is beyond a certain threshold, the multiparty communication might not be able to continue. Therefore, we need something to describe this QoS difference and present the requirements on the relative QoS.

This article will present two main achievements:

- To propose a new set of parameters and their metrics derived from the IETF IPPM One-way metrics. These metrics extends the foundation of the IP network performance metrics defined in the IPPM working group to adapt the requirement of the relative QoS of multiparty communications services. It also extends the metric concept to vector and matrix concept for network performance measurement to cover both single point measurement and multipoint measurement. The measurement methodology and results reporting algorithm of the proposed parameters, metrics, vectors and matrix is also presented. The work presented here is a part an IETF internet draft that is under the process of the 2nd IPPM working group last call and will be published as a standard RFC very shortly [2].
- Based on the proposed metrics, an optimization algorithm is developed for the relative QoS that uses dynamic resource utilization depending on network situations, which shows the relative delay and packet loss can be enhanced to meet their requirements of, as an example, online gaming services [3].

2. One-to-Group Parameters and Metrics

Previously, all IETF IPPM QoS parameters are defined for one-to-one connections. Further attention should be put on the multiparty applications that use multicast routing protocols, e.g. the IP conferencing services and online gaming. The basic consideration is that in the multiparty communication, we have a group of people involved in the action rather than two. One may say that no matter how many people join the communication, the connections can still be treated as a set of end-to-end connections. However, we might not describe a multiparty communication by a set of end-to-end measurement metrics both because of the difficulty for understanding and the lack of convenience. For instance, an engineer might not describe the connections of a multiparty online conference in terms of one-way delay for user A and B, B and C, and C and A because people might be confused. And he might use the end-to-end metrics with the worst and the best value to give users an idea of the QoS range of the service they are providing. But it's not clear enough and might not be accurate in a big multiparty communication. Our suggestion is to use a more sophisticated way after reason-nable mathematic deriving, i.e. mean, variation etc. the new metrics will be more efficient and accurate to express the connection situation among a group of users.

We need measures to present the performance of a multiparty communication topology. A simple point-to-point metric cannot completely describe the multiparty situation. New one-to-group metrics assess performance of the multiple paths for further statistical analysis. The new metrics are named one-to-group performance metrics, and they are based on the unicast metrics defined in IPPM RFCs. One-to-group metrics are one-way metrics from one source to a group of destinations, or receivers, which are needed for:

1. Designing and engineering multicast trees and MPLS point-to-multipoint LSPs.
2. Evaluating and controlling the quality of multicast services, including inter-domain multicast.

3. Presenting and evaluating the performance requirements for multiparty communications and overlay multicast.

The One-to-group parameters should be measured based on only one source in a multiparty communication group. Whenever we say one-to-group parameters, we should associate it with a source. The Figure 1 shows this concept.

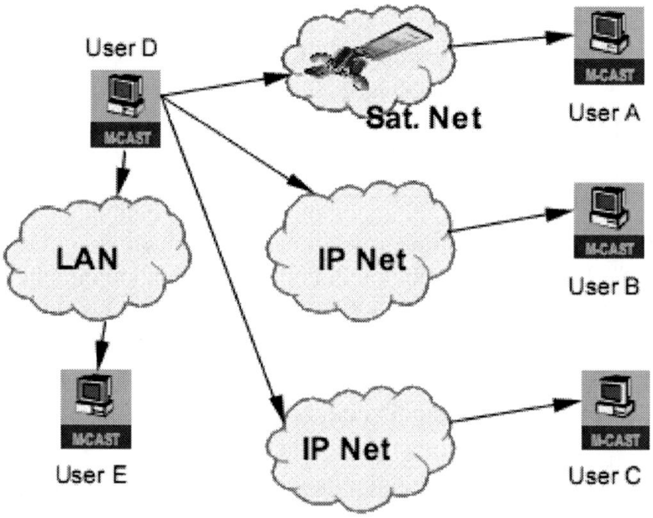

Figure 1. One-to-group measurement scenario example.

In Figure 1 user A, B, C, D and E belong to the same multicast group. User D is the only active source in the multicast group when measuring the One-to-group parameters. User B and C are connected with user D through terrestrial IP network, user E are in the same LAN with user D, and user A are connected with user D using a satellite network. The One-to-group parameters measured in this scenario should be associated with user D.

2.1. The New Terms for One-to-Group Metrics

The definition of the new One-to-group metrics and their relevant statistics need new terms other than those used for One-way metrics. They are:

- Points of interest: Points of interest are the hosts (as per [5] definition, "hosts" include routing nodes) that are measurement collection points, a sub-set of the set of hosts involved in the delivery of the packets (in addition to the source itself). Points of interest of one-to-group metrics are the intended destination hosts for packets from the source (in addition to the source itself).
- Reference point: A reference point is defined as the server where the statistical calculations will be carried out. It is usually a centralized server in the measurement architecture that is controlled by a network operator, where measurement data can be collected for further processing. The reference point is distinctly different from hosts

at measurement collection points, where the actual measurements are carried out (e.g., points of interest).

- Vector: A vector is a set of singletons (single atomic results) comprised of observations corresponding to a single source packet at different hosts in a network. For instance, if the one-way delay singletons observed at N receivers for Packet P sent by the source Src are dT1, dT2,..., dTN, then a vector V with N elements can be organized as {dT1, dT2,..., dTN}. The element dT1 is distinct from all others as the singleton at receiver 1 in response to a packet sent from the source at a specific time. The complete vector gives information over the dimension of space; a set of N receivers in this example. The singleton elements of any vector are distinctly different from each other in terms of their measurement collection point. Different vectors for common measurement points of interest are distinguished by the source packet sending time
- Matrix: Several vectors form a matrix, which contains results observed over a sampling interval at different places in a network at different times. For example, the One-way delay vectors V1={dT11, dT12,..., dT1N}, V2={dT21, dT22,..., dT2N},..., Vm={dTm1, dTm2,..., dTmN} for Packet P1, P2,...,Pm, form a One-way delay Matrix {V1, V2,...,Vm}. The matrix organizes the vector information to present network performance in both space and time. A one-dimensional matrix (row) corresponds to a sample in simple point-to-point measurement.

2.2. One-to-Group Metrics

There are totally three one-to-group vectors defined to measure the one-way performance between a source and a group of receivers. They are:

1. Type-P-One-to-group-Delay-Vector collects the set of Type-P-one-way-delay singletons between one sender and N receivers. It contains following parameter:

   - Src, the IP address of a host acting as the source.
   - Recv1,..., RecvN, the IP addresses of the N hosts acting as receivers.
   - T, a time.
   - dT1,...,dTn, a list of times.
   - Type-P, the specification of the packet type.
   - Gr, the receiving group identifier. The parameter Gr is the multicast group address if the measured packets are transmitted over IP multicast. This parameter is to differentiate the measured traffic from other unicast and multicast traffic. It is OPTIONAL for this metric to avoid losing any generality, i.e. to make the metric also applicable to unicast measurement where there is only one receiver.

   The value of a Type-P-One-to-group-Delay-Vector is a set of Type-P-One-way-Delay singletons [6], which is a sequence of times (a real number in the dimension of seconds with sufficient resolution to convey the results).

   The definition of this vector is that given a Type-P packet sent by the source Src at time T, and the N hosts { Recv1,...,RecvN } which receive the packet at the time

{T+dT1,...,T+dTn }, or the packet does not pass a receiver within a specified loss threshold time, then the Type-P-One-to-group-Delay-Vector is defined as the set of the Type-P-One-way-Delay singletons between Src and each receiver with value of { dT1, dT2,...,dTn }, where any of the singletons may be undefined if the packet did not pass the corresponding receiver within a specified loss threshold time.

2. Type-P-One-to-group-Packet-Loss-Vector collects the set of Type-P-One-way-Packet-Loss singletons between one sender and N receivers. It has the following parameters:

- Src, the IP address of a host acting as the source.
- Recv1,..., RecvN, the IP addresses of the N hosts acting as receivers.
- T, a time.
- Type-P, the specification of the packet type.
- Gr, the receiving group identifier, OPTIONAL.

The value of a Type-P-One-to-group-Packet-Loss-Vector is a set of Type-P-One-way-Packet-Loss singletons [7] as:

- T, time the source packet was sent
- L1,...,LN a list of Boolean values

The definition of this vector is that Given a Type P packet sent by the source Src at T and the N hosts, Recv1,...,RecvN, the Type-P-One-to-group-Packet-Loss-Vector is defined as a set of the Type-P-One-way-Packet-Loss singletons between Src and each of the receivers {T, <L1=0|1>,<L2=0|1>,..., <LN=0|1>}, where the Boolean value 0|1 depends on receiving the packet at a particular receiver within a loss threshold time.

3. Type-P-One-to-group-ipdv-Vector collects the set of Type-P-One-way-ipdv singletons between one sender and N receivers. This metric contains the following parameters:

- Src, the IP address of a host acting as the source.
- Recv1,..., RecvN, the IP addresses of the N hosts acting as receivers.
- T1, a time.
- T2, a time.
- ddT1, ...,ddTn, a list of times.
- Type-P, the specification of the packet type.
- F, a selection function non-ambiguously defining the two packets from the stream selected for the metric.
- Gr, the receiving group identifier. The parameter Gr is the multicast group address if the measured packets are transmitted over IP multicast. This parameter is to differentiate the measured traffic from other unicast and multicast traffic. It is OPTIONAL in the metric to avoid losing any generality, i.e. to make the metric also applicable to unicast measurement where there is only one receiver.

The value of a Type-P-One-to-group-ipdv-Vector is a set of Type-P-One-way-ipdv singletons [8].

The definition of this vector is that given a Type-P packet stream, Type-P-One-to-group-ipdv-Vector is defined for two packets transferred from the source Src to the N hosts { Recv1,...,RecvN }, which are selected by the selection function F as the difference between the value of the Type-P-One-to-group-Delay-Vector from Src to { Recv1,..., RecvN } at time T1 and the value of the Type-P-One-to-group-Delay-Vector from Src to {Recv1,...,RecvN } at time T2. T1 is the wire-time at which Src sent the first bit of the first packet, and T2 is the wire-time at which Src sent the first bit of the second packet. This metric is derived from the Type-P-One-to-group-Delay-Vector metric.

For a set of real numbers {ddT1,...,ddTn}, the Type-P-One-to-group-ipdv-Vector from Src to { Recv1,...,RecvN } at T1, T2 is{ddT1,...,ddTn} means that Src sent two packets, the first at wire-time T1 (first bit), and the second at wire-time T2 (first bit) and the packets were received by { Recv1,...,RecvN } at wire-time {dT1+T1,...,dTn+T1}(last bit of the first packet), and at wire-time {dT'1+T2,...,dT'n+T2} (last bit of the second packet), and that {dT'1-dT1,...,dT'n-dTn} ={ddT1,...,ddTn}.

For any pair of selected packets, the difference dT'n-dTn is undefined if:the delay dTn to Receiver n is undefined, OR the delay dT'n to Receiver n is undefined.

2.3. One-to-Group Sample Statistics

The one-to-group metrics defined above are directly achieved by collecting relevant unicast one-way metrics measurements results and by gathering them per group of receivers. They produce network performance information which guides engineers toward potential problems which may have happened on any branch of a multicast routing tree.

The results of these metrics are not directly usable to present the performance of a group because each result is made of a huge number of singletons which are difficult to read and analyze. As an example, delays are not comparable because the distance between receiver and sender differs. Furthermore they don't capture relative performance situation a multiparty communication.

From the performance point of view, the multiparty communication services not only require the support of absolute performance information but also information on "relative performance". The relative performance means the difference between absolute performances of all users. Directly using the one-way metrics cannot present the relative performance situation. However, if we use the variations of all users' one-way parameters, we can have new metrics to measure the difference of the absolute performance and hence provide the threshold value of relative performance that a multiparty service might demand. A very good example of the high relative performance requirement is online gaming. A very small difference in delay might result in failure in the game. We have to use multicast specific statistic metrics to define the relative delay required by online gaming. There are many other services, e.g. online biding, online stock market, etc., that require multicast metrics in order to evaluate the network against their requirements. Therefore, we can see the importance of new, multicast specific, statistic metrics to feed this need.

We might also use some one-to-group statistic conceptions to present and report the group performance and relative performance to save the report transmission bandwidth.

Statistics have been defined for One-way metrics in corresponding RFCs. They provide the foundation of definition for performance statistics. For instance, there are definitions for minimum and maximum One-way delay in [6]. However, there is a dramatic difference between the statistics for one-to-one communications and for one-to-many communications. The former one only has statistics over the time dimension while the later one can have statistics over both time and space dimensions. This space dimension is introduced by the Matrix concept as illustrated in Figure 2. For a Matrix M each row is a set of One-way singletons spreading over the time dimension and each column is another set of One-way singletons spreading over the space dimension.

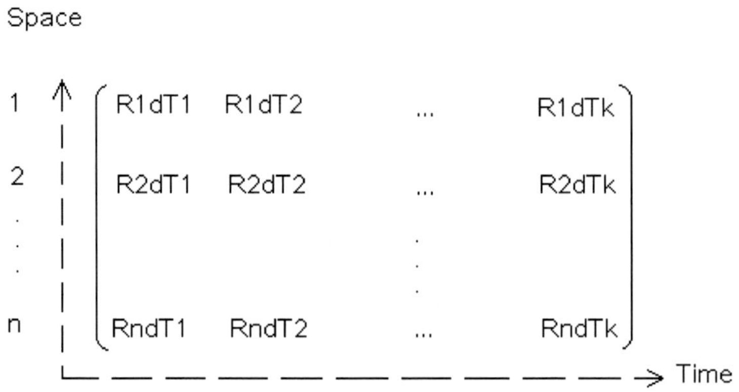

Figure 2. Matrix M (n*k).

In Matrix M, each element is a one-way delay singleton. Each column is a delay vector contains the One-way delays of the same packet observed at M points of interest. It implies the geographical factor of the performance within a group. Each row is a set of One-way delays observed during a sampling interval at one of the points of interest. It presents the delay performance at a receiver over the time dimension.

Therefore, one can either calculate statistics by rows over the space dimension or by columns over the time dimension. It's up to the operators or service provides which dimension they are interested in. For example, a TV broadcast service provider might want to know the statistical performance of each user in a long term run to make sure their services are acceptable and stable. While for an online gaming service provider, he might be more interested to know if all users are served fairly by calculating the statistics over the space dimension. This article does not intend to recommend which of the statistics are better than the other.

To save the report transmission bandwidth, each point of interest can send statistics in a pre-defined time interval to the reference point rather than sending every one-way singleton it observed. As long as an appropriate time interval is decided, appropriate statistics can represent the performance in a certain accurate scale. How to decide the time interval and how to bootstrap all points of interest and the reference point depend on applications. For instance, applications with lower transmission rate can have the time interval longer and ones with higher transmission rate can have the time interval shorter.

Moreover, after knowing the statistics over the time dimension, one might want to know how these statistics are distributed over the space dimension. For instance, a TV broadcast service provider had the performance Matrix M and calculated the One-way delay mean over the time dimension to obtain a delay Vector as {V1,V2,..., VN}. He then calculated the mean of all the elements in the Vector to see what level of delay he has served to all N users. This new delay mean gives information on how good the service has been delivered to a group of users during a sampling interval in terms of delay. It requires twice as much calculation to have this statistic over both time and space dimensions. This kind of statistics is referred to as 2-level statistics to distinguish them from 1-level statistics calculated over either space or time dimension. It can be easily proven that no matter over which dimension a 2-level statistic is calculated first, the results are the same. I.e. one can calculate the 2-level delay mean using the Matrix M by having the 1-level delay mean over the time dimension first and then calculate the mean of the obtained vector to find out the 2-level delay mean. Or, he can do the 1-level statistic calculation over the space dimension first and then have the 2-level delay mean. Both two results will be exactly the same. Therefore, when defining a 2-level statistic there is no need to specify the order in which the calculation is executed.

Many statistics can be defined for the proposed one-to-group metrics over either the space dimension or the time dimension or both. This article treats the case where a stream of packets from the Source results in a sample at each of the Receivers in the Group, and these samples are each summarized with the usual statistics employed in one-to-one communication. New statistic definitions are presented, which summarize the one-to-one statistics over all the Receivers in the Group. In this article, only delay related statistics are presented. for a receiver and for an entire group as illustrated by the matrix below.

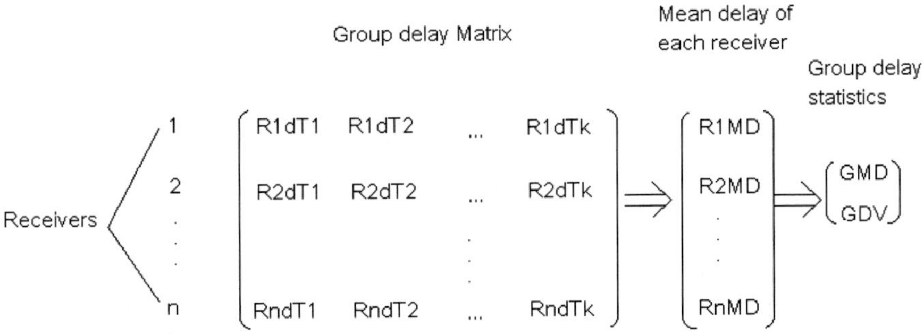

Figure 3. Group delay statistics.

Based on Figure 3, we can define three statistic metrics relevant to One-to-group delay metrics defined above.

Type-P-One-to-group-Receiver-n-Mean-Delay is to define the Delay Mean at each Receiver N, also named RnDM in Figure 3. We obtain the value of Type-P-One-way-Delay singleton for all packets sent during the test interval at each Receiver, as in [6]. For each packet that arrives within threshold of its sending time, TstampSrc, the one-way delay singleton (dT) will be the finite value TstampRecv[i] - TstampSrc[i] in units of seconds. Otherwise, the value of the singleton is Undefined. We can have the RnDM using the following formula:

$$RnMD = \frac{1}{k}\sum_{i=1}^{k} Tstamp\mathrm{Re}\,cv[i] - TstampSrc[i] \quad (1)$$

Type-P-One-to-group-Mean-Delay is to define the Mean One-way delay calculated over the entire Group, also named GMD in Figure 3. It is to measure the overall QoS for a multiparty communication group. The definition of the Type-P-One-to-group-Mean-Delay is the mean of a one-way delay, measured simultaneously on all of the group members except of the active source. The word "simultaneously" implies the one-way parameter should be measured based on the same sample interval at each user. It can be calculated using the above RnMD with the following formula:

$$GMD = \frac{1}{n}\sum_{i=1}^{n} RnMD[i] \quad (3)$$

Type-P-One-to-group-Delay-Variation, also named GDV in Figure 3, can be defined to measure how the QoS varies among all receivers in the multiparty communication group. The definition of the Type-P-One-to-group-Delay-Variation is the population standard deviation of the Type-P-One-to-group-Receiver-n-Mean-Delay of all receivers. It can be then calculated using the following formula:

$$GDV = \sqrt{\frac{1}{n}\sum_{i=1}^{n}\left(RnMD[i] - GMD\right)^2} \quad (4)$$

2.4. Discussion on Group-to-One and Group-to-Group Metrics

We note that points of interest can also be selected to define measurements on group-to-one and group-to-group topologies. These topologies are beyond the scope of this article, because they would involve multiple packets launched from different sources. However, this section gives some insights on these two cases.

The measurements for group-to-one topology can be easily derived from the one-to-group measurement. The measurement point is the host that is acting as a receiver while all other hosts act as sources in this case.

The group-to-group communication topology has no obvious focal point: the sources and the measurement collection points can be anywhere. However, it is possible to organize the problem by applying measurements in one-to-group or group-to-one topologies for each host in a uniform way (without taking account of how the real communication might be carried out). For example, one group of hosts < ha, hb, hc, ..., hn > might act as sources to send data to another group of hosts < Ha, Hb, Hc, ..., Hm >, and they can be organized into n sets of points of interest for one-to-group communications: < ha, Ha, Hb, Hc, ..., Hm >, < hb, Ha, Hb, Hc, ..., Hm >, < hc, Ha, Hb, Hc, ..., Hm >, ..., < hn, Ha, Hb, Hc, ..., Hm >

3. Relative QoS Optimization Algorithm for Multiparty Communications Using One-to-Group Metrics

As a good example of using these proposed new vectors and metrics, a relative QoS optimization algorithm based on the DiffServ framework has been proposed for online gaming services. To describe the algorithm, the relative delay was chosen to be the study objective. The proposed algorithm can dynamically monitor the delays for all clients in a client-server based topology and manipulate the priority of each client's traffic corresponding to the network situation to guarantee that the relative delay is kept under a predefined threshold without breaking the absolute delay bound. Although only the relative delay was chosen as the study objective, our algorithm can be extended to other relative parameters, such as relative jitter and packet loss ratio.

Some research efforts have been put to reduce the difference between all user delays in the online gaming service by adding additional entities to the network. We can use term GDV defined in previous section to present this difference here. [9] and [10] proposed to use delay control entities or proxies on both server and user side to decrease the relative delay variation while increase the absolute delay. Our thought is more concentrate on developing algorithms based on already existing technologies rather than introducing more complexity to the network. Moreover, the idea to increase the absolute delay is not a good choice, as real-time applications are all vulnerable to long absolute delays. Our proposed algorithm is to utilize the measurement methodologies and parameters proposed in previous section to solve this relative QoS issue based on DiffServ networks.

As we all know, the fundamental of DiffServ is to differentiate services by classifying the traffics. It implies relative QoS for different traffic classes. For instance, some algorithms manipulate the traffic priorities on routers to let some traffic pass through more quickly while others have to wait for a longer time. So our basic idea is to assign the users who are suffering worse delay a higher priority traffic class to decrease the absolute delay in one hand and, in another hand, improve the delay relative to other users. However, there are more questions to be answered to support this algorithm.

3.1. Algorithm Environment Assumptions

What environment will the algorithm be deployed? Despite of the DiffServ environment, the trend of the multiparty communication is to utilize the multicast technologies to use the bandwidth more efficiently and enable one-to-many communication. The algorithm proposed in [11] could be one of possible solutions to enable different QoS classes for individual multicast branches. Also, the communication topology will be based on centralized server and distributed clients. It is because that to support fully meshed multicast connections will be typically difficult as the changes of the sources can make the delay change much more often and that will trigger much more traffic class modifications. The complexity and the dynamics of the fully meshed multicast might be too difficult to be efficiently supported in the Internet. Client-server based topology is highly practical for many multiparty communications mentioned before. Actually, online gaming currently has been implemented based on this topology for billing requirement. Furthermore, the client-sever topology implies single source multicast. Source Specific Multicast (SSM) [12] will be used to enable the multicast routing. The multicast only happened when the server acts as a source and sends the same information to all clients. Clients have to use unicast to send data to the server and allow server to update all the rest clients. This is essential for a centralized server and distributed client topology.

3.2. Class Modification for Multicast Traffic

To apply the defined One-to-group metrics, we only consider the multicast traffic flow from the server to clients here. We consider the unicast and multicast transmission separately with respect to the fact that two routing algorithms might use different paths and might suffer from different delays. The delay for each multicast branch has to be measured on each client rather than on the server. Then all clients should send the measured one-way delays to the server on which the One-to-group delay matrix will be formed for the GDV calculation. If the GDV is higher than the pre-set threshold, the class modification function will be triggered.

To trigger the class modification, the server will periodically calculate the current GDV value by collecting the One-to-group delay matrix for the multicast group. The period to calculate the GDV marks the crucial interval that will impact the efficiency of the algorithm. It can be derived using the following formula:

$$T_{\text{GDV}} = D_{Link} \times 2 + T_{Tran} \tag{4}$$

where TGDV is the GDV calculation interval, DLink is the link delay and TTran is the source transmission interval. Equation 4) shows clearly that the GDV calculation interval should be equal to the double of the link delay plus the source transmission interval. This is because that the server has to wait long enough for one signalling procedure finishing before it starts another signalling procedure. It has also to wait for the next data packet arrival after the signalling procedure finished in order to get the modified delay for the next GDV calculation.

The server sets up a threshold value for the GDV, which can be various to satisfy different requirements of different applications. For instance, FPS (First Person Shooting) online game will have much higher requirement on GDV than a videoconference service. If the calculated GDV is bigger than the threshold, it will trigger the delay modification function to upgrade the class of the traffic from the client who is currently suffering from the worst delay to give it higher priority till the threshold is satisfied. And if the threshold cannot be satisfied when the traffic from the client already has the highest priority, the server will degrade the traffic from the client with the shortest delay to a lower priority. At last, if the GDV threshold still cannot be satisfied, that means the network situation is beyond the optimisation limit. Therefore, the server can either give up optimisation or notify the client with the worst delay to modify its connection situation.

There is a reason to increase the traffic class to give the client with the worst delay a higher priority rather than decrease those with best delay. The multimedia interactive applications have high requirement on absolute delay, which can be represented by the GMD in Equation 2). Therefore, the better choice is to improve the mean delay at first by increasing the priority of the client with worst delay unless it cannot reduce the GDV below the threshold value. When the server manages to lower a client traffic priority, it has to check if the resulted mean delay is higher than another threshold required by the application to avoid the absolute delay requirement being abandoned. This implies the system has an assumption that any violation of the GDV threshold is due to the network situation becoming worse rather than better. The weak point of this assumption is that the priorities of the traffic from clients will become higher and higher. For instance, we have A, B and C three connections to the server. In the beginning, the GDV for all of these three connections satisfies the threshold in the server. Connection A suddenly suffers the worst delay and the server upgrades its priority. Later, the network situation for connection A becomes much better and results in a much shorter delay. This might rise up a new violation to the GDV threshold. However, the server will not degrade the priority for connection A but upgrade connection C, which currently suffers the worst delay, to satisfy the threshold. If this situation repeats, three connections will be upgraded to highest priority at last before the serve managed to degrade them. For the users, this is not economic since they will have to pay for this high priority that is not necessary. There are some means to avoid this. One is to set up both the lower bound and upper bound for mean delay. So the server will check the upper mean delay bound to decide if it should degrade the priority for a connection first rather than always upgrade the priority. Another method is to let the server remember two delays for each connection collected at the last two continuous measurement time points. Before it executes the class modification function, it will have to check the reason of the GDV violation to know whether it's because one connection suffers from a worse delay caused by the dynamic network or another connection benefits from a better delay.

3.3. Simulation for the Relative Qos Optimisation Algorithm

With the proposed QoS optimization algorithm in mind, a simulation was built up using *ns2* to verify its availability and testify how much it can improve the relative QoS in a multiparty Internet gaming environment. In the simulation, 9 nodes, R_i ($i \in [1, 9]$), work as routers. R_1, R_3, R_4, R_6, R_7 and R_9 are edge routers as well as Markers and Demarkers. Link delays are configured for the link between these routers so each three of them present a domain. R_1, R_2 and R_3 present a domain; R_4, R_5 and R_6 present another domain; and the rest three routers present the third domain. All domains have been configured with the same link delay. Each of the three game clients, G_1, G_2 and G_3, was connected with one game server, GS, through one of the three domains via the corresponding edge routers. 6 UDP cross-sources, CS_j ($j \in [1, 6]$), and their 6 destination sinks, SN_k ($k \in [1, 6]$), are also connected through three domains as shown in Figure 4 to generate the background traffics. Each of these cross-sources has a Pareto on-off application flow attached to a UDP agent and they will send traffics with Pareto distribution to the simulation network.

We name links connecting end users and the corresponding edge routers as edge link and links between routers as core link. Edge links always have bigger bandwidth than the core links like the real networks.

In the simulation, All of the six cross-sources, CS_j ($j \in [1,6]$), were configured to generate traffic heavily enough to introduce long queuing delay for all the three clients and trigger the traffic class modification procedure. For other network situation, please refer to [13]. A new cross-source, CS_7, was connected to the network and began to generate traffic at 15th second with the highest priority after the simulation started. It stopped at the 25th second after 10 seconds raising congestion at the edge router R_1. We are expecting that our algorithm can realize that only increasing the traffic priorities will not able to solve the RDV problem in this scenario and it will try to approach an optimisation by decrease priorities of some traffic.

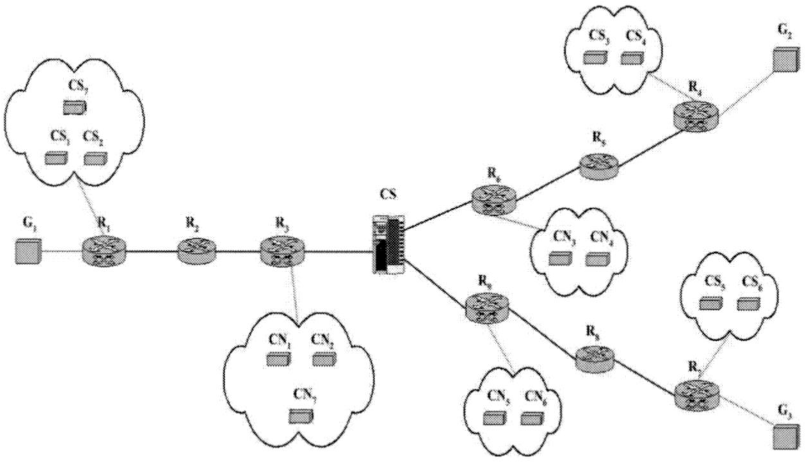

Figure 4. Simulation configuration layout.

One error was found that the server sent out one extra signalling packet. This error was caused by the large packet delay in the heavily loaded network. The server did not receive packets with updated priority after one GDV calculation period, please refer to Equation 4), due to the large network delay. Therefore, it made the wrong decision that another class modification procedure should be triggered and sent out an extra signalling packet to the corresponding client. The client found its traffic already had the highest priority and ignored this signalling packet. Thus, we had totally 1 extra signalling packet. It can be easily removed by setting a longer GDV period by adding an estimate factor corresponding to network load to the right side of the Equation 4).

It also showed that the algorithm successfully adjusted traffics from all clients to the right traffic classes and resulted in a much better mean GDV from 2.8500e-2s in a best-effort network to 2.6000e-3s in an optimized network. Figure 5 shows the GDV result curves for both cases with and without our algorithm. We can clearly see in Figure 5 that from the right beginning to the very last of the simulation, our optimisation algorithm made the QoS GDV lower than the Non-QoS GDV.

Totally 12 priority upgrading procedures were successfully executed during the simulation as well as 4 priority degrading procedures. We need to be reminded here that in our simulation, increase of priority means decrease of the traffic class number. All the traffic decrease procedure happened between 15th second and 25th second when the traffic with highest priority generated by the CS_7. That means during that period of time, the GDV threshold cannot be satisfied even all traffics from clients have the highest priority. Then the algorithm managed to lower the priority of the traffics with the lowest absolute delay to decrease the GDV. And clearly the connection between the server and Client G_3 was mostly affected in this case.

The simulation results showed that the proposed algorithm can provide less relative delay variation in both heavily and lightly loaded networks. With well-defined traffic class constraints, the simulation shows that very small transmission overhead will be required by the proposed algorithm to achieving better relative delay variation in a lightly loaded network. The algorithm can provide more benefit on relative delay variation in a heavily loaded network as well as improve the packet loss situation when relevant class constraints are defined. Figure 5 is an example of the simulation results. It can be seen the relative delay variation has been optimized using the proposed algorithm, showed as red dash line, comparing to the normal situation, showed as blue solid line.

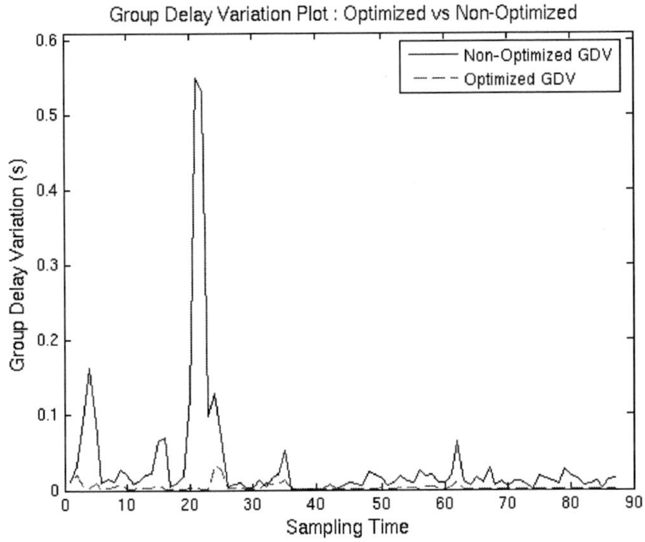

Figure 5. Group Delay Variation enhancement.

4. Conclusions

We introduced relative QoS in the beginning of this article as a new concept for multiparty communications and defined a set of One-to-group metrics to measure and present it based on the One-way metrics defined in IETF IPPM working group. We also presented how to derive statistics from these metrics using the Matrix concept and three statistic metrics have been defined for group delay as an example.

As an example of using these One-to-group metrics, a relative QoS optimization algorithm based on the DiffServ framework has been proposed for online gaming. To describe the algorithm, the One-to-group delay metric and its statistics group delay variation was chosen to be the study objective. The proposed algorithm can dynamically monitor the delays for all clients in a client-server based topology and manipulate the priority of each client's traffic corresponding to the network situation to guarantee that the relative delay is kept under a predefined threshold without breaking the absolute delay bound. The simulation results showed that the proposed algorithm can provide less group delay variation in a heavily loaded network.

References

[1] L. Liang, Z. Sun, and D. He, "New Parameters and Metrics for Multiparty Communications," 1st Conference on Next Generation Internet Networks Traffic Engineering (*NGI 2005*), Rome, Italy, 18th-20th April, 2005.

[2] E. Stephan, L. Liang and A. Morton, " IP Performance Metrics (IPPM): Spatial and Multicast", *IETF 5644*, October 2009.

[3] L. Liang, Z. Sun and H. Cruickshank, "Relative QoS Optimisation for Multiparty Online Gaming in DiffServ Networks," *IEEE Communication Magazine*, Vol. 43, No. 5, pp 75-83, May, 2005.

[4] ITU-T Rec. Y.1540, "Internet Protocol Data Communication Service - IP Packet Transfer and Availability Performance Parameters," ITU-T Study Group 13, Dec 2002.

[5] V. Paxson, G. Almes, J. Mahdavi, M. Mathis, "Framework for IP Performance Metrics," *IETF RFC 2330*, May 1998.

[6] Almes, G., Kalidindi, S., and M. Zekauskas, "A One-way Delay Metric for IPPM", *RFC 2679,* September 1999.

[7] Almes, G., Kalidindi, S., and M. Zekauskas, "A One-way Packet Loss Metric for IPPM", *RFC 2680*, September 1999

[8] Demichelis, C. and P. Chimento, "IP Packet Delay Variation Metric for IP Performance Metrics (IPPM)", *RFC 3393*, November 2002.

[9] Yow-Jian Lin, Katherine Guo, and Sanjoy Paul, "Sync-MS: Synchronized Messaging Service for Real-Time Multi-Player Distributed Games," 10th IEEE International Conference on Network Protocols (ICNP'02), November 12 - 15, 2002.

[10] Katherine Guo, Sarit Mukherjee, Sampath Rangrarjan, and Sanjoy Paul, "A Fair Message Exchange Framework for Distributed Multi-Player Games," the Second Workshop on Network and System Support for Games (NetGames'2003), May 2003.

[11] Giuseppe Bianchi, Nicola Blefari-Melazzi, Giuliano Bonafede and Emiliano Tintinelli, "QUASIMODO: Quality of Service-Aware Multicasting over DiffServ and Overlay Networks", *IEEE Network*, Vol 17, No. 1, January 2003.

[12] S. Bhattacharyya, Ed., "An Overview of Source-Specific Multicast (SSM)," *RFC 3569*, July 2003.

[13] L. Liang, Z. Sun and H. Cruickshank, "Relative QoS Optimisation for Multiparty Online Gaming in DiffServ Networks," *IEEE Communication Magazine*, Vol. 43, No. 5, May, 2005, pp 75-83..

In: Recent Advances in Providing QoS and Reliability... ISBN 978-1-61761-858-1
Editors: N. Wang, G. Pavlou and M. Boucadair

Chapter 5

QoS Deployment and Operation on SuperJANET, the UK Academic and Educational Research Network

***Michael Mackay*[*1], *Christopher Edwards*[1], *Tim Chown*[*2] and *Victor Olifer*[3*]**

[1]Computing Department, InfoLab21, South Drive, Lancaster University, Bailrigg, Lancaster, UK
[2]School of Electronics and Computer Science, University of Southampton, Southampton, UK
[3]JANET (UK), Lumen House, Library Avenue, Harwell Science and Innovation Campus, Didcot, UK

Abstract

In response to the ongoing efforts in driving Quality of Service (QoS) protocols and standardisation, partners within the UK academic community led by JANET (UK) undertook an extensive investigation into the viability of deploying and using a QoS service in the SuperJANET production network. Within the scope of this five year project, the partners investigated many of the key aspects of QoS deployment and operation including hardware configuration, flow monitoring and overall application performance, both in the core and at the edge, to determine the optimal approach to ensuring network service quality.

The ultimate aim of this work was to establish a set of guidelines for best practise with regard to QoS and thus lay the groundwork for a full end-to-end QoS deployment in the SuperJANET network. In practice, we found that while a DiffServ-based QoS service can be deployed and operated over SuperJANET, quality in the core may be more efficiently supported by using other techniques such as over-provisioning, and quality issues at the edge may not require a 'full' QoS deployment. As a result, the main

* [m.mackay, ce] @comp.lancs.ac.uk.
* tjc@ecs.soton.ac.uk.
* Victor.Olifer@ja.net.

conclusion of the project was that DiffServ would not be enforced end-to-end over SuperJANET and instead a 'QoS-transparent' approach would be adopted whereby differing levels of QoS support can be enforced at the edge as needed while over-provisioning is pursued in the core.

1. Introduction

Despite the years of research and development put into defining the underlying protocols and mechanisms, practical deployments and use of Quality of Service (QoS) in production networks is still perhaps one of the most challenging aspects of modern networking. Moreover, the lack of extensive deployments to date has given rise to the belief that the complexity and cost of QoS deployments cannot be justified and that the pursuit of alternative solutions will ultimately yield more viable results. It is this uncertainty that we aim to address in this work.

1.1. Recent Developments in QoS

An extensive body of existing work on QoS has been developed over the last 10 years and cannot be fully described here but in essence, the purpose of QoS is to provide a means to support network prioritisation for specific applications, users or streams to meet specific service requirements. Such prioritisation will also be very useful for participating network providers to control the types and volume of traffic sent over their infrastructure instead of relying on the existing fair-usage mechanisms in TCP/IP and other protocols. It also has the potential to be lucrative as extra charges can be levied for the more demanding network requirements. Over time, DiffServ [1] has emerged as the dominant QoS protocol in the research field primarily as it can scale to support wide-scale deployments by treating packets based on their Per Hop Behaviour (PHB).

However, the complexity of deploying and operating this functionality is also widely acknowledged [2] as not only must there be mechanisms to enforce traffic prioritisation in the network, including admission control and per-hop handling, but also a range of supporting functionality. This includes a monitoring service to ensure proper network operation, network provisioning functionality to properly pre-configure core and access routers, and the means to negotiate SLAs between customers and network operators. Moreover, once this policy is in deployed in the network, some policing (enforcement) techniques are required to ensure that the bounds for each traffic class are not exceeded.

1.2. QoS on SuperJANET

SuperJANET[1], the UK academic and research network, is managed by JANET (UK) (formerly UKERNA). SuperJANET is a multi-domain hierarchical network, consisting of three discrete domains: the core SuperJANET backbone [3], the twenty or so Regional

[1] Since renamed simply as JANET, i.e. JANET Core, JANET Regional Networks, etc.

Networks (RNs) and the Campus Networks, which represent JANET end-users (Universities and other Higher Education Institutions, Further Education organisations, schools and research councils). Since the rollout of the 10Gbps SuperJANET backbone in 2002, the core network has always maintained sufficient capacity to avoid congestion. This is also true for most of the 2.5Gbps access links from the core to the Backbone Access Routers (BARs) which connect the Regional Networks. However, there were always a number of Regional Network and Campus links that were not of sufficiently provisioned and as a result frequently experienced congestion. Further, increasing growth in traffic volumes across SuperJANET raised the potential of more congestion occurring which could create difficulties for the large-scale deployment of production VoIP, videoconferencing and Content Delivery services. Moreover, the SuperJANET architecture itself poses interesting challenges for supporting QoS, in particular when establishing common services across the core and Regional Networks that may have differing vendors, platforms and administration. An overview of the SuperJANET core is shown in Figure 1.

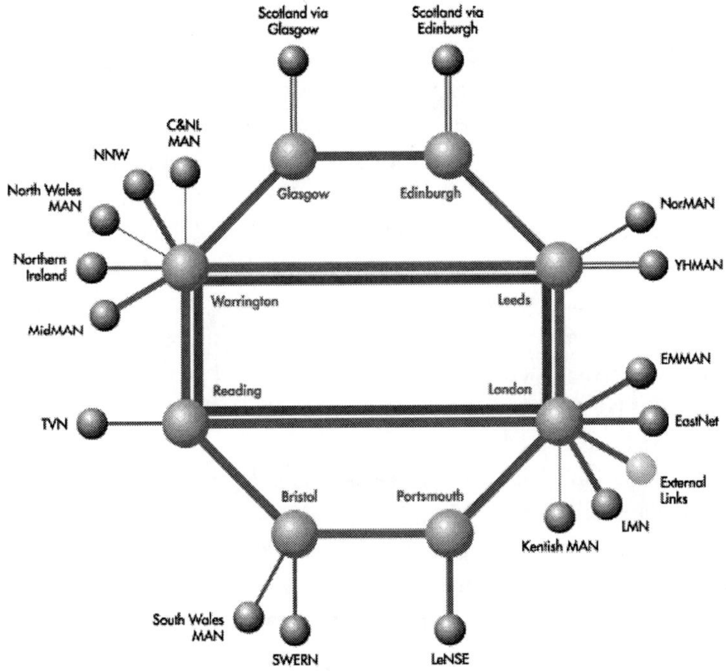

Figure 1. SuperJANET4 core in 2001.

The JANET QoS Development Project was established in January 2002 with the following objectives:

- Define an open, non-proprietary framework for QoS services that, as far as possible, will not exclude any Regional Network or SuperJANET organisation.
- Assess the effort required to deploy and manage QoS services on the production multi-domain and multi-vendor network.
- Evaluate the effectiveness of QoS services for applications used by the SuperJANET community.

- Evaluate the capability of modern routers for supporting QoS services.

Phase 1 of the project began in 2002 and ran until 2004 with the goal of assessing the benefits of QoS on SuperJANET. Then, Phase 2 of the project ran from November 2005 until December 2007, to investigate the feasibility of QoS production services for the SuperJANET community.

The remainder of this chapter is organised as follows. Section 2 describes the work done in Phase 1 and section 3 described the work done in Phase 2 of the project. Section 4 provides an analysis of our results in the broader context of QoS and we conclude in section 6.

2. QoS Development Project Phase 1

JANET (UK) initiated the project at the beginning of 2002by inviting members of the UK academic community to participate. The project was intended to represent the aggregation of QoS-related research efforts in the UK and many influential academic institutions working in this area were involved including the University of Manchester, Swansea University, University of Southampton, Lancaster University and Imperial College. These groups were also supported by the Regional Networks through which they connected.

The DiffServ model was selected for the initial trial service across SuperJANET and three levels of QoS service were selected for exploration: IP Premium, Best Effort (BE), and Less-than-Best Effort (LBE). A single unified 'IP Premium' service was used here to minimise the issues caused by different QoS prioritisation implementations on different router platforms. After consultation, the group then selected VoIP and videoconferencing [4] for the IP Premium service as they were considered to be the most important, time-sensitive applications for the SuperJANET community. The effects of bulky Grid applications using LBE on BE traffic was also selected for investigation as part of a LBE service trial. All other applications on the network were to be classified as BE traffic to minimise the potential for disruption to our testing.

The main aim of the QoS trials was to assess the behaviour of time-sensitive application traffic on the production network at times of high congestion. As such, traffic behaviour was examined under two conditions: when application traffic was processed as BE (i.e. receiving 'common' priority) and when the same traffic was processed as a higher priority DiffServ class. The first phase of the project was also interesting in evaluating the challenges of deploying a full DiffServ deployment and testing its ability to support multiple QoS classes (IP Premium, BE and LBE) on an end-to-end basis.

2.1. Network Configuration

After selecting the elements of SuperJANET that would be used, i.e. between the partner edge networks, the next task was to configure of network equipment to support QoS. A phased deployment was adopted to decrease the risk of IP Premium traffic impacting on the SuperJANET production service (LBE traffic should not distort BE traffic as it should not be given precedence). Prior to standardisation of IETF-recommended DSCP (Differentiated Service Code Points) values [5], the partners selected the most appropriate settings for marking traffic classes such that IP Premium traffic was marked as DSCP 46, Best Effort traffic as DSCP 0, and LBE traffic as DSCP 8.

By the end of 2003, all routers in the core and the selected BAR routers on SuperJANET were configured to support the three QoS classes. Access links to the participating Regional Networks in the trial were also configured to accept IP Premium and LBE traffic from the participants. All other access links into SuperJANET were configured to remark any IP Premium and LBE packets from sites not participating in the trial as normal BE traffic to ensure they did not affect our tests. By March 2004, all areas of SuperJANET (including the respective parts of the Regional Networks and Campus Networks) had also been configured and activated with QoS and the trials were ready to begin.

In terms of equipment configuration, most Border Access Routers (BARs) and all core routers on the SuperJANET backbone were Cisco GSRs but a few BARs in the project were Cisco 7507s, such as that connecting to Lancaster. A sample GSR QoS configuration that was used is given in [6]. For the individual partners, a range of Cisco, Juniper and other vendor equipment was used and while the majority of these scenarios were completed with no problems, we did encounter some minor issues. For example, Manchester University found a number of caveats when configuring QoS on the Cisco 6500. Equipment configuration issues are covered in detail in the individual partner Phase 1 deliverables [7].

2.2. Testing Process

The main series of tests were carried out between March-May 2004 by all six Universities, their Regional Networks, and JANET (UK). The project partners each carried out a number of end-to-end tests across the production SuperJANET network to verify the applicability and possible benefits of DiffServ for the most popular traffic types in the multi-domain SuperJANET environment.

The tests were conducted according to a predefined test plan, which provided descriptions of the test scenarios, outlined generic network diagrams, and outlines the measurement and monitoring tools [8]. In additional to the end-to-end testing, the plan also included some elements of local testing, mainly for configuration verification, etc, and testing under various degrees of natural and artificial congestion. The testing in Phase 1 focussed on evaluating QoS support in the network core but, as discussed above, the IP Premium traffic was first validated over local networks before trailing was conducted between sites during times of natural load. Additionally, end-to-end testing was done under network-at-risk periods where controlled artificial congestion could be injected into the network. A diagram of the testing paths used over SuperJANET is given in Figure 2. Lancaster, Manchester and Swansea University tested the IP Premium service, with the VoIP trial led by Manchester and the video-conferencing trial led by Swansea. The University of Southampton and Imperial College tested the LBE service using the AccessGrid [9] application.

A range of subjective and objective evaluation techniques were used for the IP Premium testing. In terms of the subjective testing, each application was observed for a range of parameters (e.g. echo, cracking or word clipping for VoIP) under the differing conditions. For the objective testing, a bespoke testing infrastructure was employed to measure specific QoS metrics including one way delay, jitter, packet loss, and misordering.

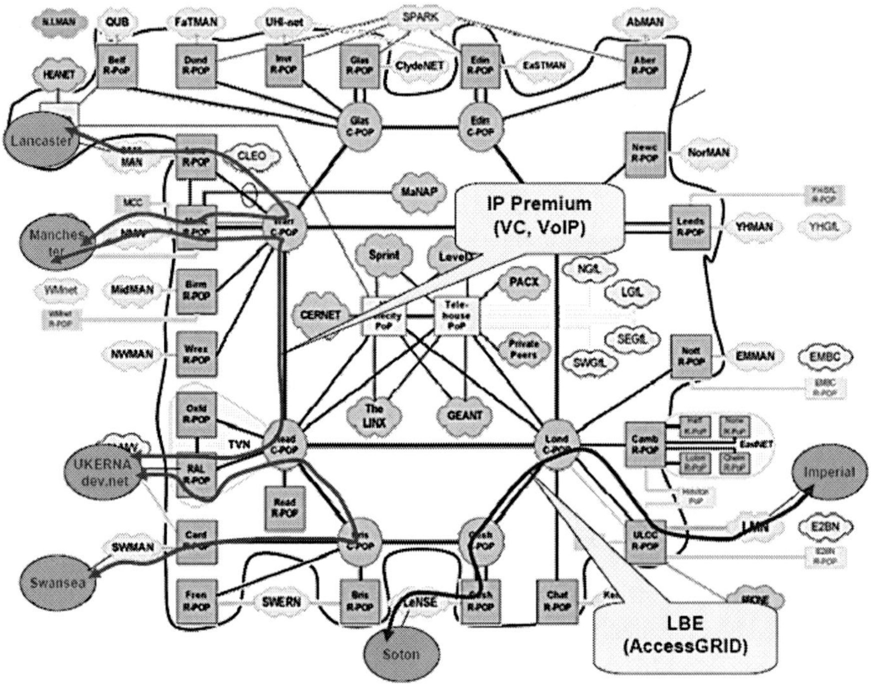

Figure 2. QoS testing over SuperJANET.

The infrastructure included real-world applications (based on videoconferencing, VoIP and Grid transfers), traffic-generating tools (mainly IPerf and RUDE/CRUDE) and a monitoring infrastructure based on IPerf and Cisco's SAA. A detailed outline of the testing plan used in each case can be found in the test plan document and partner deliverables.

2.3. Testing Results

The test results showed clear benefits for the VoIP and videoconferencing traffic during periods of severe and long-term BE congestion. For example, despite a load of almost 150% BE traffic on the SuperJANET core routers, they still successfully served IP Premium traffic at the proper rate via the priority queue as shown in Figure 3a. LBE probe traffic was also processed almost without loss and delay even when BE traffic was congesting the link as its rate was far lower than the routers LBE bandwidth guarantee as shown in Figure 3b. This guaranteed percentage of bandwidth for LBE is intended to keep established sessions active during such congestion so the effect on this traffic is less severe.

In contrast however, the benefits of using QoS during periods of only moderate network load were less conclusive and require justification. For example, if load on a router never exceeds 50%, a reasonable figure, then QoS functionality is largely redundant. This was somewhat disappointing as it is clearly unrealistic to deploy such a complex service if its benefits are only felt when network load is very high. The testing also revealed unexpected behaviour in terms of QoS support on specific platforms requiring further investigation. In one case LBE unicast traffic was given priority over multicast BE traffic, contrary to the expected result.

a)

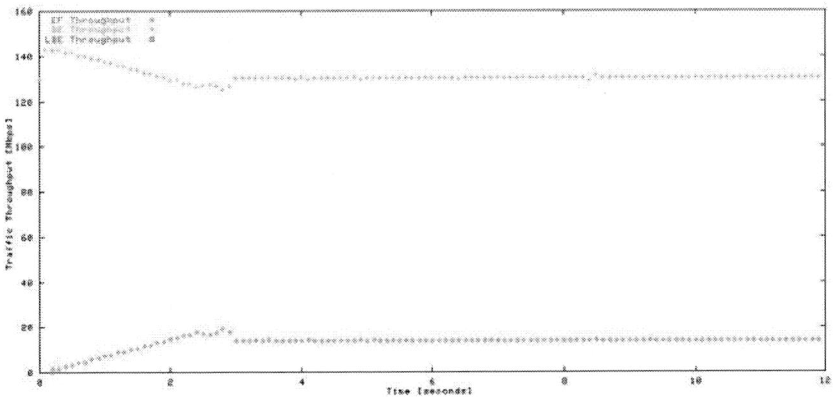

b)

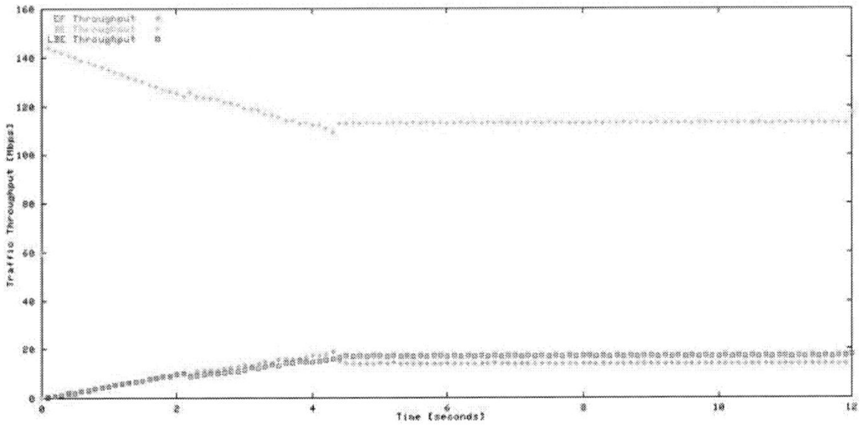

Figure 3. Typical Premium IP testing results: a – IP Premium and BE testing results. b – IP Premium, BE and LBE testing results.

During testing, the behaviour of the IP Premium applications was compared both subjectively and objectively and both while QoS was active and disabled. An example of this quantitative/qualitative testing approach is shown in Figure 4. Here, Figure 4a shows the qualitative results while Figure 4b shows the corresponding quantitative observations. During severe congestion periods, participants observed different types of distortion on the BE voice traffic during VoIP sessions, and on the BE video-conferencing traffic for both voice and video during the VC sessions. Other more severe symptoms of network congestion included calls being dropped unexpectedly or session initiation failures. These distortions were not observed when the traffic was served as IP Premium.

The LBE tests in Phase 1 aimed primarily to evaluate the ability of the routers to provide the guaranteed minimum LBE bandwidth during BE and IP Premium bursts, and to allow available bandwidth to be consumed during periods of low IP Premium and BE activity. As shown in Figure 5, the results were quite positive as it was found that, as BE traffic rises to claim the majority of the network resources (top), LBE traffic was still given an adequate proportion of the link bandwidth (bottom), allowing a minimal flow to be maintained during congestion periods.

a)

07:45	An initial call was placed to Lancaster with the VoIP 'phones before congestion was applied as a control test. **The subjective call quality was "crystal clear"** (despite the fact that at this stage it was being given no priority), **no packet loss was observed and jitter varied from 4 to 6ms.**
07:56	Traffic was then added to the link, using RUDE to create 140Mbps of traffic (25Mbps Premium, 110Mbps of BE and 5Mbps of LBE) from a Zone B traffic generator to Zone C traffic generator (see figure 11).
08:05	A (BE) Call was placed from Lancaster to Manchester: **Manchester saw a maximum jitter of 8ms** (from phone statistics) **with zero packet loss. Lancaster observed a maximum jitter of 6ms** (jitter varied from 4 to 6) **with zero packet loss.** Subjectively, the call quality seemed unaffected for both sites.
08:10	Manchester then changed the traffic passing from B to C, using RUDE, to 145Mbps (25Mbps of Premium, 115Mbps of BE and 5Mbps of LBE).
08:11	Lancaster placed another BE call to Manchester: **Manchester's 'phone recorded packet loss and experienced degraded call quality ("clipping/crackling" but still perfectly usable – every word comprehensible). The maximum jitter recorded on both 'phones was only 7ms. Lancaster saw no packet loss and maintained a clear call quality.** It was at this point we realised that this was because both sites were congesting their test component of the link in effectively the same direction, i.e. the Manchester to Lancaster direction. This meant that the traffic being received by Lancaster was only competing with general background traffic: This would explain Lancaster's receiving an unaffected call at this point.
08:20	Since it was more convenient for Manchester to reverse the direction of test traffic flow, Manchester then started to generate 134Mbps of traffic from C to B (a RUDE mix of 15Mbps Premium, 113Mbps BE and 6Mbps LBE). The reason we altered the class mix of traffic was because we had noticed far more Premium packet loss than we would have expected over the test link at Manchester (even taking into account that the Premium class was at almost the maximum threshold set). We wanted to see if, as expected, the premium loss went back down to zero with this traffic mix before increasing the levels again as before.
08:38	**With the Manchester test traffic at 134Mbps, a new call was raised from Lancaster: At both ends the call appeared crystal clear with the same low jitter values recorded. However, we were still experiencing 10-15% premium packet loss.**
08:45	At this point we ran out of time before we had a chance to up the traffic levels at Manchester again or indeed change the VoIP call to be classified as Premium.

b)

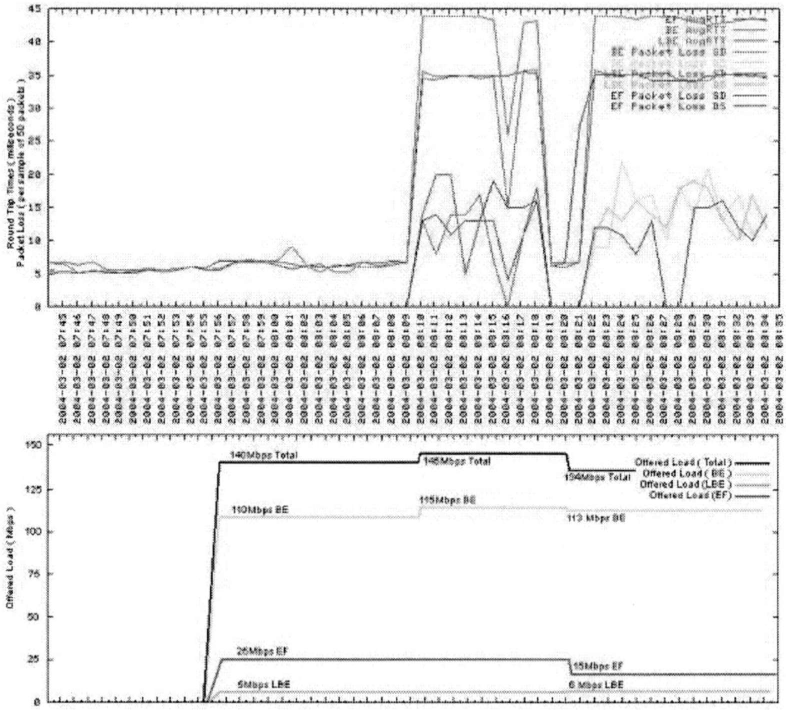

Figure 4. Quantitative/Qualitative test results for a VOIP session between Lancaster and Manchester: a – Qualitative testing results. b – Quantitative testing results.

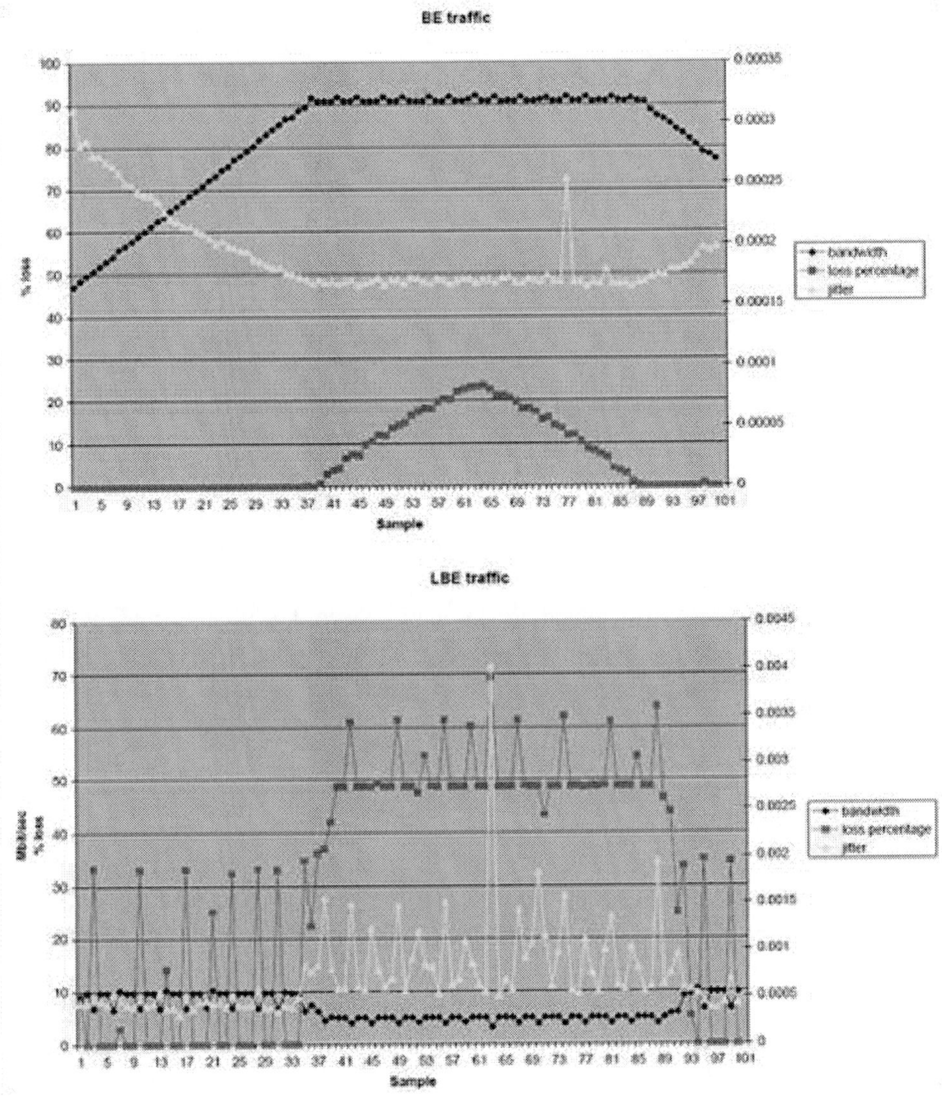

Figure 5. Typical LBE testing results.

2.4. Phase 1 Summary and Analysis

Overall, we were encouraged by the success of Phase 1 of the project, both in terms of configuring QoS on the end-to-end network and in testing its effectiveness in prioritising different traffic flows. Our results showed that the IP Premium service gave a significant benefit to selected applications, especially during periods of severe network congestion. Also, the LBE tests showed positive results using all the available bandwidth on the network after IP Premium and BE traffic was processed. Our success in configuring different vendors' routers and switches according to the DiffServ model and common policy rules showed that, despite the diverse character of configuration commands and mechanisms across the

SuperJANET core and the participants' campus and regional networks, the final results were both consistent and positive.

At the same time, phase 1 emphasised the substantial effort required to properly plan, deploy and maintain a QoS service on this scale. Also, some unexpected and peculiar behaviour was observed on routers and switches when traffic classes were not treated according to the demands of the selected applications. However, these tended to be relatively minor in nature.

3. QoS Development Project Phase 2

Based on our successful experience and results of running QoS across core multi-vendor domains in Phase1, in 2005 the project partners recommended continuing work in QoS by establishing Phase 2 of the QoS Development Project. The intention was to now focus on areas such as multi-domain provisioning and administration, interaction with new technologies such as multicast, IPv6, wireless and ADSL; and providing QoS on low-speed 'last mile' links and through specialised networks.

Phase 2 of the project also aimed to build on Phase 1 with the goal of ultimately establishing an end-to-end production QoS service across SuperJANET. The main project objectives were therefore to refine the application requirements and QoS classes defined in Phase 1 and to finalise the DiffServ model to be used. This included defining policy rules, provisioning and admission control procedures, implementing network reservation models and monitoring support, and agreeing inter-domain (SLA) models.

Moreover, this phase also aimed to explore the impact of QoS on other technologies commonly employed by operators and end users in SuperJANET such as caching, firewalls, VPNs, multicast and media gateways. The participants in Phase 2 of the project were the same as Phase 1 with the exception of Imperial College withdrawing and SSDN and Kentish Man being included. In line with the updated objectives, Phase 2 of the project was organised as shown in Figure 6.

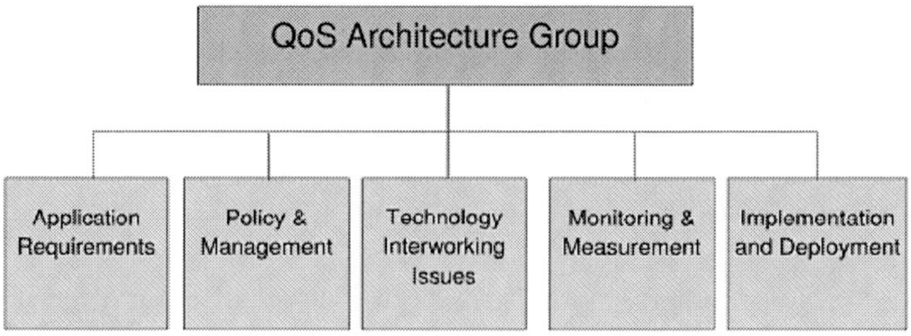

Figure 6. Project Phase 2 work areas.

It was also decided that, as in Phase 1, each partner would focus their efforts on investigating a specific aspect of QoS such as LBE, Video Conferencing using the JANET Video-Conferencing Service (JVCS), multicast and in-depth QoS deployment and operation issues. Detailed descriptions of this work, including test plans, results, and equipment configurations, are again available in the respective partner deliverables [10].

3.1. QoS Deployment Efforts

To build on our successes in Phase 1 of the project, deployment efforts now focused on enabling QoS at the network edge, i.e. across the Regional Networks (RNs) and into the customer sites. Cumbria and North Lancashire MAN (CandNLMAN) and Scottish Schools Digital Network (SSDN) focussed their efforts in this area. However, while CandNLMAN did deploy and test QoS with some success, SSDN eventually pursued a more practical approach.

SSDN is the primary educational network for Scotland, connecting schools and colleges across the region. Based on the test results of running QoS over SuperJANET in Phase 1, the partners proceeded from the basis that QoS is not effective in the core unless the network is under very heavy load. Hence the purpose of this trial was first to explore the best approach to QoS on heavily over-provisioned links. After thoroughly monitoring and analysing the traffic in their network, it was found that most applications currently use BE (including VoIP and JVCS) with no ill effect. Moreover, a survey undertaken among SSDN customers found little interest for QoS among the respondents. As such, a policy of sustained over-provisioning was adopted as the overall approach to QoS in SSDN and supporting strategies were explored instead. Of particular relevance in this case were Content Delivery Infrastructures which could be deployed to support the high-availability of popular and commonly used educational resources under the Glow Project.

A parallel effort to the above was undertaken in CandNLMAN but, in this case, QoS trialling was done on the basis that some edge customers simply could not be over-provisioned due to technical constraints. CandNLMAN provides the educational network in North-West England and a diverse infrastructure has been deployed to overcome the challenging terrain. Here, a range of fibre (in the core), wireless radio links and xDSL is used to connect the regions' schools as shown in Figure 7.

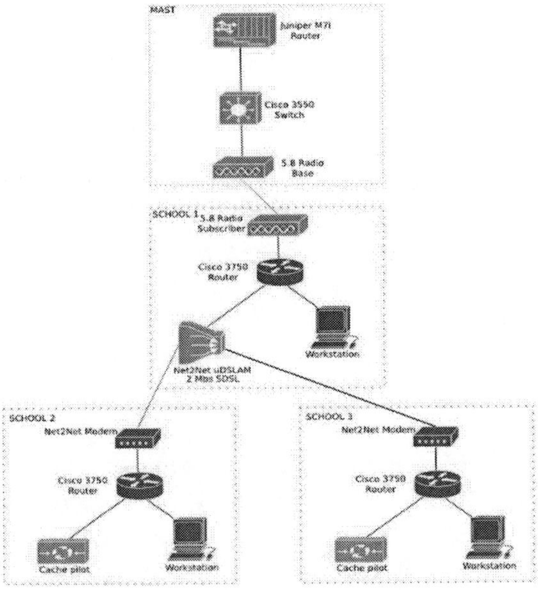

Figure 7. Example of a typical CandNLMAN scenario.

As with SSDN, a monitoring and analysis phase was first conducted and a range of traffic was seen on the network including standard web traffic, network control traffic, VoIP/VC traffic and others. In line with the findings of Phase 1, VoIP and VC traffic was selected for prioritisation and the remainder was made BE with the exception of network control traffic which was marked with the highest priority in this case.

In the first evaluation phase the network router equipment, primarily the Cisco 3550 and the Juniper M7i, were configured for QoS and tested with Agilent N2X traffic generators to establish their performance when handling multiple priority queues under load are shown in Figure 8. The testing then moved on to edge equipment including the Cisco 3750, ADSL/SDSL DSLAM and modem devices and, for the wireless links, the Alvarion radio Subscriber Units. Typical results of this, for the Cisco 3550.

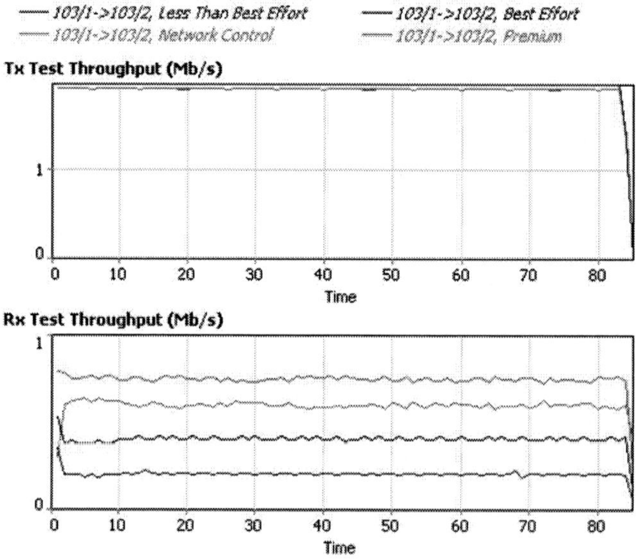

Figure 8. QoS configuration results for the Cisco 3550.

In terms of configuration, it was found that the QoS functionality performed well in the core equipment, working in a manner consistent with our expectations. The only caveat was some results which suggested fine-tuning of the Juniper queuing configuration was necessary to get the weightings expected. The edge equipment also demonstrated that QoS support was possible in every case but some more so than others. For example, we found that the Cisco 3750 worked as expected in testing but, while the SDSL DSLAM equipment worked well, the SHDSL modems exhibited erroneous behaviour under QoS testing. This pattern was also repeated with the ADSL equipment where the DSLAM devices worked well but the results for the modems were inconsistent. In contrast, both the 5.8 Ghz radio Access Unit (AU) and Subscriber Unit (SU) worked as expected in the testing scenarios.

The second phase of testing involved actually deploying QoS into the network in an attempt to improve Video Conferencing performance. This was done at two locations where network congestion was suspected to be the cause of poor performance. In these trials, QoS support was deployed between Lancaster University and the Wordsworth Museum (over a DSL-based network) and Waberthwaite School (over a radio link) on the basis that they were prime examples of where QoS could be used to benefit end users. In both cases however, QoS deployment was successful but video conferencing performance was not improved and other issues were since identified as being the cause of the poor performance experienced. In the case of the Wordsworth Museum, a poor-quality DSL link was identified as the probable cause while at Waberthwaite School, an under-performing host machine was found to be at fault. However, that QoS was successfully deployed and tested in both cases was a valuable result in itself and justified the primary hypothesis of the work.

3.2. QoS-Enabled JVCS Trial

Also, in Phase 2 of the project, Swansea University investigated the benefits of a production QoS service on the national JANET Video Conferencing Service (JVCS) application. As before, network monitoring equipment was first deployed at each location where the VC Multipoint Control Units (MCUs) were located during June 2006. This provided us with metrics on the network service available to these locations. The next task then involved investigating the ability of the MCUs, and the Polycom Media Gateway Controller (MGC) devices, to set and respect DSCP values.

In order to then verify that the MCUs were marking IP packets with QoS values, it was necessary to capture the IP packets and inspect the DSCP values. This was conducted at the JVCS Management Centre in Edinburgh as it provided the most accessible location for the connection of testing devices. In order to perform the packet capture, a Network Test Access Point (TAP) was connected to the appropriate MCU network interfaces. The Network TAP used for this purpose was a NetOptics 10/100BaseT Teeny TAP which is an in-line, passive, zero delay device capturing full duplex traffic flows. Then, a TANDBERG T150 video-conferencing endpoint was used as a test device to receive videoconferencing calls from the MCU and the IP traffic in both directions was captured using Ethereal running on two laptops.

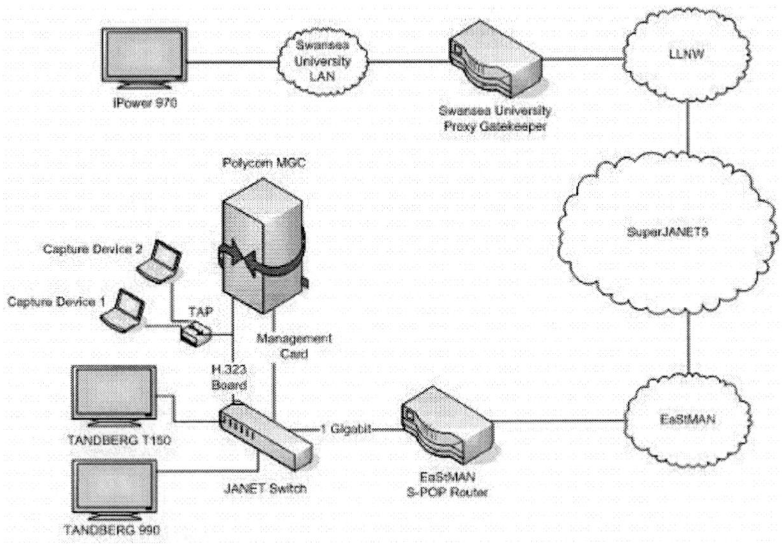

Figure 9. test bed used for JVCS trialling.

In addition, a TANDBERG 990 connected to the same network switch and a Polycom iPower 970 MCG located at Swansea University were used during the testing. A test plan was then prepared that involved making controlled changes to either the videoconferencing endpoint or the MCU, observing the results, and recording whether they were as anticipated. The tests were first conducted over the LAN that the development MCU was connected to, before later tests were then conducted over the Regional Networks and SuperJANET Backbone as shown in Figure 9.

Details of the test plan and our results are included in the Swansea deliverable but, in summary, we found that it is indeed possible to mark traffic on JVCS MCUs to any value between DSCP 0 and 63, as shown in Figure 10.

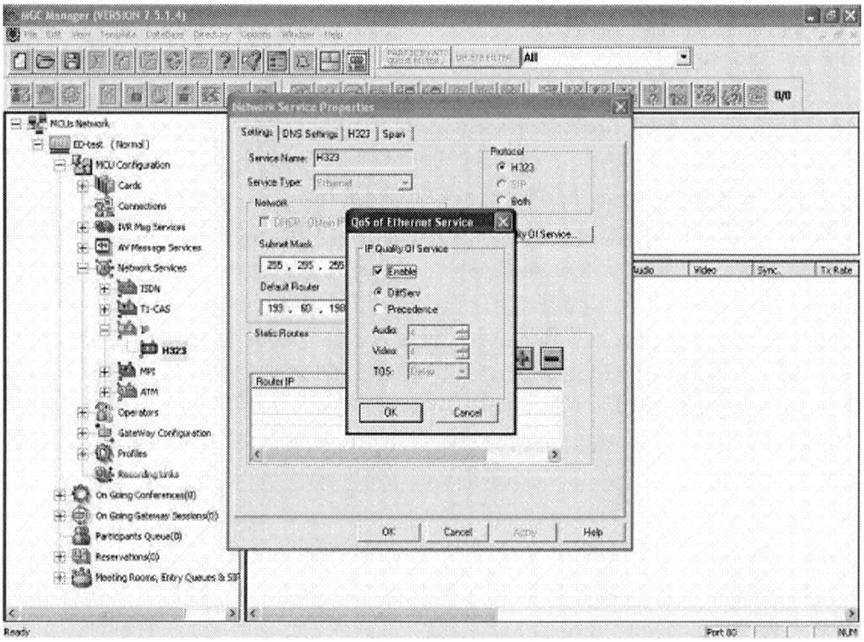

Figure 10. Configuring the JVCS MCUs to use Diffserv.

This is applied at the system level and will affect all endpoints in all conferences (unless manually overridden). This would therefore permit a production marking service to be deployed if required. However, it is not currently possible to set different DSCP values for different endpoints so, in effect, a single static DSCP must be chosen which is either applied or not to endpoints in a video-conference. Also, the MCU must be restarted if any changes are made to the DSCP values, which is far from ideal.

3.3. LBE Evaluation

The University of Kent connects to SuperJANET via the Kentish MAN and currently hosts the UK Mirror Service. However, concerns have always existed with the Mirror's traffic as it consumes a high percentage of the RN's link into SuperJANET and therefore has the potential to starve other traffic. This network was therefore seen as an ideal choice for participation in the LBE QoS trials. The aim here was to configure QoS on the Kentish MAN network such that non-Mirror traffic would take precedence over Mirror traffic in the event of congestion but also to ensure that, during congestion, Mirror traffic would still receive a guaranteed minimum bandwidth.

As the first step, Netflow monitoring was configured on all core routers to determine the DSCP values currently being generated throughout the network. Several DSCP values were detected including; BE, Premium, Network Control and others but critically not LBE. The next step was to then remark all traffic at the ingress into the Kentish MAN core as BE. Once this was done, the core was again monitored for a short period to ensure there were no unforeseen repercussions of this change. Finally, the domain was reconfigured to honour markings on all traffic from the University of Kent domain so Mirror traffic was remarked to LBE and all other traffic to BE.

In this case the network core used for the trials consisted of five Cisco 6500s, each with a 16 port Gigabit Ethernet fibre LAN module. Within each port, there were three transmit queues: two with standard priority and one with high priority. A Weighted Round Robin (WRR) scheduling algorithm was used in the hardware output queues as this guarantees a minimum amount of bandwidth to each class of service and also allows each class to use the link's available bandwidth if unused. WRR was configured by mapping LBE to the low priority standard queue and BE to the high priority standard queue. The strict priority was queue was not used for the LBE trials.

For the testing, the Realtime UDP Data Emitter (RUDE) and Collector for RUDE (CRUDE) [11] were used to generate, send and capture traffic streams. The testing was conducted between July and November 2006 to evaluate the ability of the configuration to fulfil the project aims. However, a number of configuration issues and unanticipated events were encountered which limited the success of the trials.

The first series of testing was done to correctly configure and tune the WRR ratios for each class. Initially, 10% of the total bandwidth was assigned for LBE and the aim was to saturate the link and validate this LBE limit. However, due to erroneous configuration on the core routers, BE traffic was affected more by congestion than LBE and the assumption was that the values allocated to these ratios were inappropriate and 10% is excessive for LBE. The next tests attempted to first saturate the link with LBE background traffic in an attempt to demonstrate that it can use all available bandwidth before secondly demonstrating that the minimum bandwidth guarantee for LBE is honoured whilst the link is saturated with BE traffic. Once again, the BE traffic was affected the same or worse than LBE but in this case when the link was fully congested, it was LBE traffic that was at least now being dropped as opposed to BE, as shown in Figure 11.

Several factors affected the LBE test results, notably the difficulty in correctly configuring the end-to-end link for accurate testing and in generating streams of traffic to truly achieve saturation of these links. Ultimately however, the tests did not generate the expected results and, after investigation, this was found to be due to the QoS configuration on the SuperJANET links under test. During some of the tests we did see that LBE traffic was affected when BE was introduced, as was the intention, but this was not consistent throughout the trial. Unfortunately, at this point (November 2006), the scheduled network upgrade to SuperJANET5 got underway effectively ending the possibility of any further testing being performed here.

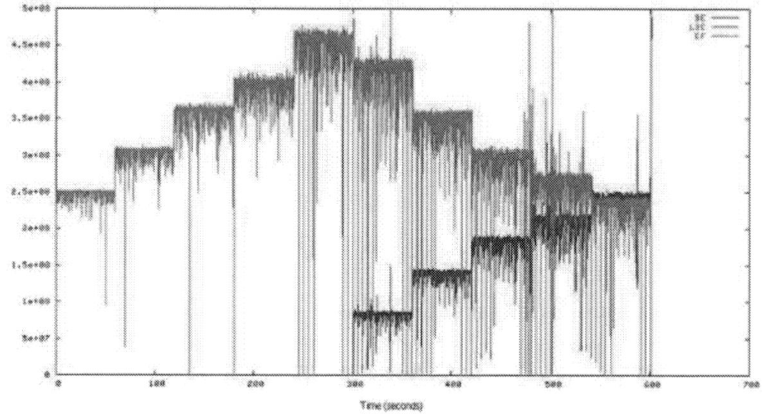

Figure 11. LBE test results showing LBE link utilisation dropping in response to increased BE traffic.

3.4. JANET (UK) Approach to QoS

By December 2006, sufficient work had been carried out by the participants to understand the complexities involved in deploying and maintaining an operationally stable QoS service across SuperJANET. It was found that the network core and most of the Regional Networks maintained sufficient capacity to transfer all traffic within acceptable timeframes, regardless of the class assigned. Based on these findings, the project participants concluded that the overheads required in effectively configuring and maintaining production QoS services outweighed the benefits experienced. However, it was also widely acknowledged that the access links between SuperJANET user sites and the Regional Networks were potential congestion points as they do not always have sufficient capacity to serve all user application traffic at the required quality.

As a result of our work, in March 2007 JANET (UK) released a statement on its policy towards QoS in the network core [12]. This statement summarised the JANET (UK) approach to QoS by defining that traffic on the SuperJANET backbone will not be subject to QoS treatment as the infrastructure is sufficiently over-provisioned to avoid congestion. It also indicated that while DSCP packet markings would also not be enforced, they would not be remarked at ingress, meaning that the network backbone would effectively be QoS transparent, allowing all marked traffic to pass through unchanged. This has the immediate benefit of minimising the specific functionality required as no admission control, per-flow forwarding or policing mechanisms are needed in this case. However, the latest version of the JANET (UK) Netsight monitoring system will retain the ability to monitor QoS parameters (delay, jitter) by request. Overall, this clarified the initial JANET (UK) policy on QoS [13] and meant that the deployment of a DiffServ service on SuperJANET would not be pursued beyond this point.

Phase 2 of the QoS project concluded in December 2007 having successfully demonstrated and evaluated end-to-end QoS on the SuperJANET network. As such the project was deemed to have been a success based on the body of work produced, despite the decision not to deploy a full production QoS service and instead pursue a more pragmatic solution. The project helped to define the JANET (UK) position on QoS, develop a set of guidelines for QoS users on SuperJANET and develop a longer-term policy towards potential uptake in the future. The project also resulted in the publication of the JANET (UK) recommended DSCP marking scheme for use on SuperJANET [14] which outlines the recommended DSCP values on SuperJANET and the QoS Technical Guide [15] which embodies a set of guidelines for QoS. This later document is the ultimate deliverable of the project which provides a guideline for RN and Site administrators considering the deployment of QoS in their networks. This report provides an introduction to the project, a discussion of QoS mechanisms and relevant technologies used, and a detailed analysis of QoS at every level of SuperJANET (Core, RNs and Sites). The report also describes the use of QoS to support applications such as VoIP and videoconferencing and provides configuration examples on common hardware. It also provides a starting point for finding further information on supporting QoS and Managed Bandwidth Services (MBS) in this scope and introduces the JANET (UK) QoS service desk [**16**] which was also established as a result of the project.

4. Analysis of Our Results

The results of the JANET QoS Development Project can be summarised as follows; Phase 1 showed the viability and benefits of using DiffServ QoS to support popular applications such as VoIP and videoconferencing, especially under periods of network congestion. However, it also showed that provisioning such a production service on an end-to-end basis would be a major technical challenge. Phase 2 of the project then built on this to develop a generic model that would create the basis for a stable, consistent and maintainable QoS service across the SuperJANET core and Regional Networks. This included looking at deploying QoS outside of the core and towards the access network to support an end-to-end service. Ultimately however, it was found that alternative approaches to QoS were preferable due to the significantly reduced complexity and overheads involved.

A major strength of this work is that a large volume of the testing was done over production networks in both phases of the project, providing a unique opportunity to evaluate QoS in 'real' large-scale environments. The suite of QoS functionality we considered was extensively evaluated, both quantitatively and qualitatively, to determine the benefits of enabling it in the network. Our results showed that traffic prioritisation can effectively favour premium traffic over Best Effort on a scalable end-to-end basis and that this can enhance the Quality of Experience for users of demanding applications. The project also demonstrated that QoS can be configured relatively easily in the core on popular equipment from vendors like Cisco and Juniper and that it is possible to support this right to the edge, depending on the equipment deployed. However, some areas that we examined (especially in Phase 2) where not so easy to effectively demonstrate and test, particularly in large production networks, such as the LBE testing, which was hampered by the complexity of deploying new services in highly intricate operating environments.

These results demonstrate that end-to-end QoS is technically possible on large, national networks such as SuperJANET, with multiple different RNs in place, especially where there exists some over-arcing authority and the will to govern its usage and policies. However, this work also highlights that even in this case there are significant issues to consider in terms of practicality (e.g. equipment heterogeneity) and management (DSCP marking policy, admission control, monitoring). More significantly however, our results demonstrate that unless there are specific requirements that necessitate the use of 'formal' QoS techniques, the benefits of QoS do not become evident until the network is dangerously congested and that in most other circumstances, other forms of QoS can yield similar results.

As a result of our work, towards the conclusion of the QoS Project, JANET (UK) policy shifted away from pursuing a DiffServ-based QoS service towards making the network core QoS transparent whilst ensuring that it is always sufficiently provisioned for the current traffic load. While this could be seen as a failure to achieve one of the major project aims, the JANET QoS Policy does support the use of QoS for end users, as DSCP markings are still carried, and in special circumstances where explicit provisioning and Managed Bandwidth services can be considered. This should therefore be seen as what we believe to be a fair compromise for SuperJANET as end-to-end QoS can still be supported to some extent beyond the bounds of the network. This approach to QoS is also by no means unique as over-provisioning in the network core is commonly used by operators to ensure there is sufficient capacity to treat all traffic as IP Premium [17]. This approach is obviously more expensive in terms of hardware costs and is not an 'elegant' solution but it is far more straight-forward to deploy and manage.

This contrast between the ideal of deploying full QoS and the practicality of employing realistic solutions is also at the core of the debate between the need for QoS and the general lack of deployment to date [18]. The cost and complexity of deploying QoS is well-known to be a major barrier to its wider deployment and so alternatives are often selected in its place. What we believe we are actually seeing here is a spectrum of 'QoS deployments' ranging from DiffServ to over-provisioning with a range of viable options in between. Each solution in this scope offers some trade-off between cost and service and, in the absence of a universally applicable approach to QoS, administrators are simply selecting the path that suits them best. This opens an interesting avenue of investigation into what exactly constitutes a QoS deployment. For example, while not enforcing any of the standards or protocols, simply over-provisioning the network to ensure that all traffic is reasonably free of delay and loss, can represent a form of QoS in itself. QoS solutions can also be applied, using network or application-specific methods where congestion is predicted, in effect facilitating end-to-end QoS without necessarily employing full configuration and management mechanisms.

We believe that this represents an interesting area of investigation for further work into the future of QoS. Given this starting point, it should be possible to identify the forms of QoS that are available, and the complexity and benefits that can be expected during deployment, depending on the scope of a given scenario. This could also provide useful guidance into the best forms of QoS for administrators considering deploying it in their networks. Ultimately however, one of our greatest concerns is in trying to find some cohesion between this piecemeal adoption of network quality mechanisms to support wider end-to-end solutions for users. Many formal QoS protocols rely on the end-to-end paradigm as a fundamental aspect of their operation and the danger here is that the lack of a unified approach could 'break' QoS in any real sense. We believe that this work would provide a useful step towards overcoming this.

5. Conclusion

The JANET QoS Development Project was conducted from 2002 to 2007 and, during this time, academics throughout the UK together with JANET (UK) explored the potential of using production QoS services on the SuperJANET network. Project partners investigated every aspect of QoS including deployment and configuration, performance, operations and management, and its impact on services and applications. Our results indicate that while DiffServ-based QoS can, and has, been deployed on an end-to-end basis in large-scale networks such as SuperJANET, the operational overheads involved are significant and perhaps even prohibitively so.

Moreover, in the second phase of the project we examined the complexities of end-to-end QoS solutions and evaluated alternative QoS approaches such as LBE-only and over-provisioning. Our findings here generally suggest that this form of QoS can provide much the same performance as 'classic' end-to-end Premium IP via DiffServ in many cases but at a much lower cost. This would seem to largely corroborate the findings of the academic community in recent years [18], along with other 'QoS' deployments in industry where no *de facto* approach is in place [17].

In conclusion, while we have shown that it is technically possible to build a full end-to-end QoS deployment, the effort required to support and maintain it on +20 RNs and the SuperJANET core is excessive as any 'problems' are likely to be localised to some site links and a small number of low capacity RN-SuperJANET links. These findings not only influenced the JANET (UK) approach to QoS, where over-provisioning and QoS-transparency were ultimately adopted, but opened the broader discussion into what constitutes a 'QoS deployment'. We closed with a brief discussion of further work describing how the array of QoS solutions currently being employed could be brought together to present a unified and cohesive approach to QoS.

Acknowledgments

The authors would like to acknowledge and thank the other partners from both phases of the JANET QoS Development Project for their dedication and efforts over the duration of the project.

References

[1] S. Blake et al., An Architecture for Differentiated Services, *RFC 2475*, 1998.

[2] P. Jacobs, B. Davie, Technical challenges in the Delivery of Interprovider QoS, *IEEE Communications Magazine,* Vol. 43, No. 6, pp. 112-118, 2005.

[3] JANET Website, http://www.ja.net/ (accessed Oct. 2009).

[4] JANET Video Conferencing Service (JVSC) website, http://www.ja.net/services/video/jvcs/index.html (accessed Oct. 2009).

[5] J. Babiarz, K. Chan, F. Baker, Configuration Guidelines for DiffServ Service Classes, *RFC 4594*, August 2006.

[6] Results of QoS trial tests in which UKERNA participated, http://www.webarchive.ja.net/development/qos/the-results-of-qos-trial-tests-across-janet-v1.1.pdf.
[7] Phase 1 project partner deliverables, http://www.ja.net/development/network-engineering/qos/project-phase-1/partner-deliverables.html.
[8] Testplan, http://webarchive.ja.net/development/qos/qos-testplan-final.pdf.
[9] Access Grid Website, http://www.accessgrid.org/ (accessed Oct. 2009).
[10] JANET Phase 2 deliverables, http://www.ja.net/development/network-engineering.
[11] RUDE/CRUDE Website, http://rude.sourceforge.net/ (accessed Oct. 2009).
[12] JANET QoS Statement, http://www.ja.net/development/network-engineering.
[13] JANET QoS Policy, http://www.ja.net/documents/development/network-engineering/qos/qos-policy-framework.pdf.
[14] JANET DSCP marking scheme, http://www.ja.net/documents/development/network-engineering/qos/suggested-dscp-marking-scheme.pdf.
[15] JANET QoS Technical Guide, http://www.ja.net/documents/publications/technical-guides/qos-tg.pdf.
[16] JANET Service Desk, service@janet.ac.uk.
[17] S. Bhagat, QoS: Solution Waiting For A Problem, ZNET, 2006.
[18] G. J. Armitage, Revisiting IP QoS: why do we care, what have we learned?, ACM SIGCOMM 2003 RIPQOS workshop report, *ACM SIGCOMM Computer Communication Review*, v.33 n.5, October 2003.

In: Recent Advances in Providing QoS and Reliability... ISBN 978-1-61761-858-1
Editors: N. Wang, G. Pavlou and M. Boucadair

Chapter 6

AN ARCHITECTURAL FRAMEWORK FOR INTER-DOMAIN QUALITY OF SERVICE MONITORING TO SUPPORT SERVICE ASSURANCE AND RESOURCE MANAGEMENT*

Abolghasem (Hamid) Asgari[1]
Thales Research and Technology (TRT),
Worton Drive, Reading RG2 0SB, UK

ABSTRACT

The explosive increasing amount of multimedia content to be offered in the Internet, demand the provision of new Quality of Service (QoS) enabled mechanisms and architecture to efficiently control, manage and monitor services and networks. Deployment of QoS-based services across the Internet requires a large set of providers to co-operate for expanding the geographical scope of each other's services. Appropriate means are required to enable providers to extend their QoS over multiple domains, thus enabling the providers to offer reachability to networks beyond their own domains with QoS performance levels suitable for delivery of end-to-end QoS-enabled services. In this respect, quality of service monitoring is becoming crucial to service providers for providing quantified QoS-based services and service assurance and to network providers for managing network resources at both intra and inter-domain levels. In this chapter, we discuss that for monitoring in multi-domain environment, it is essential for providers in the service delivery chain to co-operate based on an agreed framework formulating the configuration of monitoring elements and services, the execution of measurements, the composition of results, and the exchange of measurement data. This chapter proposes large-scale inter-domain QoS monitoring system by taking into account the appropriate QoS interconnection models among providers. The types of measurements to be collected by this monitoring system are discussed, as they are needed for in-service verification of

* The author would like to thank IST ENTHRONE and IST MESCAL EC project partners for their inputs and valuable discussions.
[1] Hamid.Asgari@thalesgroup.com.

offered value-added services and for resource management in performing short-term resource tuning and long-term network planning.

1. Introduction

Quality of service monitoring is becoming crucial to Service Providers2 and IP Network Providers (INP)3 for providing QoS-based services and Service Assurance [1] and for managing network resources at both intra- and inter-domain levels. The performance and traffic requirements of a requested service are described in the Service Level Agreements (SLA) and consequently its SLS (Service Level Specification) part. SLAs describe the characteristics of the service offering and the responsibilities of the parties involved for using/providing the offered service. SLAs between consumer and providers (cSLAs) are used to formulate the customer requests as well as customers' and providers' service commitments. Provider Level Service Agreements (pSLAs) are between providers. These pSLA agreements are supposed to lay the first stone for providers towards extending their geographical scope beyond their boundaries. TEQUILA project [2] partially funded by European Commission (EC) defined a set of semantics for SLSs as the basic component for defining QoS-based IP connectivity services [3]. Two types of SLS are distinguished, customer SLSs (cSLSs), and provider SLSs (pSLSs) [4]. pSLSs are meant to support aggregated traffic serving many customers. In order to ensure conformance to SLSs and detect violations, a provider may need to gather quality of service performance and traffic related measurements from multiple networks. A QoS-based monitoring system should provide information for end-to-end Service Management (SM) encompassing Service Assurance and Resource Management (RM) including Traffic Engineering in:

1. Assisting service/network providers to verify whether the QoS performance guarantees committed in c/pSLSs are in fact being met (i.e. delivered). SLSs can differ depending on the type of services offered and different SLS types have different QoS requirements that need processing different types of information. In-service verification of traffic and performance characteristics of services in progress may be required.
2. Assisting network providers in making provisioning decisions for optimizing the usage of network resources (both at intra and inter-domain levels) according to short to medium term (i.e., hours, days) changes as well as providing measurement information for long-term (i.e., months) planning in order to optimize network usage and avoid undesirable conditions. For this, it is necessary to perform QoS-based resource monitoring at traffic class, node, path, and network levels.

[2] A Service Provider is termed as the entity responsible for offering high-level QoS-based services (e.g., multimedia content) to consumers. Service Providers may not necessarily own and administer a networking infrastructure; except the infrastructure required for provisioning of offered services. Service Providers rely on the connectivity services offered by INPs.

[3] The terms INP and AS (Autonomous System) are used interchangeably throughout the chapter to denote a business entity owning a network and being responsible for its operation and the provision of network connectivity aspects.

This chapter is organized as follows. Section 2 provides a brief summary of past and present related monitoring activities. Section 3 explains the requirements for performing monitoring in multi-domain environment where multiple autonomous domains are interconnected. Section 4 describes the high-level inter-domain QoS monitoring architecture and the impact of QoS Interconnection models on its functions. Finally, conclusion is provided in Section 5.

2. Overview of Network Monitoring and Measurement Activities

There has been a number of Working Groups (WG) in the Internet Engineering Task Force (IETF) related to measurements and monitoring [5]. The IP Performance Metrics (IPPM) WG has been developing a set of standard metrics applicable to the quality, performance and reliability of Internet data delivery, but not developing metrics that characterize traffic streams. The IP Flow Information Export (IPFIX) WG has the mandate to define and develop a common traffic IP flow, the protocol to transfer IP flow data between monitoring entities, and monitoring, storing, aggregating exchanging, and reporting flow information between different systems and organizations. The Performance Metrics for Other Layers (PMOL) WG develops performance metrics for IP-based protocols and applications that operate over transport protocols. The Packet Sampling (PSAMP) is specifying a standard set of capabilities for sampling packets through statistical and other methods. The IETF also completed a number of related activities including SNMP (Simple Network Management Protocol), RMON (Remote Network Monitoring), and RTFM (Real Time Traffic Flow Measurement) [5].

There exist numerous performance monitoring tools, focusing on path performance and network-wide measurements such as the RIPE TTM, NetFlow, SFlow, NAI, Skitter, and so on. The RIPE Test Traffic Measurement (TTM) [[6] project measures IPPM-based one-way delay and packet-loss, bandwidth, etc. between installed measurement probes. National Internet Measurement Infrastructure (NIMI) [[7] is a software system for building network measurement infrastructures. The Cooperative Association for Internet Data Analysis (CAIDA) provides tools for maintaining a robust and scalable global Internet infrastructure. The CAIDA Tools site [8] contains tools and software developed by CAIDA as well as a taxonomy of available research and visualization tools including AutoFocus, Beluga, cflowd, CoralReef, iffinder, Mantra, NeTraMet, RTG, scamper, skitter.

There has been some work at the intra-domain level to use measurement information for tackling network performance degradation and managing congestion in operational networks as well as addressing service monitoring. The devised measurement tools and systems collect, analyze and visualize forms of data observed in Intranets or Internet such as network topology, traffic load, performance, and routing. An intra-domain QoS monitoring system was developed in TEQUILA project for IP-based networks [9].

There have also been some works on monitoring and measurements at inter-domain level, by EC research projects including IST- INTERMON, IST-MoMe, and IST-SCAMPI [10]. The objective of the IST-INTERMON project was to develop an integrated inter-domain QoS monitoring, analysis and modeling system to be used in multi-domain Internet infrastructure.

The proposed solution assumes that a centralized manager negotiates monitoring operation with every domain along the service delivery path. This may result in a scalability problem for the INTERMON system as the inter-domain network expands. The focus of the IST-MoMe project was the enhancement of inter-domain real-time QoS architectures with integrated monitoring capabilities. The objective of the IST-SCAMPI project was to develop an open and extensible network monitoring architecture for Internet including a passive monitoring adapter at 10 Gbps speeds, and other measurement tools [11]. IST-LOBSTER was its follow on project aimed at deploying an advanced pilot European Internet Traffic Monitoring Infrastructure based on passive monitoring sensors [12]. The MOMENT project [13] is an EC Framework Program 7 project and aimed at creating a common and open, pan-European platform by integrating the measurement infrastructures resulted from various past EC projects and other measurement-related projects. This is to design and implement a mediator architecture offering a unified interface for measurement services, able to use all data and functionalities from the existing measurement infrastructures.

A multi-domain measurement framework for monitoring network connections is also proposed in [14]. PerSONAR [15], [16] is a web services-based infrastructure for collecting and publishing multi-domain network performance monitoring. In this chapter, we focus on inter-domain QoS monitoring.

3. MONITORING IN MULTI-DOMAIN ENVIRONMENT

For multi-domain QoS monitoring, a number of aspects must be taken into consideration. It is essential for providers in the service delivery chain to co-operate based on an agreed framework formulating the configuration of monitoring elements and service, the execution of measurements, the composition of results in an appropriate way, and the exchange of measurement data between providers.

Co-operation of providers: Each provider is responsible for monitoring in its domain. Providers require sharing measurement information among them for end-to-end performance/traffic monitoring. Therefore, monitoring in multi-domain environment requires co-operation of network providers. This co-operation must be formalized somehow through a negotiation process between providers resulting in an agreement. This agreement should set a common framework based on the measurement needs and how to conduct the measurements. It is envisaged that provider level business contracts (SLA/SLS) can also encompass the necessary clauses of this framework.

Type of measurements: The framework should specify the type of measurements to be carried out. Monitoring systems should be able to provide both performance and traffic related measurements at different measurement granularities from macro-flow at QoS class levels to micro-flows. In general, the passive metrics should be measured by the monitoring system are as follows:

- *cSLS* monitoring[4] offered load measured at ingress point of source domain and throughput at egress point of destination domain, required for SM purposes.

[4] By c/pSLS monitoring, we mean monitoring related to flow/s specified in c/pSLS contracts.

- pSLS/QoS path offered load at ingress AS Border Router (ASBR) of a domain and throughput at ingress ASBR of next domain, required for both SM and RM.
- PHB (Per Hop Behavior) related throughput at routers, required for RM purposes. A PHB defined by Differentiated Services (DiffServ) framework [17] includes the differential treatment individual packets receive, implemented by queue management disciplines.
- PHB related packet discards in packets per second, required for RM purposes.
- If Multi Protocol Label Switching (MPLS) technology is used, Label Switch Paths' (LSP) offered load measured at head-end and LSP throughput at tail-end of tunnel, required for both SM and RM.

The active metrics required for both SM and RM purposes that should be measured include one-way packet delay, one-way packet loss, and delay variations experienced at various levels i.e., QoS-based IP path either end-to-end5 or hop-by-hop, LSP, and PHB.

Monitoring Configurations: The common measurement framework must specify how to conduct the measurements through a monitoring specification. It should give the appropriate guidelines for configuring monitoring elements. As an example, it should define the types of measurement packets, frequency of tests, frequency of packets in test series, etc. It should specify level of synthetic traffic providers inject into the network that should not affect the normal network operation.

Composition of results: The framework must specify how to compose or compare the measurement results appropriately [18], [19], [21]. Providers have different measurement tools to collect and aggregate data. Through this agreement, providers agree on how to conduct the measurements in terms of data format, form of data collection, measurement aggregation, sampling periods, summarization periods, reporting schedule, etc. Providers should also agree on the reporting methods and format of reports. In addition, they should agree on the type of measurements they perform such as periodical or random measurements, alarms, etc. The specification should specify how to treat the errors in measurements and how to analyze and visualize the measurement results.

Exchange of monitoring data: Multi-domain monitoring requires exchange of measurement requests and responses among providers. The monitoring data must be shared through a standardized communication protocol. Data must be exchanged reliably and securely. The protocol must provide the means to limit and detect attempts to manipulate the measurement data. Without a proper degree of security no provider would agree to share its data. Access to the measurement data should be controlled and subject to secure authorization/authentication processes.

[5] In this chapter, two distinct methods, namely end-to-end and hop-by-hop, are defined for performance measurements. These measurements are conducted between the entry point of an ingress router of a source AS and exit point of an egress router of a destination AS for end-to-end measurements or per AS hop that is between the entry point of an ingress router and exit point of an egress router of the same AS for hop-by-hop measurements.

4. Monitoring System Architecture

Any inter-domain QoS monitoring infrastructure should allow co-operation among providers while keeping intact the authority, confidentiality, and full control of each provider over its resources. This section describes large-scale inter-domain QoS monitoring infrastructure specifying the monitoring system components and focusing on inter-provider relationships and relevant measurements that can be performed.

4.1. Monitoring System Components

A monitoring system infrastructure should have distinct entities operating at each AS and functioning at different levels in order to fulfil the requirements stated in the above section. The proposed entities are namely Node, Network, and Service Level Monitors.

Node Monitors perform node-related measurements. They should be able to perform active measurements between one node and any other node in the network at path or per hop level as well as passive monitoring. A *Node monitor* collects measurement results from either meters or probes located at routers through passive or active monitoring agents. *Node Monitors* should commonly be configured with information about the metrics, the sampling and summarization periods, and threshold parameters.

Network Monitor performs network-wide post-processing of measurement data using a library of statistical functions. This monitoring component utilizes network-wide performance and traffic measurements collected by the *Node Monitors* in order to build a physical and logical network view at intra-domain level. It also utilizes network-wide monitoring information related to the inter-domain links and resources.

Service Monitor performs customer/provider related service level monitoring, auditing, and reporting. It must keep track of the compliance of the level of service provided to the SLS instances. It utilizes information provided by the node and network monitoring entities of the domains and the networks involved in the end-to-end QoS delivery chain. In addition, it can be in charge of exchanging configuration information, signaling messages and measurement information between different domains that must share monitoring results by means of a secure protocol. An attempt for signaling for QoS measurement in multi-domain environment is reported in [[21].

4.2. QoS Interconnection Models and the Inter-Domain Monitoring System

There are many models for the interconnection between providers for offering QoS-enabled services. The type of interconnection model impacts inter-domain monitoring functions. These functions are investigated for three QoS interconnection models as explained below.

4.2.1. Monitoring System in the Source-Based Interconnection Environment

In the *source-based* peering model, an INP establishes QoS peering agreements (i.e., *pSLSs*) directly with all downstream providers in the end-to-end service delivery chain to offer an end-to-end QoS service (see Figure 1). In this model, the source INP is the central point, which takes the responsibility for the overall SM including service monitoring. In this model, it is possible for the source INP to get monitoring information directly from each domain in the multi-domain chain. Figure 1 shows monitoring architecture where the source-based model is employed.

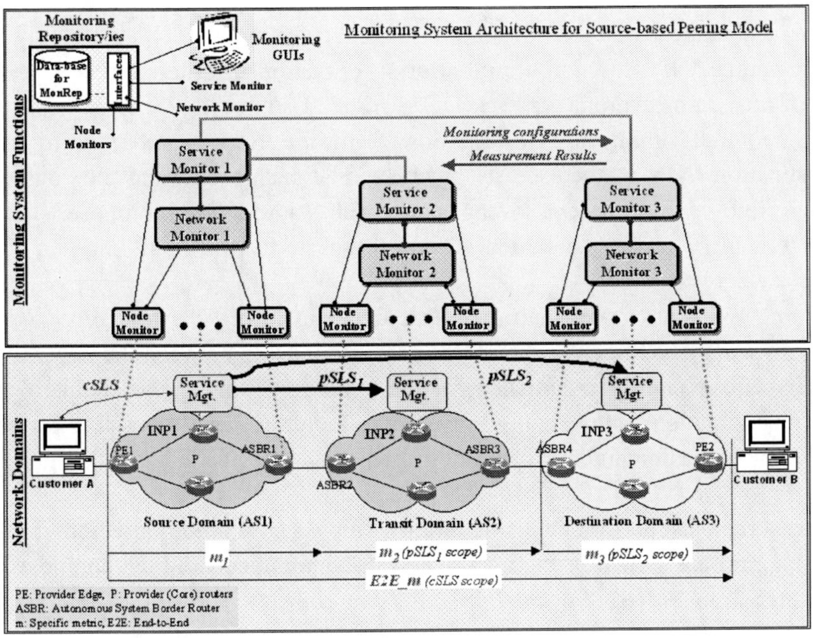

Figure 1. Monitoring system architecture for the source-based interconnection model.

Node Monitors can be configured to perform measurements on PHBs (Per Hop Behaviours) at the border routers for inter-domain or edge/core routers for intra-domain RM purposes. *Node monitors* can perform performance measurements on QoS paths using hop-by-hop method, i.e., from entry point of ASBR2 to exit point of ASBR3 of INP2 for specific QoS path. In addition, *Node monitors* can also perform end-to-end performance measurements between ingress and egress routers of two remote domains (PE1 at AS1 and PE2 at AS3, see Figure 1). Passive *cSLS* monitoring (offered load and throughput) can be performed at the ingress and egress routers. Passive *pSLS* monitoring can be performed at the border routers (e.g., at ASBR2 and ASBR3, see Figure 1).

Network monitor at each domain can deduce the AS performance view by analyzing PHBs and routes measurements. PHB QoS performance measurements can be used for managing inter-domain resources. Any intra/inter-domain RM system can then use the measured performance of the various routes in order to do route management, load balancing, and dimensioning. *Service monitor* uses the measurement data, which is collected by *network* and *node monitors* and composes the data for the use in its domain or it passes the result directly to the source INP's *service monitor*. This information includes path level performance measurements and SLS traffic statistics.

There are the following facts to consider for performing measurements when a source-based QoS interconnection model is used:

1. The source INP needs to have inter-domain topological information in order to set-up *pSLSs* and launch end-to-end monitoring operation. As source INP must know the end-to-end route (i.e., transit AS hops), end-to-end monitoring can easily be achieved by using per AS hop measurements for specific QoS path. Source INP can also directly initiate end-to-end performance measurements between its ingress router and the destination INP egress router (AS1 and AS3, see Figure 1), as there is business relationship between source and destination domains (e.g., INP1 and INP3). Hence, it can receive measurement information from the destination domain directly.
2. The source INP must initiate monitoring operation in order to receive per AS hop performance measurements. *Service monitor* at source INP can request retrieval of the required monitoring information from the *Service monitor* of transit and destination INPs as there exists business relationship between the source INP and each INP along the end-to-end path. The source INP composes per AS hop performance results obtained from these INPs for building an end-to-end service/network view.
3. Source INP knows destination INP and it can directly obtain *c/pSLS* throughput results from it as there is a direct business relationship between the two.
4. *pSLSs* are explicitly established for the source INP along the chain. If end-to-end service violation occurs, using hop-by-hop monitoring, it is possible for source INP to identify the domain/s that are not providing the service they are committed for.

The measurements performed using hop-by-hop (per AS hop) method for a specific parameter (e.g., m) are shown in Figure 1. These measurements are then composed to obtain end-to-end measurement (E2E_m) at INP1: $E2E\_m \equiv m_1 \oplus m_2 \oplus m_3$. For a discussion on how the composition of delay and loss parameters works, see Section 3.5 of [[9].

4.2.2. Monitoring System in the Cascaded Interconnection Environment

In the *cascaded* interconnection model, an INP only establishes QoS interconnection agreements with its immediate neighboring provider/s to construct an end-to-end QoS service. Each INP needs to know the QoS classes advertised and offered by its neighboring domains for mapping and binding with its own local QoS classes in order to implement its own extended QoS classes to be advertised to its customers and upstream domains. Each INP only makes *pSLS* contracts with the immediately adjacent interconnected INPs and there is no peering relationship between source INP and other transit INPs. This type of interconnection agreement provides the QoS connectivity from a customer to reachable destinations that may be several domains away. Setting-up *pSLS*s with defined scope and distinct performance characteristics between adjacent INPs is the compelling feature of this model.

Node monitors function as explained in the previous section. Except, there cannot be any end-to-end performance measurement from ingress point at AS1 and egress point at AS3 as shown in Figure 2 for specific QoS routes, as there is no business relationship between INP1 and INP3 for sending the measurement results back to INP1. Passive monitoring for *pSLS* can only be performed at the border routers. *Network monitor* at each domain builds a network view by analyzing PHBs and path measurements. *Service monitor* can compose and deduce a partial view of end-to-end performance by using its' domain measurements as well as the results received from downstream domains. Figure 2 shows monitoring system architecture for the cascaded model.

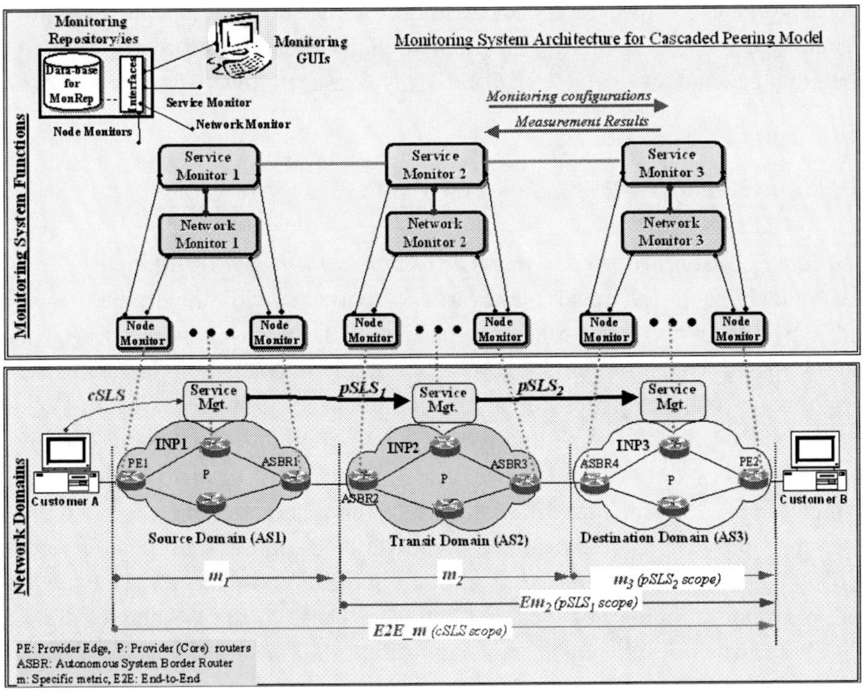

Figure 2. Monitoring system architecture for the cascaded interconnection model.

There are the following facts to consider for performing measurements when a cascaded QoS peering model is used:

1. Source INP does not need the topological information in order to set-up *pSLSs* and launch end-to-end monitoring making monitoring operation more scalable.
2. Source INP must initiate monitoring operation and it will only receive measurement results from its adjacent domain/s.
3. The end-to-end route, in all probability, may not be known to the source INP in order for it to build a complete view of the transit route. Only, the last INP (as the destination point) in the chain may be known to the source INP and it may be able to establish business relationship with that INP for monitoring purposes only. This relationship may be required for passive *cSLS* throughput monitoring.
4. The monitoring information is received by INP's *service monitor* through the adjacent domains via the monitoring protocol. Each transit INP must properly compose the results received from its adjacent INPs to build a view from its domain to the destinations for extended QoS classes offered to its customers/upstream domains.
5. Consequently, source INP's *service monitor* can then build an end-to-end view by receiving the measurement information from its neighbor/s and combining them with its own domain specific measurements.
6. *pSLS* monitoring can be performed e.g., at ASBR2 for offered load and ASBR3 for throughput as shown in Figure 2. If any service degradation is detected, it will be difficult to locate exactly the domain responsible for the service violation. Any complain has to be directed to the next INP domain in the chain by the upstream INP.

The measurements performed at each AS hop for a specific parameter (e.g., m) and they are then composed at each up-stream AS domain and builds up towards the source domain. The measurement compositions at INP2 and INP1 are as follows for parameters shown in Figure 2:

INP2: $Em_2 = m_2 \oplus m_3$ INP1: $E2E\_m = Em = m_1 \oplus Em_2$

4.2.3. Monitoring System in the Bilateral Interconnection Environment

In this model, each INP also makes *pSLS* contracts with the immediately adjacent interconnected INPs. This model relies on the use of the meta-QoS-class (*m-QC)*[6] concept [[22]. Setting-up *pSLS*s with open scope (i.e., no explicit reachability information) and no distinct performance characteristics but simple compliance with well-known m-QC behaviors between adjacent INPs is the compelling feature of this model. In this model, there is no end-to-end QoS guarantees defined and consequently there is no need to build extended QoS classes, which are the fundamental differences between this model and cascaded model. This model does not provide any end-to-end bandwidth guarantees because it enables any destination to be reached, without prior explicit indication in the *pSLS*. Each domain is engineered to support a number of local QoS classes. These local QoS classes are mapped to globally well-known *m-QC*s. Each AS advertises the *m-QC*s that it supports in its administrative domain. Other adjacent domains can make *pSLS* arrangement with this domain to make use of offered *m-QC*s. Although, inter-domain routing is *pSLS* constrained, each domain can find out whether it can reach certain destinations in an *m-QC* plane through a QoS-inferred BGP (q-BGP) protocol [23],[24]. q-BGP is the enhanced version of BGP proposed to support QoS requirements for allowing the deployment of QoS-based services. The QoS performance metrics, their characteristics and values can be exchanged between providers' domains using q-BGP UPDATE messages [[25].

The monitoring architecture and its functions are similar to the one used in the cascaded model. There are the following facts to consider for performing measurements when a source-based QoS interconnection model is used:

[1] Offered load is measured at ingress border router of a domain and throughput is measured at egress border router of the domain per *pSLS*/QoS-enabled route. This information is passed to the adjacent upstream domain/s with which this INP has *pSLS* agreements.

[2] Performance/traffic related measurements per AS hop is measured at granularity of *pSLS*/QoS-based intra-domain path.

[3] In addition to routing information, QoS measurements can be propagated to upstream domains for building end-to-end views on *m-QCs* enabled routes and services. This could help the route selection in its decision-making process..

[4] There is only business relationship between adjacent neighbors, but not between providers more than "one hop away". Hence, it is not possible to conduct end-to-end

6 An m-QC denotes an abstract well-known QoS-class, where the 'meta' term refers to a quantitative or qualitative range of values of the QoS-class performance parameters. A delay/loss-sensitive QoS-class with delay and loss value of 'very low', or delay-sensitive-QoS-class with delay value of 'low' and loss value of 'any' are typical examples of m-QCs.

performance measurements directly, as there is no end-to-end scope and business relationship with transit domains.

[5] *pSLS* monitoring is performed per AS hop and *cSLS* throughput monitoring cannot be conducted.

5. CONCLUSIONS

In order to provide access to the global Internet, providers must interact with each other. This chapter proposed a framework for inter-domain QoS monitoring taking into account the models of interactions between providers that impacts inter-domain monitoring functions. The source-based model would be difficult to manage in terms of setting-up *pSLS* contracts. But it is possible to conduct all required measurements. The cascaded and bilateral models make it possible to build IP QoS services on a global basis while only maintaining contractual relationships with adjacent providers. In cascaded model, *pSLS*s are established between adjacent INPs with defined scope and distinct performance characteristics while in bilateral model, *pSLSs* are set-up with open scope and no distinct performance characteristics. Bilateral model reflects the loosely coupled structure of Internet. The measurements to be collected by the monitoring system and limitations using both models are fully specified.

REFERENCES

[1] TeleManagment Forum: Enhanced Telecom Operations Map (eTOM), The Business Process Framework, Addendum D: *Process Decompositions and Descriptions*, GB921 D, V7.1, Jan 2007.

[2] P. Trimintzios, et al., "*Service-Driven Traffic Engineering for Intradomain Quality of Service Management*", IEEE Network Magazine, Vol. 17, No. 3, May 2003.

[3] D. Goderis et al., "Service Level Specification Semantics and Parameters", IETF Internet draft: draft-tequila-sls-02.txt, expired Aug. 2002.

[4] P. Flegkas, Ed., Mescal Delivrable D1.1: "Specification of Business Models and a Functional Architecture for Inter-domain QoS Delivery", June 2003, http://www.mescal.org/.

[5] Internet Engineering Task Force (IETF), for information on the various IETF working groups visit: http://www.ietf.org.

[6] RIPE-NCC Test Traffic Measurement web page: http://www.ripe.net/projects/ttm/ index.html.

[7] V. Paxson, J. Mahdavi, A. Adams, and M. Mathis "An Architecture for Large-Scale Internet Measurement", *IEEE Communications Magazine*, Vol. 36 No. 8, Aug. 1998, pp. 48-54.

[8] CAIDA (Cooperative Association for Internet Data Analysis) Tools web site: http://www.caida.org/tools/.

[9] A. Asgari et al., "Scalable Monitoring Support for Resource Management and Service Assurance", *IEEE Network Magazine*, Vol. 18, No. 6, Dec./Nov. 2004, pp. 6-18.

[10] European IST research projects' web site: http://www.cordis.lu/ist/, for INTERMON: http://www.ist-intermon.org/, for MoMe: http://ww.ist-mome.org/, for SCAMPI: http://ww.ist-scampi.org/.

[11] J. Coppens, et al., "SCAMPI - A Scaleable Monitoring Platform for the Internet," Proceedings of the 2nd International Workshop on IPS, Budapest, Hungary, Mar. 2004.

[12] IST-LOBSTER home page at http://www.ist-lobster.org/about/objectives.html.

[13] MOMENT (Monitoring and Measurement in the Next Generation Technologies) project website: http://www.fp7-moment.eu/.

[14] J. W. Boote, et al., "Towards multi-domain monitoring for the European research networks," *Computational Methods in Science and Technologies journal*, Vol. 11(2), 2005, pp. 91-100.

[15] A Hanemann, et al., "PerfSONAR: A service oriented architecture for multi-domain network monitoring", *Lecture Notes in Computer Science* (LNCS), Book Chapter, ISBN 978-3-540-30817-1, Springer, Volume 3826, 2005pp. 241-254.

[16] J. W. Boote, et al., "Instantiating a Global Network Measurement Framework", *LBNL Technical Report LBNL*-1452E, Jan. 2009.

[17] S. Blake, D. Black, M. Carlson, E. Davies, Z. Wang and W. Weiss, "An Architecture for Differentiated Services," *IETF Informational RFC 2475*, Dec. 1998.

[18] A. Morton, S. Van den Berghe, "Framework for Metric Composition", IETF Internet draft, <draft-ietf-ippm-framework-compagg-07>, expired May 2009.

[19] A. Morton, E. Stephan, "Spatial Composition of Metrics", IETF Internet draft, < draft-ietf-ippm-spatial-composition-08>, expires Sept. 2009.

[20] A. Hanemann, et al., "A study on Network Performance Metrics and their Composition," Emerald Group Publishing Limited, *Campus-Wide Information Systems Journal,* Vol. 23, Issue 4, 2006, pp. 268 – 282.

[21] Alban Couturier, "Signaling for QoS Measurement", Internet Draft, <draft-couturier-nsis-measure-00.txt>, expired Nov. 2003.

[22] P. Levis et al., "The Meta-QoS-Class concept: a step towards global QoS inter-domain services", *In Proc. of IEEE SoftCOM conference*, Oct. 2004.

[23] M. Howarth et al., Mescal Delivrable D1.2, "Initial specification of protocols and algorithms for inter-domain SLS management and traffic engineering for QoS-based IP service delivery and their test requirements", Jan. 2004, available at: http://www. mescal.org/.

[24] D. Griffin, M. Boucadiar, P. Morand, M. Howarth, N. Wang, G. Pavlou, A. H. Asgari, P. Georgatsos, "Interdomain Routing through, QoS-Class Planes, *IEEE Communications Magazine,* Volume 45, No. 2, Feb. 2007, pp88-95.

[25] M. Boucadiar (Ed.), "QoS-Enhanced Border Gateway Protocol, IETF Internet Draft, <draft-boucadair-qos-bgp-spec-01.txt>, expired Jan. 2006.

In: Recent Advances in Providing QoS and Reliability... ISBN 978-1-61761-858-1
Editors: N. Wang, G. Pavlou and M. Boucadair

Chapter 7

INTERCONNECTION MODELS FOR QOS-BASED IP SERVICE OFFERING

Abolghasem (Hamid) Asgari*[*1], Mohamed Boucadair[2], David Griffin[3], Panagiotis Georgatsos[4], and George Pavlou[5]
[1]Thales Research and Technology (TRT) Limited, Worton Drive, Reading RG2 0SB, UK,
[2]France Telecom, 3 Av François Château, Rennes, France
[3]University College London, Dept. of EEE, Torrington Place, London, UK
[4]Algonet S.A, Athens, Greece
[5]University of Surrey, Guildford, UK

ABSTRACT

In order to provide end-to-end QoS for the global Internet, providers must interact more closely with each other. The focus of this chapter is to evaluate new techniques for providing these interactions in propagating QoS-based agreements among the set of providers involved in the chain of inter-domain service delivery. These providers' interactions occur at the service layer that result in the establishment of QoS-aware service agreements between providers. This needs to be supported by appropriate service management and traffic engineering capabilities per provider domain as well as by BGP-based interactions. The concepts of how to build such agreements are discussed and models for inter-domain QoS peering (interconnection) are proposed (source-based, cascaded, and bilateral models). By taking into account the loosely coupled structure of the Internet, the emphasis is put on cascaded and bilateral models, in which each provider establishes agreements with its directly attached upstream peers. Along with the proposed models, targeted value-added services are identified and the methods of supporting the bi-directionality for these services are also proposed. The focus is put on specification and evaluation of bilateral model for service level peering associated with meta-QoS-class concept [1], together with BGP-based interactions that are used to construct QoS-enabled Internet.

* Hamid.Asgari@thalesgroup.com.

Keywords: Inter-domain, QoS classes, Peering, Cascade, Bilateral, SLA, SLS, q-BGP

1. INTRODUCTION

In the best-effort Internet, there exist two forms of relationships between providers for traffic exchange, underlined by respective business agreements: peering and transit [2], [3]. Peering is termed as the business relationship whereby providers reciprocally provide access only to each other's customers. Peering is a mutual non-transitive relationship between providers to exchange data between themselves, normally for no fee or charge. Transit is the business relationship whereby one transit provider offers access to all destinations in its routing table to another provider for a charge. It should be clarified that the term 'peering' normally used to denote that two providers interact with each other for the purpose of expanding the topological scope of their offered services, under any business relationship which may govern this interaction. In [4], a number of aspects is presented including the general issue of backbone interconnection, the peering (interconnection) agreements, the impact of peering in infrastructure, the future of interconnection agreements, the current state of international transit services, and so on.

Deployment of new applications and services across the Internet requires a more complex management of Internet. EMANICS was a European Commission (EC) funded project that addressed management of the Internet and complex services. The project deliverable [5] describes the problem of interacting among providers in multi-domain environments and outlines the key issues of provisioning of services in a multi-domain environment. In [6], some insights into recent operational developments are provided, describing why interconnection in the Internet has become more complex and explaining the implications for cost/revenue allocations.

Deployment of QoS-based services across the Internet requires a large set of providers to co-operate and to establish interconnection agreements for expanding the geographical scope of each other's QoS services. In a QoS-enabled Internet, enhanced agreements are required to determine the QoS levels, the traffic quantities and the destinations to be reached across the pre-existing inter-domain links, together with the agreed financial settlement terms. The intention is to enable a provider to extend its QoS over multiple domains, thus enabling the provider to offer reachability to networks beyond its own domain with QoS performance levels suitable for end-to-end QoS-enabled services. Appropriate means are required to enable providers to discover feasible offered QoS-based services. Once a path to reach a destination is discovered and QoS values associated with the path are chosen by a provider, relevant automated means are required for establishing QoS peering agreements. A provider may need to set up appropriate agreements with direct peers, or with a remote AS, or agreements may need to be established between two remote ASes upon request from a third party AS. Eurescom specified a number of organisational models for these interactions between providers and the support of inter-operator IP-based services [7]. Interactions between providers and in particular service layer interactions are required when offering QoS services across multiple domains. These interactions result in the establishment of service agreements between providers aggregating customer service traffic, which need to be supported by appropriate service management and traffic engineering capabilities per provider domain [8] as well as by BGP-based interactions [9] at the IP layer for QoS inter-domain routing purposes.

In contrast to the significant research work carried out for providing intra-domain QoS solutions, limited work has been conducted on providing inter-domain QoS solutions. Many authors have considered inter-domain traffic engineering for best effort traffic e.g., [10] and some e.g., [11] considered efficient traffic engineering negotiations between adjacent ISPs, however, this work on plain Border Gateway Protocol (BGP) does not take QoS into consideration. Using service level agreement policies to enable IP network providers agree how to distribute service-level constraints (i.e. QoS) across multiple domains is proposed in [12]. Other proposals have addressed QoS extensions to the underlying BGP [13] to enable QoS dissemination and routing across multiple Autonomous Systems (AS). However, it should be noted that all these contributions are ad hoc solutions without an integrated and systematic view of how to deploy Internet QoS in a scalable and incremental fashion. This chapter investigates the inter-domain QoS peering between providers in order to set-up a QoS-enabled Internet. The issues related to the financial settlement for inter-domain QoS services are discussed in [14]. In addition, commercial models for QoS interconnection of networks are explained in [15] focusing on the economical aspects. In [16] authors specified two main goals i.e., to identify standards that should be worked on to simplify deployment of inter-provider QoS and to identify "best common practices" that, while not requiring standardization, could ease the deployment of inter-provider QoS if agreed to by a critical mass of providers.

This chapter is organised as follows. Section 2 defines the terms used throughout this chapter. Section 3 briefly explains the QoS-class operations in order to build a QoS based Internet. Section 4 describes the inter-domain QoS peering arrangements emphasising on the hop-by-hop cascaded and bilateral models. The issues related to the bi-directional service offerings are also discussed in Section 5. In Section 6, the target services are proposed that can be constructed on top of these peering agreements. In Section 7, an implementation of a QoS-enabled Internet in a testbed is discussed and the results of evaluation are presented. Section 8 concludes this chapter.

2. DEFINITIONS AND TERMS

A '*Customer*' (subscriber) denotes an entity, which has the ability to subscribe to QoS-based services offered by 'Providers'. Customers are the target recipients of QoS-based services that are offered on the basis of respective agreements, i.e., Service Level Agreements (SLAs).

An '*IP Network Provider*' (INP[1])' offers IP connectivity services, that is services that provide reachability between hosts in the IP address space. Such 'Providers' own and administer an IP network infrastructure. For the purpose of expanding the geographical span of the offered connectivity services, INPs interact with each other, on a one-to-one peering relationship basis.

---

[1] The terms INP and AS (Autonomous System) are used interchangeably throughout this chapter to denote a business entity owning a network and being responsible for its operation and the provision of Internet connectivity aspects.

'*QoS-based service*' term denotes a service that offers a type of added value to customers, e.g. matching application and customer usage requirements. An SLA denotes an agreement that describes the characteristics of a service offering and the mutual responsibilities of the customers/providers for using/providing the offered service. The *Service Level Specification (SLS)* is an integral part of a SLA that denotes the technical characteristics of an offered service. Two types of SLS (and subsequently of SLAs) are distinguished here:

- *cSLS (customer SLS)*, established between end-customers and providers, and
- *pSLS (peer SLS)*, established between providers for exchanging traffic in the Internet with the purpose to expand the geographical span of their offered services. *pSLSs* are meant to support aggregate traffic and they are assumed to exist prior to any agreements with end customers.

'IP *Connectivity Service*' is an IP layer transport service for reaching particular destination(s) from specific source(s) in the IP address space. QoS-based connectivity services offered by INPs are divided into elementary and complex connectivity services. Elementary connectivity services as 'connectivity legs' are strictly point-to-point and uni-directional, whereas complex connectivity services may be multipoint-to-multipoint and bi-directional (e.g., VPN, server access services, etc). As such, complex connectivity services encompass a number of elementary connectivity services. SLSs may only be specified for elementary connectivity services. TEQUILA, an EC project, specified an SLS template for intra-domain QoS-based connectivity services [17].

2.1. Qos-Classes

A '*QoS-class (QC)*' denotes a basic network-wide *QoS transfer capability* of a provider domain. A QoS transfer capability is a set of attribute-value pairs, where the attributes express various packet transfer performance parameters such as one-way transit delay, packet loss and inter-packet delay variation (a.k.a., jitter), and their particular values [18]. Considering a provider domain, its QoS-classes can be distinguished as *local-QoS-classes* and *extended-QoS-classes* [19]. In addition, *Meta-QoS-Class (m-QC)* is introduced as an abstract concept. *m-QCs* rely on global understanding of QoS requirements of well-known applications. This distinction is required for capturing the notion of 'QoS capabilities' across domains, upon which QoS-based Internet services could be built. These QoS-classes are explained below.

- A local-QoS-class (l-QC) denotes a basic QoS transfer capability that can be provided by means employed in the provider domain itself. Evidently, the topological scope of an l-QC is restricted within the boundaries of the provider domain.
- An *extended-QoS-class (e-QC)* denotes a basic network-wide QoS transfer capability that can be provided by means employed not only in the provider domain but also utilising appropriate means in other (service-peering) provider domains. In other words, an *e-QC* is provided by concatenating the QoS transfer capabilities (QoS-classes) of the provider domain with appropriate capabilities (QoS-classes, *l-QC* or *e-*

QC) of other provider domains. The topological scope of an *e-QC* could therefore be outside the boundaries of the provider domain.

- A *Meta-QoS-Class (m-QC)* denotes an abstract QoS-class, where the 'meta' term refers to a quantitative or qualitative range of values of the QoS-class performance parameters. A QoS-class with delay value of 'very low' and loss value of 'very low', or delay-sensitive-QoS-class with delay value of 'low' and loss value of 'any' are typical examples of *m-QCs*. Unlike *e-QC*s that are defined end-to-end with distinct performance characteristics, *m-QCs* do not imply a predefined/engineered end-to-end-QoS [1]. *m-QCs* lays the foundations for a set of "parallel networks", one of which may be suitable for specific service/s.

From a service offering perspective, QoS-classes correspond to the performance (transfer quality) guarantees expressed in c/pSLS along with other aspects such as bandwidth, grade of service guarantees and topological scope. From a service provisioning perspective, QoS-classes segregate the network QoS-space into a number of distinct classes, aggregating user QoS traffic accordingly. In this respect, the notion of QoS-classes sets the traffic-related objectives of the inter- or intra-domain traffic engineering functions. The concept of QoS-class could be compared to the notion of DiffServ (Differentiated Services) Per Domain Behaviours (PDBs) [20]. Where an l-QC defines constant behaviour across a single domain that can be sold to other domains, but with non-standardised behaviour, an e-QC defines a "combined" l-QC behaviour, and where an m-QC defines standardised, well-known PDBs obeyed by all domains.

3. QoS-Class Operations

For a provider domain wishing to provide QoS-classes from its domain to destinations outside its domain, a number of *QC-operations* need to be performed. They are depicted in Figure 1 and outlined below, with further details in [19]. It should be noted that the purpose of these QC-operations is mainly to build *e-QC*s. The provisioning and fulfilment of QoS-based services falls under the realm of service management and traffic engineering functions and the identified QC-operations outline the required functions.

The *QC-advertisement* operation enables a provider domain to inform other providers of its QoS-class capabilities; *l-QC*s, *e-QC*s, or *m-QCs*. QoS-classes are advertised as part of respective QoS-based services (*pSLS*) through suitable methods. It is envisaged that a variety of advertising means will be used, ranging from digital marketplaces or other automated peer-to-peer processes to conventional techniques such as salespersons, newspapers and word of mouth.

The *QC-discovery* operation enables a provider domain to locate and find out the QoS-classes offered by other provider domains. This is to discover the QoS capabilities, capacities, destination prefixes and costs of service peer providers.

The *QC-mapping* operation enables a provider domain to see how to build *e-QC*s by determining suitable (according to the performance characteristics of the *e-QC*s being built) combinations of the domain's own capabilities (*l-QC*s) with the QoS-class capabilities offered by other provider domains, which were made known through the QC-discovery operation.

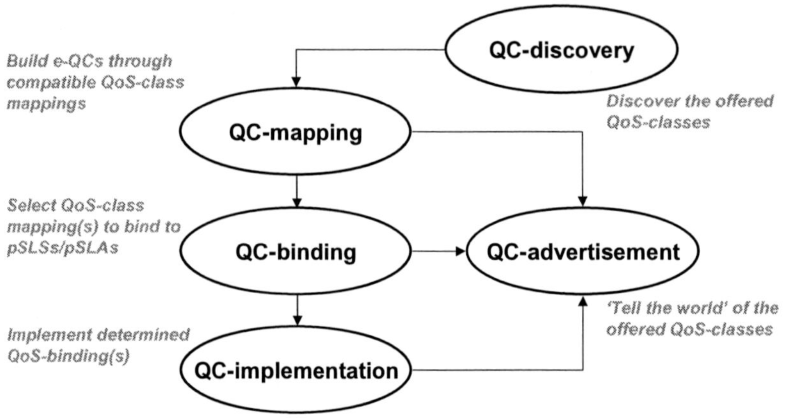

Figure 1. The QoS-class operations.

The *QC-binding* operation enables a provider domain to decide which of the possible QoS-mappings determined for building an *e-QC* will be used for actually providing this *e-QC*. The selection of a particular QoS-mapping is substantiated by negotiating corresponding *pSLSs*/*pSLAs* with appropriate service-peering providers. It should be noted that the QC-binding operation might result into a number of QoS-bindings for a given *e-QC* e.g. through different service-peering providers. The decision as to which of the established QoS-bindings will be *put in effect* in the network for actually implementing an *e-QC* as well as related routing/forwarding decisions fall into the realm of (inter-domain) traffic engineering.

The *QC-implementation* operation enables a provider domain to implement at the network (IP) layer a QoS-binding that has been determined to be in effect. The operation encompasses the necessary configurations at the IP layer required for the appropriate treatment of the packets. In particular, assuming an IP DiffServ layer, the operation entails the configuration of appropriate classifiers and traffic conditioners that allow packets entering a provider domain to receive the treatment prescribed by the *e-QC/m-QC*.

4. Inter-Domain QoS Models

Eurescom organisational models [7] are strongly influenced by experience in the telecommunications industry of provision of international telephony and other services for which network interconnection is a requirement, both in commercial and regulatory terms. We extend these organisational models and build the concepts to establish a set of inter-domain QoS interconnection models in order to set-up *pSLSs* and consequently to construct end-to-end QoS-based services across the Internet at large scale. The challenge is to propose methodologies to fulfil the requirements of new IP QoS-based services, which will be attractive both to customers and providers.

There are many models for the interconnection and service-layer interactions between providers' for offering QoS services across multiple domains. The type of inter-domain interconnection impacts the service negotiation procedures, the required signalling protocols, the path discovery through QoS binding, and path selection. The following models are considered: hub, source-based, cascaded, and hybrid.

- The *hub* model where the Service Provider (SP), as a distinct entity from INP, is the central point that negotiates and establishes *pSLSs*. Here, the SP takes the responsibility for the overall service management of any given customer IP QoS service instance. This is achieved by making *pSLS* contracts with a chain of INPs so as to create an end-to-end service.
- The *source-based* model, which is similar to the hub model, where an INP negotiates *pSLSs* directly with an appropriate number of downstream providers to construct an end-to-end QoS service. With this model, service peers are not necessarily BGP peers.
- The *cascaded* model where an INP negotiates with its immediate neighbouring provider/s the *pSLS*s having defined scope and distinct performance characteristics to construct an end-to-end QoS service. With this model, service peers can be BGP peers.
- The *bilateral* model where each INP makes *pSLS* contracts with the immediately adjacent interconnected INPs with open scope and no distinct performance characteristics.
- The *hybrid* model is combination of the source-based and the cascaded models. The value of the hybrid model is that it combines the benefits of the cascaded and source-based models. However, it also suffers from the limitations of both models [21].

Any solution for inter-domain QoS should function effectively and in a scalable manner. The three most significant models (source-based, cascaded, and bilateral) are explained in detail below.

4.1. Source-Based Model

The source-based model disassociates *pSLS* negotiations from the existing best-effort interconnection arrangements. The originating domain (central point) knows the network topology end-to-end and directly establishes *pSLS*s with a set of potential domains along the end-to-end path in order to reach a set of IP destinations, to offer an end-to-end QoS-based service. Each AS is responsible for the connection inside its domain and its inter-domain link interfaces. Figure 2 shows the source-based model where AS1 as the central point establishes *pSLSs* so that its customers can reach destinations in AS3. The scope (the source point and the reachable destinations) of the c/*pSLS*s and the QC binding operation are also shown in this figure. As an example, the intra-domain QoS capability of $l\text{-}QC_3$, $l\text{-}QC_2$, and $l\text{-}QC_1$ are supported and advertised by AS3, AS2, and AS1 respectively. AS1 as the central point discovers these QoS capabilities and constructs the $e\text{-}QC_1$ through QC mappings and bindings of the above stated *l-QC*s. This $e\text{-}QC_1$ is only known by the AS1 and is advertised only to its customers and not to other providers.

The central point requires an up-to-date topology of the Internet including the existence and operational status of the physical links between ASes for discovering and selecting end-to-end routes. In addition it needs to know the domains' advertised *l-QCs* in order to perform mapping and binding of these *l-QCs* to form *e-QC*s (e.g., $e\text{-}QC_1$).

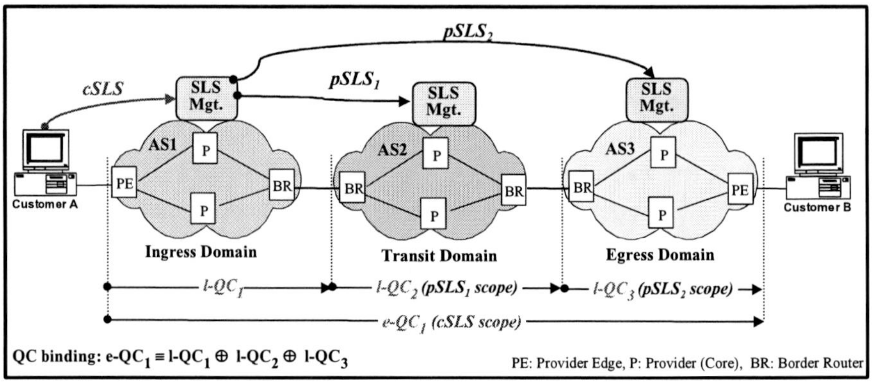

Figure 2. The source-based QoS peering model.

The combination of the above information is used for selecting the appropriate ASes as well as negotiating and establishing *pSLS* agreements. *pSLS* agreements are therefore tailored to the central point requirements. Although it is possible to find and set-up the optimal routes to the destinations since the central point has access to the overall QoS-based topology, the need for accurate topological and QoS related information of the Internet is a major drawback of this model. This may be feasible for a relatively small number of domains, but it raises scalability concerns when a large number of networks are involved. The central point may end up with many *pSLSs* to manage, which can be in the order of $O(N_d^2)$ where N_d is the number of domains in the Internet.

4.2. Cascaded Model

In the cascaded model, each INP makes *pSLS* contracts with the immediately adjacent interconnected INPs. Thus, the QoS peering agreements are between adjacent neighbours, but not between providers more than one hop away. This type of interconnection agreement provides the QoS connectivity from a customer to reachable destinations that may be several domains away. Setting-up *pSLS*s with defined scope and distinct performance characteristics between adjacent INPs is the compelling feature of cascaded model. For QoS-Class discovery and selection, each INP in the chain needs to know its adjacent neighbours and the status of related interconnection links. In addition, each INP needs to know the *e-QC*s advertised by its neighbouring domains for binding with its own *l-QC*s in order to implement its own *e-QC*s to be advertised to its customers and upstream domains. This is true for every INP involved in the chain in order to implement its *e-QC*s. Figure 3 gives an overview of the operations in this model. $l\text{-}QC_3$, $l\text{-}QC_2$, and $l\text{-}QC_1$ are supported and advertised by AS3, AS2, and AS1 respectively. AS2 discovers the AS3 capabilities and negotiates a contract (*pSLS2*) with AS3 for enabling its customers to reach destinations in AS3 with an $e\text{-}QC_2$. AS2 constructs (i.e., through QC mapping, binding, and implementation) $e\text{-}QC_2$ and advertises it. This type of process is repeated recursively to enable AS1 customers to also reach destinations in AS3, but at no point do AS1 and AS3 negotiate directly. In each step of the cascade, the upstream provider acts in the consumer role to the provider immediately downstream. It is each provider's responsibility to make appropriate *pSLS*s with the immediate downstream provider making it possible for individual customer IP QoS services to be created and managed along the entire route.

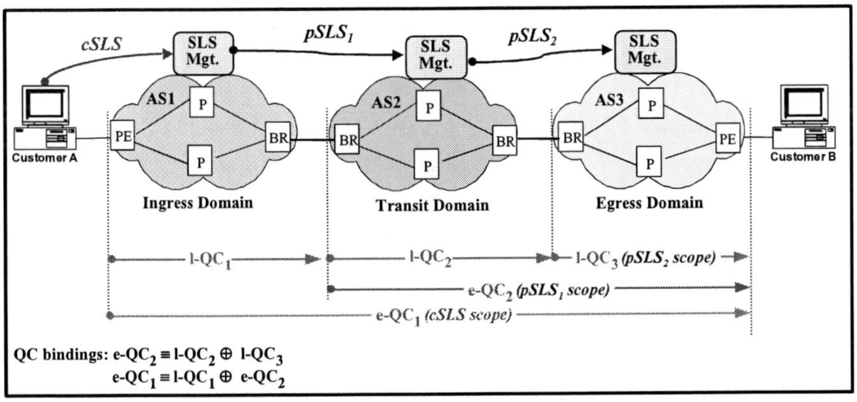

Figure 3. The cascaded QoS peering model.

With this model, a provider is able to aggregate traffic demands by establishing a single *pSLS* with its adjacent provider's domain if that traffic enters the provider's domain from the same ingress point, has the same QoS requirements, and is destined for the same destination point in spite of the fact that the traffic originated from different sources. Therefore, *pSLS* agreements can be tailored at nearly optimum level by aggregating the customers' traffic demands. As traffic demand aggregation can happen at *pSLS* level, each INP may only have a limited number of *pSLSs* to manage. Thus, an order of $O(N_d)$ of *pSLSs* needs to be established by an INP making the cascaded model more scalable. A detailed comparison between source-based and cascaded models is reported in [21].

4.3. Bilateral Model

In this model, each INP also makes *pSLS* contracts with the immediately adjacent interconnected INPs. This model relies on the use of the *m-QC* concept. Setting-up *pSLS*s with open scope (i.e., no explicit reachability information) and no distinct performance characteristics but simple compliance with well-known m-QC behaviours between adjacent INPs is the compelling feature of this model. In this model, there is no end-to-end QoS guarantees defined and consequently there is no need to build *e-QC*s, which are the fundamental differences between this model and 'cascaded model'. This model does not provide any end-to-end bandwidth guarantees because it enables any destination to be reached, without prior explicit indication in the *pSLS*. Each domain is engineered to support a number of local QoS classes (i.e. *l-QC*s). These *l-QC*s are mapped to globally well-known *m-QC*s. Each AS advertises the *m-QC*s that it supports in its administrative domain. Other domains can make *pSLS* arrangement in cascaded fashion with this domain to make use of offered *m-QC*s. Although, inter-domain routing is *pSLS* constrained, each domain can find out whether it can reach certain destinations in an *m-QC* plane through a BGP-like protocol (q-BGP) [22]. The core functions of this model are as follows:

- A globally known identifier identifies each *m-QC*.
- Establishing *pSLS*s sets off the exchange of inter-domain connectivity information per *m-QC* between service peer domains.
- Each AS announces to its service peers the network prefixes that can be reached within each *m-QC* plane through q-BGP.

These functions result in QoS-enabled Internet that can be viewed as a set of parallel planes each offering service levels associated with a specific *m-QC* and running distinct instances of q-BGP as described in [23]. The *pSLS* agreement for an *m-QC* allows the AS to benefit from their neighbour's inter-domain QoS capabilities and enabling it to reach anywhere in the QoS-Internet of that specific *m-QC*. Using the *m-QC* concept means when crossing through a set of ASes, the QoS treatment experienced by an IP datagram is "*consistent*" in all transit ASes. The term "*consistent*" means that the treatment received by the IP packets in each AS conforms to the corresponding *m-QC* definition. It does not mean that the QoS characteristics applied to the datagrams, when crossing different AS domains, are the same. The basic requirement for a domain is to have only one pSLS agreement with its adjacent domain to join an m-QC plane. This makes bilateral model much more scalable than other models.

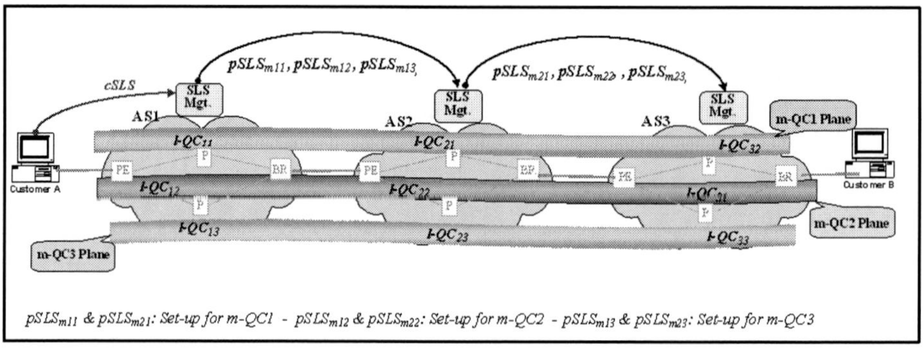

Figure 4. The bilateral QoS peering model.

4.3.1. QoS-Enhanced Border Gateway Protocol (q-BGP)

QoS-enhanced BGP is the enhanced version of BGP proposed to support QoS requirements for allowing the deployment of QoS-based services. The QoS-related information and their characteristics that are required to exchange between providers/domains can occur either at the service plane during the pSLS negotiation phase or at the routing level using q-BGP. In the first option, an identifier agreed at the pSLS negotiation phase specifying an m-QC/e-QC plane, is exchanged via q-BGP messages. QoS performance metrics and their target values are negotiated and agreed in the pSLS; they are not exchanged in the routing level by q-BGP. In the second option, the m-QC/e-QC plane identifier and the QoS performance metrics' target values are exchanged by q-BGP. Here, the QoS performance metrics to be exchanged are agreed during the pSLS negotiation phase. Therefore, q-BGP provides a number of features:

- *QoS service capabilities*: since peering entities need to know about each other's QoS service capabilities, q-BGP allows to negotiate the capabilities that a peer domain provides, and indicates what information can potentially be carried by the q-BGP messages;
- *QoS Class (QC) identifier*: this is used to distinguish the m-QC planes (or e-QCs) that have been bought by/from service peers.
- *QoS performance characteristics*: these are a set of QoS characteristics values, such as one-way packet loss and delay and inter-packet delay variation. q-BGP supports a set of QoS performance characteristics to be sent in one single q-BGP UPDATE message.

q-BGP can advertise QoS information either statically valid for a specified period, set by domains' administrators, or dynamically, obtained through measurement. Since QoS information is exchanged in q-BGP UPDATE messages, the BGP route selection process has to be modified in order to take it into account. The q-BGP route selection process differs according to whether the first or second option explained above is used. In the first option, the q-BGP route selection process is very similar to the one for classical BGP, i.e. q-BGP route selection process will choose the route that minimises the AS_PATH hops for each QC plane. It should be noted that, additional policies could also be configured. In the second option, since several QoS parameters may be advertised for a given destination, the process examines each QoS parameter in a prioritised order. Thus, the route selection process chooses the best routes by examining initially the highest priority QoS parameter. If several routes have the same weight for the highest priority parameter, the second priority parameter is considered, and this process is repeated as necessary until a route is selected.

5. Bi-Directionality Support for Complex Connectivity Services

In previous sections, QoS interconnection models have been discussed that provide elementary connectivity services. Supporting bi-directionality provides the means in offering complex connectivity services. The primary challenge is in constructing the QoS-enabled reverse path for return traffic. This section discusses providing bi-directionality using these models. This section identifies the issues, presents a discussion of the resulting implications and provides methods for resolving them.

5.1. Bi-Directionality Support in the Source-Based Model

Since the central point has access to the overall QoS-based topology and is able to establish the appropriate SLSs in forward and return directions with a set of potential domains, it can constructs e-QCs in both directions and offer a bi-directional end-to-end QoS-based service.

5.1.1. Bi-Directionality Support in the Cascaded Model

In the "cascaded model", the scope of the desired *e-QC*s for the forward direction is part of the c/*pSLS* during the negotiation phase. However, when the reverse direction is considered from the destination AS's point of view there are the following apparent issues that must be addressed when constructing bi-directional services.

Firstly, from the destination AS's point of view (AS3 in Figure 3), the destination for the traffic in the reverse direction is not known. This is due to the fact that the *cSLS* is between Customer A and AS1 and AS1 knows the 3-tuple (Source Customer, Destination Customer, *e-QC: A, B, e-QC1*) whereas AS3 is unaware of it. Thus, AS3 cannot find/verify whether there are *e-QC*s formed through QC binding operations to reach the desired return destination (e.g., Customer A) or not. Therefore, how does AS3 find the scope for the reverse direction (e.g., AS1) in order to see if any *e-QC* exists to reach AS1 customers? Secondly, every time another upstream AS forms an *e-QC* that utilises the *l-QC* of the destination AS (AS3), the scope of the return paths for AS3 extends and AS3 will not know this. Thirdly, if asymmetric QoS is required (as it is often the case), which QoS class (*l-QC*) at each AS (e.g., AS3) should be used for return traffic and how should this *l-QC* be mapped to an *e-QC* offered by the upstream AS (e.g., AS2)? The destination AS (AS3) has no explicit information to answer the above questions.

Two methods are proposed to tackle the problem of providing QoS enabled path in the reverse direction. The first method extends the single cascade with bi-directional capabilities. The second method employs uni-directional cascades in forward and reverse directions to build bi-directional services.

5.1.2. Single Cascade

One possible solution for setting up a reverse path is to negotiate *pSLSs* in the reverse direction between peer ASes with an open destination scope. This allows the upstream AS (e.g., AS4 in Figure 5) to offer the QCs to further upstream ASes (e.g., AS3) without the need for amending the scope of pre-existing downstream *pSLS*s every time the scope changes. This implements bi-directional QoS-enabled services by employing *e-QC* enabled *c/pSLSs* in forward direction and *l-QC* enabled *pSLSs* with no explicit *e-QC* binding in reverse direction. While each ISP provides the QoS environment by provisioning its network and allocating resources in the forward direction, it can provide a similar environment for return traffic in the reverse direction within its own domain. This potentially solves the bi-directionality problem at the *pSLS* level, but there are still some issues such as implementing the *e-QC*s and invoking the service, e.g. it may not provide the fine-tuned desired *e-QC* for return traffic. To provide fine-tuned desired QC as discussed in the next section, it requires the use of a signalling mechanism for communicating between the Source and Destination ASes in order to inform the Destination AS the desired QC level for return traffic. This is problematic and violates the cascaded concept, which implies relationships only between cascade neighbours, because there is no direct business relationship between the two remote ASes.

5.1.3. Multiple Unidirectional Cascades

This method allows suitable *e-QC*s to be set-up separately by the source and destination ASes. This method would potentially provide the environment for having bi-directional services using the cascaded model in both directions. Figure shows the cascaded implementation for forward direction in which the sources from AS1 (e.g., Customer A), AS2, AS3, AS4 and AS5 can reach Customer C in AS5 with the specified desired *e-QC* quality. Figure shows the establishment of cascade for reverse direction. However, there are a few implications/issues, arising from this model.

The most obvious issue is the requirement to have a suitable reverse path *e-QC*. Since the existence of this path depends on the willingness of the Destination AS to set it up, its existence and availability can be determined either during the invocation phase of the service or via some other pre-set-up means of communication between the involved ASes. This implies that there is a negotiation between Customers/ASes/third parties before invocation has taken place in order to agree the forward and reverse QoS levels. These are then mapped to *e-QC*s at each end according to the inter-domain capabilities (and pre-existing *cSLSs*) at each Source and Destination ASes.

However, additional complexity arises from multiple reverse direction cascades. As shown in Figure 5, sources from AS1 (e.g., Customer A), AS2, AS3, AS4 and AS5 can reach Customer C in AS5 with the specified desired *e-QC* quality (see Forward Cascade in Figure 5). For reverse direction, can there be only a reverse path *e-QC* for every forward path *e-QC* using the cascaded model in order to allow bi-directional QoS offering? As it is depicted in Figure 5, it may not possible to achieve this using the cascaded model starting from Destination AS. This is only possible by constructing *e-QC*s in reverse direction by using source-based model. As an example (bottom of Figure 5), $e\text{-}QC_4$ and $l\text{-}\ QC_{31}$ need to be combined to form $e\text{-}\ QC_{31}$ in reverse direction and this can only be achieved using the source-based model. The reverse cascade block in Figure 5 shows the source AS as the starting point for constructing *e-QC*s in the reverse direction and not the destination AS.

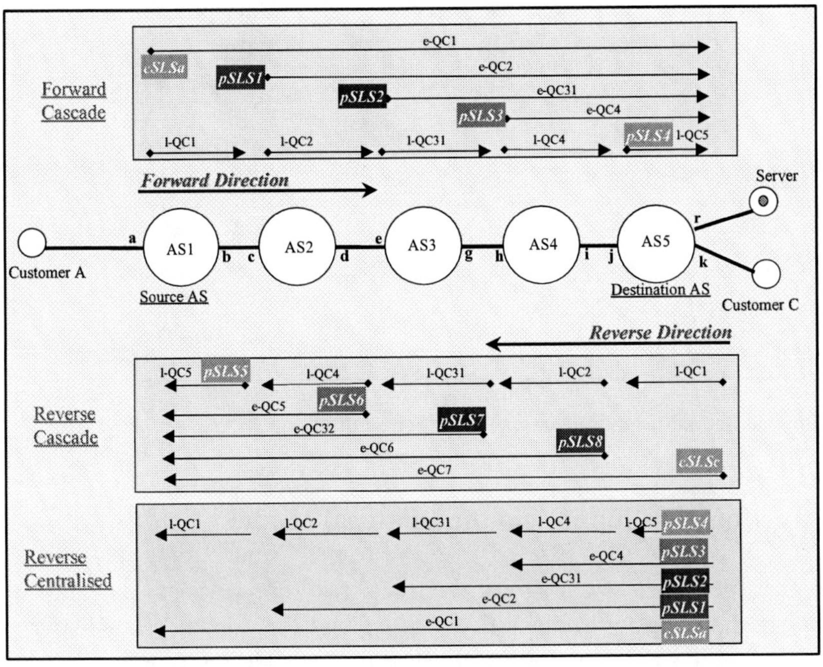

Figure 5. Bi-directionality support: e-QC bindings and SLS set-up in both directions.

In general, it is necessary to build multiple reverse cascades in the reverse direction to transport return traffic. In the forward path, the *e-QC* paths merge as they model the Destination AS. This provides the opportunity for constructing *pSLSs* downstream based on the aggregated traffic demands. However, the paths in the reverse direction de-merge as they depart from a Destination AS towards Source ASes. Consequently, for the Destination AS to provide return service to its upstream domains, multiple cascades of *e-QC*s and *pSLSs* set-ups are required. Thus, for a single forward direction cascade, there must be multiple cascades in the reverse direction, depending on the number of Source ASes that are served by a Destination AS (Figure 6). Figure 6 shows the implementation of multiple cascades in which not only they do serve to reach from customer C to sources in AS5 (with *l-QC*1 quality), AS4 (with $e\text{-}QC_{45}$), AS3 (with $e\text{-} QC_{35}$), AS2 (with $e\text{-} QC_{25}$), and AS1 (with $e\text{-} QC_{15}$) but also additional sources with desired quality from AS4 to AS3 (with $e\text{-} QC_{34}$), AS4 to AS2 (with $e\text{-} QC_{24}$), AS4 to AS1 (with $e\text{-} QC_{14}$), AS3 to AS2 (with $e\text{-} QC_{23}$), AS3 to AS1 (with $e\text{-} QC_{13}$), and AS2 to AS1 (with $e\text{-} QC_{12}$).

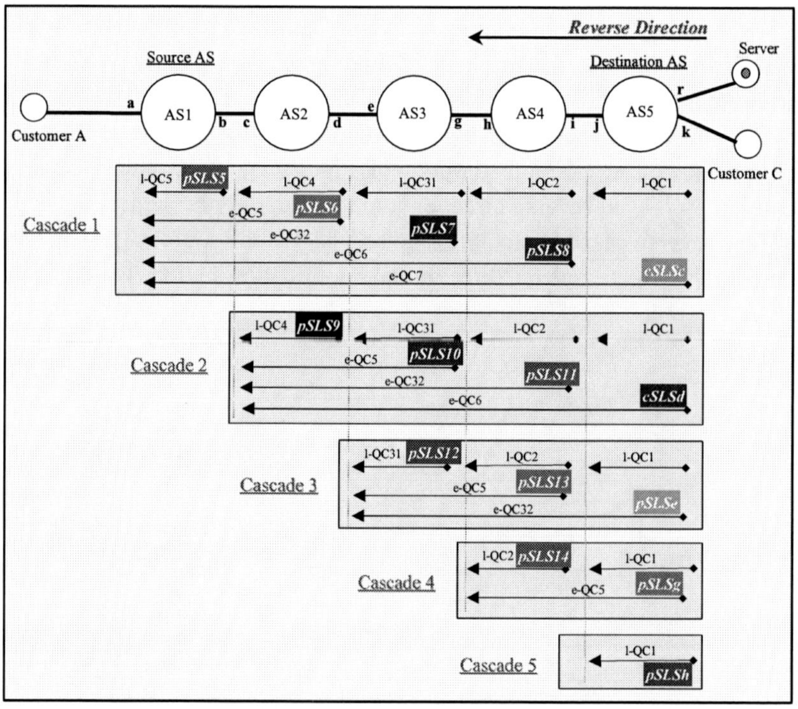

Figure 6. Implementation of multiple cascades in reverse direction.

5.2. Bi-Directionality Support in the Bilateral Model

pSLSs for specific *m-QCs* agreed between two domains are not tied to specific destinations and have no further qualifications beyond the domain's boundaries. Hence, as *pSLSs* are uni-directional and they are established for transporting traffic in forward direction, p_rSLS can be established for transporting traffic in reverse direction. The boundary for handling QoS of these two *pSLSs* are the same i.e., *m-QC* support across the domain. The performance targets for these two types of *SLSs* within the domain are also the same, e.g., *m-*

QC_1. As an alternative option, the reverse direction can be part of the *pSLS* negotiation for the forward path. Although *pSLS* and p_rSLS negotiation can be merged, the reverse direction p_rSLS can have a different bandwidth requirement, which may be specified as part of p_rSLS negotiation.

The path for forward traffic and return traffic between two remote ASes may be different depending on the q-BGP updates but the *SLS* agreements between all involved ASes are in place to handle the traffic in both directions irrespective of the paths traffic may take in forward and reverse directions. There might be a different *m-QC* requirement in the reverse direction than the forward direction. To address this, there can be application level communication between the two parties (customers) involved in order to specify the QoS requirements in either direction. This may also require having a trust relationship between the two involved ASes.

6. Target Services

Residential and corporate customers differ both at the level of the performance and traffic guarantees and geographical scope of the services they require. Residential customers may subscribe to IP services to reach any available destination at any time with better-than-best-effort service levels. The duration of the communications may be short and the frequency of interactions can be sparse. Corporate customers, on the other hands, may request specific, strong guarantees with hard upper bounds on QoS parameters and a constant bandwidth for supporting particular mission- or safety-critical applications and services such as IP VPNs in order to reach a limited set of destinations. Obviously, a range of customers could be identified between these two extreme cases, requiring hard upper bounds on delay to a large but limited set of destinations with statistically guaranteed throughput.

The 'cascaded model' can be used for services that require QoS performance guarantees for reaching specific destinations and allows end-to-end bandwidth guarantee within statistical bounds. It is able to provide a qualitative QoS service, although quantitative services can also be offered where values for packet delay and loss are specified. Inter-domain QoS services are created by constructing paths across domains that are able to statistically guarantee the required QoS. QoS services can be constructed to meet specific quantified QoS constraints.

The 'bilateral model' can used to offer better Internet connectivity services with some QoS levels, but doesn't offer any strong guarantees. It enables a provider to offer differentiated transport services, where each differentiated service is related to an *m-QC*. It is envisaged that providers throughout the Internet will implement a small number of well-known *m-QC*s. Inter-domain QoS services are then formed by using advertised paths across those domains that support a particular *m-QC*. In effect, a set of parallel "internets" will be deployed, each offering service levels associated with a specific *m-QC*. The guarantees associated with it are restricted to qualitative services, although it is anticipated that the characteristics of each *m-QC* service will rely on common application requirements and will be based on common set of characteristics of transport mechanisms such as TCP or RTP (Real-time Transport Protocol). This model prepares the grounds to address the requirements of a large population of users, while keeping the network engineering as simple as possible by supporting relaxed service guarantees.

7. Implementing and Evaluating the QoS-Enabled Internet

This section firstly presents how pSLSs are established between adjacent domains for specific m-QCs. The benefit is there will be at most one pSLS per m-QC between domains for a connectivity leg. This scales very well. There is no need for fine-grained pSLS establishment based on the scope. As explained in section 5.3, bi-directionality is easily achievable.

Secondly, it shows how parallel Internets can be constructed and how QoS routing can be achieved at inter-domain level by using q-BGP. Some tests have been conducted to validate the meta-QoS-class concept and setting-up parallel Internets by:

- Validating the implementation of l-QCs in each domain, using Linux traffic control features [24];
- Validating, at the data plane level, DSCP swapping (marking/remarking) between ASes as explained in section 3 in order to signal an inter-domain QC (m-QC);
- Validating the QoS-inferred inter-domain routing protocol, q-BGP, including its capability to advertise and select inter-domain QoS routes per meta-QoS-class plane.

7.1. The Testbed Configuration

A testbed was deployed to represent the hierarchical Internet topology as shown in Figure 7. This testbed comprises of eight autonomous systems employing a number of Linux-based routers. Each router has a number of interfaces and represents a single AS, except AS4, which is composed of three routers. In a single router AS, router acts as AS Border Router. In AS4, no QoS-inferred intra-domain routing protocol is used, only static routes are configured. All routers are additionally connected through an interface to a network that is used for testbed configuration.

All routers have DiffServ capabilities for traffic classification, traffic conditioning and various scheduling disciplines. To implement different classes of service, the HTB (Hierarchical Token Bucket) scheduling discipline [25] is used. Ingress re-marking is achieved by using IP FILTER [26] and DSCP egress re-marking is achieved by using DSMARK queuing discipline [27]. Four l-QCs are configured in each AS. A bandwidth threshold is also configured for each l-QC. Shaping and policing are also configured respectively at the egress and ingress interfaces in order to control bandwidth usage as agreed during pSLS negotiation between two adjacent ASes.

q-BGP is used as the inter-domain routing protocol. pSLSs are agreed between all adjacent domains for four m-QCs in order for each AS to have at least one q-eBGP session (i.e. q-BGP session between two different routers of different ASes) with its adjacent ASes. Consequently, q-BGP is activated at the boundaries of each domain and a full q-BGP mesh is configured within the AS4 domain. This creates a full connectivity for all parallel m-QC planes across the testbed. q-iBGP sessions (i.e. q-BGP session between two routers of the same AS) are established between all AS4 border routers. The q-BGP configuration is pSLS driven. Information related to establish pSLSs is stored in a repository. This information is retrieved for q-BGP configuration. q-BGP is able to advertise QoS routes either with dynamically obtained QoS values or static QoS values configured by administrators.

A commercial routing protocol suite (ZebOS) [28] has been used to implement q-BGP features by enhancing its classical BGP in order to support QoS information exchange and route selection, including QoS service capabilities, QoS_NLRI messages, l-QC definition, instructing q-BGP to instantiate a RIB for a particular QC plane, QoS-enabled route selection process by taking into account the QoS parameters, and implementation of new CLI commands for easing q-BGP configuration. In the case of route selection process, the q-BGP implementation allows a "precision," x, to be configured in the route selection process. This precision is used when comparing two routes having similar QoS characteristics: if the two routes have QoS values that are within x% of each other they are said to be identical.

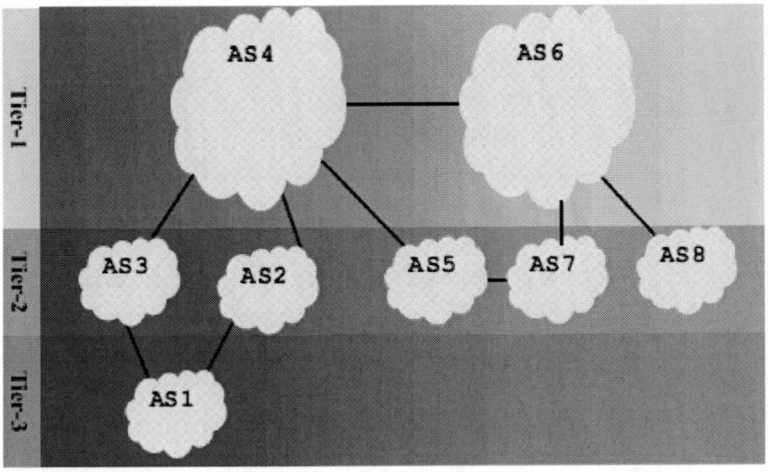

Figure 7. The deployed testbed topology.

7.1.1. q-BGP Configuration

The following parameters must be configured in border routers in order to activate q-BGP between two ASes:

- A list of network prefixes and QoS planes in which the prefixes will be advertised.
- A number of local QCs, where each l-QC is uniquely identified by a DSCP value.
- A number of optional or mandatory QoS performance and traffic metrics. Figure 8 is a configuration example of an l-QC identified by a DSCP value of 10, and characterised by a bandwidth (reserved rate) of 5000Kbits with the highest priority mandatory QoS parameter regarded as the first selection criterion for q-BGP route selection process. An optional maximum one-way delay (owd) in milliseconds is also configured with a priority less than the one for the reserved rate parameter. Since this parameter is optional, a q-BGP announcement will be injected to this m-QC plane even if the announcement does not indicate a one-way delay value.

- A list of IN and/or OUT QoS ROUTE-MAP rules – these rules describe the QC Bindings for m-QC planes by mapping them to local DSCP values. Inter-domain DSCP values are agreed between adjacent ASes during the pSLS negotiation phase and are used in q-BGP announcements (i.e. the QoS Class Identifier). Thus a dedicated DSCP value signals a given m-QC on the inter-domain links. At the ingress interface q-BGP must therefore be aware of the mapping between agreed inter-domain DSCP values (representing an m-QC) and the local DSCP value (representing the corresponding l-QC). Similarly at the egress, q-BGP must be aware of the mapping between the l-QC's DSCP value and the outgoing DSCP value of the corresponding m-QC. Therefore, the classical BGP ROUTE-MAP as implemented by ZebOS is modified in order to perform the DSCP binding operations. Figure 9 illustrates an ingress ROUTE-MAP rule, setting the value of QoS Class Identifier contained in a q-BGP QoS NLRI attribute to 4 if the QoS Class Identifier field of received q-BGP announcements is set to 5. This configuration allows q-BGP to inject the announcements received with a QoS Class Identifier of 5 into the q-RIB identified by the local-qos-class 4.

```
ZebOS# configure terminal
ZebOS(config)# local-qos-class 5
ZebOS(local-qos-dass)# qos-class-id 10
ZebOS(local-qos-dass)# qos-inf reserved-rate 5000 priority 1 mandatory precision 5
ZebOS(local-qos-dass)# qos-inf max-owd 50 priority 2 optional
```

Figure 8. Configuration setting for l-QC.

```
ZebOS# configure terminal ZebOS(config)# route-map QOS_IN permit 3
ZebOS(config-route-map)# match qos-class-id QCID 5
ZebOS(config-route-map)# set local-qos-class 4
```

Figure 9. An example for route-map set-up.

7.2. Experimental Results

7.2.1. PSLS Set-up Operation

Figure 10 shows a simplified pSLS established between two adjacent domains for the purpose of conducting the relevant proof of concept tests. Subsequent to pSLS set-up, the management entity of each AS domain must configure the DSCP binding in its border routers and traffic filters in order to control the received traffic from its service peers based on the agreed pSLSs as discussed in previous section. Then, q-BGP process is automatically provided with appropriate information that will control the advertisements that is sent to and received from neighbouring domains.

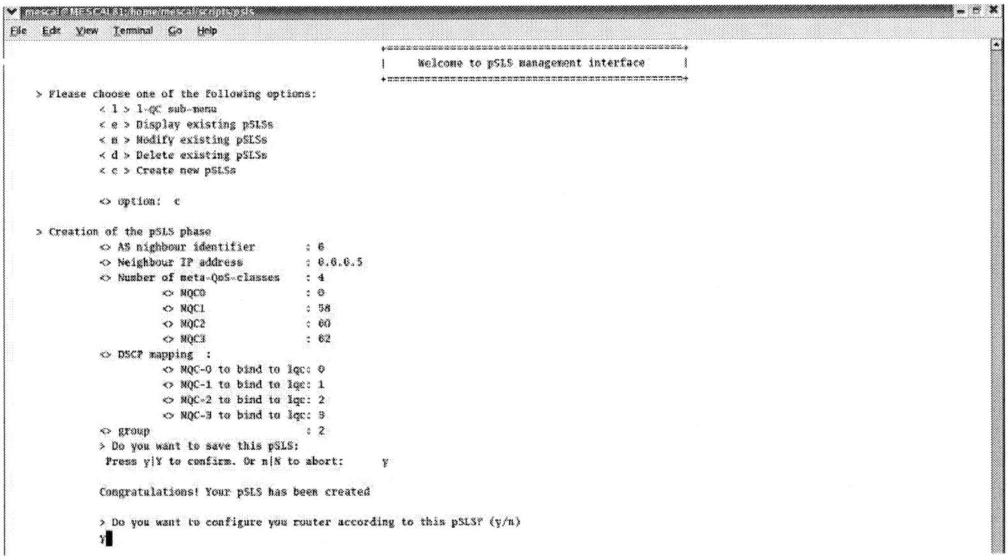

Figure 10. pSLS set-up between two adjacent domains.

7.2.2. q-BGP Route Selection

Experiments have been conducted to show how q-BGP can be configured to route packets belong to different m-QC planes coming from the same source and destined for the same destination via different routes. Two tests are conducted for displaying the path selected by BGP for best-effort plane with that selected by q-BGP for a QoS-enabled. A ping tracker, developed in MESCAL, is used to track and show the path selected by q-BGP and then used by a ping request in order to reach at given destination. Figure 11 and Figure 12 show the results of two tests conducted in the testbed. Figure 11 is a snapshot of the ping tracker showing the path of a best-effort ping request sent from a source prefix in AS1 towards a destination prefix in AS8. This figure shows that q-BGP selected the path of AS1-AS2-AS4(R2)-AS4(R3)-AS6-AS8 for ping request and reply indicated by red lines, using the classical route selection process. In the second test, all routers in the testbed are configured to prioritise the average one-way delay (avg-owd) parameter. The router in AS1 received q-BGP advertisements that gave an avg-owd to AS8 of 250 ms via AS2 and 150 ms via AS3. Hence, when a QoS ping request with a specific DSCP value is sent from AS1, q-BGP selects the path AS1-AS3-AS4(R1)-AS6-AS8 for ping request, as the avg-owd in this path is lower. While the ping reply gets uses the path of AS8-AS6-AS(R3)-AS4(R1)-AS3-AS1. This test shows that two separate uni-directional paths are used for request and reply messages based on the pSLS agreements already established. This shows that not only q-BGP computes a different optimise route to the best effort route for QoS-enabled traffic by taking into account the QoS class and QoS parameters but also it can select two different forward and return paths for an application depending on the m-QC planes set-ups.

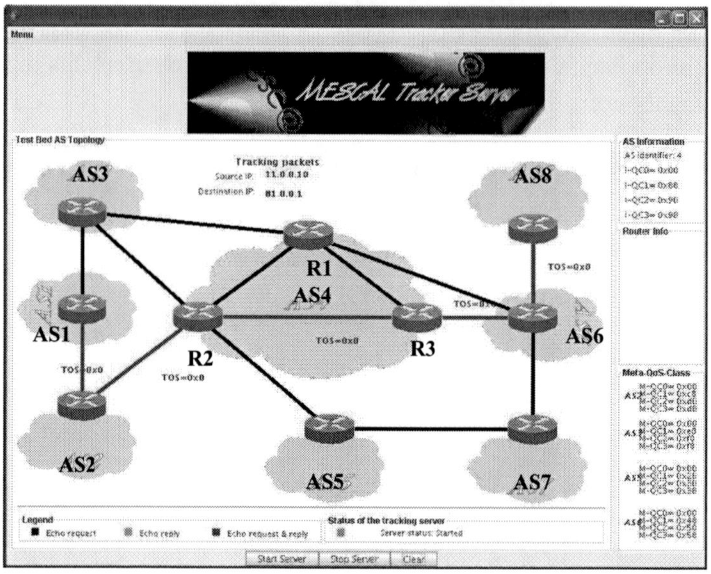

Figure 11. Path selected by BGP in best-effort plane.

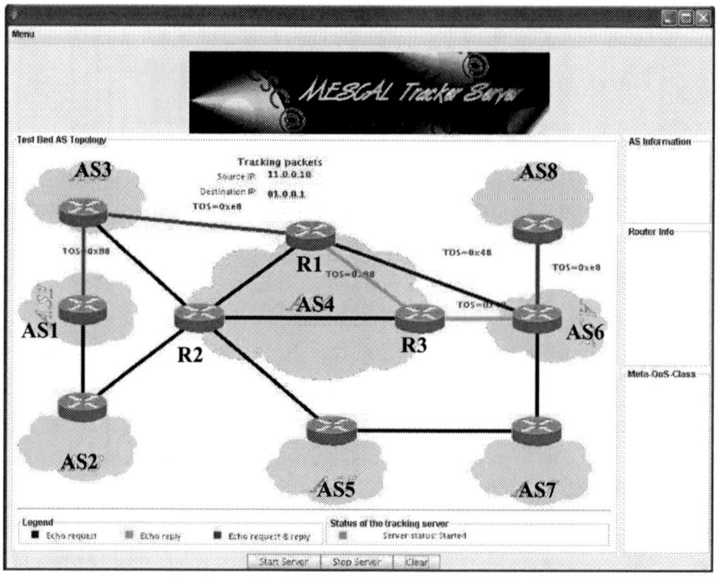

Figure 12. Paths selected by q-BGP for ping request/reply messages in an m-QC-plane.

8. CONCLUSION

In order to provide access to the global Internet, providers must interact with each other; there cannot be a single provider offering global Internet coverage. The aim of this chapter was to propose and evaluate the models of interactions between providers best suited for inter-domain QoS service delivery. The concepts to establish a set of inter-domain QoS peering models have been discussed in order to construct end-to-end QoS-based services across the Internet at large scale. Different peering models are explained. A single point of control for the service instances is the compelling feature of the source-based model. The use of the source-based model for more than a few interconnected INPs would be increasingly difficult to manage. Providers would prefer to offer services which reflect current Internet structure and for whom the use of the source-based model would be inappropriate in many instances. The cascaded model makes it possible to build IP QoS services on a global basis while only maintaining contractual relationships with adjacent providers. Hence, the cascaded model is more scalable than the source-based model. A limitation of the cascaded model is that it gives the service initiator less control of the whole IP service path. In Bilateral model, *pSLSs* are set-up between adjacent INPs with open scope and no distinct performance characteristics. This reflects the loosely coupled structure of Internet and the current behaviour of BGP. An INP needs to have only one pSLS agreement with its adjacent domain to join an m-QC plane. This makes bilateral model much more scalable than other models.

The complexity for supporting for bi-directional services was discussed in this chapter. The main issue in the cascaded model is how to construct the QoS-enabled reverse path for return traffic. Some issues with cascaded model have been identified in order to provide bi-directional services and discussed the resulting implications. These are to do with finding the source/s for return traffic, changing/extending of the scope of the return path, and the selection and mapping of *l-QC*/*e-QC* for the return direction. Two methods for enabling providers to offer bi-directional services have been proposed. Providing bi-directionality in using bilateral model causes less complication, because 1) *pSLSs* are based on the *m-QCs* 2) q-BGP is used to get the reachability information within an *m-QC* plane. In this model, there is no strict end-to-end QoS guarantee in forward direction hence there is no need to create a reverse path with a strict end-to-end QoS guarantee. Using cascaded and bilateral models, a number of target services can be supported. Bilateral model prepares the grounds to address the requirements of a large population of users, while keeping the network engineering as simple as possible by supporting relaxed service guarantees.

ACKNOWLEDGMENTS

The work described in this chapter has been carried out in the IST MESCAL project, which is partially funded by the Commission of the European Union. The authors would like to acknowledge the contribution of their colleagues in the MESCAL project for their contributions to the ideas presented in this chapter.

REFERENCES

[1] P. Levis, M. Boucadair, P. Morand, P. Trimintzios, The Meta-QoS-Class concept: a step towards global QoS inter-domain services, In proceeding of IEEE International Conference on Software, Telecommunications and Computer Networks (SoftCOM 2004), Oct. 2004.

[2] W.B. Norton, Internet Service Providers and Peering, Draft 2.7, May 2009, available at: www.nanog.org/papers/isp.peering.doc.

[3] S. Lippert, G. Spagnolo, Internet Peering as a network of relations, *Telecommunications Policy*, Vol. 32, issue 1, pp. 33-49, Feb. 2008
[4] C. Silva Ponce de Leo′n, Intra-regional Internet connectivity still an ongoing assignment, *Elsevier Telecommunications Policy* 29 (2005), pp. 367–386.
[5] B. Stiller, D. Hausheer, (Editors), Development of a Multi-provider Model, an SLM Model, and Service Provisioning Concepts, EMANICS Deliverable 8.2, July 2007, available at http://www.emanics.org/.
[6] P. Faratin, D. Clark, P. Gilmore, A. Berger, Complexity of Internet Interconnections: Technology, Incentives and Implications for Policy, The 35th Annual Telecommunications Policy Research Conference, George Mason University, September 2007, http://people.csail.mit.edu/wlehr/Lehr-Chapters.html.
[7] Eurescom Project P1008, Inter-operator interfaces for ensuring end-to-end IP QoS, Deliverable 2, Selected Scenarios and requirements for end-to-end IP QoS management, Jan. 2001, available at http://www.eurescom.de/public/projects/p1000-series/P1008/.
[8] P. Trimintzios, G. Pavlou, P. Flegkas, P. Georgatsos, A. Asgari, E. Mykoniati, Service-driven Traffic Engineering for Intra-domain Quality of Service Management, IEEE Network, special issue on Network Management of Multiservice, Multimedia*, IP-based Networks*, Vol. 17, No. 3, May/June 2003, pp. 29-36.
[9] Y. Rekhter, T. Li (Editors), A Border Gateway Protocol 4 (BGP-4), *IETF RFC 1771,* Standards Track, Mar. 1995.
[10] B. Quoitin, C. Pelsser, L. Swinnen, O. Bonaventure, S. Uhlig, Interdomain traffic engineering with BGP, *IEEE Communications Magazine*, Vol. 41, Issue 5, May 2003, pp. 122-128.
[11] N. Feamster, J. Borkenhagen, J. Rexford, Guidelines for Interdomain traffic engineering, *ACM Computer Communications Review*, Oct. 2003.
[12] P. Pongpaibool, H.S. Kim, Providing end-to-end service level agreements across multiple ISP networks, *Computer Networks*, 46 (2004), pp. 3-18.
[13] L. Xiao, K. Lui, J. Wang, K. Nahrstedt, QoS extension to BGP, In IEEE Proceeding of ICNP2002 Conference, Paris, 2002, available at http://www.ieee-icnp.org/2002/papers/2002-10.pdf.
[14] P. Georgatsos, J. Spencer, D. Griffin, P. Damilatis, H. Asgari, J. Griem, G. Pavlou, P. Morand, Provider-level Service Agreements for Inter-domain QoS delivery, A chapter in "Quality of Service in the Emerging Networking Panorama" book, Book Series: *Lecture Notes in Computer Science*, Springer Berlin / Heidelberg Publisher, ISBN978-3-540-23238-4, Sept. 2004, pp. 368-377.
[15] B. Briscoe, S. Rudkin, Commercial Models for IP Quality of Service Interconnect, *BT Technical Journal Special Edition on IP Quality of Service*, 23(2), April 2005, pp. 171-195.
[16] S. Amante, et al., Inter-provider Quality of Service, White chapter draft 1.1, prepared by the Quality of Service Working Group, MIT Communications Futures Program (CFP) Nov. 2006.
[17] D. Goderis, et al., Service level specifications semantics, parameters, and negotiation requirements, IETF Internet-Draft, draft-tequila-sls-02.txt, expired Feb. 2002.

[18] IETF's IPPM working group, RFC 2330 (Framework for IPPM), RFC 2679 (one-way delay), RFC 2680 (one-way packet loss), RFC 3393 (delay variation), visit: http://www.ietf.org/dyn/wg/charter/ippm-charter.html.

[19] P. Flegkas, et al., Mescal Project Deliverable D1.1, Specification of Business Models and a Functional Architecture for Inter-domain QoS Delivery, June 2003, available at: http://www.mescal.org/.

[20] K. Nichols, B. Carpenter, IETF DiffServ Working Group, RFC 3086, Definition of Differentiated Services Per Domain Behaviors and Rules for their Specification, April 2001.

[21] H. Asgari, et al., Mescal Project Deliverable D1.4, Issues in MESCAL Inter-Domain QoS Delivery: *Technologies, Inter-operability, and Financial Settlement*, Jan. 2004, available at: http://www.mescal.org/.

[22] M. Howarth, et al., MESCAL Project Deliverable D1.2, Initial specification of protocols and algorithms for inter-domain SLS management and traffic engineering for QoS-based IP service delivery and their test requirements, Jan. 2004, available at: http://www.mescal.org/.

[23] D. Griffin, J. Spencer, J. Griem, M. Boucadair, P. Morand, M. Howarth, N. Wang, G. Pavlou, A. Asgari, P. Georgatsos, Interdomain Routing through QoS-Class Planes, *IEEE Communications Magazine,* Vol. 45, Issue 2, Feb. 2007, pp. 88-95.

[24] B. Hubert, et al., Linux Advanced Routing and Traffic Control HOWTO, Published v1.0.0, Mar. 2004. Available at http://lartc.org/.

[25] M. Devera, HTB User Guide, May 2002, available at http://luxik.cdi.cz/~devik/qos/htb/userg.pdf.

[26] D. Reed, IP Filter, Version v4.1.30, Documentation available at: http://coombs.anu.edu.au/~avalon/.

[27] W. Almesberger, J.H. Salim, A. Kuznetsov, Differentiated Services on Linux, *In proceeding of GLOBCOM'99*, Vol. 1B, Dec. 1999, pp. 831-836.

[28] ZeBos, ZebOS Advanced Routing Suite, ip infusion Company, www.ipinfusion.com.

In: Recent Advances in Providing QoS and Reliability... ISBN 978-1-61761-858-1
Editors: N. Wang, G. Pavlou and M. Boucadair

Chapter 8

INTER-DOMAIN PATH COMPUTATION WITH MULTIPLE QOS CONSTRAINTS

G. Bertrand[*1,2]***, S. Lahoud***[*3]***, M. Molnár***[*4] ***and G. Texier***[1,2]

[1] Institut TELECOM ; TELECOM Bretagne; RSM

[2] Rue de la Châtaigneraie, CS 17607, 35576 Cesson Sévigné Cedex, France

[3]. Université européenne de Bretagne, France

[4]. IRISA – Université de Rennes 1

ABSTRACT

The Internet has become the unifying infrastructure for a wide range of applications. In particular, the Internet supports recent services, such as IPTV or VoIP, with much more stringent requirements than the legacy web-browsing application. Therefore, novel mechanisms are required to guarantee an appropriate level of end-to-end quality of service (QoS) for specific traffic flows. In addition, the traffic of many services traverses the networks of multiple operators before reaching the end-user. As these operators have typically competing interests and possibly conflicting policies, the future Internet will require mechanisms involving several network operators to provide QoS guarantees beyond the domain boundaries. Specifically, inter-domain routing and traffic engineering play a fundamental role for ensuring that the flows are routed on end-to-end paths with appropriate QoS performance. Thus, it is important to provide efficient solutions to the fundamental inter-domain QoS routing problem, which consists in computing paths subject to QoS constraints. Due to the important applications of this problem, many solutions have been proposed. However, most of these solutions do not consider the specific issues introduced by the division of a network into domains. Therefore, they cannot realistically be applied for computing inter-domain multi-constrained paths.

In this chapter, we provide a synthesis of recent advances in multi-constrained inter-domain routing. In particular, we present two innovative path computation approaches that can be applied in the Path Computation Element (PCE) framework, as well as in novel architectures based on extended IP routing protocols. The proposed solutions allow

* {gilles.bertrand; geraldine.texier}@telecom-bretagne.eu.

* samer.lahoud@irisa.fr.

* molnar@irisa.fr.

the computation of inter-domain paths with a reasonable complexity and without degrading the QoS level. Therefore, the results described in this chapter open interesting perspectives for enhancing the performance of QoS routing and for engineering inter-domain traffic.

1. INTRODUCTION

The Internet supports a growing number of services ranging from the legacy web browsing to the more recent online gaming and voice over IP. These services have heterogeneous requirements, quantified by various Quality of Service (QoS) metrics related to service availability, packet loss ratio, bandwidth, delay, and so on. The ability to determine a path fulfilling these multiple requirements is essential for providing value-added services with satisfying performance. For instance, traffic flows corresponding to low-loss, low-delay services should be routed on paths that can guarantee a low packet-loss ratio and a low transmission delay.

In the future Internet, services with performance guarantees are expected to be deployed across domain boundaries. Therefore, multiple domain owners, such as network operators or service providers, will participate in the delivery of end-to-end QoS guarantees [1]. In particular, novel mechanisms are required to enable the network operators to route the inter-domain QoS traffic on paths with appropriate end-to-end performance. For instance, the future Internet architecture needs mechanisms to exchange information about the performance of the available paths. Moreover, it requires suitable algorithms to compute paths fulfilling the service requirements. Finally, if a connection-oriented model is adopted, signaling techniques are also required to setup the paths.

This chapter presents a synthesis of recent advances in inter-domain traffic management, with a focus on the routing of inter-domain traffic subject to multiple QoS constraints. There are two main approaches for the routing of inter-domain flows with stringent QoS requirements. The first approach is connection-oriented and involves the configuration of inter-domain tunnels (label switched paths) for the priviledged traffic. This approach typically requires the cooperation of the traversed domains to compute and to configure a path with appropriate performance. For instance, the Path Computation Element (PCE) framework [2, 3, 4] describes mechanisms for the collaborative computation of constrained inter-domained paths. The second approach uses recent extensions of IP routing [5, 6, 7] to support the advertisement of QoS paths, in addition to the default path with best-effort performance. With this approach, the domains forward their QoS traffic on QoS paths and their best-effort traffic on the default routes.

Considering the technological context, we study algorithmic solutions that allow network equipments to compute multi-constrained inter-domain paths. We require distributed path computation procedures to preserve the routing autonomy of the traversed domains and to avoid the disclosure of confidential information outside the domains. Moreover, the computational complexity and the signaling overhead introduced by these path computation methods must remain reasonable, to preserve the scalability of the network. Finally, the proposed solutions should be integrable with existing technologies, such as the PCE framework, or extensions of IP routing. We present the first solutions that satisfy these requirements; these solutions pave the way for novel inter-domain traffic management techniques with enhanced QoS performance.

The remainder of this chapter is organized as follows. In Section 2, we introduce the inter-domain multi-constrained path computation problem. In particular, we describe the requirements for acceptable solutions to this problem. Section 3 describes two approaches for solving the problem. The first relies on online computations; whereas, the second enables the domains to autonomously compute an aggregate representation of their state in advance. After comparing these two approaches, we describe their integration into existing network architectures, in Section 4. In particular, we present the required extensions of the PCE framework, and of IP routing protocols.

2. THE INTER-DOMAIN MCP PROBLEM

Often, QoS routing requires the satisfaction of several criteria such as limited delay, jitter, packet losses, etc. For a given route request with QoS criteria, a route corresponding to a given set of limitations should be computed. If the source and the destination are in different domains, then both the intra-domain and inter-domain routing algorithms are concerned: they should take into account the QoS request and the solution must satisfy the end-to-end QoS criteria. Figure 1 illustrates a route request from the source node s in domain D_1 to the destination node t in domain D_3. In this example, each network link is characterized by two additive link values and the path computed between s and t should satisfy the following QoS criteria: the first metric of the path should be less than $W_1 = 11$ and the second one should be less than $W_2 = 14$. The path computation should determine such a *feasible path* (which corresponds to the QoS criteria), if one exists. We will see in this section that the computation of multi-constrained paths is a hard computational problem. Moreover, the inter-domain QoS routing adds more difficulty due to the distribution and the confidentiality of the information in such contexts. In the following, these main challenges are briefly highlighted.

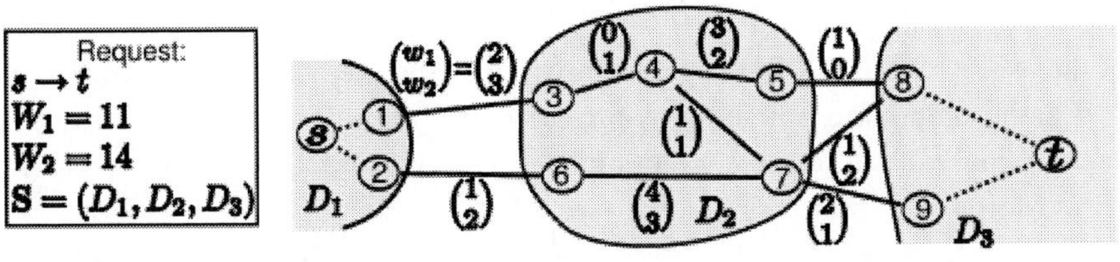

Figure 1. An example of inter-domain MCP problem with two integer-valued metrics.

2.1. Multi-Constrained Path Computation

The computation of a path subject to multiple constraints related to independent additive link-weights is a difficult problem even inside a single domain. The basic problem is called the multi-constrained path (MCP) problem and resides in finding a feasible path that satisfies the constraints. The problem of finding a feasible multi-constrained path which is optimal with respect to a length function is called the *multi-constrained optimal path* (MCOP) problem [8]. MCP and MCOP problems consider only additive constraints, because, first, constraints related to bottleneck metrics (*e.g.*, bandwidth) can be easily treated by edge pruning and, second, positively-valued multiplicative constraints can be transformed into additive constraints by using a logarithm function.

We consider a network represented by a directed graph $G=(V,E)$ where V is the set of vertices or nodes and E the set of edges or links. Each edge $e \in E$ is associated with K additive and positive weights denoted as $w_k, k=1..K$. We assume that at least one of the K weights associated with an edge e is different from zero. The set of paths between two nodes $s \in V$ and $t \in V$ is denoted as $P_{s \to t}$. Each path p is associated with K weights which are $w_k(p) \equiv \sum_{e \in p} w_k(e), k=1..K$. Moreover, a length function $c(p)$ can be associated with the path p subject to K constraints. This length is used to determine the best path, i.e. the shortest path according to the considered length. The most appropriate path length function, defined in Reference [9], expresses the critical value of the path with respect to the constraints:

$$c(p) = \max_{i=1..K} \left(\frac{w_i(p)}{W_i} \right) \quad (1)$$

Intuitively, $c(p)$ enables to select the path that is the furthest from violating the constraints. With this path length function, a path p is feasible if and only if $c(p) \leq 1$. The two fundamental problems, namely MCP and MCOP, can now be formulated as follows [10, 8].

Problem (MCP - Multi-Constrained Path) Given a source s and a destination t, K constraints $W_k, k=1..K$, find a path $p \in P_{s \to t}$ such that $w_k(p) \leq W_k$, for $k=1..K$.

Any solution of the problem MCP is called a *feasible path*.

Problem (MCOP - Multi-Constrained Optimal Path) Given a source s and a destination t, K constraints W_k, find a feasible path $p^* \in P_{s \to t}$ such that for every other feasible path $p \in P_{s \to t}$, $c(p^*) \leq c(p)$.

Both the MCP and MCOP problems are NP-complete [11]. An overview of multi-constrained path computation methods is provided in Reference [8]. Exact solutions for the MCP problem include brute-force solutions (*e.g.*, depth first search with backtracking). Several brute-force algorithms including search-space reduction mechanisms have been described in the literature (*e.g.*, SAMCRA [9], H_MCOP [10]). Due to the computational intractability of the MCP and MCOP problems, the time complexity of brute-force algorithms grows exponentially, in the worst-case. Thus, several approximation algorithms have been described. For example, Jaffe's algorithm [12] is an approximation algorithm addressing the MCP problem with two constraints. This algorithm determines two positive multipliers d_1 and d_2, and optimizes the length function $d_1 w_1(p) + d_2 w_2(p)$. According to [8], Jaffe's algorithm can be extended to an arbitrary number of constraints. In References [13, 14], Kuipers and Van Mieghem assert that the NP-complete behavior of the MCP problem emerges only in specially constructed graphs with edge weights carefully chosen. Xue *et al.*

[15, 16] have proposed recently several approximated solutions with provable performance guarantees for the MCP problem.

Nevertheless, recent work shows that most of the instances of the multi-constrainted path computation problems applied to networking can be solved exactly [13, 14]. Several exact solutions are described in the literature (*e.g.,* SAMCRA [9], H_MCOP [10]) but these algorithms are adapted to a single domain context. An additional difficulty arises when the path computation concerns multiple routing domains.

2.2. Inter-Domain Path Computation

The second difficulty of the inter-domain path computation resides in the fact that wide networks, such as the Internet, are partitioned into several routing domains and several operators operate independently for the routing. In particular, an Autonomous System (AS) represents an operator's network with homogeneous routing policies. Inside a domain, the routing algorithm is defined by the operator. The domains are interconnected by Border Nodes (BN) and they operate the inter-domain routing according to their respective policies. Path computation across multiple domains typically occurs when the source and the destination nodes of the path belong to different domains. The entity responsible for the computation may be the source note itself, the intermediate BNs, or dedicated computation elements such as the Path Computation Element (PCE) [17]. A path computation entity uses its own vision of the state of the domains in order to compute a feasible path. An objective function may also be optimized during the computation procedure.

The efficiency of the computation depends on the amount of information that is available on the computation entities. This is a key issue for the inter-domain path computation due to the limited information that is spread outside the domain borders. Three scenarios are defined depending on the domain visibility level: multi-domain visibility, partial visibility and local domain visibility [18]. Ideally, an entity with *multi-domain visibility* may have enough information to compute the entire path. However, achieving this information scenario may not be practical given the requirement that a domain should never advertise resources and topological information outside its boundaries. In practice, each operator prefers to preserve the entire control on its domain and resource and topology information is considered to be confidential for each domain and may be hidden from other domains. More realistically, it may have a *partial visibility* of the network: full information about its own domain and information about the connectivity between domains, as well as about the resource availability across other domains. In this case, the computation entity cannot provide the end-to-end path explicitly, but it can provide explicit path segments to reach its BNs and provide a domain-level path to the destination domain. Alternatively, in a *local domain visibility* scenario, the visibility of the computation entity is limited to its own domain and to its connectivity to other domains. In this case, it can provide explicit path segments to reach its BNs but cannot provide a domain-level path to the destination domain.

Generally, the routing problem can be solved in two phases. First, a sequence of domains is identified between the source and the destination; in this phase, the granularity of the routing decision corresponds to the domain level representation. Second, a feasible path is selected from the set of available paths with respect of the QoS criteria and the granularity of the routing decision corresponds in this phase to the router level representation. In the following, we suppose that the first routing problem level is solved, thus a domain sequence is pre-computed. This domain sequence is used as a input for the inter-domain MCP problems.

In order to illustrate the general path computation problem across multiple domains, let us consider the scenario in Figure 2. In this figure, node s in domain D_1 is trying to communicate with node t in domain D_3. A path, subject to a set of constraints, should be computed to enable nodes s and t to communicate. According to the assumptions presented above, a preliminary sequence of domains is computed, i.e. domains D_1, D_2, and D_3, fulfilling some policy or business constraints. Hence, the path computation problem consists of computing a path from s to t traversing successively domains D_1, D_2, and D_3. This computation can be performed by the source node s if it has sufficient topology or resource information on the three domains. Otherwise, the path computation can be distributed on the intermediate border nodes, or offloaded onto dedicated per-domain entities such as PCEs. For instance, when the domains D_1, D_2, and D_3 belong to a single management organization, one computation entity may have sufficient information to perform end-to-end efficient computations. Otherwise, when these domains belong to concurrent organizations, topology and resource information may not be spread outside the domain border. Thus, the computation result is less efficient unless some collaboration is introduced between per-domain computation entities.

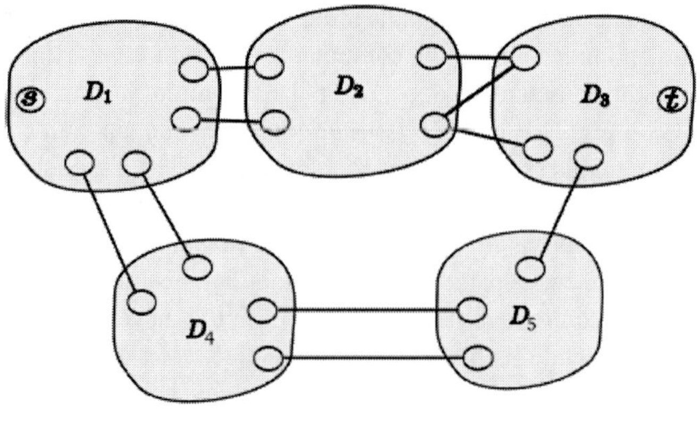

Figure 2. General scenario for path computation across multiple domains.

2.3. Requirements for the Inter-Domain MCP Problem

The requirements for an efficient solution of the inter-domain MCP problem can be summarized as follows:

- find efficient distributed algorithms for the per-domain computations resolving the scalability and the computational complexity problems, and providing good quality computed paths,

- preserve the autonomy of the domains by allowing each domain to control and operate the paths that traverse it even if tight contracts and cooperation exist between the operators,
- find good mechanisms to exchange information among the domains taking into account the confidentiality, the communication overhead and the visibility issues.

In the following sections, the main elements of efficient inter-domain MCP computations are presented and illustrated using two different approches.

3. Approaches for Computing Inter-Domain MCPs

Following the requirements presented in the previous section, the computation of constrained inter-domain paths is essentially applicable in small sets of domains bound by particular peering agreements. In addition, this computation must be distributed in order to preserve the autonomy of the domains and the scalability of the network. In this chapter, two distributed approches are presented for the multi-constrained path computation problem. These approaches rely on three building blocks, as illustrated in Figure 3: (1) the formulation of a per-domain problem, (2) an algorithm that solves the per-domain problem, and (3) a method for propagating and for combining the per-domain computation results to determine the end-to-end path. The variants of these building blocks lead us to propose two main methods for computing inter-domain MCPs: an on-line computation approach and an autonomous computation approach. We describe the common elements between these approaches, before detailing their specificities.

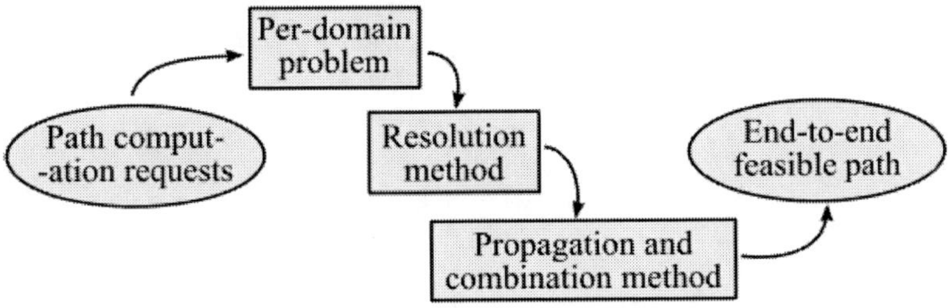

Figure 3. Building blocks of distributed solutions to the inter-domain MCP problem.

3.1. Elements of Distributed Solutions

3.1.1. Per-Domain Problem

In the following, we formulate the inter-domain problem as a combination of local per-domain problems. This enables to distribute the path computation operations among the traversed domains. Moreover, the efficiency of the computed inter-domain paths depends on the output of the local computations. Thus, the design of per-domain problems is driven by the search for path segments that lead to an efficient inter-domain solution without breaking the aforementioned confidentiality and scalability requirements.

Consequently, the computation process should integrate a method for evaluating the quality of the paths. Precisely, we use the concept of *dominance* in order to evaluate the quality of the paths computed by each traversed domain. The dominance expresses the idea that a path is "better" than another. In particular, this concept enables us to discard non-optimal paths early, and thus, to simplify the computation operations. A path p is *dominated* by a path p', with the same source and destination, if $w_k(p') \leq w_k(p)$ for all considered weights w_k with k in $[1..K]$ and if there is a k in $[1..k]$ for which $w_k(p') < w_k(p)$. For instance, consider two paths p_1 and p_2 between the same nodes and such that $\vec{w}(p_1) = (7,9)^T$ and $\vec{w}(p_2) = (6,5)^T$, then, p_2 dominates p_1. Previous work on the intra-domain MCP problem [31] shows that to compute optimal MCPs, intermediate nodes should memorize only feasible non-dominated intermediate paths. In particular, this result enables us to formulate the per-domain problem for inter-domain MCP computations: every domain must compute a well-chosen set of feasible non-dominated paths to enable the selection of efficient inter-domain MCPs. In accordance with this result, we detail subsequently two approaches, which use different formulations of the per-domain problem.

3.1.2. Solution of the Per-Domain Problem

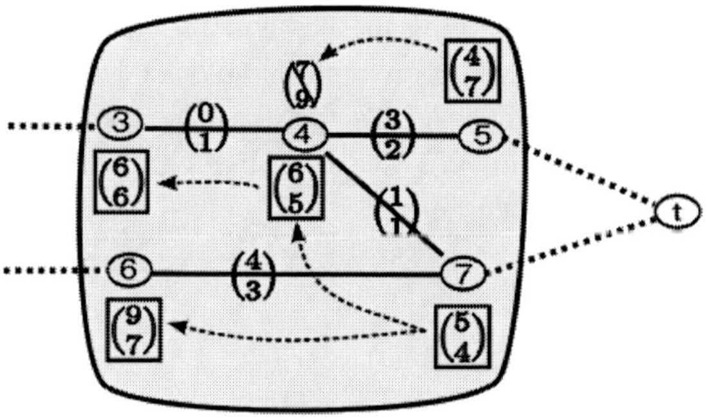

Figure 4. Simplified operations of the extended RDA in a domain for the constraints $W_1 = 11$ and $W_2 = 14$.

We propose a novel extended Reverse Dijkstra's Algorithm (RDA) [19], which calculates the non-dominated feasible paths from various sources to a destination. The reverse nature of the algorithm is chosen in accordance with the propagation direction and the combination of the per-domain results as introduced in section 3.1.3. This algorithm solves the per-domain MCP problems. Figure 4 provides a simplified overview of the operations of our algorithm on a small example: the purpose of the operations is to find the non-dominated feasible paths from the entry BNs 3 and 6, to a specific destination t outside the considered domain, through the exit BNs 5 and 7. The considered constraints are the following: $W_1 \leq 11$ and $W_2 \leq 14$. The calculation progresses from the right to the left of Figure 4.

The algorithm uses a queue structure that contains the shortest paths from every intermediate node to the destination. Suppose that the queue is initialized with two initial paths from the BNs 5 and 7 to t. Our extended RDA runs a loop. During each iteration, it picks inside the queue a path p whose weights are the furthest from the considered path constraints. Then, the algorithm *relaxes* p, which means that it evaluates the weights of the paths from the neighboring nodes of the source of p that have p as suffix. The algorithm adds the discovered paths to the queue if they are feasible and not dominated by any path in the queue. If a new path dominates one or more paths of the queue, then the dominated paths are discarded. The loop runs while the queue contains at least one element that has not been relaxed or discarded. Finally, the algorithm finds the feasible non-dominated paths from the entry BNs 3 and 6.

During its operations, the extended RDA does not discard any non-dominated feasible path. Thus, it guarantees to find the solutions to the considered per-domain MCP problems, if they exist. Its termination is guaranteed because the algorithm relaxes one path during each iteration of the loop and the number of paths in a domain is finite.

3.1.3. Propagation and Combination of the Per-Domain Results

The inter-domain path computation procedure needs to propagate and to combine the segments computed by every traversed domain (the solutions of the per-domain problems), to determine the end-to-end path for a specific request. Figure 5 depicts the operations of the propagation and combination procedures. The destination domain advertises to the upstream domain a set of paths for a destination network and specifies the performance of these paths. Usually, the per-domain results are propagated from the destination domain toward the source. For instance, the propagation operations can rely on the procedures defined for the PCE framework [4] or on an extended routing protocol that periodically advertises the available paths for a destination network and a class of service. Every domain proceeds the propagated information to determine the paths that it will advertise to the neighboring upstream domains. This operation consists in combining the results of the per-domain problem and the paths advertised by the downstream domains. Finally, the source domain determines the feasible end-to-end paths for its request thanks to the received path advertisements.

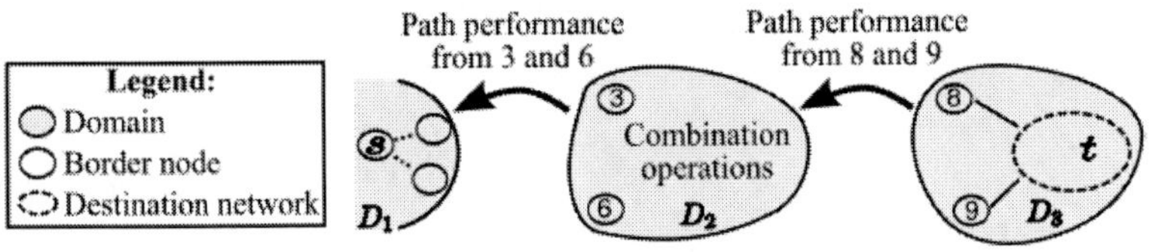

Figure 5. Advertisement and combination of the available constrained routes.

3.2. Proposed Approaches for Inter-Domain MCP

We propose two approaches, referred to as *online* and *autonomous*, to solve the inter-domain MCP problem. The online computation approach for the inter-domain MCP problem consists of serving the path computation requests on the fly. The advantage of this approach is that the path computation entities use the most recent information about the network state to answer the requests. However, frequent request arrivals burden the path computation entities with frequent computation operations. Alternatively, with the autonomous computation approach, every domain periodically computes an aggregate representation of its state. This representation consists of a set of path segments that enable neighboring domains to efficiently compute end-to-end paths. The advantage of an autonomous approach is that the operations for computing the domain representation are not repeated for every request; thus, the total path establishment delay is reduced. However, the path computation can rely on obsolete network state information.

3.2.1. Online Computation Approach

In the following we provide the details for the on-line computation approach focusing on the building blocks presented in Figure 3. Consider a computation request for a path from a node s to a node t in the network represented in Figure 6 and subject to the constraints $W_1 \leq 11$ and $W_2 \leq 14$. If backward propagation is used, the online path computation operations begin in the destination domain D_3. Inside each domain, these operations rely on our extended RDA. The extended RDA provides a set of feasible non-dominated paths, denoted as P^*, spanning from the entry nodes of domain D_3 to the destination node t of the considered path computation request. The paths in P^* are the solutions of the following per-domain problem.

Problem (Per-domain MCP problem for online computations) Given a computation request for a path with destination t and traversing a domain sequence $S = (D_1, D_2 \ldots)$, a domain D_i in the sequence S of traversed domains, and a set P^* of paths from the entry BNs of the next domain D_{i+1} to t, find all the non-dominated feasible paths from the entry BNs of D_i to t that have a suffix in P^*.

In the example, P^* includes two non-dominated paths from BN 8 and one path from BN 9, as represented in Figure 6. The set P^* is propagated upstream, toward the computation entity in domain D_2. This computation entity extends its local vision of the network topology with the paths in P^* and computes the feasible non-dominated paths from the entry BNs 3 and 6 toward t using our extended RDA. Then, it advertises these paths to its neighboring upstream domain (D_1), which is the source domain. Finally, D_1 is able to compute an end-to-end feasible path.

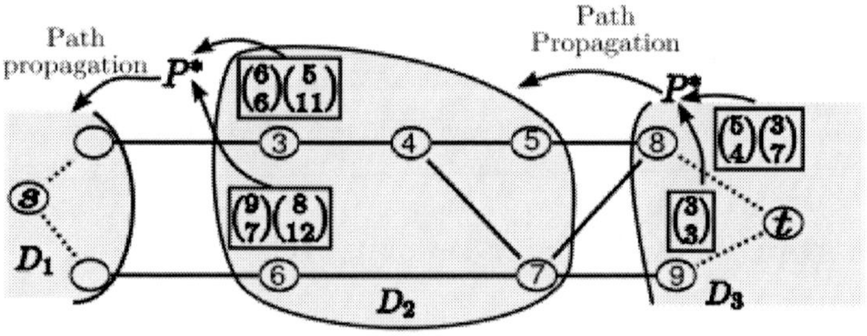

Figure 6. Propagation of the results of the online per-domain computations.

The operations of the extended RDA performed in domain (D_2) are detailed in Figure 7. The purpose of the operations is to find the non-dominated feasible paths from the entry BNs 3 and 6 to the destination t of the request. To compute these paths, the algorithm uses a queue structure that contains the shortest paths from every intermediate node to t. This queue is initialized with paths from the entry-BNs of the neighboring downstream domain, nodes 8 and 9, to t. In the example, the queue starts with two different paths from 8 to t and a path from 9 to t. The calculation progresses from the right to the left of Figure 7. The first path selected starts from node 9 and its weights are $(3,3)^T$ because the alternative paths in the queue (two paths from node 8) are closer to the constraints. Then, the algorithm *relaxes* p : it evaluates the weights of the paths from the neighboring nodes (node 7) of the source of p (node 9) that have p as suffix. The algorithm adds the discovered paths to the queue if they are feasible and not dominated by any path in the queue. In the example, the path from node 7 with weights $(5,4)^T$ is added to the queue. If a new path dominates one or more paths of the queue, then the dominated paths are discarded. The loop is repeated while the queue contains at least one element that has not been relaxed or discarded. Finally, the algorithm finds the feasible non-dominated paths from the entry BNs 3 and 6. For example, it discovers the path with weights $(6,6)^T$ from the entry BN 3 to t through the nodes 3-4-7-9. During its operations, the algorithm does not discard any non-dominated feasible path.

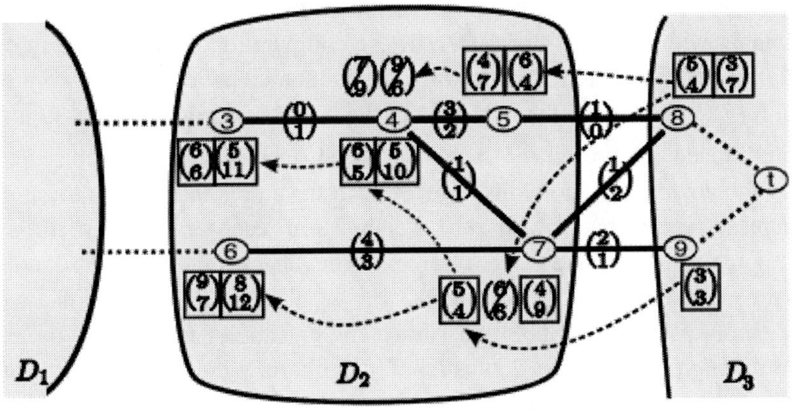

Figure 7. Operations of the extended RDA in a domain with the online approach with the constraints $W_1 = 11$ and $W_2 = 14$.

3.2.2. Autonomous Computation

In the present section, we describe a second approach for solving the inter-domain MCP problem. This approach allows autonomous computations inside each domain. With this approach, each domain solves a per-domain problem, without considering a specific request and without using the results of the computations in other domains. This contrasts with the online approach where the computations inside each domain depend on the results of the computations in the downstream domains.

In an autonomous approach, the per-domain problem depends on the path constraints: we postulate that the considered domains agree on a set of constraint vectors for which they compute the path performance. Every constraint vector represents a specific class of service. With these assumptions, we define the per-domain problem as follows.

Problem (Per-domain MCP problem for autonomous computations) Given a network represented by a valued graph $G(V, E, \vec{w})$, a constraint vector $\vec{W}$, and a specific domain

$D \subset V$, find the non-dominated feasible paths from the entry BNs of D to the entry BNs of any neighboring domain $D' \subset V$ of D.

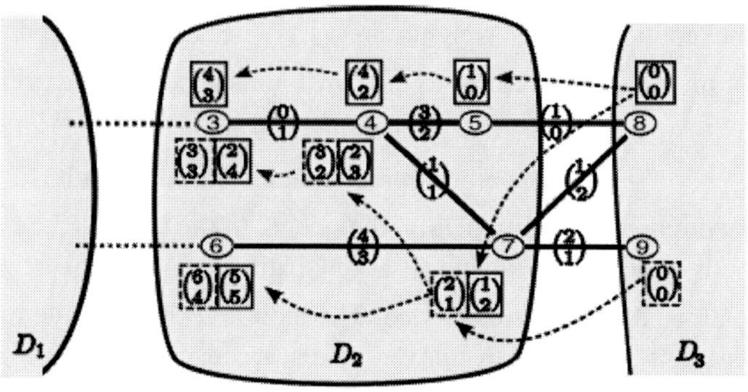

Figure 8. Operations of the extended RDA in a domain with the autonomous approach for the class of service with the constraints $W_1 = 11$ and $W_2 = 14$.

Figure 8 depicts the operations for the resolution of the per-domain problem inside a particular domain with our extended RDA. These computation operations progress from the right to the left of the figure and provides the non-dominated path segments from each ingress of a domain, for example D_2, to the ingresses of the neighboring domains.

When introduced for the online case, the initial queue elements represented the paths advertised by the downstream domains. However, in the autonomous case, these initial queue elements represent empty paths with zero weights from each entry BN of the neighboring downstream domains toward the current domain. This enables independent operations inside every domain. For instance, in Figure 8, the computation starts with two elements representing empty paths from BN 8 and BN 9. The extended RDA relaxes the initial empty paths from the ingresses of the downstream neighboring domains to discover the non-dominated feasible paths, according to the constraint vector, from the neighboring nodes. During this operation, the algorithm compares the memorized paths for each destination ingress independently. For example, the path with the weights $(3,3)^T$ to the destination ingress 9, does not dominate the path with the weights $(4,3)^T$ to the destination ingress 8. The operations of the extended RDA end when all the memorized paths have been relaxed or discarded: at this moment, the algorithm has found all the non-dominated feasible paths from the ingresses of the domain to the ingresses of the neighboring downstream domains.

Figure 9 illustrates the operations for combining the results of the per-domain computations. When the domain D_2 receives the paths computed by a downstream neighboring domain D_3 for a specific request, it combines the results of its per-domain computations and the received paths. For instance, it combines the path with weights $(3,3)^T$ from node 3 to node 9 with the path from node 9 to the request destination t, which leads to a path with cost $(6,6)^T$ from node 3 to t. During the combination operations, the procedure discards the dominated paths. For example, the path with weights $(7,8)^T$ is dominated by the path $(6,6)^T$ from the same node.

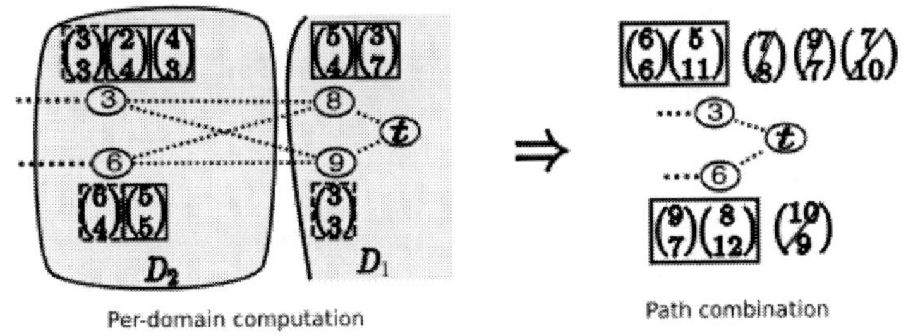

Figure 9. Propagation and combination of the per-domain results with the autonomous approach.

3.2.3. Comparison of the Proposed Approaches

As the MCP problem is NP-complete [11], the complexity of the extended RDA is prohibitive for particular network configurations. Nevertheless, previous work on Tamcra [20] and Yuan's limited-path heuristic [21] shows that it is possible to bound the worst-case complexity of MCP computations by including only a given number of paths in the path computation process. We use this strategy to bound the complexity of the per-domain operations with our extended RDA, by arbitrary limiting the maximum number of memorized paths during the computation operations. The price that we pay for the complexity improvement is the loss of the guarantee to find the best available path for a given set of constraints. To investigate the trade-offs between computation complexity and path performance, we compare our heuristics with limited complexity and exact solutions.

We consider specific topologies to assess the performance of our solutions in extreme situations 22, 23]. We consider a chain of three domains, in accordance with the average length of the domain-level paths in the Internet [24]. Every domain has a square-grid topology with twenty-five nodes and we study two kinds of domain inter-connections. In the Single Link (SL) topology, the bottom-right node of every domain is connected to the top-left node of the downstream domain. In the Full Mesh (FM) topology, every node of every domain is connected to every node of the downstream domain. We evaluate the performance of the exact online and autonomous approaches, as well as the performance of the corresponding heuristics with bounded complexity. In the simulations, we consider path computation requests with stringent QoS constraints, to evaluate the performance of our procedures in worst-case conditions [23].

Figure 10 presents an example of simulation results for the following performance metrics. The Success Rate (SR) quantifies the percentage of simulated requests for which the path computation procedures find feasible end-to-end paths. As we simulate a worst-case scenario, the network does not contain any feasible path for some requests: SR is not equal to 100%, even for exact methods. The cost (C) is the lowest value of the function $c(p) = \max_{k\in[1..K]}\left(\frac{w_k(p)}{W_k}\right)$ among the paths returned by the path computation procedure. It indicates the performance margin of these paths with respect to the most restrictive QoS metric. In addition, we measure the maximum number α of paths memorized in the computation queue for any node. This quantity indicates the complexity of the path computation operations and is arbitrarily limited in the heuristics. We present an example of simulation results with $\alpha \le 1$ for the online approach and $\alpha \le 3$ for the autonomous approach (we explain these origin of these values in the next paragraph). Finally, we evaluate the number of feasible non-dominated paths returned by the path computation procedures. We denote this quantity as NP.

Both exact approaches return the same solutions: the non-dominated feasible end-to-end paths. Thus, their performance is the same for SR, C, and NP. However, their complexity, evaluated through the values of α , depends on the considered topology and on the density of the domain inter-connections. More importantly, the simulations show that the heuristic approaches, which memorize a limited number of paths from every intermediate node, compute paths with quasi-optimal performance. Precisely, the values of SR and C for these heuristics are close to the optimal values, which are obtained by exact methods. However, we note that the autonomous approach requires memorizing more intermediate paths to reach the same level of performance as the online approach. For example, the results in Figure 10 correspond to an autonomous approach memorizing at most three paths from every node and to an online approach memorizing at most one path from every node. The origin of this performance difference is that the resolution of the per-domain MCP problem considered for the autonomous approach requires the memorization of more non-dominated feasible paths than for the online approach.

To conclude this performance evaluation, the simulation results exhibit a trade-off between the online and the autonomous approaches: the online approach has lower memory requirements than the autonomous approach for equivalent performance; nevertheless, the autonomous approach is less sensitive to the frequency of the request arrivals, and thus, scales better in the case of frequent requests.

	SR [%]		C [%]		α		NP	
Topology	*SL*	*FM*	*SL*	*FM*	*SL*	*FM*	*SL*	*FM*
Online, exact	66	56	89.3	72	8	2	5	1
Online, heuristic	64	56	89.8	72	1	1	1	1
Autonomous, exact	66	56	89.3	72	5	8	5	1
Autonomous, heuristic	66	50	89.4	72	3	3	4	1

Figure 10. Simulation results in a worst-case scenario.

4. From Best Effort Actual Networks to QoS-Able Next Generation Networks

4.1. Toward QoS-Aware IP Networks

Best-Effort inter-domain routing is performed by domains which use BGP protocol to select and advertise routes to neighboring domains according to routing policies. Several European projects, such as AQUILA [25], EuQoS [26, 27, 28, 29], TEQUILA, MESCAL [6], and AGAVE [30], have studied the problem of inter-domain QoS management. BGP is complex but universally deployed and Fonte *et al.* have exposed in [5] the challenge to adapt it. The evolution of BGP to enable QoS routing implies a coordination between the domains to possibly find an end-to-end inter-domain path that respects multiple QoS constraints. One main issue is to enable the propagation to neighbors of multiple paths for the same destination fulfilling different QoS constraints. Cisco proposes BGP multipath [31] that extends BGP to perform load sharing by storing several paths for the same destination in the routing table. This adaptation is important but not sufficient since BGP multi-path still selects and propagates only one best path to neighbors. Work is in progress to modify the UPDATE messages exchange to advertise multiple paths. The most recent work is proposed by Watson *et al.* in [32]. They propose to define a new BGP capability to negotiate the exchange of adapted UPDATE messages where the routes are designated by a prefix and a Path Identifier. In [33], Zhang *et al.* show that another issue is the reduction of the set of paths exchanged. Benmohamed *et al.* use the notion of dominance in [34] to propagate only worthwhile paths to perform QoS routing.

A parallel can be done between the autonomous approach presented in section 3.2.2 and BGP. It reflects the distinction between the domains interconnection and the traffic forwarding service offered within a domain to its neighbors. This characteristic is inherent to BGP and incarnated by the usage of two distinct protocols: eBGP and iBGP. iBGP maintains the communication between the BNs of the same domain, and thus the forwarding of the external traffic within the domain. Similarly, the solution to the per-domain problem exposed in 3.2.2, is in charge of the computation of the routes and their performance within the domain between the ingress nodes and each entry BN of the neighboring downstream domains. Like eBGP, the segment combination method in 3.2.2 burdens the propagation of the paths between the domains with additional information on the performances that can be expected from these paths. The autonomous approach addresses the domain visibility requirements of BGP since the exchanged information is restricted to the announcement of the performances between the border nodes of a domain, hiding the concrete implementation of the path within the corresponding domain.

Even after the proposed evolutions that enable BGP to advertise more than one route for a destination and to take QoS into account in the path selection algorithm, BGP still entails important limitations to be fully a QoS-aware protocol. Although the RFC 3221 [35] indicates that the scalability, the stability, and the convergence time of BGP must not be affected by the QoS extensions, the well-known instability of BGP, shown in [36], has important consequences on the convergence, thus on the offered QoS. More generally, any path reconfiguration may jeopardizes the paths already established with respect to QoS constraints. In particular, a change in the routing performed can outcome with unpredictable delay variations, which may be harmfull for application requiring QoS. This limitation partially justifies the routing solution that relies on oriented connected protocols like MPLS-TE.

4.2. Toward QoS-Aware Next Generation Networks

Traffic Engineering (TE) offers an alternative to implement inter-domain QoS routing by the establishment of Label Switched Paths (LSPs) in a Multi-Protocol Label Switching (MPLS) TE architecture described in [37]. The trend in standardization is to extend MPLS-TE mechanisms to enable the establishment of constrained LSPs at the inter-domain level, as presented by Dasgupta *et al.* in [38]. In [17], Farrel *et al.* specifies the PCE architecture that offers a mechanism to distribute the computation of constrained paths with guaranteed performance. Douville *et al.* [39] show that these mechanisms can be coupled advantageously with a multi-domain service plane for automatic inter-domain provisioning. With the

Backward Recursive PCE-based Computation (BRPC) procedure, the PCE working group proposes a path computation algorithm and a mechanism to propagate the path computation results from the destination domain to the source domain. The propagation is based on a multipoint-to-point tree structure, named *Virtual Shortest Path Tree* (VSPT) that represents a path by an aggregated virtual link. Bradford *et al.* in [40] show that this structure enforces the confidentiality requirement inherent to inter-domain computations.

The online and the autonomous approach, presented in section 3 can be efficiently implemented with the PCE architecture provided minor adaptations on the data structure used to propagate the segments of eligible paths already identified. The main limitation of the VSPT is its tree structure that allows to keep only one path from each entry border node. The spirit of the VSPT is to keep the best path from each BN to the destination, although it may not be possible to identify locally the best intermediate segment in a multi-constrained context. This implies that the VSPT structure in the MCP case should be extended to be able to propagate several paths from the same entry-BN and thus may not be a tree .

4.3. The QoS Inter-Domain Routing during the Transition from IP to NGN

The extension of the traffic engineering feature to inter-domain routing is still under standardization and it will take time before being deployed. Above all, the QoS inter-domain routing is possible if every domain on the path implements it. During the transition from the Best-Effort IP network towards QoS-aware NGN, the propagation of QoS eligible paths can be performed by the evolution of BGP presented in section 4.1. Each domain is responsible for the internal computation of the paths between its bordure nodes and participates to the distributed computation of a feasible path either with an autonomous or an online approach.

5. CONCLUSION

In this chapter, we have introduced the problem of routing inter-domain flows on paths with guaranteed performance for multiple QoS metrics. In particular, we have described the requirements for acceptable solutions to this problem, as well as the building blocks for such solutions. Moreover, we have presented two approaches, enabling online or autonomous computations in the traversed domains. We have illustrated these approaches on simple examples. As the considered path computation problem is intractable in the general setting, we have provided efficient heuristics based on the online and the autonomous computation approach. The proposed inter-domain MCP computation procedures make the computation of inter-domain constrained paths tractable in practice, without degrading the QoS. Furthermore, we have described the methods to integrate these procedures with existing protocols and architectures. To conclude, the elements presented in this chapter open interesting perspectives for improving the performance of inter-domain routing and traffic engineering. They pave the way for the on-demand setup of inter-domain paths with guaranteed performance, and thus, will provide an enhanced flexibility in the deployment of services with stringent QoS requirements, such as IPTV.

REFERENCES

[1] G. Bertrand, S. Lahoud, M. Molnár, G. Texier, *Intelligent Quality of Service Technologies and Network Management: Models for Enhancing Communication*, chapter QoS Routing and Management in Backbone Networks. IGI Global, Hershey, Pennsylvania, USA, 2010.

[2] F. Aslam, Z.A. Uzmi, A. Farrel, Interdomain Path Computation: Challenges and Solutions for Label Switched Networks. *IEEE Communications Magazine*, 45(10):94 --101, 2007.

[3] JP. Vasseur, A. Ayyangar, R. Zhang, A Per-Domain Path Computation Method for Establishing Inter-Domain Traffic Engineering (TE) Label Switched Paths (LSPs). RFC 5152, 2008.

[4] JP. Vasseur, R. Zhang, N. Bitar, JL. Le Roux, A Backward-Recursive PCE-Based Computation (BRPC) Procedure to Compute Shortest Constrained Inter-Domain Traffic Engineering Label Switched Paths. RFC 5441, IETF, 2009.

[5] A. Fonte, M. Curadoa, E. Monteiro, Inter-domain Quality of Service Routing: Setting the Grounds for the Way Ahead. *Annals of Telecommunications*, 63(11--12):683--695, 2008.

[6] [6] M.P. Howarth, M. Boucadair, P. Flegkas, N. Wang, G. Pavlou, P. Morand, T. Coadic, D. Griffin, A. Asgari, P. Georgatsos, End-to-end quality of service provisioning through inter-provider traffic engineering. *Computer Communications*, 29(6):683--702, 2006.

[7] N. Kumar, G. Saraph, End-to-End QoS in Interdomain Routing. *ICNS '06: Proceedings of the International conference on Networking and Services*, pages 82, Washington, DC, USA, 2006. IEEE Computer Society.

[8] F. Kuipers, P. Van Mieghem, T. Korkmaz, M. Krunz, An overview of constraint-based path selection algorithms for QoS routing. *IEEE Communications Magazine*, 40(12):50-55, 2002.

[9] P. Van Mieghem, H. De Neve, F. Kuipers, Hop-by-hop quality of service routing. *Computer Networks*, 37(3-4):407--423, 2001.

[10] [10] T. Korkmaz, M. Krunz, Multi-constrained optimal path selection. *Twentieth Annual Joint Conference of the IEEE Computer and Communications Societies (INFOCOM)*, pages 834-843, 2001.

[11] Z. Wang, J. Crowcroft, Quality-of-Service Routing for Supporting Multimedia Applications. *IEEE Journal on Selected Areas in Communications*, 14(7):1228--1234, 1996.

[12] J.M. Jaffe, Algorithms for finding paths with multiple constraints. *Networks*, 14:95--116, 1984.

[13] F.A. Kuipers, P. Van Mieghem, The impact of correlated link weights on QoS routing. *Twenty-Second Annual Joint Conference of the IEEE Computer and Communications Societies (INFOCOM)*, pages 1425-1434, 2003.

[14] P. Van Mieghem, F.A. Kuipers, Concepts of exact QoS routing algorithms. *IEEE/ACM Transactions on Networking*, 12(5):851--864, 2004.

[15] G. Xue, A. Sen, W. Zhang, J. Tang, K. Thulasiraman, Finding a path subject to many additive QoS constraints. *IEEE/ACM Transactions on Networking*, 15(1):201--211, 2007.

[16] G. Xue, A. Sen, W. Zhang, J. Tang, K. Thulasiraman, Polynomial time approximation algorithms for multi-constrained QoS routing. *IEEE/ACM Transactions on Networking*, 16(3):656--669, 2008.

[17] A. Farrel, J.P. Vasseur, J. Ash, A Path Computation Element (PCE)-Based Architecture. RFC 4655, 2006.

[18] A. Farrel, J.P. Vasseur, A. Ayyangar, A Framework for Inter-Domain Multiprotocol Label Switching Traffic Engineering. RFC 4726, 2006.

[19] R.K. Ahuja, T.L. Magnanti, J.B. Orlin, *Network Flows: Theory, Algorithms, and Applications*. Prentice-Hall, Inc., New Jersey, 1993.

[20] H. De Neve, P. Van Mieghem, TAMCRA: a tunable accuracy multiple constraints routing algorithm. *Computer Communications*, 23(7):667--679, 2000.

[21] X. Yuan, Heuristic algorithms for multiconstrained quality-of-service routing. *IEEE/ACM Transactions on Networking*, 10(2):244--256, 2002.

[22] G. Bertrand, S. Lahoud, G. Texier, M. Molnár, Computation of Multi-Constrained Paths in Multi-Domain MPLS-TE Networks. *Fifth Conference on Next Generation Internet Networks (NGI), Aveiro, Portugal*, 2009.

[23] G. Bertrand, S. Lahoud, M. Molnár, G. Texier, Inter-Domain Path Computation with Multiple Constraints. Technical report, 1902, IRISA, IRISA - Campus de Beaulieu - 35042 Rennes Cedex, 2008. http://hal.inria.fr.

[24] T. Bu, D. Towsley, On distinguishing between Internet power law topology generators. *Twenty-First Annual Joint Conference of the IEEE Computer and Communications Societies (INFOCOM)*, pages 638--647, 2002.

[25] B.F. Koch, H. Hussmann. *Architectures for Quality of Service in the Internet*, chapter Overview of the Project AQUILA (IST-1999-10077), pages 1084. Springer Berlin / Heidelberg, 2003.

[26] O. Dugeon, E. Mingozzi, G. Stea, L. Bisti, Provisioning QoS in inter-domain traffic engineering. *Annals of Telecommunications*, 63:545--557, 2008.

[27] A. Fonte, E. Monteiro, M. Yannuzzi, X. Masip-Bruin, J. Domingo-Pascual, A Framework for Cooperative Inter-Domain QoS Routing. *EUNICE*, pages 91-104, Secaucus, NJ, USA, 2005. Springer-Verlag New York, Inc.

[28] X. Masip-Bruin, M. Yannuzzi, R. Serral-Gracia, J. Domingo-Pascual, J. Enriquez-Gabeiras, M. Callejo, M. Diaz, F. Racaru, G. Stea, E. Mingozzi, A. Beben, W. Burakowski, E. Monteiro, L. Cordeiro, The EuQoS system: a solution for QoS routing in heterogeneous networks [Quality of Service based Routing Algorithms for Heterogeneous Networks]. *IEEE Communications Magazine*, 45(2):96-103, 2007.

[29] M. Yannuzzi, A. Fonte, X. Masip-Bruin, E. Monteiro, S. Sanchez-Lopez, M. Curado, J. Domingo-Pascual, *Quality of Service in the Emerging Networking Panorama*, chapter A Proposal for Inter-domain QoS Routing Based on Distributed Overlay Entities and QBGP, pages 257-267. Springer Berlin / Heidelberg, 2004.

[30] M. Boucadair, P. Levis, D. Griffin and N. Wang, M. Howarth, G. Pavlou, E. Mykoniati, P. Georgatsos, B. Quoitin, J. Rodriguez Sanchez, M.L. Garcia-Osma, A Framework for End-to-End Service Differentiation: Network Planes and Parallel Internets. *IEEE Communications Magazine*, 45(9):134-143, 2007.

[31] Cisco Documentation. BGP Best Path Selection Algorithm.
[32] D. Walton, Advertisement of Multiple Paths in BGP. draft-ietf-idr-add-paths-00, work in progress, IETF, 2009.
[33] T. Zhang, Y. Cui, Y. Zhao, L. Fu, T. Korkmaz, *Scalable BGP QoS Extension with Multiple Metrics*. International conference on Networking and Services (ICNS'06), July 2006, p. 80.
[34] L. Benmohamed, C. Liang, E. Naber, A. Terzis, QoS Enhancements to BGP in Support of Multiple Classes of Service. *IEEE Military Communications Conference (MILCOM)*, pages 1-7, 2006.
[35] G. Huston, Commentary on Inter-Domain Routing in the Internet. RFC 3221, 2001.
[36] J. Rexford, J. Wang, Z. Xiao, Y. Zhang, BGP routing stability of popular destinations. *IMW '02: Proceedings of the 2nd ACM SIGCOMM Workshop on Internet measurment*, pages 197--202, New York, NY, USA, 2002. ACM.
[37] E. Rosen, A. Viswanathan, R. Callon, Multiprotocol Label Switching Architecture. RFC 3031, 2001.
[38] S. Dasgupta, J.C. de Oliveira, J.P. Vasseur, Path-Computation-Element-Based Architecture for Interdomain MPLS/GMPLS Traffic Engineering: Overview and Performance. *IEEE Network*, 21(4):38-45, 2007.
[39] R. Douville, J.L. Le Roux, J.L. Rougier, S. Secci, A Service Plane over the PCE Architecture for Automatic Multidomain Connection-Oriented Services. *IEEE Communications Magazine*, 46(6):94--101, 2008.
[40] R. Bradford, J.P. Vasseur, A. Farrel, Preserving Topology Confidentiality in Inter-Domain Path Computation Using a Key-Based Mechanism. draft-ietf-pce-path-key-05, work in progress, IETF, 2008.

In: Recent Advances in Providing QoS and Reliability... ISBN 978-1-61761-858-1
Editors: N. Wang, G. Pavlou and M. Boucadair

Chapter 9

COMBINING INTELLIGENT ROUTE CONTROL WITH BACKBONE TRAFFIC ENGINEERING TO DELIVER GLOBAL QOS-ENABLED SERVICES

***A. Fonte*[1]*, M. Pedro*[2]*, M. Curado*[3]*, E. Monteiro*[4]*, and F. Boavida*[5]**

Department of Informatics/CISUC, University of Coimbra, Portugal

ABSTRACT

A global quality of service enabled Internet requires standard mechanisms to support the inter-autonomous systems quality of service connection. Two core components of the required functionality are the quality of service-enabled Border Gateway Protocol and the off-line backbone Traffic Engineering. Each of these approaches is, by itself, rather limited. Although the first enables the propagation of quality of service related messages and the latter potentially helps to improve the end-to-end quality of service, they both fail to achieve fast reaction to topology or path quality changes, as well as to users' requirements. Existing solutions have shown that these limitations can be partially addressed by employing Intelligent Route Controllers at multi-homed stub autonomous systems. Unfortunately, the ability of both parties, i.e., stub autonomous systems and Internet Service Providers, to choose their own routing policies does not necessarily lead to the best routing of IP packets in the Internet. In effect, each party seeks to control its traffic according to its own goals without considering the effects over the traffic or network of the other party. In this chapter the integration of Intelligent Route Controllers and off-line Traffic Engineering mechanisms is proposed to overcome the identified issues. The results show that this combination can produce synergistic interactions between Intelligent Routing Control and Traffic Engineering.

[1]afonte@dei.uc.pt.
[2] macpedro@dei.uc.pt.
[3] marilia@dei.uc.pt.
[4] edmundo@dei.uc.pt.
[5] boavida@dei.uc.pt.

1. INTRODUCTION

Providing Quality of Service (QoS)-enabled services across Autonomous Systems (AS) boundaries is a very complex problem. QoS policies and services in one AS might be significantly different from those in other AS. In addition, an AS only controls its own network resources and just discloses a small part of its internal information (e.g. configurations or policy details) due to business constraints.

Recently, some research projects have addressed the important problem of inter-domain QoS and provided a full description of the functionality required to support inter-AS QoS connections [1,2]. The two key pieces of the proposed functional architectures are QoS-enabled Border Gateway Protocol (q-BGP) and off-line backbone Traffic Engineering (TE) for inter-domain QoS. On the one hand, q-BGP enables an AS to propagate to its peers BGP messages containing the information about the QoS connectivity services that it can provide (e.g., bandwidth and latency bounds, pricing and penalties) [3]. On the other hand, the off-line backbone TE enables an Internet Service Provider (ISP) to select the neighbor AS that will carry the customer traffic according to the network resource optimization objectives (e.g., the minimization of bandwidth consumption and the improvement of load-balancing) [4,5]. Therefore, the off-line backbone TE enables an AS to provide QoS connectivity services to the customers, as well as to identify the need of establishing new peering QoS relationships with neighbor autonomous systems.

The functionalities described have the potential to improve the QoS across AS boundaries. However, they may not completely achieve the following design requirements of inter-domain QoS: (1) Fast reaction to link failure and quality degradation; and fast recovery; (2) Being centered on user's perceived QoS level. In fact, q-BGP is not prepared to react in short timescales, without decreasing significantly the end-to-end QoS. And, the off-line TE at ISPs is only focused on local and coarse-grained traffic optimizations, being executed at large timescales, due to the complexity involved in the routing optimization process. Consequently, additional mechanisms operating at shorter timescales are needed to meet finer end-to-end QoS requirements of user applications.

The limitations identified above can be partially addressed by employing Intelligent Route Controllers (IRC), also called Smart Route Controllers (SRC), at multi-homed stub AS, as they provide a holistic way in which an AS solves locally end-to-end traffic challenges (e.g., latency, or loss rate bounds) through shifting some traffic between ISPs in short timescales [6,7]. By adopting Smart Route Controllers, the end-to-end performance or quality is improved without the need to change BGP routers and without the need of cooperation of the ISPs along the data paths.

Figure 1 illustrates a simple scenario of two autonomous systems employing Smart Route Controllers, where the SRC of AS2 might improve the performance of the outbound traffic toward the remote stub AS, AS3, through switching among the AS3-ISP1-ISP3 and AS3-ISP1-ISP4-ISP5 paths, across ISP3 and ISP5, respectively. A recent study reveals that this potential improvement in performance may reach up to 40% [8].

Unfortunately, the ability of both parties, i.e., multi-homed AS and ISPs, to choose their own routing policies does not necessarily lead to the best routing of IP packets in the Internet. In effect, each party seeks to control its traffic according to its own goals without considering the effects over the traffic or network of the other party. In short, a major challenge of the research on Traffic Engineering and Internet Routing architectures is to accommodate this tussle.

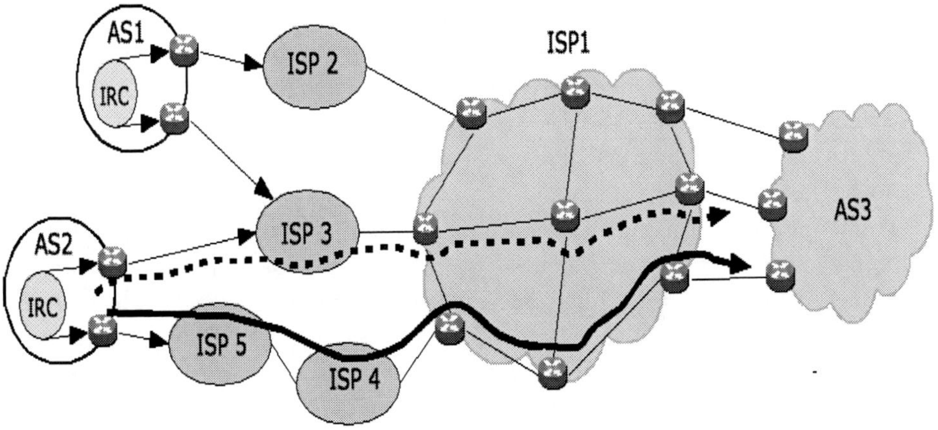

Figure 1. A simple scenario of two multi-homed stub ASes employing smart routing control.

This chapter comprises two main sections. In the first section, a broad overview of the use of Intelligent Route Controllers is provided, including their design principles and main algorithms. The effectiveness of using IRCs in networks where traffic differentiation is done per class is addressed by extensive simulation studies. In particular, path stability, traffic performance and reaction to path outages are evaluated in a scenario where IRCs are integrated within existing functional architectures in order to deliver QoS-enabled services. In the second section, a proposal of a novel Intelligent Routing Control-Traffic Engineering (IRC-TE) cooperative framework is described and evaluated through a large-scale performance study based on a realistic scenario. The results will show that this framework can produce synergistic interactions between Intelligent Routing Control and Traffic Engineering.

2. Intelligent Routing Control Framework

This section describes the design principles that play a key role in the success of inter-domain quality of service routing architectures and it details the main functions of Intelligent Route Controllers. Simulation results show how IRC can contribute to an improved traffic performance in a network where traffic differentiation is class-based.

2.1. Design Principles

Three key design principles of the inter-domain routing architecture, which are essential in enabling inter-domain QoS, are described in this subsection. Here, the doors of Intelligent Routing Control (IRC) to achieve the goals behind these principles are also open.

2.1.1. Decoupled Performance/QoS Routing Control from BGP

The inter-domain routing of IP packets toward a given prefix involves four basic functions: Route Discovery, Route Filtering, Path Selection and Packet Forwarding [9].

- Route Discovery - At least a single route connecting both source and remote ASes should be discovered to ensure end-to-end connectivity between both ASes. To achieve this goal, each AS uses external BGP (eBGP) to propagate the best-learned routes to its neighbouring ASes, and uses internal BGP (iBGP) to distribute the routes inside the AS.
- Route Filtering - This function concerns the filtering of routes to be accepted from or to be advertised to the neighbouring ASes. Each AS can configure the import route filters of BGP routers to filter unwanted routes and/or to influence the selection of the remaining routes. It can also configure the export route filters of BGP routers to manipulate the route attributes or control whether a given route would be propagated to neighbour ASes.
- Path Selection - From the set of routes that passes import filters, BGP decision process ranks and selects the best routes to be installed in local RIB (routing information base). The best routes that pass export filters are then propagated to neighbouring ASes.
- Packet Forwarding - Once the best routes are chosen and installed in the local Routing Information Base (RIB), the BGP daemon of a router feeds the IP forwarding table so that IP packets can be forwarded along these routes.

Unfortunately, Routing Filtering and Path Selection are increasingly complex functions due to the growth of the Internet and the addition of new features to BGP [10,11]. Thus, any changes to the existing routing filtering and path decision processes to support QoS policies may difficult router configuration. In short, to face the BGP lack of QoS support, the addition of new features (e.g., new attributes and decision criteria) should be avoided.

Principle: Path control limitations of current inter-domain routing should be addressed in a separated and distributed route control layer.

To reduce the involved complexity needed to improve the quality of inter-domain routing of IP packets, standalone IRCs (or pairs of IRCs located at remote ASes) select the best routes on behalf of BGP, according to QoS goals. In other words, the BGP decision process is still used, but most routing intelligence is within IRCs. Therefore, signaling messages exchanged between IRCs are carried out by this out-of-BGP-band layer.

2.1.2. Fast Link/QoS Failure Reaction and Recovery

Inter-domain routing based on BGP is not prepared to react quickly to link failures. At the Internet scale, the BGP fail-over process may take several minutes [12,13]. To address this issue several improvements were proposed to reduce the number of messages distributed between BGP routers after a link failure. Unfortunately, even with these improvements, the convergence time scale still is on the order of a few minutes, which does not really fit the performance/QoS requirements of mission-critical or real-time traffic.

Principle: An AS should be able to detect link/QoS failures and recovery at a short enough timescale, without degrade significantly the end-to-end quality.

To achieve this goal, an IRC must react much faster than the BGP layer to link or QoS failures. Therefore, an IRC system relies on end-to-end QoS monitoring along every link connecting the AS to the Internet. Then, when an IRC detects quality violations against specified thresholds for a given traffic flow, it adapts on-the-fly the local routing behaviour. In this situation an alternative path that is able to bypass the network link failure or congestion is selected. In other words, IRCs enhances the end-to-end QoS of the underlying BGP layer by tweaking route attributes in very short timescales given that no BGP messages will be ever spawned.

2.1.3. Being Centered on User's Perceived QoS Level.

Operators can employ inter-domain Traffic Engineering to meet the traffic challenges of local autonomous systems, such as load-balancing or minimizing the maximum utilization of peering links. This type of Traffic Engineering is usually performed by tweaking BGP route attributes in order to change an arbitrary number of routes according to the computed solution.

When the traffic demands are stable, the inter-domain traffic engineering optimizations potentially result in network operation points close to the optimum. However its major drawback is that traffic objectives are not centered on the user's perspective of network quality. This means that upon finding a new optimal routing pattern it gives no guarantees that the end-to-end quality properties for a particular traffic aggregate are compliant with the QoS requirements (e.g., one-way delays or round-trip times bounds). Even though quality centered traffic engineering is used, it potentially requires much more processing and route tweaks than the traditional scheme, due to the higher dynamics of end-to-end performance metrics.

Principle: In order to improve the user's perceived QoS, the ASes should be centered on end-to-end QoS objectives.

To achieve this goal, an IRC employs both performance monitoring and path selection processes centered on end-to-end performance objectives. By using this approach, an IRC can follow the path quality and adapt the routing of individual traffic aggregates to the real-time network conditions. As a result, this implies that IRCs are not suitable to transit ASes, in particular to large transit ASes such as Tier-1 or Tier-2 ISPs, because adapting the routing of the traffic aggregates to network conditions might require changing a large number of paths, and the effects of managing large amounts of inter-domain traffic in short timescales are unpredictable.

2.2. IRC Key Functions

Figure 2 presents a logical diagram of an IRC, which captures the common functionalities from BGP-based IRCs [6,14,15,16]. The main running activities of an IRC in every routing cycle are the following. First, an IRC derives the traffic demands and captures the quality of all available paths. Then, it does an on-line processing to compute the required path changes. Finally, it issues command scripts to routers with the corresponding BGP tweaking. These activities are described in detail in the next subsections.

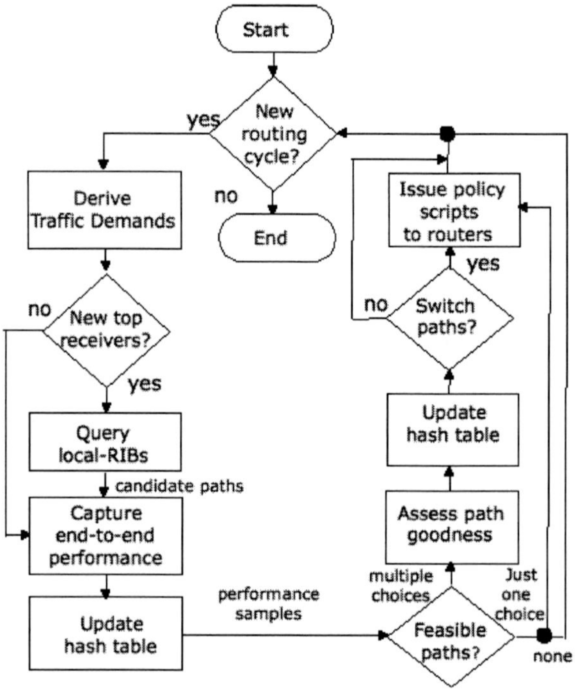

Figure 2. Intelligent Route Controller logical presentation.

2.2.1. Path Monitoring

IRCs are composed of a Path Monitor (PM) component, which has the role of capturing, on a real-time basis, the quality attributes of paths (e.g., one-way delay (OWD), one-way-loss (OWL) or avail-bw (available bandwidth)). In this process, two monitoring methods can be employed independently or combined to derive the estimates of quality attributes of paths:

- Active measurement monitoring - the PM component is endowed with a mechanism to spawn, at a given frequency, small probes targeting the remote destination through every available link connecting the local AS to the Internet. The streams of probes are then monitored to determine the quality of the user/network, assuming implicitly that the values measured from the probes represent accurately the perceived quality of a user/network. Methods like ICMP time-stamp Request and Reply with a specific mark on the Differentiated Services Code Point (DSCP) field of IP packets (e.g., set to AF11 (Assured Forwarding Class 1 Low)) can be used to derive quality metrics, such as the One-way delay (OWD) or Round-Trip Time (RTT) [17].
- Passive measurement monitoring - Usually, the PM collects samples of data packets to derive incoming or outgoing traffic volumes. This is especially important to avoid the self-load effect, and the resulting path instability. Moreover, the PM can also derive other performance or quality attributes over the available path options. For instance, instead of using active probing, the PM might use the TCP acknowledgment mechanism to derive the RTTs. More specifically, the PM can monitor pairs of TCP segments (sent by local TCP sources) and the corresponding TCP acknowledgements (sent by the remote TCP sinks).

Synchronization between probes and the overhead introduced are two issues that must be addressed. The first can be avoided by adding randomization in the sampling times and the second by using a conservative-enough frequency of probes, while keeping efficient routing [6,18].

2.2.2. Dynamic Path Switching

Dynamic path switching is the key technique used by IRC systems to get better end-to-end performance [6,14,15,16]. With this approach, the IRC selects, in every routing cycle, the next-hop ISP to forward packets depending of the quality attributes of paths. However, in practice, after collecting the quality measures, the IRC uses a cost or utility function, denote by $M(.)$ or $U(.)$, to determine whether one path performs better than another. More precisely, for instance, the $M(.)$ expression might be given by a positive quantity -a cardinal value- direct or inversely proportional to the smoothed quality measurement, depending on whether this measurement is additive or concave (e.g., $M \propto latency$ or $M \propto \frac{1}{bandwidth}$).

Knowing that an alternative path performs better than the active path is not a sufficient condition to pick it due to stability issues. Therefore, three path switching policies are considered:

- Choose Best-Choose Best policy (CBCB) - According to the CBCB policy, the IRC switches paths whenever it finds better paths in terms of QoS. So, for each destination, the IRC picks the path that has the smallest value of the chosen metric independently of any QoS bound;
- Choose Best-Choose Good policy (CBCG) - Similarly to the CBCB policy, the IRC switches paths whenever it finds better paths in terms of QoS. However, there is an important difference; here, the IRC is aware of the end-to-end quality bounds, so that if the quality of a path does not fit these bounds, it is enough to pick any alternative good path;
- Choose Good policy (CG) - According to the CG policy, the IRC only switches paths if their QoS characteristics are not sufficient to handle traffic QoS requirements. So, in that case, it picks any good alternative path.

2.2.3. Shifting Traffic over ISPs

IRCs must then change the route BGP attributes reflecting the path descending order (i.e., from the best to the worst path). Two simple solutions to implement the traffic optimizations are by means of the LOCAL-PREFERENCE or MED route attributes change, as described next.

Local-Preference Tweaking: The LOCAL-PREFERENCE attribute indicates the degree of preferences for a route as compared to other available routes for the same prefix (a higher LOCAL-PREFERENCE means more preferred). Therefore, if we denote P = [P1,P2,...,Pk] as the path descending order, and the corresponding vector of routing costs, denoted as M = [C1,C2,...,Ck], the simplest mapping is the linear mapping as in equation (1). It would allow the mappings between each Ci and its LOCAL-PREFERENCE value of the cardinal type.

$$Local - pref(P_i) = p_{min} + \left\lfloor (p_{max} - p_{min})\left(1 - \frac{C_i}{max[C_1, C_2,..., C_k]}\right)\right\rfloor + \Delta Tie \quad (1)$$

where Local-pref(Pi) denotes the LOCAL-PREFERENCE to assign to Pi within a range [pmin,pmax] and ΔTie denotes a small optional Tie-breaking factor that may be add by the IRC to the LOCAL-PREFERENCE value to tie-break equally good routes.

The biggest advantage of a solution based on LOCAL-PREFERENCE tweaking is that it overrides any other route attribute. However, this implies that when an IRC uses it for traffic engineering purposes it may violate local business policy (unless two LOCAL-PREFERENCE ranges are used, one for enforcing business policies and other for traffic engineering purposes).

MED Tweaking: In this case, the mapping between the routing costs and MED values is similar to Eq. (1), except that the preferred routes have lower MED values. However, with this solution the MEDs are only compared if the routes have equal AS path lengths, which may limit the effectiveness of the traffic optimizations deduce by the IRC system.

2.3. Simulation Study

Intelligent Route Controllers were evaluated using the following path switching policies - choose-best-choose-best (CBCB), choose-best-choose-good (CBCG) and choose-good (CG), when the Differentiated Services (Diffserv) feature [19] is enabled or disabled, resulting on four pairs of simulation scenarios:

1. CBCB IRCs and Diffserv on (CBCB-DSon) / CBCB IRCs and Diffserv off (CBCB-DSoff);
2. CBCG IRCs and Diffserv on (CBCG-DSon) / CBCG IRCs and Diffserv off (CBCG-DSoff);
3. CG IRCs and Diffserv on (CG-DSon) / CG IRCs and Diffserv off (CG-DSoff);
4. BGP and Diffserv on (BGP-DSon) / BGP and Diffserv off (BGP-DSoff).

The simulations were performed using the J-Sim [20] simulator in which the functionalities of the IRCs were implemented.

Figure 3 illustrates a simplified picture of the network model used. The simulated network aims at representing a multi-service part of the Internet composed by access ISPs able to provide some limited QoS services to their customers, and an over-provisioned Internet core (composed by Tier 1 and big Tier 2 ISPs).

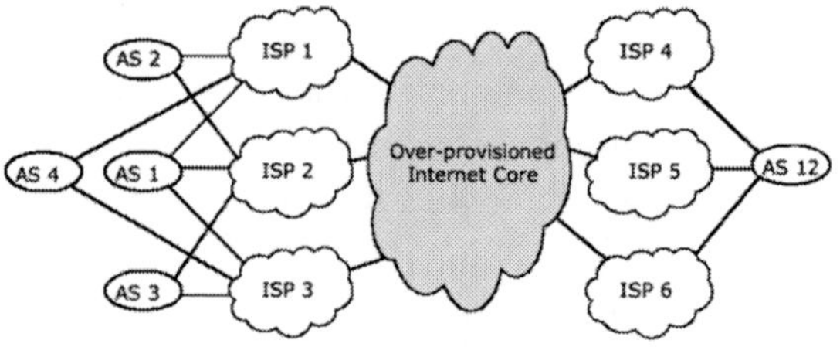

Figure 3. Network model.

In this set-up, the tests were conducted using a traffic mix consisting of Voice over IP (VoIP) calls, video calls, prioritized data, and Web traffic. When Diffserv feature is enabled, packets are classified and forwarded using the standard Expedited Forwarding (EF), Assured Forwarding (AF11 and AF21), and Best-Effort (BE) traffic classes, respectively [21,22].

During all the experiments, it is assumed that a service-level specification (SLS) was previously exchanged between remote multihomed stub domains, based on maximum OWDs for each service. These maximum OWDs tolerated per-service were chosen to represent reasonable but demanding values for the kinds of traffic sources considered. Thus, the OWD bound for voice and video traffic was set at 100ms, and at 400ms for prioritized data and web traffic, which are in accordance with the E-model Rating from ITU's G.107/G.114 recommendations [23,24].

2.3.1. Performance Metrics and Objectives

The first objective is to assess how much IRCs aid to improve end-to-end network quality. This is shown by evaluating: (i) the average end-to-end OWD (or latency), denoted as *owd*, and (ii) the traffic transfer efficiency for the different traffic flows, denoted as *Ef*. The efficiency for a traffic class is defined by $Ef = \frac{F_D}{C_O}$, where F_D is the total throughput at destinations D, and C_O is the corresponding total throughput sent by source domains O.

The second objective is to study how IRCs contribute to the overall network stability under variable QoS dynamics. The performance indicator is the total number of path switches needed to meet the latency constraint for each kind of traffic.

The third objective is to find the overall efficiency of each IRC path switching policy and BGP. The overall efficiency is given by an Efficiency index (see Eq. (2)), which represents the relative number of path switches that were needed to obtain a given latency and traffic transfer efficiency. Lower values for this index indicate better overall efficiency, i.e., that there is a better trade-off between the number of path switches, the averaged OWD and the traffic efficiency; and so the IRC path switching policy is more efficient.

$$Efficiency\ index = PSindex\left(\frac{d}{d_{max}}\right)\left(\frac{100}{Ef}\right) \tag{2}$$

where *PSindex* is a path shifts index computed, as follows.

$$PSindex = \begin{cases} \dfrac{PS}{PS_{ref}} & , if\ PS \geq PS_{ref} \\ \dfrac{abs\left(PS - PS_{ref}\right) + PS_{ref}}{PS_{ref}} & , if\ PS < PS_{ref} \end{cases} \tag{3}$$

where PS_{ref} is the number of path switches performed by the IRC adopting a given reference policy.

In the evaluations of the overall efficiency, the CG policy was used as the base reference. Thus, the *PSindex* is given by the number path switches performed by other policies normalized by the number of path switches performed by the IRC CG policy. Otherwise, the

PSindex is given by a penalty that depends of the number of path switches that would be done by the IRC police to achieve the same performance of the IRC CG policy.

Finally, the fourth objective is to compare the path failover time that a stub AS gets when it uses an IRC system with the time BGP needs to detect and recovery from the same path outages. In the tests, the interval of times between the instant of the occurrence of the failure and the instant of the path switch at the AS source of traffic were recorded. We also recorded the times needed to recovery the throughput on the destination.

2.3.2. Results

The first results concern the latency obtained with the different IRC path switching policies and BGP. The cluster of figures 4 illustrates the Complementary Cumulative Distribution Functions (CCDF) of the traffic latencies. If the probability of the OWD is greater than or equal to x is high (i.e., P(OWD $\geq$ x) is high), it means that there is a high likelihood that the traffic will suffer a latency greater than or equal to x. In turn, figure 5 presents the averaged latencies for each traffic.

Two main conclusions can be drawn from the analysis of these results. First, the IRC architecture substantially enhances end-to-end QoS when compared with a pure BGP model. On the one hand, when Diffserv feature is disabled and IRCs are switched OFF, under stressful traffic load, BGP is not capable of supporting ITU's performance bounds. In particular, figure 4 shows that the BGP-based scheme presents a likelihood of violation of all OWD bounds greater than 95%. On the other hand, when IRCs are switched ON, figure 4 shows that all IRC policies for all traffic classes have a likelihood of violation of the maximum bounds greater than 50%. This is not necessarily bad given that the simulations were carried out under stressful traffic load. Another observation is that the CG policy presents longer tails, so that for less important traffic classes (i.e., data prioritized and Web traffic), there is a probability greater than 10% that the latency exceeds 500 ms. This would be expected, since the CG policy only reacts to QoS violations.

Second, Diffserv clearly shows its effectiveness to protect the most important traffic classes, since all the traffic classes have OWDs within the ranges allowed, except for web traffic, and sometimes, for the interactive data prioritized traffic when BGP is enabled. Although this may sound surprising, this is only possible due to a strong efficiency penalization of the data prioritized traffic and web traffic. Figure 6 clearly shows that, especially for the BGP case; in fact, more than 60% of web traffic is dropped.

Next, the discussion of the IRC path switching policies on controlling the number of path switches is performed. Figure 7 presents the total number of path switches registered for each policy. As one would guess, the IRC path switching algorithm based on CBCB policy presents the larger number of path switches, since according to CBCB policy, an IRC switches paths whenever a better path is found. This is especially evident when Diffserv is disabled, and particularly for the less important traffic classes. As it would be expected, the IRC path switching algorithm based on CG policy provides the best performance in terms of the number of path switches. However, this is not necessarily good given that this policy only reacts when there is a clear violation of the performance bound. As mentioned before, longer tails in the cluster of figures 5 clearly show that this policy might allow unacceptable latencies.

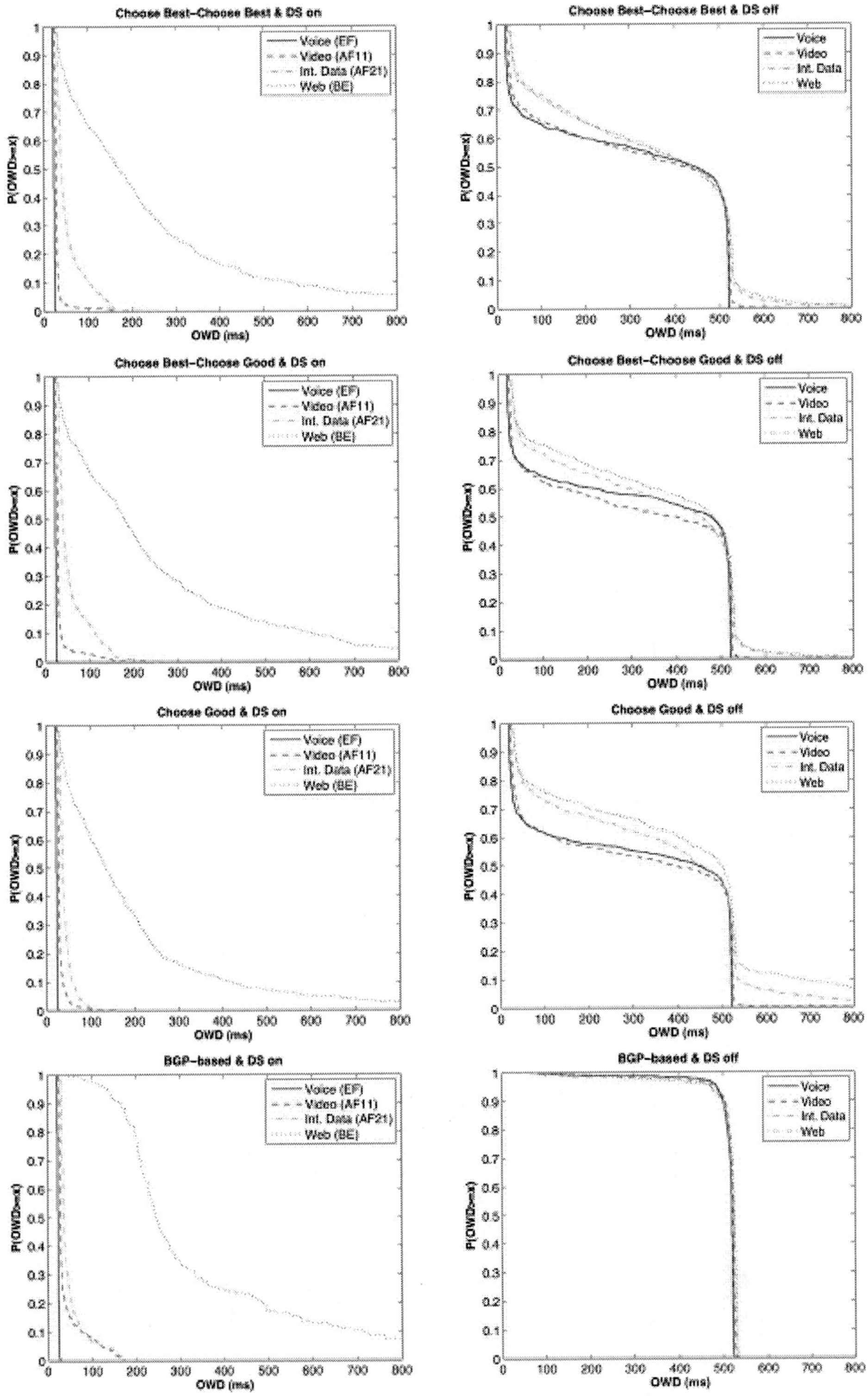

Figure 4. Complementary Cumulative Distribution Function (CCDF) of OWDs for each traffic (Left) whether Diffserv feature is enabled or (Right) Diffserv feature is disabled.

Figure 8 depicts the overall performance index results. As it would be expected, BGP presents the weaker overall efficiency. On the other hand, the CG policy appears to be the most efficient scheme, at least in absolute terms. These results show that just a small number of path switches is enough to improve dramatically the performance of traffic in terms of latency and efficiency.

However, combining these results with the ones from the figure 4, where, as earlier mentioned, it is possible to observe that the CB policy presents long tails, we consider the CBCG policy as the most balanced scheme. In other words, a few number of extra path switches performed by an IRC using this policy allows to avoid episodes of high latency. On contrary, the results of figure 8 also clearly show that a number of path switches larger than necessary might not lead to performance improvements. This is especially evident when the Diffserv feature is enabled.

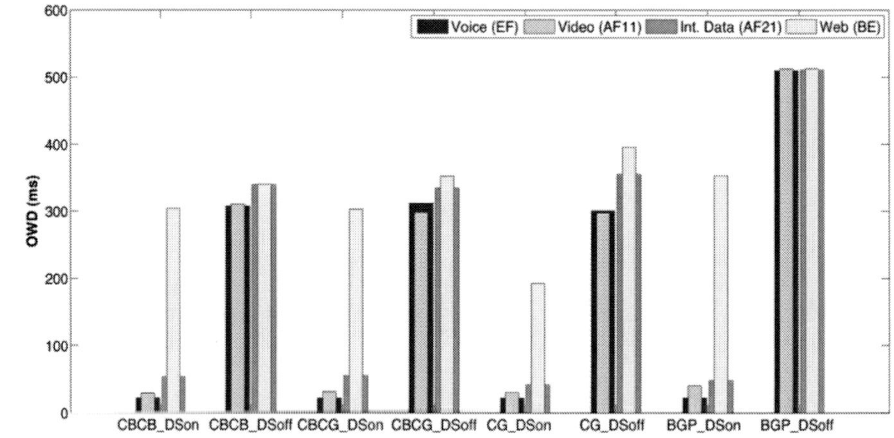

Figure 5. Average OWD for each traffic.

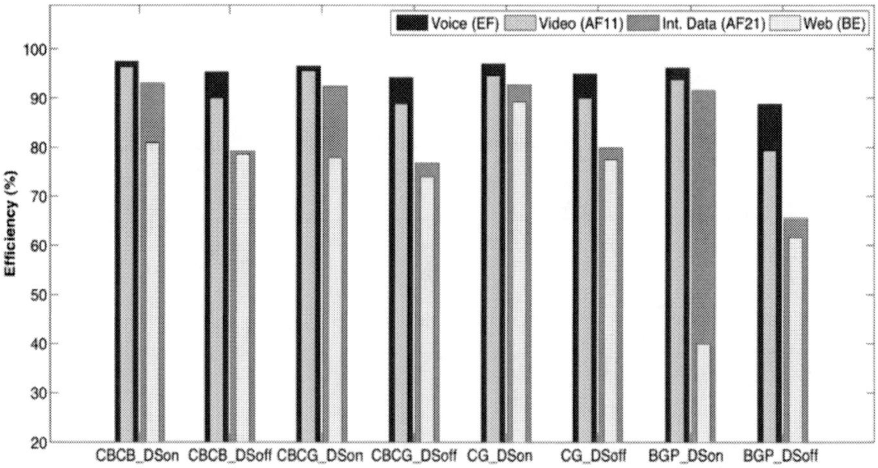

Figure 6. Transfer Efficiency for each traffic.

Finally, in this section we try to assess how the IRCs are able to manage and react to a remote link failure. Figure 9 contrasts the results obtained when the IRCs are in use against the results obtained by BGP. We have aggressively configured small KEEPALIVE and HOLD timer values (30 and 90 seconds respectively) so as to increase the speed of reaction of BGP. From Figure 9 we can observe that in case of links failures occurring a few hops away from a certain AS, the IRCs are able to react, on average, between 3-4 times faster than the time that BGP needs to converge to new route. In addition, since the IRCs gather end-to-end measurements their responsiveness becomes independent of the place where the remote link failure occurs. As a result, IRCs are also able to reduce performance degradations (e.g. packet loss and latency) or service outages arising from inaccurate routing states during BGP transient fail-over periods.

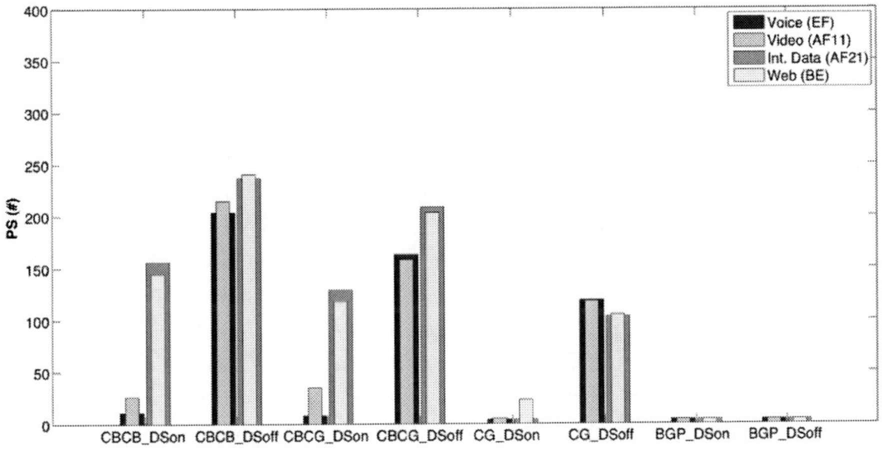

Figure 7. Total path shifts for each traffic.

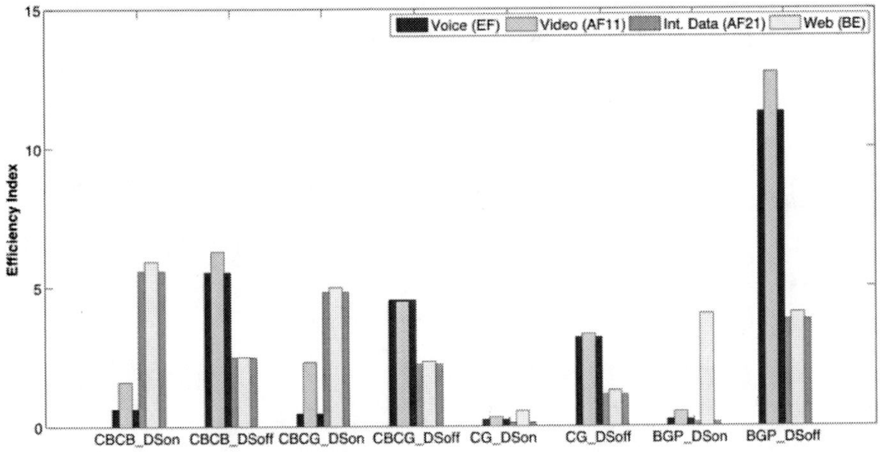

Figure 8. Global Efficiency Index for each traffic.

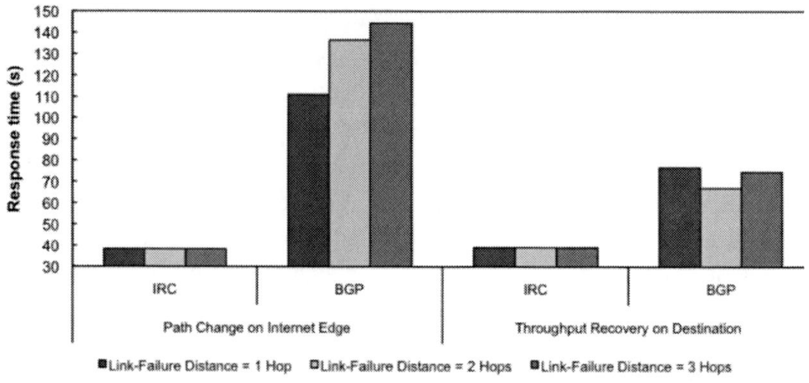

Figure 9. Contrasting the response time to a link failure.

3. Combining IRC with Backbone Traffic Engineering

The benefits of employing Intelligent Routing Control (IRC) are evident from the technical and economical perspectives [14,15,25]. However, IRC mechanisms commonly rely on the selfish routing approach. They allow stub ASes to perform outbound traffic optimization, but the target optimum is only local since the paths (or transit providers) are greedily selected. In other words, selfish routing makes IRCs unaware of the effects of their route choices over transit ASes. The practical result is that the networks of transit ASes may become far away from optimal performance regimes, and congestion can occur on intra or inter-domain links of their networks. This is caused by the increased difficulty to get accurate forecasts of traffic demands, due to rapid route changes performed by IRC [26].

Similarly, selfishness is also a common attribute to Traffic Engineering boxes for transit ASes. So, in turn, these controller boxes compute a new local routing solution to return networks of transit ASes to the optimal regime taking into account current traffic demands and local traffic objectives. Unfortunately, resulting route changes can then interact with IRCs by changing the end-to-end quality of traffic; so that IRCs react to this quality change by adapting the routing in stub ASes. This way uncoordinated routing changes attempting to face congestion can produce cycles of influence between stub ASes and ISPs. Figure 10 summarizes the control actions of IRC and TE boxes over the traffic, and corresponding interactions between both boxes.

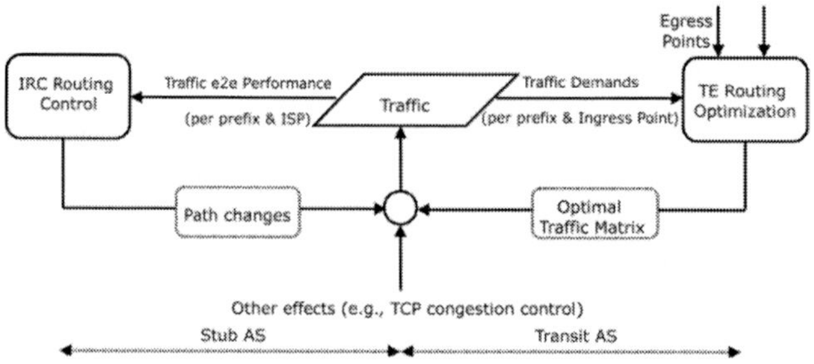

Figure 10. Model of actions of IRC and TE boxes over traffic.

To address the above issues, this section considers a conceptually general and simple distributed out-of-BGP-band cooperative approach able to support in some sense coordinated inter-domain routing decisions among stub and transit AS for the context (but not limited) of the future QoS-aware Internet. The particularity of this approach is that it allows IRCs finding 'social' optimums by honouring both individual stub and transit AS preferences (or constraints) regarding the carrying (or admission of new) traffic amounts of certain traffic class (TC) aggregates.

To summarize, the proposed approach is motivated and well suited to:

1. Protect stubs ASes from performance and QoS violations against end-to-end performance and quality bounds;
2. Improve the traffic demands predictability over transit ASes;
3. Reduce selfish costs, i.e., traffic performance losses, TE performance losses and routing instability.

Starting from some background on inter-domain Traffic Engineering heuristics, this section provides a broad overview of an IRC-TE cooperative scheme, including a description of the main mechanisms and algorithms that integrate the IRC-TE cooperation framework, and finally some results demonstrating the framework's feasibility.

3.1. Backbone Traffic Engineering Heuristics

Let us first briefly describe a typical inter-domain backbone TE process in an ISP network with a set of ingress points I, a set of egress points E and a set of reachable prefixes P. The inputs of TE process are the incoming traffic demands (TD), the egress point choices for each prefix $p \in P$ (given by BGP) and the egress point capacities. Its output is the optimal ID routing i.e., the routing that ensures the optimal performance regime according to a given traffic objective. Then, at a given timescale t this process is repeated as the traffic demands might fluctuate over the time. In this section, we focus on fluctuations due to routing changes in multihoming users employing IRC. Following, these users are referred, simply as IP network customers (INCs).

More formally, the predicted TD over the ISP $k \in K$ for the slot time t is represented by the matrix $D_{(k,t)}$, where K is the set of ISPs and each entry $D_{(k,t)}(i,p)$ is the predicted TD over ingress point i of ISP k for prefix p. If each INC $h \in H$ has T data transfers at rates $x_h(p)$ to distribute over its ISPs, then each entry of $D_{(k,t)}$ is defined as in equation (4).

$$D_{(k,t)}(i,p) = \sum_{h}\sum_{p} x_h(p).r_{(h,k,t)}(i,p) \tag{4}$$

where H is the set of INCs and $r_{(h,k,t)}(i,p) \in \{0,1\}$ is an indicator function to select whether the route from INC h to prefix p via ingress point i of ISP k is active (i.e., True (1), False(0)).

On the other hand, we represent the egress resources of ISP k as C_k, where each entry $C_k(e)$ is the capacity at each egress point e. And, we represent the inter-domain routing from

ISP k as $\varepsilon_{(k,t)}$, where each entry $\varepsilon_{(k,t)}(i,e,p) \in \{0,1\}$ is an indicator function that tells whether the $D_{(k,t)}(i,p)$ is assigned to the egress point e.

The border egress router selection (BERS) problem being addressed is the following: *How to assign each entry of traffic demands $D_{(k,t)}(i,p)$ to an egress point e, so as to optimize a certain traffic performance objective.*

In this section, a typical objective, the min-max link utilization, is encoded in BERS problem to ensure that egress link utilization is at lowest levels and thereby to minimize congestion. Other objectives can also be encoded in BERS (e.g., min-cost routing or maximum business profit) [27]. Before proceeding, let first define the link utilization of e for a routing $\varepsilon_{(k,t)}$ as:

$$U_e = \sum_i \sum_p \frac{\varepsilon_{(k,t)}(i,e,p).D_{(k,t)}(i,p)}{C_k(e)} (i,p),\ \varepsilon_{(k,t)} \text{ is a routing.} \tag{5}$$

Objective - Minimizing the Maximum Link Utilization (min-MLU). One possibility for the BERS problem would be to minimize the maximum link utilization, i.e.,

$$\min \max U_e,\ \forall e \in E,\ \varepsilon_{(k,t)} \text{ is a routing.} \tag{6}$$

This objective is subject to the following constraints:

$$\sum_i \sum_p \varepsilon_{(k,t)}(i,e,p).D_{(k,t)}(i,p) \le C_k(e),\ \forall e \in E \tag{7}$$

$$\text{with} \sum_e \varepsilon_{(k,t)}(i,e,p) = 1,\ \forall i \in I \tag{8}$$

The BERS goal to be addressed is to minimize traffic objective (6). The capacity constraint (7) ensures that the total resource requirements of the traffic flows assigned to each egress point do not exceed the available contracted capacity. The assignment constraint (8) guarantees that each traffic flow is assigned to exactly one egress point e.

The BERS algorithm used is based on a genetic single objective version of [5]. The algorithm, belonging to the class of evolution strategies used in optimization, resembles the process of biological evolution, where each individual is described by its genetic code, called a chromosome. In turn, each chromosome is composed of individual genes. In the problem in hand, a gene is the assignment of a single aggregate traffic flow to an egress point of the ISP, and an individual (i.e., a chromosome) is a potential solution.

The basic algorithm steps are presented in figure 11, Algorithm (1). It starts with the creation of the initial generation, where the individuals are created randomly. Then, an evaluating step based on the proposed objective function (6) follows. After that, and for a number of generations, a new generation of children is created and compared with the corresponding generation of parents. From this comparison the better elements will compose the next generation of parents. The last of the generations is the aimed TE solution.

Algorithm 1: Basic steps of the genetic Backbone Traffic Engineering algorithm.

```
1: Create the initial parent generation;
2: Evaluate the generation;
3: for a number of generations do
4: Create the child generation;
5: Evaluate both generations together;
6: Rank both generations together;
7: Replace worst parents with better children;
8: end for
```

Figure 11. Basic algorithm steps.

3.2. IRC-TE Cooperative Framework

Generically introducing a certain degree of cooperation in the routing decisions can reduce selfishness. In the case addressed, this corresponds to incorporate ISP feedback signals into the path decision process of IRCs, so that the paths would be selected given the observed path quality and the associated ISP feedback. A path is thus characterized by a tuple of attributes including the path quality measures and ISP feedback signals.

The mechanisms used aims, on the one hand, to compute ISP feedback signals from the current ISP network regime; and, on the other hand, to compare a pair of path tuples. However, the exact mechanisms design depends of the nature of the ISP feedback signals. To narrow the space of possible solutions, the following design decisions were made:

1. *ISP feedback signals advertise ISP route prices* to carry the amount of traffic from stub AS customers employing IRC. These prices depend of local target traffic objectives of the ISP (see (e));
2. *ISP route prices are advertised through an opaque metric.* The exact mapping function used to calculated this metric is not shared between ISPs and stub AS customers employing IRC. This way stub AS customers employing IRC have no possibility to uncover the goals or procedures employed by ISPs;
3. *The opaque metric values are bounded to* $[0,1]$ to enable fair comparisons between different ISP route prices formulations, and to avoid normalization to mix these prices with path performance attributes;
4. *ISP route prices are dynamically adapted by ISPs* in response to ISP load changes and deviations from a predefined target range. This target range is defined taking into account the optimal regime of the ISP network previously set by the ISP Traffic Engineering process for a given traffic objective;
5. *Use of MIAD (Multiplicative Increase Additive Decrease) policy to adapt the maximum values for ISP route prices.* This mechanism has been introduced to ensure that the ISP can effectively repulse/attract traffic from/to its network in order to keep ISP load within the target range. Further details are given in figure 12.

3.3. Utility-Based IRC Algorithm

The Utility-based Intelligent Routing Control algorithm relies on the notion of utility function [28]. In the design of the solution proposed, it is consider that each IRC middlebox has a utility function associated with each traffic class. Therefore, it can determine the IRC/end-User degree of satisfaction after shifting a traffic aggregate to a given path.

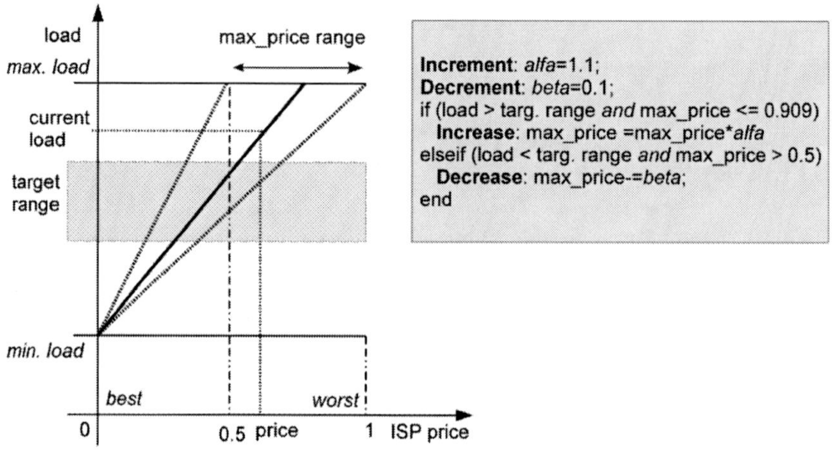

Figure 12. Mapping of ISP performance measures to agnostic values.

Denoting generically d as the delay measured (OWD or RTT) at the INC_i throughout the path offered by the ISP_k, there are a reasonable number constraints concerning utility values $U(d)$:

1. $U(d):[0,d_{max}]\rightarrow[0,1]$, If the path offers a delay higher than the delay bound dmax its utility is zero;
2. $lim_{d\rightarrow 0^+}U(d)=1$, since the delay tends to zero, the utility tends to zero;
3. $U'(d)\leq 0$, since the utility should decrease as the delay increases;
4. $U''(d)>0$, to make the utility more sensitive as the delay approaches the delay bound.

In this design, a modified sigmoid utility function is used, since it fits these constraints (see equation 9). In addition, its parameter α is set to 0.0125 to allow the utility to follow the shape of the E-model Rating from ITU's G.107/G.114 recommendations [23,24].

$$U(d)=\begin{cases}1-\dfrac{2}{1-exp(-\alpha(d-d_{max}))} & , if\, d\in[0,d_{max}[\\ 0 & , if\, d>d_{max}\end{cases} \quad (9)$$

where α determines the steepness the curve.

As described previously, ISPs use feedback signals (i.e., route prices) to indicate their willingness regarding the traffic being injected into their networks by a given stub AS customer. So, each Cooperative IRC (C-IRC) computes the surplus, defined as the difference between the utility and the route price, and selects the path with the maximal surplus. Figure 13, Algorithm 2 details the Utility-based IRC algorithm.

Algorithm 2: IRC($\{P,A,C\}$)

Require: $\{P\}$ – vector of the set of AS paths for a prefix p
$\{A\}$ – matrix of the set of performance/QoS attributes
$\{p\}$ – vector of criteria representing the ISP route prices
$\{d_{max}\}$ – delay traffic bound
Ensure: P_x - the active path fits traffic goals toward prefix p
1: *Wait* for changes in the QoS attributes
2: /* Basic IRC path selection process */
3: Compute the vector of Utilities U
4: Identify the set of feasible paths P'
$[P',U'] \leftarrow \{P_i \in P : U_i(d_i) > 0\}$
5: **if** $\|P'\| \neq 0$ **then**
6: /* Identify the highest rank path $P_i \in P'$, which gives the maximal surplus*/
$x' = argmax\ \chi(\{P',U'\}) = U_i(d_i) - p_i, \forall P_i \in P'$ /* the ranking function χ compares the surplus of all feasible paths*/
7: **if** $\|x'\| > 1$ **then**
8: /* If there is more than one path equally good, apply the standard BGP process to break the ties*/
$P'' \leftarrow \{P_i \in P' : i = x'\}$
$x' \leftarrow BGPTie(P'')$
9: **end if**
10: Switch traffic towards p from P_x to $P_{x'}$
11: $P_x \leftarrow P_{x'}$
12: **end if**
13: /* End of IRC path selection process */

Figure 13. Utility-based IRC algorithm.

3.4. Simulation Evaluation

For performance studies, four IRC-TE combinations were considered depending on whether IRC and TE mechanisms were switched ON or OFF, and the IRC-TE cooperation was enabled or disabled. The results presented were obtained using a realistic simulation model built from BGP routing table dumps and data traces collected at each of the 23 nodes of the GÉANT pan-European academic network [29]. In this model, the GÉANT network employs a genetic inter-domain TE algorithm, and ASes (representing European countries) connected to GÉANT employ IRC.

In accordance with the best traffic engineering practices, it is assumed that both IRC and TE boxes only focus on the traffic toward top receivers, the so called popular prefixes or destinations, which are a small fraction (i.e., about 5 - 10%) of the total number of receivers. This assumption arises from the property of traffic demands of GÉANT being consistent with a Zipf-like distribution [30]. Thus, after a route summarizing process followed by the flow rankings computation based on the individual contributions of each flow to the total volume of traffic, 296 popular destinations among a total of 16150 prefixes were identified. The popular destinations were identified such the sum of their individual traffic volumes is a fraction of 99% of total traffic volume.

A last point to note concerning the simulation model is that the AS-level topology used in the simulations is composed of 731 ASes and corresponding peerings, which were inferred from the GÉANT BGP routing table dumps taking only into account the popular destinations. Further details about GÉANT traffic and the AS-level topology are presented in figures 14 and 15.

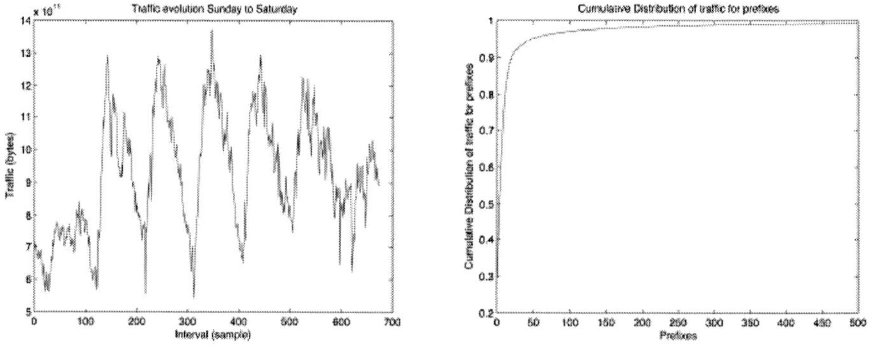

Figure 14. GÉANT Traffic: (left) Weekly Traffic evolution; (right) Distribution of Traffic volumes.

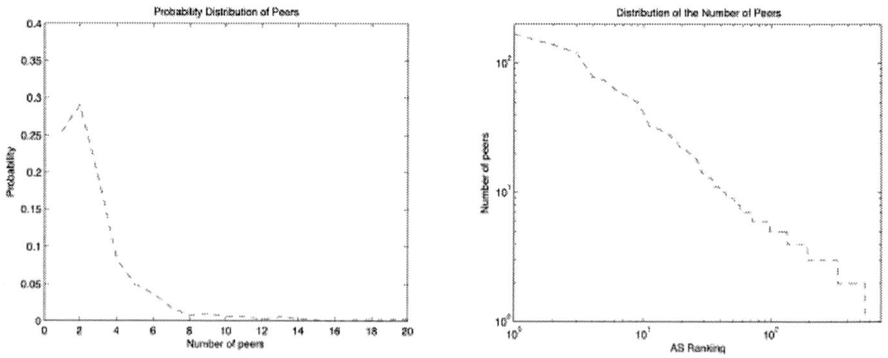

Figure 15. AS-Level topology: (left) Probability of a number of peers; (right) Distribution of the number of peers.

The results reported in figures 16-18 allow an evaluation of the IRC-TE cooperative framework and its ability to produce synergistic interactions between IRC and TE. Synergistic interactions has a threefold meaning:

I. latency measured with IRC-TE cooperation is equal or better than the latency measured without IRC-TE cooperation;

II. link utilization with IRC-TE cooperation is lower than link utilization without IRC-TE cooperation;

III. and, the total number of path switches with IRC-TE cooperation is smaller than the number of path switches without IRC-TE cooperation.

Otherwise, the interactions between IRC and TE are antagonistic.

The results reported in figures 16 and 17 show the averaged latency for each destination and the median of the link utilization in egress links of GÉANT for all four IRC-TE combinations. They reveal two significant observations concerning the cooperative IRC-TE scheme. First, it can ensure a performance similar to the one obtained by the scheme without IRC-TE cooperation. Second, it can improve the link utilization of the ISP network. In figure 17, the median link utilization presents lower values across the simulation. This is particularly evident in figure 17 across the interval of samples [150,440]. On contrary, the selfish IRC may hurt the TE performance especially for higher loads, which is across the interval of samples [550,640].

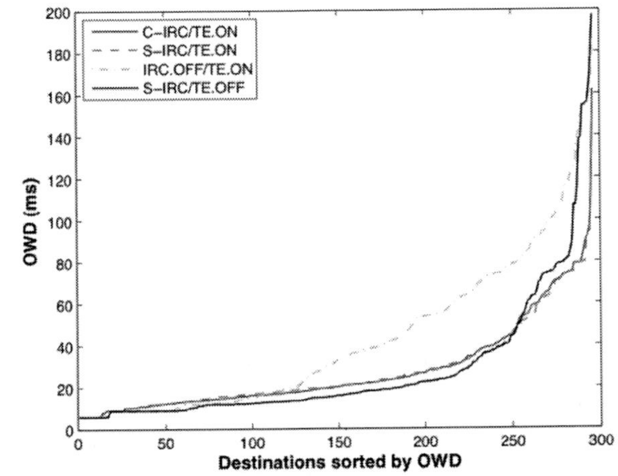

Figure 16. Latency measured for each destination.

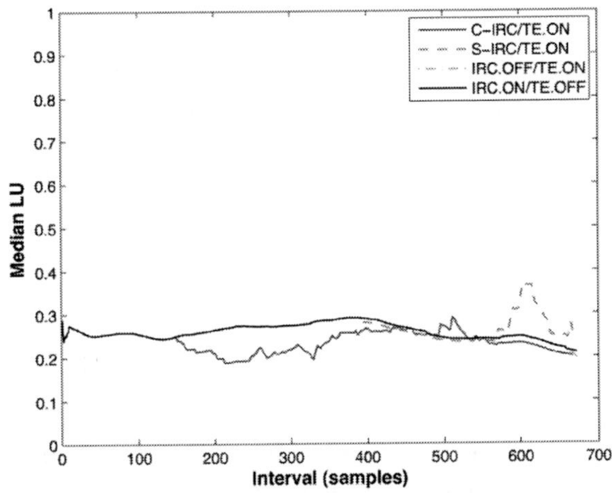

Figure 17. Median of Link Utilization.

IRC stability is discussed next. Figure 18 shows the total number of path switches for all IRC-TE combinations.

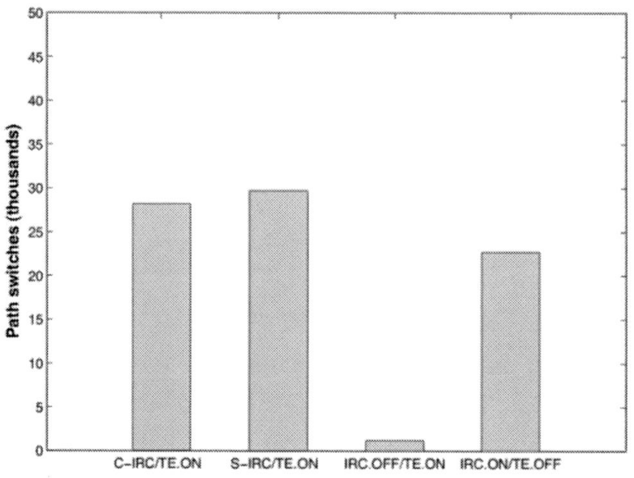

Figure 18. Total number of path switches performed by IRCs.

What we see is, first, TE is clearly antagonistic to IRC, since both IRC/TE.ON combinations need a few more thousands of path switches than the IRC.ON/TE.OFF combination in order to meet the same OWD constraint. However, it appears that this is compensated by better OWD distributions. Second, there is an overall stability benefit from combining IRC and TE according to a cooperative scheme. In fact, this combination roughly needs less 7% of the total number of path shifts needed by the IRC-TE combination without cooperation.

To sum up, these results, as a first main conclusion, they substantiate the claim on the reduction of the effectiveness of TE due to IRC route control. In other words, this means that although TE is able to adapt efficiently the inter-domain routing to traffic demands fluctuations due to the sources, it might be unable to accommodate traffic changes due to IRCs. As a second main conclusion, these results show that a cooperative IRC-TE scheme can produce synergistic interactions between IRC and TE.

4. Conclusion

In this chapter, multihoming intelligent routing control has been introduced as an alternative approach in enabling inter-domain quality of service routing. First, the main design principles of intelligent route controllers and their algorithms were presented. Results from a simulation study have shown that intelligent routing control can substantially enhance end-to-end quality of service when compared with a pure Border Gateway Protocol (BGP) model.

Given that intelligent routing control and inter-domain traffic engineering can interact due to selfish routing changes, a novel framework that combines both mechanisms in order to produce synergistic interactions was described.

The novelty of this framework is due to the mutual cooperation between intelligent routing control and traffic engineering, and on the use of out-BGP-band signaling. Specifically, this mechanism supports the exchange of feedback signals between traffic engineering and intelligent routing control, that notify intelligent route controllers from route price modifications due to traffic load changes over the internet service provider (ISP) network. A significant feature of feedback signals is their agnosticism to ISP traffic objectives.

Based on a utility-based algorithm, an intelligent route controller can integrate ISP feedback signals into its routing decision process, and find 'social' optimums, honouring both individual stub and transit preferences. Performance results were presented and demonstrated the feasibility of this framework both in terms of stability and traffic performance.

REFERENCES

[1] X. Masip-Bruin, M. Yannuzzi, R. Serral-Gracia, J. Domingo-Pascual, J. Enriquez-Gabeiras, M. Callejo, M. Diaz, F. Racaru, G. Stea, E. Mingozzi, A. Beben, W. Burakowski, E. Monteiro, L. Cordeiro, The EuQoS System: A Solution for QoS Routing in Heterogeneous Networks, in *IEEE Communications Magazine*, 45(2):96-103, February 2007.

[2] M.P. Howarth, P. Flegkas, G. Pavlou, N. Wang, P. Trimintzios, D. Griffin, J. Griem, M. Boucadair, P. Morand, H. Asgari, P. Georgatsos, Provisioning for Inter-domain quality of service: the MESCAL approach, *IEEE Communications Magazine,* June 2005.

[3] G. Cristallo, C. Jacquenet, Providing Quality of Service Indication by BGP-4 Protocol: the QOS NLRI attribute, IETF draft, IETF, 2002.

[4] K.H. Ho, N. Wang, P. Trimintzios, G. Pavlou, Traffic Engineering for Inter-domain Quality of Service, Proc. London Communications Symposium (LCS), London, UK, September 2003.

[5] M. Pedro, E. Monteiro, F. Boavida, An Approach to Off-line Inter-domain QoS-Aware Resource Optimization, in Proc. of the Networking 2006, pp. 247-255, Networking 2006, Coimbra, Portugal, May 2006.

[6] R. Gao, C. Dovrolis, E.W. Zegura, Avoiding Oscillations due to Intelligent Route Control Systems. In the Proc. of *IEEE INFOCOM 2006*, Barcelona, Spain, April 2006.

[7] M. Yannuzzi, X. Masip-Bruin, E. Marin-Tordera, J. Domingo-Pascual, A. Fonte, E. Monteiro, Improving the Performance of Route Control Middleboxes in a Competitive Environment, in *IEEE Network*, Vol. 22, no. 5, Sep./Oct. 2008.

[8] A. Akella, B. Maggs, S. Seshan, A. Shaikh, R. Sitaraman, A Measurement-Based Analysis of Multihoming. In the Proc. of *ACM SIGCOMM 2003*, Karlsruhe, Germany, 2003.

[9] Y. Rekhter, A Border Gateway Protocol 4 (BGP-4), IETF RFC 4271, January 2006.

[10] BGP Analysis Reports, http://bgp.potaroo.net/index-bgp.html, Web page accessed at June 2009

[11] T. Bates, R. Chandra, D. Katz, Y. Rekhter, Multiprotocol Extensions for BGP-4, *IETF RFC 4760*, IETF (2007).

[12] C. Labovitz, R. Wattenhofer, S. Venkatachary, A. Ahuja, The impact of internet policy and topology on delayed routing convergence, In Proc. of *IEEE INFOCOM* 2001, April 2001.

[13] C. Labovitz, A. Ahuja, A. Bose, F. Jahanianitz, Delayed internet routing convergence, In *IEEE/ACM TRANSACTIONS ON NETWORKING*, VOL. 9, NO. 3 (2001).

[14] Cisco Systems, Inc., Performance Routing.
[15] Internap Networks Inc., Flow Control Platform.
[16] M. Yannuzzi, A. Fonte, X. Masip-Bruin, M. Curado, J. Domingo-Pascual, E. Monteiro, S. Sanchez-Lopez, On the Advantages of Cooperative and Social Smart Route. In Proc. of ICCCN 2006, Arlington, Virginia, USA, October 2006.
[17] J. Postel, Internet Control Message Protocol, *IETF RFC792*, September 1981.
[18] A. Fonte, J. Martins, M. Curado, E. Monteiro, Stabilizing Intelligent Route Control: Randomized Path Monitoring, Randomized Path Switching or History-Aware Path Switching?, in Proc. of the 11th IFIP/IEEE International Conference on Management of Multimedia and Mobile Networks and Services Management of Converged Multimedia Networks and Services (MMNS 2008), Samos Island, Greece, September 2008.
[19] S. Blake, D. Black, M. Carlson, E. Davies, Z. Wang, W. Weiss, An Architecture for Differentiated Services, *IETF RFC 2475*, December 1998.
[20] J-Sim Homepage, http://www.j-sim.org.
[21] [V. Jacobson, K. Nichols, K. Poduri, An Expedited Forward-ing PHB, *RFC 2598*, IETF, June 1999.
[22] J. Heinanen, F. Baker, W. Weiss, J. Wroclawski, Assured Forwarding PHB Group, *RFC 2597*, IETF, June 1999.
[23] ITU-T Recommendation G.107: The E-Model, a computational model for use in transmission planning, 2003.
[24] ITU-T Recommendation G.114: One-way transmission time, 2003.
[25] R. Dai, D. Stahl, A. Whinston, The economics of smart routing and QoS, In Proc. of the Fifth Inter. *Workshop on Networked Group Comm* (NGC'03), 2003.
[26] R. Teixeira, N. Duffield, J. Rexford, M. Roughan, Traffic Matrix Reloaded: The Impact of Routing Changes, in Proc. of PAM, March 2005.
[27] T. Bressoud, R. Rastogi., Optimal Configuration for BGP Route Selection. In Proc. of IEEE INFOCOM 2003, San Francisco, USA, April 2003.
[28] H. R. Varian, Microeconomics Analysis, third edition. W. W. Norton and Company, Inc., 1992.
[29] S. Uhlig, B. Quoitin, J. Lepropre, S. Balon, Providing public intradomain traffic matrices to the research community, *Journal of SIGCOMM Comput. Commun. Rev.*, 2006.
[30] W. Fang, L. Peterson, Inter-as traffic patterns and their implications. In Proceedings of the 4th Global Internet Symposium, December 1999.
[31] A. Fonte, M. Pedro, E. Monteiro, F. Boavida, Analysis of Interdomain Smart Routing and Traffic Engineering Interactions, in Proc. of IEEE Globecom 2007 Internet Protocol Symposium, Washington, DC, USA, November 2007.
[32] G. Almes, S. Kalidindi, M. Zekauskas, A one-way delay metric for IPPM, IETF, *RFC 2679*, September 1999.

In: Recent Advances in Providing QoS and Reliability... ISBN 978-1-61761-858-1
Editors: N. Wang, G. Pavlou and M. Boucadair

Chapter 10

SELF-PROTECTING MULTIPATHS (SPM): EFFICIENT RESILIENCE FOR TRANSPORT NETWORKS

Michael Menth[1]
University of Würzburg, Institute of Computer Science, Germany

ABSTRACT

The self-protecting multipath (SPM) is a simple and efficient end-to-end protection switching mechanism for transport networks. It distributes the traffic of a demand between two nodes according to a specific load balancing function over several disjoint paths and redistributes it if one of them fails. The load balancing functions can be optimized so that backup capacity in the network is optimally shared by multiple demands in various failure scenarios. As a result, resilience against all link and node failures can be achieved with only little extra capacity and in capacitated networks more protected traffic can be carried with the SPM than with other resilience mechanisms. The SPM is rather simple which facilitates its deployment in practice. This chapter explains the SPM in detail, distinguishes it from other, similar mechanisms, shows how the load balancing functions can be optimized, and illustrates the superior performance of the SPM.

1. INTRODUCTION

The self-protecting multipath (SPM) has been first published in [1]. It carries a traffic demand d between two routers in a network and protects the transmission against network failures. The path layout $P_d = (p_d^0, \dots, p_d^{k_d-1})$ of the SPM for a demand d consists of k_d disjoint parallel paths p_d^i that are explicitly established between two routers as depicted in Figure 1. The traffic is distributed over them according to a load balancing function l_d^f that indicates the traffic fraction that should be carried over each of them. If paths fail, the source node sees a pattern f_d of failed and working paths in the SPM for demand d and redistributes

[1] menth@informatik.uni-wuerzburg.de.

the traffic over the working paths according to another SPM-specific load balancing function l_d^f that depends on the observed failure pattern f_d. Thus, the SPM redistributes traffic only when one of its partial paths is affected by a network failure. To detect a failure pattern f_d, the source node must check whether each partial path within a SPM is working. This also includes partial paths that do not carry any traffic. They act as sensors in the network, give feedback about the network health, and can also trigger traffic shifts if they fail.

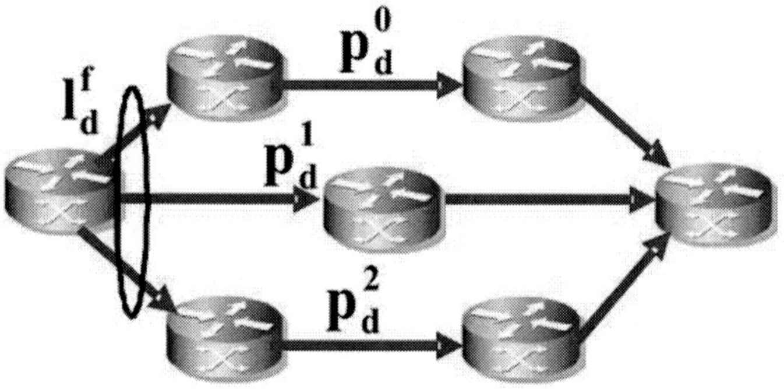

Figure 1. The SPM distributes the traffic of a demand $\boldsymbol{d}$ over $\boldsymbol{k_d}$ disjoint paths $P_d = (p_d^0, \ldots, p_d^{k_d-1})$ according to a load balancing function l_d^f which depends on the pattern f_d of failed and working paths.

When the traffic matrix and the link capacities are given for a network, the routing and the load balancing functions of the SPM can be configured in an optimized way so that link utilizations are low under normal conditions and in failure scenarios. This requires that the transmission capacity of the links can be shared by different paths. Similarly, joint capacity provisioning and SPM configuration can minimize the required backup capacity in networks where links still need to be provisioned with capacity. To quantify and compare “backup efficiency”, we use the maximum link utilization in capacitated networks and the required backup capacity normalized by the primary capacity in uncapacitated networks.

The SPM can be implemented by any connection-oriented communication technology that allows to establish disjoint partial paths. Backup efficiency can be realized only when transmission capacity can be shared among different paths. Multiprotocol Label Switching (MPLS) technology has theses features. Therefore, it is interesting to implement the SPM in MPLS. The disjoint paths can be set up as label switched paths (LSPs) between a pair of routers, and the head-end router distributes the traffic over these LSPs according to a load balancing function l_d^f As an alternative, the SPM may also be implemented in Carrier Ethernet technology.

1.1. Basic SPM

The basic SPM uses load balancing functions l_d^f that partition traffic rates arbitrarily. However, this cannot be easily achieved in practice. Packets of a single flow should be forwarded over the same interface to avoid out-of-order delivery at the destination. Therefore, simple packet-based round-robin mechanisms or extensions of them cannot be used. Instead, hash-based load balancing algorithms guarantee that packets of the same flow are forwarded over the same interface [2]. These algorithms achieve a desired split ratio only in the long run with possibly significant deviations at particular instances. Therefore, it is rather hard to realize a desired traffic distribution with sufficient accuracy on a short time scale.

1.2. Integer SPM (iSPM)

The integer SPM (iSPM) constrains the load balancing function l_d^f to values 0 and 1, i.e., the traffic between two routers is carried only over a single partial path. Hence, the load balancing function l_d^f becomes a path selection function. In contrast to the basic SPM, the iSPM does not need complex load balancing algorithms. Nevertheless, the iSPM has about the same backup efficiency as the basic SPM, especially in networks with a small or moderate node degree [3].

1.3. Failure-Specific SPM (fSPM)

The failure-specific SPM (fSPM) is another obvious extension of the basic SPM. Its source node uses a load balancing function that requires the knowledge of failed elements on the paths instead of the failure pattern f_d only. Thus, the source node requires a different load balancing function for every possible combination of link and node failures that affects the multipath structure of the SPM and relies on the fact that this information can be quickly provided to the source node under failure conditions. Hence, the fSPM is significantly more complex than the basic SPM or the iSPM. However, the fSPM can hardly increase the backup efficiency of the basic SPM [4].

2. Comparison with other Resilience Mechanisms

We compare the SPM with various other resilience mechanisms that are applicable in similar environments as the SPM or that have a similar structure [5].

2.1. Resilience Mechanisms for Similar Environments

The SPM is a resilience mechanism for packet-switched communication networks that allow capacity sharing among arbitrary flows on their links. We give a brief overview of some other mechanisms that are applicable for the same environment.

IP Routing and Rerouting

In intra-domain IP networks, routing follows the least-cost paths according to administrative link costs. They are the shortest paths with respect to this cost metric. The hop count metric sets all link costs to 1 and leads to the shortest paths in terms of hop count. In case of a failure, distributed routing algorithms find the next shortest paths and connectivity is restored after some time (in the order of seconds). Thus, restoration is used, i.e., backup paths are not established a priori but only when needed. The SPM is intended to react clearly faster (in the order of 100 ms), and its failover time depends mainly on the failure detection time.

Several least-cost paths possibly exist for a source and destination pair. Single shortest path (SSP) routing chooses just one of them for data forwarding while equal-cost multipath (ECMP) routing splits traffic equally over all interfaces that are part of a shortest path to the destination. Equal-cost paths are not necessarily disjoint, but may consist of partial paths that fork and join several times.

The path layout of IP routing can be controlled only indirectly by assigning appropriate link costs to links. Modifying the cost of a single link possibly changes layout of paths between several source and destination pairs. Given the topology, the link capacities, and the traffic matrix of a network, the link costs can be optimized so that the maximum utilization of all links in the network is minimized both under failure-free conditions [6] and for a limited set of failure scenarios [7; 8]. Optimization can also be performed using other objective functions besides the maximum link utilization [9].

End-to-End Protection Using Explicit Primary and Backup Paths

In connection-oriented networks, a disjoint backup path can protect the transmission of traffic on a primary path. This is called end-to-end protection. The disjoint primary and backup paths are established at the time of the connection setup. The source node detects whether the primary path fails and then switches the traffic from the primary to the backup path. This principle called protection switching requires that a failure on the primary path is detected and reported to the head-end node, and works quite fast. End-to-end protection is a wide-spread principle and is applied, e.g., in MPLS networks.

The SPM also implements end-to-end protection. However, its partial paths are not explicit primary and backup paths. They are rather equal since all of them can basically carry traffic in failure-free and in failure scenarios which is determined by the load balancing function. Moreover, the primary/backup path concept deviates traffic from the primary path to the backup path only when the primary path fails while the SPM may also redirect traffic when one of its paths fails that does not carry any traffic. The primary/backup path mechanism can be optimized by choosing an appropriate layout for the primary and backup paths. The SPM has additional degrees of freedom: the path layout for multiple paths and the load balancing functions for different failure patterns can be chosen. This makes the SPM more flexible than the mere primary/backup path concept.

MPLS Fast Reroute

MPLS fast reroute (MPLS-FRR) provides faster protection in MPLS networks than end-to-end protection [10]. FRR techniques in general achieve fast protection since nodes detecting a failure immediately switch traffic to backup paths instead of notifying the source node. This requires backup paths starting at every node along an LSP. Two options exist: facility backup [11] and one-to-one backup [12]. Facility backup installs local bypass LSPs around links and nodes to implement link and node protection. One-to-one backup is LSP-oriented and installs detour LSPs starting at every node of an LSP and ending at its tail-end router. To reduce the number of connection states in the routers, the detour LSPs can be merged at some merge point when they share the same downstream paths.

IP Fast Reroute

The end-to-end protection and MPLS-FRR techniques are based on the connection concept. Therefore, they are not applicable in connectionless IP networks. To achieve faster protection than IP restoration, IP fast reroute (IP-FRR) provides local backup paths [13]. If a next hop fails in an IP network, loop-free alternates (LFAs) [14; 15] deviate traffic to alternative neighbor nodes that can route the traffic to the destination without using the failed node. Such alternative nodes do not always exist and, thus, LFAs cannot achieve protection of all link or node failures. In the not-via mechanism [16], a special address is used to tunnel a packet that encounters a next-hop failure on its path and guides it to the next-next-hop where the packet is decapsulated. As a result, the backup path layout of not-via addresses is similar to the facility backup option for node protection in MPLS-FRR. More approaches exist [17; 18; 19], but they are currently not being standardized so that it is not likely to see them deployed in the near future.

Other Mechanisms

The authors of [20] propose a set of optimum primary and backup paths. Their assumption is that any node is informed about failed elements in the network and can activate failure-specific backup paths that do not need to be disjoint. This is quite complex since it requires fast dissemination of exact failure information through the network during outages and source nodes possibly need to switch traffic although none of its paths has failed. In contrast, the SPM switches its traffic to other partial paths only if its source node detects that at least one of its partial paths is broken. Segment protection [21] protects subpaths by backup paths and presents thereby a hybrid between link protection and end-to-end protection.

2.2. Resilience Mechanisms with Similar Structures

There are various other mechanisms for resilience and traffic engineering that take advantage of explicit multipath structures [5]. To avoid confusion with them, we present them and explain differences to the SPM.

Demand-Wise Shared Protection

Demand-wise shared protection (DSP) is a survivability concept initially proposed in [22] for optical networks. A demand is the entirety of flows between two nodes. Bandwidth for a specific demand is reserved on several paths in the network. It is dedicated to particular flows and part of it is reserved for backup purposes. If one of the paths fails, the flows are redirected over other paths belonging to the same demand. The backup bandwidth is shared only among the flows of the same demand. In contrast, the SPM takes advantage of capacity sharing among flows with different source or destination nodes.

Protection Cycles

Protection cycles (p-cycles) [23] have been originally proposed for ring-based optical networks where the transmission direction can be reconfigured within milliseconds. Thus, they are suitable for physical layer protection scheme, e.g., WDM or SONET networks, but they can also be adapted to be used in other technologies.

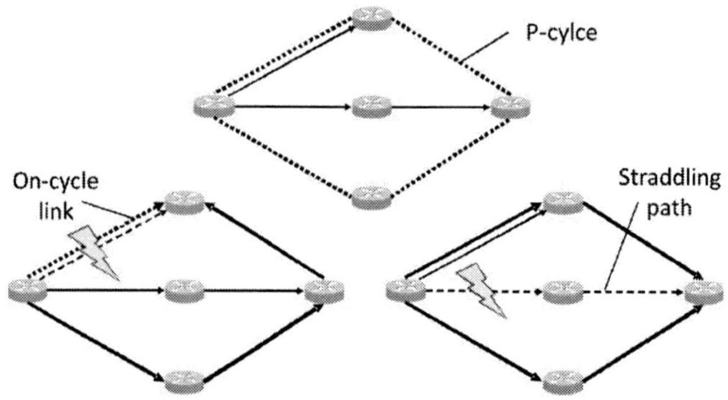

Figure 2. Protection by p-cycles for on-cycle links and straddling paths.

Figure 2 explains the idea of p-cycles. If an on-cycle link fails, protection is achieved by operating the cycle in the opposite direction. If a straddling link or path fails, its traffic can be rerouted over both parts of the cycle. Hence, p-cycles provide local protection. This requires fast signalling so that backup resources can be signalled on demand. Backup resources are not dedicated to specific connections in advance. Therefore, backup capacity sharing among different connections is possible. The p-cycles can be configured so that protection with only little backup capacity can be achieved. While p-cycles require cycle-oriented resource management, the SPM does not need to follow such rules.

TeXCP

TeXCP [24] is rather a dynamic traffic engineering mechanism than a protection mechanism. It distributes traffic over a multipath structure consisting of single paths between source and destination. A load balancing algorithm adjusts the traffic distribution over the paths according to feedback from probes sent along the paths. The objective of this method is to minimize the maximum link utilization in the network. The multipath structure consists of not necessarily disjoint paths and can be implemented, e.g., by MPLS. In contrast, the SPM has pre-configured load balancing functions and can redistribute traffic quickly in case of a failure.

3. Optimized Configuration of the SPM

The optimization of a resilience mechanism improves its configuration so that it works well for a limited set of protected failure scenarios $\mathcal{S}$, e.g. all single link and node failures. There are various optimization goals. For capacitated networks, the maximum utilization of all links in all protected failure scenarios $\mathcal{S}$ should be minimized for a given traffic matrix and link capacities. For network planning, when links are not yet provisioned, the overall link capacities required to carry the traffic under failure-free conditions and in all protected failure scenarios should be minimized. The overall link capacity is just one example and other objectives like installation costs can be of more interest.

The configuration of the SPM comprises both the path layout and the load balancing functions that depend on the pattern of failed and working paths. Their joint optimization is possible, but it is computationally not feasible for medium-size or large networks. Therefore, we present a linear program for the optimization of the load balancing functions which can be applied if the path layout of the SPM is already given. We first explain how an appropriate path layout can be obtained for an SPM, then formalize the structure of the SPM, and eventually explain how the load balancing functions for the basic SPM can be optimized for various objectives using linear programs. The section closes with some remarks about optimization of iSPM and fSPM.

3.1. Path Layout

The SPM consists of disjoint paths so that the remaining paths are still working if a single path fails due to the failure of a single network element. A very intuitive method to find link- or node-disjoint paths in a network is based on the shortest path algorithm. The disjoint paths are obtained iteratively: once a shortest path between a pair of nodes is found, its links and interior nodes are removed from the topology. When no additional path can be found, the algorithm stops. This simple approach cannot always find disjoint paths (see Figure 3) although a disjoint paths solution exist, or it may not always find the shortest disjoint paths (see Figure 4). Therefore, disjoint-shortest paths algorithms should be used. A good overview can be found in Bhandari's book [25]. The k-disjoint shortest paths algorithm finds up to k shortest paths if so many are available in the network. Setting k to a smaller value yields fewer disjoint shortest paths with possibly shorter path lengths.

3.2. Modelling Spms for Linear Programs

We formulate linear programs for the optimization of the load balancing functions. To that end, we present some general notation and conventions for the description of network concepts, failure scenarios, and load balancing functions.

Impact of the wrong selection of the first shortest path:

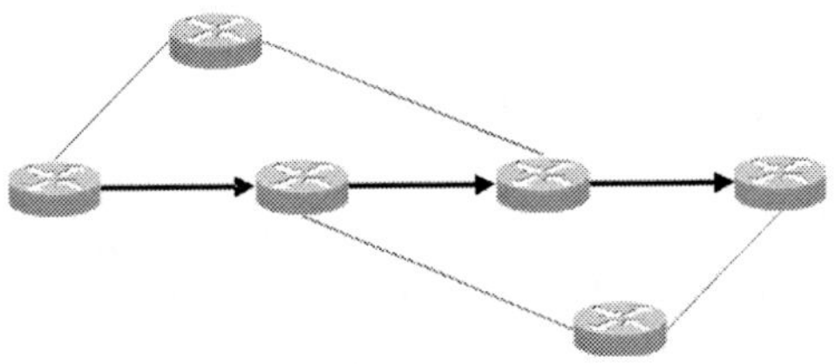

Figure 3. A disjoint path cannot be found.

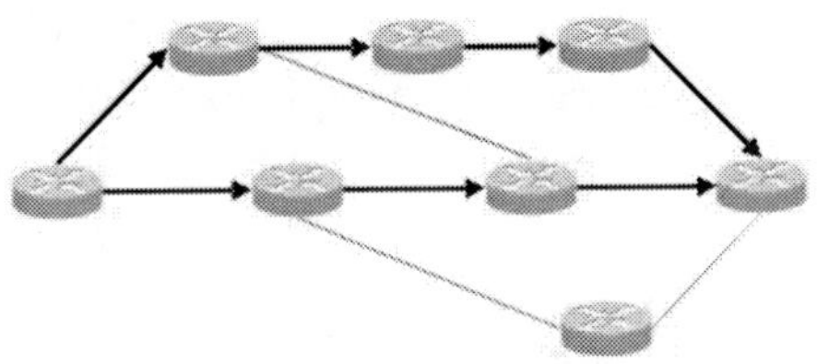

Figure 4. The length of the shortest disjoint paths is increased.

General Notation

Let $\mathbb{X}$ be a set of elements, then $\mathbb{X}^n$ is the set of all $\boldsymbol{n}$-dimensional vectors and $\mathbb{X}^{n\times m}$ is the set of all $n \times m$-matrices with components taken from $\mathbb{X}$. Vectors x $\in \mathbb{X}^n$ and matrices X $\in \mathbb{X}^{n\times m}$ are written bold and their components are written as

$$\mathrm{x} = \begin{pmatrix} x_0 \\ \vdots \\ x_{n-1} \end{pmatrix} \text{and} = \begin{pmatrix} x_{0,0} & \cdots & x_{0,m-1} \\ \vdots & \ddots & \vdots \\ x_{n-1,0} & \cdots & x_{n-1,m-1} \end{pmatrix}.$$

The scalar multiplication $c \cdot \mathbf{v}$ and the transpose operator T are defined as usual. The scalar product of two n-dimensional vectors u and $\mathbf{v}$ is written with the help of matrix multiplication $\boldsymbol{u}^{\mathsf{T}}\mathrm{v} = \sum_{i=o}^{n-1} u_i \cdot v_i$. Binary operators $\circ \in \{+, -, \cdot\}$ are applied componentwise, i.e. $\mathrm{u} \circ \mathrm{v} = (u_0 \circ v_0, \dots, u_{n-1} \circ v_{n-1})^{\mathsf{T}}$. The same holds for relational operators $\circ \in \{<, \leq, =, \geq, >\}$, i.e. u $\circ$ v is true if $\forall\, 0 \leq i < n{:}\, u_i \circ v_i$ holds. For simplicity reasons we define special vectors $\mathbf{0} = (0,\dots,0)^{\mathsf{T}}$ and $\mathbf{1} = (1,\dots,1)^{\mathsf{T}}$ with context-specific dimensions.

Network Concepts

A network $\mathcal{N} = (\mathcal{V}, \mathcal{E})$ consists of $n = |\mathcal{V}|$ nodes and $m = |\mathcal{E}|$ unidirectional links. The links are numbered $0 \leq i < m$ and represented as unit vectors $\mathrm{e}_\mathrm{i} \in \{0,1\}^m$, i.e., $(e_i)_j = 1$ if $i = j$, and $(e_i)_j = 0$ if $i \neq j$ with $0 \leq j < m$. We denote the traffic aggregate between routers $\mathrm{v_i} \in \mathcal{V}$ and $\mathrm{v_j} \in \mathcal{V}$ by the demand $d = (i, j)$ and the set of all demands by $\mathcal{D} = \{d = (i,j) : 0 \leq i,j < n \, and \, i \neq j\}$. The traffic rate associated with each demand $d \in \mathcal{D}$ is $c(d)$ and is given by the traffic matrix.

A single path p between two distinct nodes is a set of contiguous links represented by a link vector $\boldsymbol{p} \in \{0,1\}^m$. The path layout of an SPM for demand d is a multipath $\mathrm{P_d}$ that consists of k_d single paths $\mathrm{p_d^i}$ for $0 \leq i < k_d$. They are link- and possibly also node-disjoint except for their source and destination nodes. The multipath is represented by a vector of single paths $\mathrm{P_d} = (\mathrm{p_d^0}, \dots, \mathrm{p_d^{k_d-1}})$. Thus, a multipath is described by a matrix $\mathrm{P_d} \in \{0,1\}^{m\times k_d}$

Failure Scenarios

A failure scenario s is given by a set of failed links and nodes. The set of protected scenarios $\mathcal{S}$ contains all outage cases for which the SPM should protect the traffic from being lost and also the failure-free scenario $\emptyset$. The failure indication function $\phi(\mathrm{p}, \mathrm{s})$ yields 1 if a path p is affected by a failure scenario s; otherwise, it yields 0. The failure pattern of a multipath $\mathrm{P_d}$ is the vector $\mathrm{f_d(s)} = (\phi(\mathrm{p_d^0}, \mathrm{s}), \dots, \phi(\mathrm{p_d^{k_d-1}}, \mathrm{s}))^{\mathsf{T}}$ and indicates the failed single paths in failure scenario s. Thus, with a failure pattern of $\mathrm{f_d} = \mathbf{0}$, all paths are working while for $\mathrm{f_d} = \mathbf{1}$ connectivity cannot be maintained by the SPM.

Normally, all demands $d \in \mathcal{D}$ are active. If routers fail, some demands disappear which leads to a traffic reduction that is expressed by the failure scenario specific set of aggregates $\mathcal{D}_s$.

- No Traffic Reduction (NTR): We assume hypothetically that failed routers lose only their transport capability for transit flows but they are still able to generate or receive traffic. Therefore, we have $\mathcal{D}_s = \mathcal{D}$.

- Source Traffic Reduction (STR): If a certain router fails, all demands with this source node disappear.
- Full Traffic Reduction (FTR): We assume that demands with failed source or destination are stalled.

Load Balancing Functions

For each demand $d \in \mathcal{D}$ there is one SPM, and each SPM has a load balancing function to distribute the traffic of its demand d over its k_d disjoint paths. If certain paths fail, which is indicated by the failure pattern $f_d(s)$, the load balancing function shifts the traffic to the remaining working paths. Thus, the SPM needs a load balancing function l_d^f for each failure pattern $f_d \in \{0,1\}^{k_d}$. It should be optimized for all failure patterns $\mathcal{F}_d^{\mathcal{S}} = \{f_d(s): s \in \mathcal{S}\}$ that occur in the protected failure scenarios $s \in \mathcal{S}$. Since the load balancing function $l_d^f \in (\mathbb{R}_0^+)^{k_d}$ describes a distribution, it must obey

$$1^T l_d^f = 1 \tag{1}$$

Furthermore, failed paths must not be used, i.e.

$$f_d{}^T l_d^f = 0 \tag{2}$$

3.3. Optimization of Load Balancing Functions for Capacitated Networks

We present a linear program to optimize the load balancing functions for all SPMs in a network so that the maximum utilization ρ_{max} of all links in all protected failure scenarios $s \in \mathcal{S}$ is minimized [26]. The assumption is that all link capacities and the traffic matrix are given and that the path layout $P_d, d \in \mathcal{D}$ is also provided for all SPMs.

The bandwidths are denoted by a vector $b \in (\mathbb{R}_0^+)^m$ which carries a capacity value for each link. Similarly, the vector indicating the traffic rates on all links, which are induced by a specific SPM P_d, a load balancing function l_d^f, and a specific failure pattern $f \in \mathcal{F}_d^{\mathcal{S}}$, is calculated by $P_d \cdot l_d^f \cdot c(d)$.

In packet switched networks, resources are not physically bound to traffic aggregates. If traffic is rerouted due to an outage, the released resources can be immediately reused for the transport of other traffic. Under this assumption, the capacity constraints are

$$\forall s \in \mathcal{S}: \sum_{d \in \mathcal{D}_s} P_d \cdot l_d^{f_d(s)} \cdot c(d) \leq b \cdot \rho_{max} \tag{3}$$

and must be met for all protected failure scenario $s \in \mathcal{S}$. The scalar ρ_{max} is the value of the maximum link utilization and needs to be minimized. Thus, the objective function is

$$\rho_{max} \rightarrow \min . \tag{4}$$

The free variables to be set are $\mathrm{l}_\mathrm{d}^\mathrm{f} \in (\mathbb{R}_0^+)^{k_d}, d \in \mathcal{D}, \mathrm{f} \in \mathcal{F}_d^S$ and the maximum link utilization ρ_{max} itself. The following constraints must be respected in the optimization process to obtain valid load balancing functions and to avoid overload on the links.

- (C0): Equation (1) assures that the load balancing function is a distribution.
- (C1): Equation (2) assures that failed paths are not used.
- (C2): Equation (3) assures that the bandwidth suffices to carry the traffic in all protected failure scenarios.

These constraints constitute a linear program that can be efficiently solved for networks with up to about 100 nodes.

3.4. Joint Optimization of Load Balancing Functions and Link Capacities

We present a linear program for the joint optimization of the load balancing functions for all SPMs and the link capacities in a network. Its objective is to minimize the overall network capacity required to carry the traffic in all protected failure scenarios $s \in \mathcal{S}$ [27]. The assumption is that only the network topology and the traffic matrix are given and that links are not yet capacitated. Furthermore, the path layout $\mathrm{P}_\mathrm{d}, d \in \mathcal{D}$ is also provided for all SPMs. The link capacities b must be set in such a way that Equation [3] is met when setting the value for the maximum link utilization ρ_{max} to a fixed desired value. The objective function is the minimization of the overall bandwidth:

$$\mathbf{1}^\mathrm{T}\mathrm{b} \rightarrow \min . \tag{5}$$

Thus, the free variables to be set are $\mathrm{l}_\mathrm{d}^\mathrm{f} \in (\mathbb{R}_0^+)^{k_d}, d \in \mathcal{D}, \mathrm{f} \in \mathcal{F}_d^S$ and the link bandwidth vector b. Again, the constraints C0 – C2 must be met whereby ρ_{max} is set to a fixed desired value. Also this linear program can be efficiently solved for networks with up to about 100 nodes.

3.5. Optimization of the iSPM

The integer SPM (iSPM) is a special case of the basic SPM where the load balancing functions can take only the values 0 and 1 instead of any real values between 0 and 1. If the solution of the linear programs presented above is limited to integer solutions, they are significantly more complex to solve so that optimization using linear programs is not feasible for real-world problem instances. An efficient heuristic algorithm for the optimization of the load balancing functions in capacitated networks has been presented in [3]. Its evaluation has shown that networks with up to 200 nodes can be easily optimized and the backup efficiency of the iSPM is only little worse than the one of the basic SPM. Especially in networks with an average node degree up to 5 the backup efficiency of the iSPM optimized with this heuristic is at most 5% worse than the one of the basic SPM.

3.6. Optimization of the fSPM

The failure-specific SPM (fSPM) is an extension of the basic SPM. The difference between them is that the load balancing functions of the fSPM $\mathrm{l}_\mathrm{d}^\mathrm{s}$ depend on the exact failure scenario s on the affected partial paths instead of the failure pattern $\mathrm{f_d}$ observed by the source node of the basic SPM. The linear programs presented above can be easily adapted to optimize the load balancing functions of the fSPM. This has been done in [4]. Although the number of load balancing functions $\mathrm{l}_\mathrm{d}^\mathrm{s}, d \in \mathcal{D}, \mathrm{s} \in \mathcal{S}, \mathrm{f_d}(\boldsymbol{s}) \neq \mathbf{0}$ for the fSPM is much larger than the number of load balancing functions $\mathrm{l}_\mathrm{d}^\mathrm{f}, d \in \mathcal{D}, \mathrm{f} \in \mathcal{F}_d^{\mathcal{S}}$ for the basic SPM, its evaluation has shown that the computation time required for the solution of the linear program has increased only by little; it took only 16% longer than for the basic SPM in the investigated cases. However, the improvement in backup efficiency is negligible so that fSPM is not an interesting option for implementation in practice due to its increased operational complexity.

4. Performance Results

The SPM requires only very little backup capacity to protect single link and node failures [27]. In capacitated networks, significantly more protected traffic can be transmitted than with conventional single shortest path (SSP) routing [26]. This backup efficiency of the SPM depends on the underlying network structure. When networks are tightly provisioned for protected single failures $\mathcal{S}$, the minimized backup capacity might not suffice to accommodate backup traffic from unprotected multi-failure scenarios $s \notin \mathcal{S}$ [28]. However, this also holds for other routing and resilience mechanisms when the network is capacitated only for rerouted traffic resulting from a limited set of protected single failures $s \in \mathcal{S}$. These findings are illustrated in the following.

We apply the SPM to networks with different characteristics to investigate their backup efficiency. The networks under study are the COST239 which has been used in the COST239 project [29] and the Labnet network which has been used in the KING project [30]. Their topologies are depicted in Figure 5 and Figure 6. In the following studies, the COST239 network is associated with a traffic matrix proportional to the city cites [30] and the Labnet is accompanied with a homogeneous traffic matrix. The networks are assumed to have equal link capacities.

In addition, we study a large number of randomly constructed networks using the algorithm given in [30]. It allows to control the number of nodes n, the average node degree $\delta_{avg} = \frac{m}{n}$ where m is the number of unidirectional links, as well as the maximum deviation δ_{max}^{dev} of the node degree of a single node from the average node degree δ_{avg}. The construction algorithm is based on the Waxman model [31] so that close nodes are more likely to be connected than distant nodes. For these random networks we assume equal traffic matrices and equal link capacities.

In the remainder, the path layout of the SPMs is calculated using the k-disjoint-shortest-path algorithm [25] and at most $k = 5$ link- and node-disjoint paths between source and destination are tried to be found. Furthermore, the set of protected failure scenarios $\mathcal{S}$ comprises all single link and node failures. Hence, at most one partial path of an SPM fails.

The optimization methods assume the full traffic reduction (FTR) option when nodes fail (see Section 0).

Topologies of networks under study

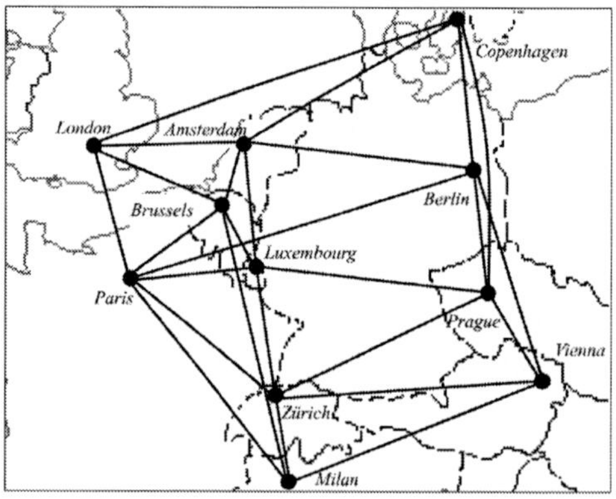

Figure 5. The COST239 network has 11 nodes and 52 links; it has a highly resilient structure due to the large average node degree $\boldsymbol{\delta_{avg}}$.

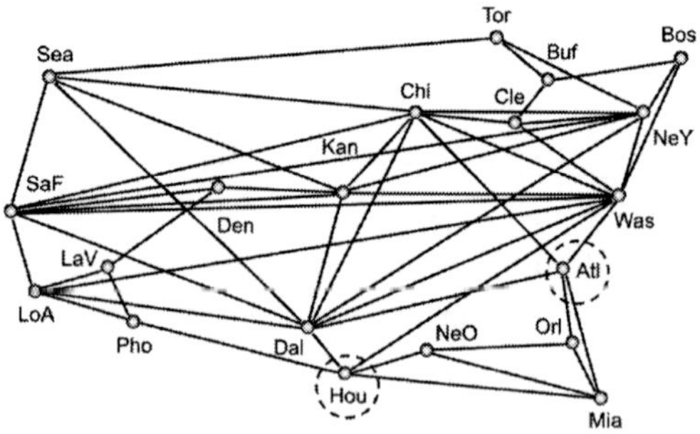

Figure 6. The Labnet has 20 nodes and 106 links; the simultaneous failure of Hou and Atl effects a separation of the network into two disconnected islands.

4.1. Impact of Network Structure on Backup Efficiency

We consider the overall capacity C_S^X that is required to carry the traffic matrix with resilience mechanism X under all protected failure scenarios S (failure-free conditions, single link and node failures). We compare this capacity to the minimum capacity $C_\emptyset^X$ that is required to carry the traffic matrix under failure-free conditions. We use single shortest path (SSP) routing based on the hop-count metric for comparison since this yields the smallest value for $C_\emptyset^{SSP}$. We calculate the relative required backup capacity for SSP routing and rerouting by $B_S^{SSP} = \frac{C_S^{SSP} - C_\emptyset^{SSP}}{C_\emptyset^{SSP}}$ and obtain a value of 78% for the COST239 network.

Furthermore, we calculate the path layout for all SPMs in the COST239 network using the k-shortest paths algorithm. We jointly optimize the load balancing functions and the link capacities according to the method described in Section 0 while setting $\rho_{max} = 1$. As a result, the overall capacity C_S^{SPM} to carry the traffic without loss under all single link and node failures is minimized. We compute the relative required backup capacity by $B_S^{SPM} = \frac{C_S^{SPM} - C_\emptyset^{SSP}}{C_\emptyset^{SSP}}$ and obtain a value of 23%for the COST239 network. This is extremely little backup capacity compared to SSP routing and rerouting and shows the very good backup efficiency of the SPM.

We investigate the relative required backup capacity for SSP and SPM depending on network characteristics using a large number of randomly constructed networks. We vary the network size n, the average node degree δ_{avg} , the maximum deviation δ_{dev}^{max} of the nodes from the average node degree, and construct 5 sample networks for each configuration. We average for these 5 sample networks the average number of disjoint paths per node pair and also the relative backup capacity. These data are compiled in Figure 7. They show that the SPM requires clearly less backup capacity than SSP. The relative backup capacity significantly depends on the average number of disjoint parallel paths in the network. In contrast, the number of nodes n and the maximum deviation from the average node degree δ_{dev}^{max} have a rather small impact.

We consider the optimization of load balancing functions for capacitated networks. We minimize the maximum link utilization δ_{max}^{SPM} for all single link and node failures for the basic SPM and calculate this value δ_{max}^{SSP} also for SSP routing and rerouting. We define $\gamma_{SSP}^{SPM} = \frac{\delta_{max}^{SSP}}{\delta_{max}^{SPM}} - 1$ as the protected capacity gain by SPM compared to SSP. Applied to the COST239 network, we get $\gamma_{SSP}^{SPM} = 1.09$. Thus, the SPM can carry more than twice the traffic that SSP can handle with protection. This again reveals an excellent backup efficiency for the SPM.

We extend this study to sample networks in analogy to above, and Figure 8 shows its results. The protected capacity gain is always positive and increases clearly with the average number of disjoint parallel paths in the network. In larger networks it also tends to be larger than in smaller networks. Under certain conditions, the SPM can carry 250% more protected traffic than SSP. This can be explained as follows. The probability for a mismatch between the capacity of a link and its carried traffic under SSP routing and rerouting increases with the network size. Therefore, the maximum link utilization ρ_{max}^{SSP} also increases. In contrast, the SPM steers traffic around bottleneck links and avoids large maximum link utilizations ρ_{max}^{SPM} which works well when the network has multiple disjoint paths.

Backup efficiency in random networks: basic SPM vs. single shortest path IP routing and rerouting.

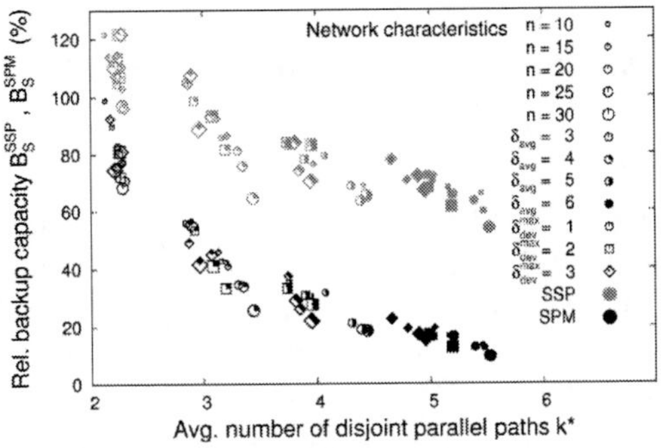

Figure 7. Relative backup capacity in uncapacitated networks.

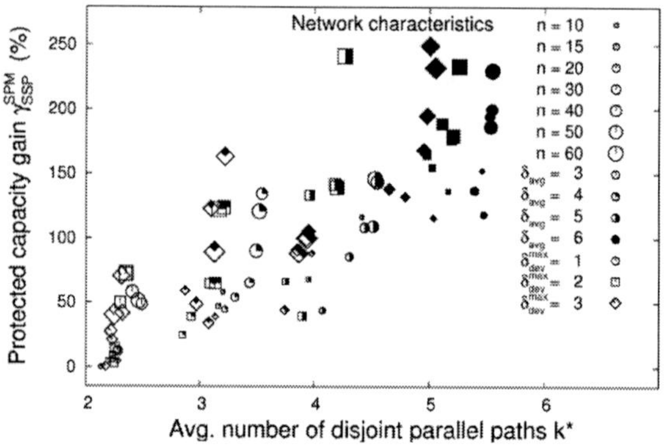

Figure 8. Protected capacity gain in networks with equal link capacities.

In [32] we have compared the backup efficiency of the SPM and the following other resilience mechanisms:

- SSP: single shortest path routing
- optSSP: optimized SSP using the heuristic in [8]
- ECMP: equal-cost multpath routing
- optECMP: optimized ECMP using the heuristic in [8]
- PB: disjoint primary and backup path routing (obtained through simple 2-disjoint shortest paths calculation)
- optPB: optimized primary and backup path routing (obtained as a special case of the iSPM with only two partial paths per multipath)
- Bypass: standard MPLS-FRR facility backup
- impBypass: MPLS-FRR facility backup with the simple improvement presented in [11]
- Detour: standard MPLS-FRR one-to-one backup
- impDetour:MPLS-FRR one-to-one backup with the simple improvement presented in [12]

The SPM is clearly superior to all other resilience mechanisms with regard to backup efficiency. While optSSP, ECMP, optECMP, PB, optPB were more backup-efficient than SSP, impDetour, Detour, impBypass, and especially Bypass turned out to be less backup-efficient than SSP.

4.2. Traffic Loss Due to Unprotected Multi-Failures

The SPM requires only little backup capacity to protect single link failures. If only little backup capacity is provided, some traffic is possibly lost in case of unprotected multi-failures when there is insufficient backup capacity. This issue has been investigated in [28] and compared with SSP and ECMP routing and rerouting. The Labnet in Figure 6 was used for the analysis in [28] together with a homogeneous traffic matrix to facilitate the evaluation. Single link failures cannot partition the Labnet in two parts, but the simultaneous failures of nodes Hou and Atl effect a separation of the network into two disconnected islands.

The SPM has optimized load balancing functions for single path failures. If two paths fail, some interpolation between suitable load balancing functions should quickly yield a valid load balancing function for that case. If the SPM has only two disjoint paths, the failure of an element in each of these paths disconnects the corresponding traffic aggregate. In such a situation, the connectivity is lost until the failure is repaired (SPM-INTR), or it is restored by changing the transport paradigm for this specific aggregate from the connection-oriented SPM to connectionless SSP or ECMP forwarding (SPM-SSP, SPM-ECMP).

Traffic loss can be due to overload because of rerouted flows and missing backup capacity (A); it can be due to node failures so that demands starting and ending in the failed nodes are lost (B); it can also be due to unavailable paths when a network is disconnected by failures (C). Sufficient backup capacity can minimize only the lost traffic due to (A). Link failures are more likely than router failures. Similarly, double link failures ($\mathcal{S}_{LL}$), link and router failures ($\mathcal{S}_{LR}$), and double router failures ($\mathcal{S}_{RR}$) have different probabilities and also different impact. Averaging over all of them obscures the impact of the different failure classes, therefore, they are analyzed and reported separately.

Failure set	SSP	ECMP	SMP-INTR	SPM-SSP	SPM-ECMP
$\mathcal{S}_{LL}$	0.436	0.315	2.089	2.059	2.021
$\mathcal{S}_{LR}$	10.890	10.807	12.966	13.018	12.968
$\mathcal{S}_{RR}$	21.035	20.965	23.321	23.426	23.356
$\mathcal{S}_{all}$	0.508	0.388	2.164	2.134	2.096

Figure 9. Lost traffic due to double failures in %.

Double link failures can cause traffic loss only due to (A). Figure 9 shows that double link failures lead to an average traffic loss of 0.436% and 0.315% for SSP and ECMP routing in the Labnet network when it was capacitated very tightly for single link and node failures only. The SPM leads to significantly more traffic loss in the order of 2% whereby the exact SPM variant has only little impact on the lost traffic. Link and router failures lead to lost traffic due to (A) and (B). They lead to 10% lost traffic due to (B). The remaining lost traffic is due to (A) which is caused by missing backup capacity. This is about 0.85% for SSP and ECMP while it is about 3% for the SPM. Double router failures lead to lost traffic due to (A), (B). About 19.47% lost traffic is due to (B). One out of 190 possible double router failures leads even to lost traffic due to (C) so that additional 11.84% traffic is lost in that particular case. Averaged over all double failures, this increases the lost traffic only by 0.06% and has quite little impact. Hence, SSP and ECMP lose about 1.5% traffic due to missing capacity (A) while the SPM variants lose about 3.9% traffic due to missing capacity (A). When the results for the different double failure scenarios are weighted by their probabilities, SSP and ECMP lead to 0.5% and 0.39% lost traffic while the SPM mechanisms lead to about 2.1% lost traffic. Hence, the SPM leads to clearly more average traffic loss than SSP or ECMP routing and rerouting in case of double failures due to the minimized backup capacity. However, the traffic loss is not tremendously higher. These numbers were obtained from a rigid analysis assuming that capacity is provided very tightly. This is of course not realistic.

Sets of protected failures	SSP	ECMO	SPM-INTR	SPM-SSP	SPM-ECMP
S_L, S_R	93%	77%	48%	48%	48%
S_L, S_R, S_{LL}	183%	143%	103%	119%	115%
$S_L, S_R, S_{LL}, S_{LR}, S_{RR}$	238%	207%	117%	172%	168%

Figure 10. Required network resources in capacity units and relative required backup capacity in percent for the resilience against different protected failure scenarios $\boldsymbol{S}$.

Although the average lost traffic due to missing capacity in case of double failures is rather small, providing enough capacity to avoid missing backup capacity for all double failures is quite expensive. Figure 10 shows how much relative backup capacity is required for the same mechanisms as above to avoid traffic loss due to missing capacity for different sets of protected failure scenarios. Thereby, the SPM remains optimized for single failures and the backup capacity required for double failures is calculated for the different strategies (SPM-INTR, SPM-SSP, SPM-ECMP). The figure shows that the protection against double failures requires significantly more backup capacity than for single failures. The capacity savings of the SPM compared to SSP and ECMP remain and even increase. In contrast to protection against single failures, the different SPM strategies (SPM-INTR, SPM-SSP, SPM-ECMP) require different backup capacity values when double failures are protected.

Conclusion

The SPM is a simple protection switching mechanism for connection-oriented, packet-switched networks. Therefore, it may be applied, e.g., in MPLS or Carrier Ethernet networks. The SPM sets up several disjoint paths and transmits traffic over them according to a load balancing function that depends on the set of failed paths. Optimization of the load balancing functions can minimize the required backup capacity dramatically or maximize the protected capacity in capacitated networks. Hence, the SPM is simple and provides fast fail-over at low cost. It is a compelling protection switching mechanism for future transport networks.

Acknowledgment

The author would like to thank Ulrich Spoerlein for his valuable inputs in preparing the manuscript as well as David Hock and Matthias Hartmann for proof-reading.

References

[1] 1. M. Menth, A. Reifert, J. Milbrandt, Self-Protecting Multipaths - A Simple and Resource-Efficient Protection Switching Mechanism for MPLS Networks. In: 3rd *IFIP-TC6 Networking Conference (Networking)*, Athens, Greece (May 2004) 526-537.

[2] 2. R. Martin, M. Menth, M. Hemmkeppler, Accuracy and Dynamics of Hash-Based Load Balancing Algorithms for Multipath Internet Routing. In: *IEEE International Conference on Broadband Communication, Networks, and Systems (BROADNETS)*, San Jose, CA, USA (October 2006).

[3] 3. R. Martin, M. Menth, U. Spoerlein, Integer SPM: Intelligent Path Selection for Resilient Networks. In: *IFIP-TC6 Networking Conference (Networking)*, Atlanta, GA, USA (May 2007).

[4] 4. M. Menth, R. Martin, U. Spoerlein, Failure-Specific Self-ProtectingMultipaths – Increased Capacity Savings or Overengineering? In: *International Workshop on Design of Reliable Communication Networks (DRCN)*, La Rochelle, France (October 2007).

[5] 5. M. Menth, R. Martin, A.M.C.A. Koster, S. Orlowski, Overview of Resilience Mechanisms Based on Multipath Structures. In: I*nternational Workshop on Design of Reliable Communication Networks (DRCN)*, La Rochelle, France (October 2007).

[6] 6. B. Fortz, M. Thorup, Internet Traffic Engineering by Optimizing OSPF Weights. In: *IEEE Infocom*, Tel-Aviv, Israel (2000) 519–528.

[7] 7. B. Fortz, M. Thorup, Robust Optimization of OSPF/IS-IS Weights. In: *International Network Optimization Conference (INOC)*, Paris, France (October 2003) 225–230.

[8] 8. M. Menth, M. Hartmann, R. Martin, Robust IP Link Costs for Multilayer Resilience. In: *IFIP-TC6 Networking Conference (Networking)*, Atlanta, GA, USA (May 2007).

[9] 9.M. Hartmann, D. Hock, C. Schwartz, M. Menth, Objective Functions for Optimization for Resilient and Non-Resilient IP Routing. In: 7th *International Workshop on Design of Reliable Communication Networks (DRCN)*, Washington, D.C., USA (October 2009).

[10] 10. P. Pan, G. Swallow, A. Atlas, RFC4090: Fast Reroute Extensions to RSVP-TE for LSP Tunnels (May 2005).

[11] 11. R. Martin, M. Menth, K. Canbolat, Capacity Requirements for the Facility Backup Option in MPLS Fast Reroute. In: I*EEE Workshop on High Performance Switching and Routing (HPSR)*, Poznan, Poland (June 2006) 329 – 338.

[12] 12. R. Martin, M. Menth, K. Canbolat, Capacity Requirements for the One-to-One Backup Option in MPLS Fast Reroute. In: *IEEE International Conference on Broadband Communication, Networks, and Systems (BROADNETS)*, San Jose, CA, USA (October 2006).

[13] 13. S. Rai, B. Mukherjee, O. Deshpande, IP Resilience within an Autonomous System: Current Approaches, Challenges, and Future Directions. *IEEE Communications Magazine* 43(10) (October 2005) 142–149.

[14] 14. A. Atlas, A. Zinin, RFC5286: Basic Specification for IP Fast Reroute: Loop-Free Alternates (September 2008).

[15] 15. R. Martin, M. Menth, M. Hartmann, T. Cicic, A. Kvalbein, Loop-Free Alternates and Not-Via Addresses: A Proper Combination for IP Fast Reroute? accepted for Computer Networks (2009).

[16] 16. S. Bryant, S. Previdi, M. Shand, IP Fast Reroute Using Not-via Addresses. http://tools.ietf.org/id/draft-ietf-rtgwg-ipfrr-notvia-addresses-04.txt (July 2009).

[17] 17. S. Nelakuditi, S. Lee, Y. Yu, Z.L. Zhang, C.N. Chuah, Fast Local Rerouting for Handling Transient Link Failures. *IEEE/ACM Transactions on Networking* 15(2) (April 2007) 359–372.

[18] 18. M. Menth, R. Martin, Network Resilience through Multi-Topology Routing. In: 5th *International Workshop on Design of Reliable Communication Networks (DRCN),* Island of Ischia (Naples), Italy (October 2005) 271 – 277.

[19] 19. T. Cicic, A.F. Hansen, A. Kvalbein, M. Hartmann, R. Martin, M. Menth, Relaxed Multiple Routing Configurations for IP Fast Reroute. In: *IEEE Network Operations and Management Symposium (NOMS)*, Salvador de Bahia, Brazil (April 2008).

[20] 20. K. Murakami, H.S. Kim, Optimal Capacity and Flow Assignment for Self–Healing ATM Networks Based on Line and End-to-End Restoration. *IEEE/ACM Transactions on Networking* 6(2) (April 1998) 207–221.

[21] 21. C.S. Ou, S. Rai, B. Mukherjee, Extension of Segment Protection for Bandwidth Efficiency and Differentiated Quality of Protection in Optical/MPLS Networks. Optical Switching and Networking: *A Computer Networks Journal 1*(1) (January 2005) 19 – 33.

[22] 22. A.M.C.A. Koster, A. Zymolka, M. Jäger, R. Hülsermann, Demand-Wise Shared Protection for Meshed Optical Networks. *Journal of Network and Systems Management* 13(1) (2005) 35-55.

[23] 23. W.D. Grover, D. Stamatelakis, Cycle-Oriented Distributed Preconfiguration: Ring-Like Speed with Mesh-Like Capacity for Self-Planning Network Restoration. In: *IEEE International Conference on Communications (ICC).* (Jun 1998) 537–543.

[24] 24. S. Kandula, D. Katabi, B. Davie, A. Charny, Walking the Tightrope: Responsive Yet Stable Traffic Engineering. In: *ACM SIGCOMM*, Philadelphia, PA, USA (August 2005).

[25] 25. R. Bhandari, Survivable Networks: Algorithms for Diverse Routing. Kluwer Academic Publishers, Norwell, MA, USA (1999).

[26] 26. M. Menth, R. Martin, U. Spoerlein, Optimization of the Self-Protecting Multipath for Deployment in Legacy Networks. In: *IEEE International Conference on Communications (ICC)*, Glasgow, Scotland, UK (June 2007).

[27] 27. M. Menth, R. Martin, U. Spoerlein, Network Dimensioning for the Self-Protecting Multipath: A Performance Study. In: *IEEE International Conference on Communications (ICC)*, Istanbul, Turkey (June 2006).

[28] 28. M. Menth, R. Martin, U. Spoerlein, Impact of Unprotected Multi-Failures in Resilient SPM Networks: a Capacity Dimensioning Approach. In: *IEEE Globecom*, San Francisco, California, USA (November 2006).

[29] 29. P. Batchelor, B. Daino, P. Heinzmann, D. Hjelme, R. Inkret, H. Jäger, M. Joindot, A. Kuchar, E. Le Coquil, P. Leuthold, G. de Marchis, F. Matera, B. Mikac, H.P. Nolting, J. Späth, F. Tillerot, B. Van Caenegem, N. Wauters, C. Weinert, Study on the Implementation of Optical Transparent Transport Networks in the European Environment - Results of the Research Project COST 239. *Photonic Network Communications* 2(1) (2000) 15–32.

[30] 30. M. Menth, Efficient Admission Control and Routing in Resilient Communication Networks. PhD thesis, University of Würzburg, Faculty of Computer Science (July 2004).

[31] 31. B.M. Waxman, Routing of Multipoint Connections. *IEEE Journal on Selected Areas in Communications* 6(9) (1988) 1617–1622.

[32] 32. M. Menth, R. Martin, M. Hartmann, U. Spoerlein, Efficiency of Routing and Resilience Mechanisms in Packet-Switched Communication Networks. accepted for European Transactions on Telecommunications (ETT) (2009).
[33] 33. R. Martin, M. Menth, U. Spoerlein, Integer SPM: Intelligent Path Selection for Resilient . Networks. In: *IFIP-TC6 Networking Conference (Networking)*, Atlanta, GA, USA (May 2007).

In: Recent Advances in Providing QoS and Reliability... ISBN 978-1-61761-858-1
Editors: N. Wang, G. Pavlou and M. Boucadair

Chapter 11

RELIABILITY ANALYSIS OF PROTECTION METHODS FOR THE FUTURE INTERNET BACKBONE

Piotr Cholda and Andrzej Jajszczyk
AGH University of Science and Technology, Krakow, Poland

ABSTRACT

This chapter presents the use of reliability modeling to predict some values that describe the operation of selected recovery (in this case, protection) methods in the future backbone, concentrating on optical networks. Fundamentals of reliability modeling are presented, along with the metrics that can be used and methods to obtain them. Then, examples of models are given, including: no recovery, dedicated protection, shared APS protection, ring protections, and protection based on p-cycles. This chapter is appended with a few problems to individual solving for an interested reader.

1. INTRODUCTION: PRIMER ON RELIABILITY MODELING

In this section the basic reliability measures used in the communication network context are presented. Then, simple reliability assessment methods are given. Generally, we do not focus here very much on the reliability terminology. It is assumed that such terms as *normal state*, *failure* or *fault* are intuitively understandable. The basic definitions and concepts related to the reliability field with the application to communication and computer sciences can be found, for example, in [1].

1.1. Reliability Measures

The most basic and frequently used measure to describe the recovery performance of communication networks is the *reliability function*. According to ITU-T E.800 Recommendation [1] the reliability is defined as 'the probability that an item can perform a required function under stated conditions for a given time interval'. More precisely in the mathematical sense, $R(t)$ is the probability that no failure happens in interval $[0, t)$. If T is defined as an operating (up) time:

$$R(t) \equiv \Pr\{T > t\}$$

$R(t)$ is a function of time t with the following properties [2]:

$$\begin{cases} R(0) = 1 \\ \bigwedge_{0 \le t_1 \le t_2} R(t_1) \ge R(t_2) \\ \lim_{t \to \infty} R(t) = 0 \end{cases}$$

Then, we can define the failure cumulative distribution function (CDF; lifetime distribution) $F(t)$ as the probability that one or more failures happen in interval $[0, t]$:

$$F(t) \equiv \Pr\{T \le t\} = 1 - R(t)$$

Then, the failure (lifetime) probability density function can be defined as follows:

$$f(t) = \frac{dF(t)}{dt} \leftrightarrow F(t) = \int_0^t f(t)\, dt$$

(*Instantaneous*) *Failure rate* $\lambda(t)$ is determined as [1]: 'the limit, if this exists, of the ratio of the conditional probability that the time to failure T of an item falls within a given time interval $(t, t + \Delta t)$ to the length of this interval Δt when Δt tends to zero, given that the item is in a state to perform a required function at the beginning of the time interval.' This measure can also be identified with the hazard rate and is, in general, expressed as follows:

$$\lambda(t) = \lim_{\Delta t \to 0} \frac{\frac{\Pr\{t \le T \le t + \Delta t\}}{\Pr\{T > t\}}}{\Delta t} = \lim_{\Delta t \to 0} \frac{F(t + \Delta t) - F(t)}{\Delta t \times R(t)} = \frac{\frac{dF(t)}{dt}}{R(t)} = \frac{\frac{d[1 - R(t)]}{dt}}{R(t)}$$
$$= -\frac{dR(t)}{dt} \times \frac{1}{R(t)} = -\frac{d[\ln R(t)]}{dt}$$

It appeared to be a quite simple differential equation which, after solving, gives the following result:

$$R(t) = e^{-\int_0^t \lambda(t) dt}$$

We can note that if $f(t)$ has an exponential distribution, i.e., when:

$$f(t) = \lambda e^{-\lambda t}$$

the reliability function equals:

$$R(t) = e^{-\lambda t}$$

This means that in such a case the failure rate is constant and equal to λ. The assumption of the exponential, i.e., the memory-less continuous distribution, is often proper for hardware in its typical operation period (so-called 'useful life time' [3]). It is also proper in the case of cable failures, i.e., the memory-less assumption is met. When $f(t)$ has an exponential distribution, calculations of reliability related parameters are considerably simplified. Moreover, homogeneous Markov models can be applied.

MTTF (*Mean Time to Failure*) is the expectation of the duration of the operating time of an item. It is calculated from the instant of time when it goes from a down state to an up state (after a corrective maintenance action) until the next failure occurrence [1]. Therefore, it is the mean value of function $f(t)$:

$$MTTF = E[T] = \int_0^\infty tf(t)dt = \int_0^\infty tdF(t) = -\int_0^\infty tdR(t) = -\int_0^\infty t\frac{dR(t)}{dt}dt = \int_0^\infty R(t)dt - tR(t)|_0^\infty$$
$$= \int_0^\infty R(t)dt$$

This result is possible to obtain since $R(t)$ approaches zero faster than t approaches ∞ [3]. If failure function $f(t)$ is modeled as the exponential distribution, then:

$$MTTF = \frac{1}{\lambda}$$

Repair time is often assessed as *Mean Time to Repair* (*Recovery, Restoration*) *MTTR*, i.e, in the expected value of such a distribution. *MTTR* is calculated in an analogous way as *MTTF*, i.e., on the basis of a hazard function. In this case it is a (*instantaneous*) *repair rate* $\mu(t)$. This is a parameter analogously defined to the failure rate. It happens quite frequently that an assumption is made that the repair time distribution has an exponential character. If it is true, the repair rate will be a constant and:

$$MTTR = \frac{1}{\mu}$$

Although this assumption is doubtful, it is usually held, because it considerably simplifies calculations and does not have a very large influence on the accuracy of the obtained assessments, especially if:

$$MTTF \gg MTTR \gg 0$$

Although the reliability function is the one most often used in the theoretical analysis, there is one measure which is commonly used for practical purposes in the communication recovery field. It is the *availability* metric. ITU-T Rec. E.800 [1] defines so-called *instantaneous availability* $A(t)$ as 'the probability that an item is in an up state at a given instant of time t.' On this basis more useful measures are defined:

- *Mean availability* $\overline{A(t_1, t_2)}$: the normalized integral of the instantaneous availability in a given time interval (t_1, t_2):

$$\overline{A(t_1, t_2)} = \frac{1}{t_2 - t_1} \int_{t_1}^{t_2} A(t)dt$$

- *(Asymptotic/Steady-state) Availability: the limit, if this exists, of the instantaneous availability when the time tends to infinity:*

$$A = \lim_{t \to \infty} A(t)$$

- *(Asymptotic) Unavailability: the parameter which is a probabilistic complement of the availability:*

$$U = 1 - A$$

We are mostly interested in the (steady-state) availability which can also be intuitively understood as [4]: 'the probability of finding the item (system, network, connection, etc.) in an operating state at any time we want its service.'

If *MUT* represents the *Mean Up Time* (the time interval during which an item is in an up state, i.e., a state of an item characterized by the fact that it can perform a required function, assuming that the external resources, if required, are provided [1]) and *MDT* represents the *Mean Down Time*:

$$A = \frac{MUT}{MUT + MDT}$$

If exponential times both for failure and repair times are assumed, we have:

$$\begin{cases} MUT = MTTF \\ MDT = MTTR \end{cases}$$

Thus:

$$A = \frac{MTTF}{MTTF + MTTR}$$

1.2. Reliability of Complex Structures

Here we present also some reliability models, i.e., the models used to predict the reliability measures of communications networks [1].

When we calculate reliability-related metrics we have two basic options for which they will be calculated:

- the two-terminal reliability/availability, etc.;
- the all-terminal reliability/availability, etc.

The above terms are related to the network context. If a network consists of N nodes, the all-terminal reliability/availability is defined as the probability that all N nodes are connected, whereas the two-terminal reliability/availability is calculated for selected source node s and termination (sink) node t, and equals the probability that these nodes are connected (therefore, it is also called s-t reliability). Nodes are connected if there is an operational path between them on which traffic can be transported.

According to [1] a *reliability block diagram* (RBD) is defined as a 'block diagram showing, for one or more functional modes of a complex item, how faults of the subitems represented by the blocks, or combinations thereof, result in a fault of the item.' When we assume that faults and repairs (generally, the behavior from the reliability viewpoint) of these sub-element blocks are statistically independent, what is usually the case, we can often easily calculate the overall reliability or availability. The relations between diagram blocks can be different. Those related to series, parallel and k-out-of-n structure are relatively simple to analyze. The methods to find the appropriate values are presented below.

A series reliability system is one in which all n components are so interrelated that the entire system will fail if any one of its components fails [3]. If the reliability function of component i equals $R_i(t)$, the reliability function for a series system is equal to:

$$R_s(t) = \prod_{i=1}^{n} R_i(t)$$

And consequently, for availabilities/unavailabilities we have:

$$A_s = \prod_{i=1}^{n} A_i = \prod_{i=1}^{n} (1 - U_i)$$

A serial structure is shown in Figure 1.

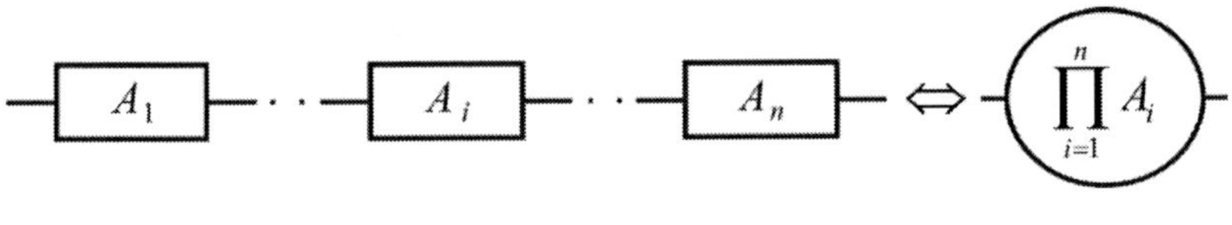

Figure 1. Series reliability structure.

If unavailability values are not high $U \ll 1$ (typically, $U \ll 10^{-3}$), what is usually the case in the telecommunications field, a useful simplification can be used [4]:

$$A_s = \prod_{i=1}^{n} (1 - U_i) \approx 1 - \sum_{i=1}^{n} U_i \leftrightarrow U_s \approx \sum_{i=1}^{n} U_i$$

If we assume that the lifetime of component i is exponentially distributed with parameter λ_i we can calculate the failure rate of a series system as follows:

$$R_s(t) = \prod_{i=1}^{n} R_i(t) = \prod_{i=1}^{n} e^{\lambda_i t}{}_i = e^{-t\sum_{i=1}^{n}\lambda_i}$$

We can see that the lifetime of such a structure will be also exponentially distributed with failure rate:

$$\lambda_s = \sum_{i=1}^{n} \lambda_i$$

Consequently, *Mean Time to Failure* of this structure will be:

$$MTTF_s = \frac{1}{\sum_{i=1}^{n}\lambda_i} = \frac{1}{\sum_{i=1}^{n}\frac{1}{MTTF_i}} = \frac{\prod_{i=1}^{n} MTTF_i}{\sum_{i=1}^{n}\prod_{j\neq i} MTTF_j}$$

On the other hand, a parallel reliability system is one that will fail only if all of its components fail [3]. The reliability function for a parallel reliability structure is equal to:

$$R_p(t) = 1 - \prod_{i=1}^{n}[1 - R_i(t)]$$

On this basis, the availability for the parallel structure can be assessed:

$$A_p = 1 - \prod_{i=1}^{n}(1 - A_i) = 1 - \prod_{i=1}^{n} U_i \leftrightarrow U_p = \prod_{i=1}^{n} U_i$$

A parallel structure is shown in Figure 2.

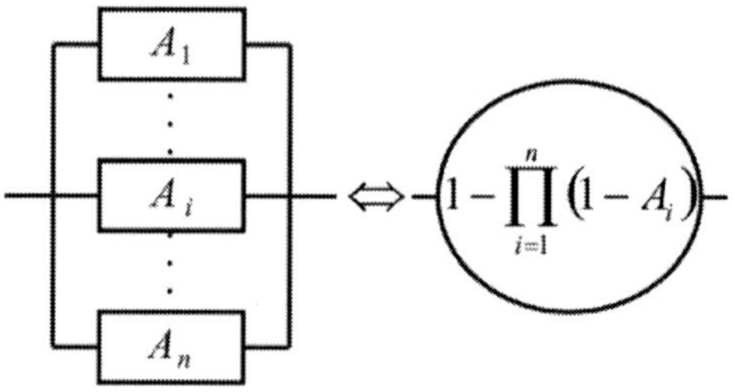

Figure 2. Parallel reliability structure.

In the case of a series system, *MTTF* was calculated with the assumption that the failure PDF is of an exponential character. This task is more complex in the case of a parallel structure. If all components of such a structure have the same failure rate λ, we can calculate *MTTF* for the whole structure. The details are omitted here. They can be found in [3]. We can calculate *Mean Time to Failure* of a parallel structure as follows:

$$MTTF_p = \frac{\sum_{i=1}^{n} \frac{1}{i}}{\lambda} = MTTF \sum_{i=1}^{n} \frac{1}{i}$$

k-out-of-*n* system, where $k \le n$, is a system consisting of *n* components which requires that at least *k* components are operating to ensure that the whole system is up. In the general case, the reliability of such a system is quite complex. We can simplify the calculations significantly if the reliability functions of all components are identical and equal to $R(t)$. Then, the system can be modeled by the usage of the binomial distribution:

$$R_{k|n}(t) = \sum_{r=k}^{n} R_i^r(t)[1 - R_i(t)]^{n-r}$$

We can note that if $k = n$, the system reduces to the series system and while $k = 1$, the system reduces to the parallel system. *MTTF* of the *k*-out-of-*n* reliability structure is also difficult to calculate. Nonetheless, if all component lifetimes are exponentially distributed with the same failure rate λ, we obtain that [3]:

$$MTTF_{k|n} = \frac{\sum_{i=k}^{n} \frac{1}{i}}{\lambda} = MTTF \sum_{i=k}^{n} \frac{1}{i}$$

Some systems can be characterized by RBDs which are not simple series or parallel ones, but can be reduced to them (series-parallel systems). The methodology is related to the iterative reductions of series/parallel parts to one single block with the substitute reliability/(un)availability calculated according to the given part.

There are also structures which can be properly described by RBDs but cannot be solved by using the ‘reduction methodology’ because they do not form series-parallel structures (bridges, stars) or they contain the same block more than once. In such a case, more complex and effort requiring methods must be used. The so-called enumeration method is most universal, in fact. It consists in enumerating all possible combinations of the up/down state of the components and summing up the probability of all states which are related to the probabilistic event in which a connection among all *k* nodes of the node set exists. In telecommunications practice, it consists in enumerating all groups of similar events where at least one of the possible connections among nodes is up. As all combinations are mutually exclusive events, we can add their probabilities to obtain the probability that a path between both nodes exists (i.e, the reliability or availability of the connection). The method is effective if it is simple to enumerate all events fostering the up state of the connection. The all/two-terminal reliability of protection ring and *p*-cycles is calculated below according to the method.

Models presented so far are called combinatorial models, as they present the reliability-related situation only as a combination of different conditions related to an operating or faulty state, but do not take into account time relations, e.g., order of faults and repairs of some elements. Such relations are covered by more complex models, known as state space models. The simplest group of methods is known as Markov models. *Markov chain* can be defined as a stochastic process whose dynamic behavior is such that probability distributions for its future development depend only on the present state and not on how the process arrived in that state [3]. Additionally, the state space is countable. Here, only simple Markov chain models are used, namely the subclass of continuous time Markov chains (CTMC). They are related to the Poisson distribution of the number of event occurence in a time unit, e.g., a failure or a repair (thus, failure or repair time has an exponential distribution). These are so-called *homogeneous* Markov chains in which transition rates are not dependent on time. In these models, the probability of a transition from one state to another in a very short period of time Δt is given by $z\times\Delta t$ where z is the transition rate. Here z is identical with the failure or repair rate (e.g., λ for failures). Moreover, the probabilities of more than one transition in time Δt are infinitesimally small.

As defined in [1], the *state transitions diagram* is 'a diagram showing the set of possible states of an item and the possible one step transitions between these states.' Such diagrams are commonly used for visualization of the modeling with the help of a Markov chain and will be used in further sections. In such a diagram, the considered states are connected by arrows with the determined values of transition rates. There are two types of Markov models interesting for us: the reliability and availability ones. The reliability model for a single backup system (a working element and a backup element) is shown in Figure 3. There are three states: s_0 is related to the situation where both elements are working property, s_1 is related to the situation where one element is faulty, but another is working properly, and s_2 concerns the situation where both elements are faulty. The arrows represent transitions rates. The rate of transition between s_0 and s_1 is 2λ as both elements can fail. The rate of transition between s_1 and s_2 is only λ as only one element remaining operational can fail. When we enter the so-called absorbing state s_2 it means that the fault is treated as catastrophic and generally it cannot be repaired or a system is treated as non-repairable. On the other hand, it is possible to transit from state s_1 and s_0 with repair rate μ. The reliability function is the probability of being either in states s_0 or s_1. The Markov availability model, adequate for systems where we do not have the absorbing state, and the system is treated as repairable, is given in Figure 4. The only difference for this simple situation is related to the transition from s_2 and s_1 where we consider a possible repair of one of two faulty elements. The availability is the probability of being either in states s_0 or s_1.

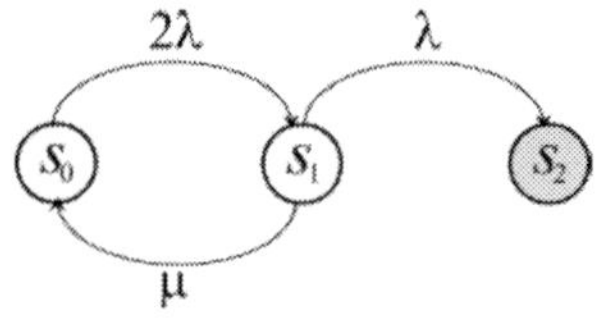

Figure 3. State diagram for Markov chain reliability model.

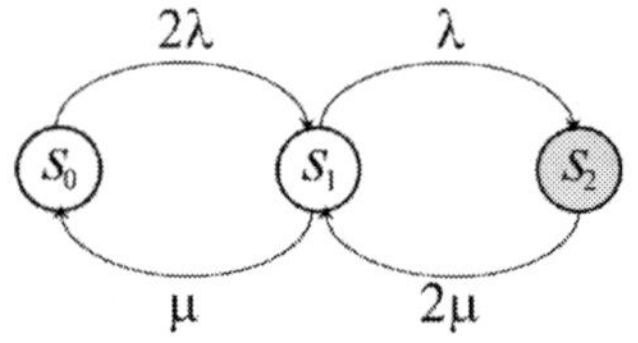

Figure 4. State diagram for Markov chain availability model.

In the case of *MTTF* calculation on the basis of the Markov model, it is necessary to use the reliability model and use the definition formula. The value is easily obtained when the reliability function is trasformed by the the Laplace transform $L\{s\}$. Then, its limit where s tends to 0 gives *MTTF* values [5]. Here, we do not present how to solve Markov models. The methods can be found in the comprehensive bibliography on this topic.

2. Overview of Protection Methods

Before a failure, protected data are transmitted on a working (primary) path. After a failure, the data are switched onto another path (recovery, alternative, backup path) or another segment (or even link) of the path. The recovery path can be established in several ways. It can or cannot be fully disjoint with the working path. Recovery procedures are usually classified depending on the following three criteria (for detailed classification see [6]): the recovery path provisioning method, the level of recovery resources overbooking, and the scope of the procedure. The *link* (or local) methods bypass only a single faulty node or link, whereas the *segment* methods involve larger parts of a path. Its special case, the *global* method (known also as end-to-end or path procedure) safeguards the whole working path. The *protection* procedures are based on recovery paths established in advance, whereas in the *restoration* techniques recovery paths are established or even computed after the failure. Protection switching actions can be more or less predefined but the common feature is that the protection path or the set of possible protection paths is designated while the working path is established. Although a restoration path can be known before a failure occurs, it is more frequently changed and the resources are never reserved until it is necessary.

In *dedicated* (1+1) protection traffic is simultaneously transmitted on the working and recovery paths. The end node selects better signal or rather traffic from a pre-defined path. The working and recovery paths are generally disjoint. In *shared* (M:N) protection working and recovery paths are established before a failure occurrence. In the case of a link failure, data are switched onto one of N recovery paths, but if more than the predefined number of M working paths (usually only one, 1:N) are faulty, some traffic will be lost. Signaling mechanisms are also necessary to enable the coordination. We can also speak of Shared Backup Path Protection (SBPP) in which links of recovery paths are shared among different connections which are not subject to the same single failures.

Ring recovery methods are special cases of dedicated or shared protection [7]. In *Unidirectional Path-Switched Ring* (UPSR) each pair of nodes is connected by two separate paths. These paths do not share any common nodes or links with the exception of the source and sink nodes. Traffic from the source node is transmitted simultaneously in both directions: clockwise on the working path and counterclockwise on the protecting path. The working path is located on a fiber which is different from the fiber carrying the protection path. In the case of any working path element failure, the sink node starts to receive signal from the protecting path. From the reliability standpoint UPSR can be described as dedicated protection. The structure of such a ring is shown in Figure 5.

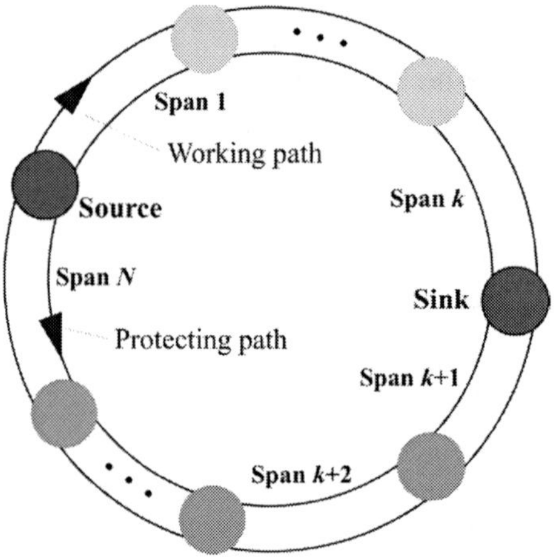

Figure 5. Unidirectional Path-Switched Ring.

In *Bidirectional Line-Switched Ring* (BLSR), the nodes are connected by four fibers (there are also 2-fiber BLSRs, but we do not consider them here). Working traffic in a BLSR can be carried on both directions along the ring, usually on the shorter of the two possible paths. The working connection as well as the protecting connection use separate pairs of fibers.

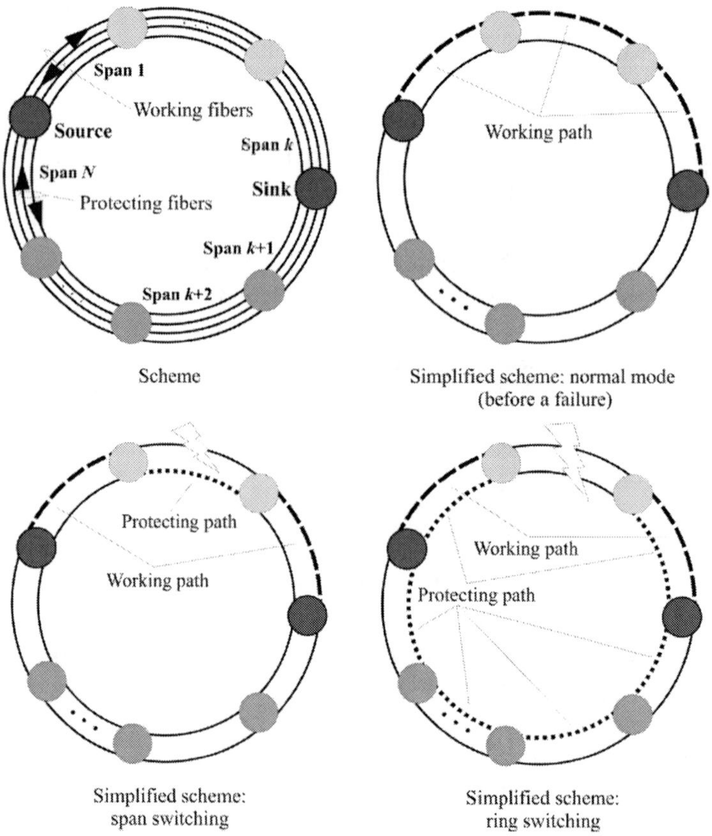

Figure 6. Bidirectional Line-Switched Ring.

The BLSR topology and its behavior during failures are presented in Figure 6. It is important to note that in the case of a failure the BLSR reacts in two ways. Span switching consists in rerouting traffic from the working fibers to the corresponding protecting fibers, i.e., between the same nodes. It is possible that only one of the corresponding fibers fails. Usually, this concerns the situation where only transponders fail because the working and protecting fibers are not disjoint. However, in our analyzes we assume that this is also the case and failures of the corresponding working and protecting fibers are statistically independent. In the case of ring switching which is related to the fault of all four fibers between two nodes, the data are rerouted around the ring on the protecting fibers. From the reliability point of view, BLSR represents the shared method.

p-Cycle is the abbreviation of the technique called *preconfigured protection cycle* [4]. Analogously to rings, *p*-cycles can be treated as protection schemes, because the resources are reserved and allocated before a failure occurs. Unlike rings, they are very flexible. Networks characterized by a high average nodal degree are the ones in which *p*-cycles show their best effectiveness. Therefore, *p*-cycles are best suited to mesh topologies which are perceived as the topologies of next generation networks. A *p*-cycle consists of predefined and pre-allocated spare resources in some spans forming a closed path in a network (Figure 7). There are two types of spans whose failures are recovered by a *p*-cycle: on-cycle spans and straddling spans. In an *on-cycle span* (e.g., link *A-B* in Figure 7), the protected (working) capacity is jointly allocated with spare capacity which forms the *p*-cycle.

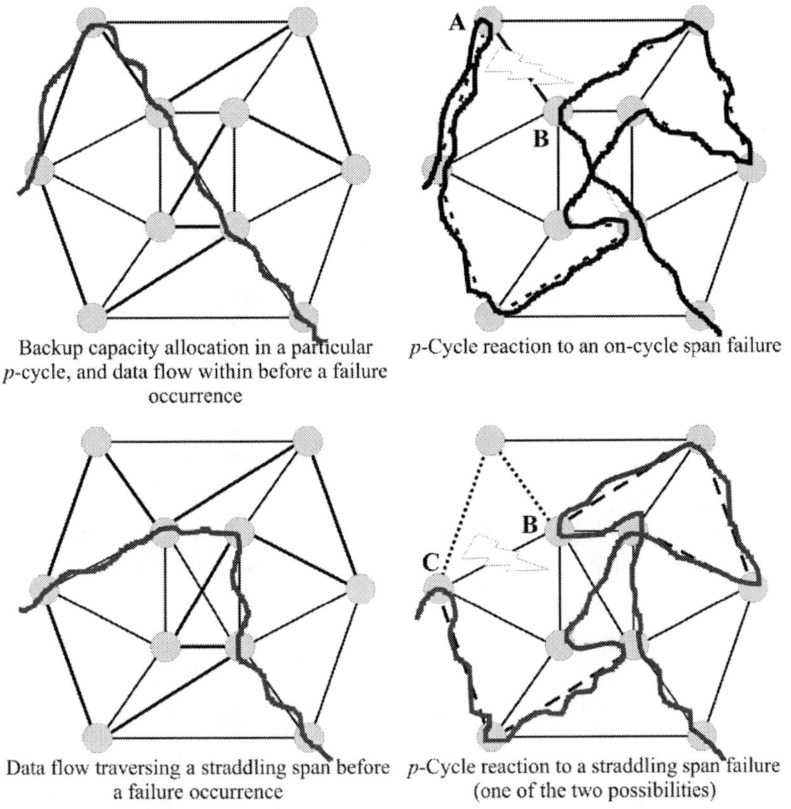

Figure 7. General concept of a p-cycle (based on [4]).

It is not the case with a straddling span. If an on-cycle span fails, the working capacity is recovered due to the usage of the spare capacity in a *p*-cycle. Then the operation of a *p*-cycle is similar to BLSR ring switching. In the case of a *straddling span* failure, two possible recovery paths are provided by a *p*-cycle. A straddling span (e.g., link *C-B* in Figure 7) is a link which does not belong to a *p*-cycle, but two nodes incident to it form a *p*-cycle. It can be seen that the number of straddling spans is responsible for the fact that the redundancy ratio of *p*-cycles is potentially very good.

3. Examples of Modeling

3.1. Example 1: Unprotected Connection

During calculations, it is assumed that the failures of the elements are statistically independent. An unprotected connection consists only of a working path. The recovery (alternative) path is not used. The connection is interrupted when any of its elements fails. Thus, its availability equals simply an availability of a path on which this connection is established. As a path we consider a set of L links/spans and N nodes through which a signal from an input node (source) to an output node (sink) is transmitted. From the reliability standpoint, this is a series structure, i.e., the structure remaining in the operation state only if all of its elements are in the up state. Therefore, the availability of an unprotected path A_U is determined as:

$$A_U = \prod_{i=1}^{L} A_{L_i} \times \prod_{j=1}^{N} A_{N_j}$$

where A_{L_i} is the availability of link/span i; A_{N_j} is the availability of node j.

3.2. Example 2: Dedicated Protection

The simplest protection scheme, dedicated (1+1) protection is shown in Figure 8. From the reliability point of view it is a parallel-series structure with hot standby, because traffic is carried both through the working and the protection paths all the time. The parallel structure means that only if all n paths fail, the connection is down. Therefore, the availability of the whole connection using the dedicated protection A_{1+1} will be calculated as follows:

$$A_{1+1} = A_{So} \times A_{Sp} \times [1 - (1 - A_{WP})(1 - A_{PP})] \times A_{Sw} \times A_{Si}$$

where A_{So}, A_{Si} are the availabilities of the source and sink node, respectively; A_{WP} is the availability of the first path (working path), and A_{PP} is the availability of the second path (protection path); A_{Sp}, A_{Sw} are the availabilities of a splitter and switch, respectively.

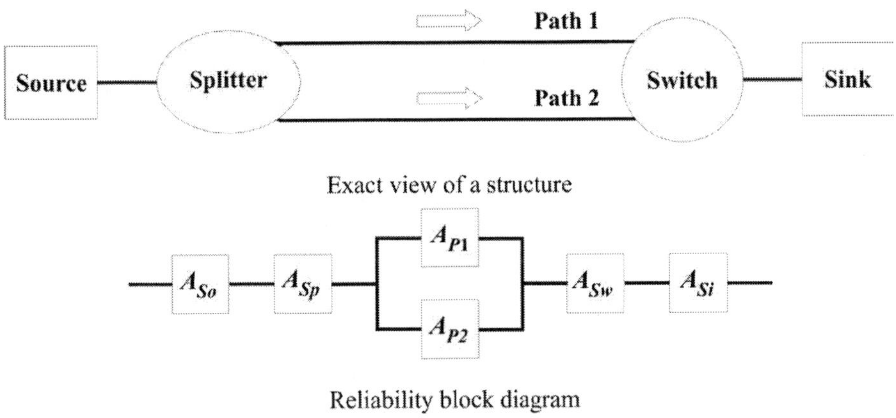

Figure 8. Dedicated protection case.

3.3. Example 3: Unidirectional Path-Switched Ring

Using the example of a Unidirectional Path-Switched Ring (UPSR), a particular case of the dedicated protection, we present how to practically calculate the availability. If we assume that the availabilities of all nodes are equal and each span is of an identical length (which means that also the availabilities of all spans are equal) the availability of a connection between two nodes in a UPSR A_{UPSR} is given by the following formula (cf. the reliability block diagram shown in Figure 9):

$$A_{UPSR} = A_N \times [1 - (1 - A_{WP})(1 - A_{PP})] \times A_N$$
$$= A_N^2 \times \left[1 - \left(1 - \prod_{i=1}^{k} A_S \times \prod_{i=1}^{k-1} A_N\right)\left(1 - \prod_{i=k+1}^{n} A_S \times \prod_{i=k+1}^{n} A_N\right)\right]$$

where A_N, A_S, A_{WP}, A_{PP} are the availabilities of a node, a span, the working and the protection path, respectively; k is the number of spans between source and sink nodes; n is the total number of spans in the ring.

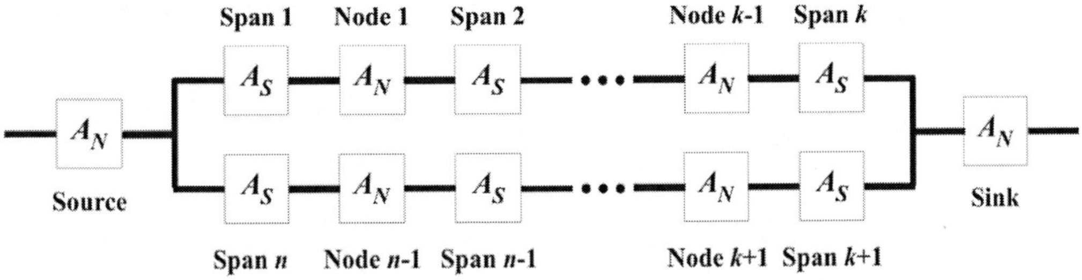

Figure 9. Reliability block diagram for a connection established in UPSR.

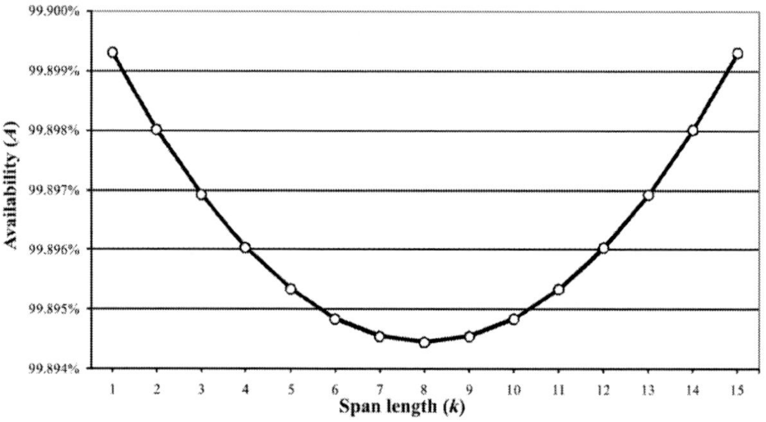

Figure 10. Comparison of connection availabilities in a UPSR.

The availability function achieves its minimum in the case of the connection between the most distant nodes (the nodes which are present at the opposite sides of the ring). Figure 10 illustrates the way the availability is changing depending on the length of the protection path ($A_N = A_S = 99.95\%$, $n = 16$). The graph is symmetrical: the availabilities calculated for connections which can be characterized by span length k are characterized by values equal to those calculated for connections of span length $n-k$. It also means that the connection from X to Y has the same availability as the connection from Y to X.

3.4. Example 4: Shared Protection

Except for the 1:1 protection case, that from the reliability standpoint has the same structure as the 1+1 protection, schemes describing shared protection form non-series-parallel structures (an example: Figure 11). We employ a simplified model which reduces all switches to one. Therefore, it will be possible to apply calculations for the k-out-of-n reliability structure. We will calculate the availability of the 1:N protection scheme $A_{1:N}$, i.e., for the N-out-of-(N + 1) reliability structure. In such a method, one protection path is shared by N working paths. For clarity, we disregard unnecessary details such as the source/sink nodes availability as is commonly practiced. The following formula considers only the availability of the 'parallel' part (serially connected blocks related to the availabilities of source, sink and switches are removed):

$$A_{1:N} = \prod_{i=1}^{N} A_i + \sum_{i=1}^{N} (1 - A_i) \prod_{j \neq i} A_j = \sum_{i=1}^{N} \prod_{j \neq i} A_j - \mathrm{N} \prod_{i=1}^{N+1} A_i$$

where A_i is the availability of path i (A_{N+1} for the protection path).

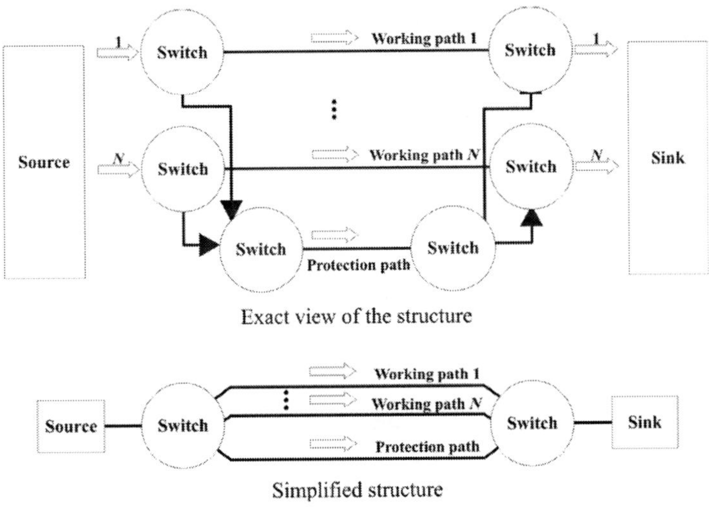

Figure 11. N shared protection.

We take into account N+1 probabilistic events in the state enumeration method: one in which all of N working paths are in the up state, and N similar events in which one (in each event different) of the working paths fails, but all the remaining paths (including the protection one) are up. The availability calculated according to the presented method concerns the probability that the whole protected traffic will be carried properly. We have to remember, however, that even if some working paths and the protection path fail, the rest of the traffic (i.e., that o working paths in the up state) will be transmitted. Therefore, we consider the best case, i.e., the all-terminal availability.

As a numerical example, we compare three different protection topologies: three working connections with the same availabilities are to be protected. The following schemes are compared: the 1:3 protection; the topology in which each working path has its own protection path, it is in fact the 1+1 protection applied three times (six paths in total); and the 3:3 protection (three protection paths shared by three working paths). The complex analytical formula for the last case is based on the 3-out-of-6 structure. The results are presented in Figure 12. We can see that the 1:3 protection results in a large increase of the availability in relation to unprotected connections. The gain is especially visible in the case when availabilities of the working paths are small (even if availabilities of protection paths are relatively low). It is the least reliable but the most cost efficient scheme of the three compared. Moreover, from the reliability point of view, the 3:3 protection is the most favorable, even better than applying the 1+1 protection for each working path separately. The reason is that in the case of the 3:3 protection the scheme is more flexible. When one of the working paths fails, the traffic is rerouted on the protection path. And again, when this path fails, the traffic can be rerouted again. It is impossible in the case of the 1+1 protection.

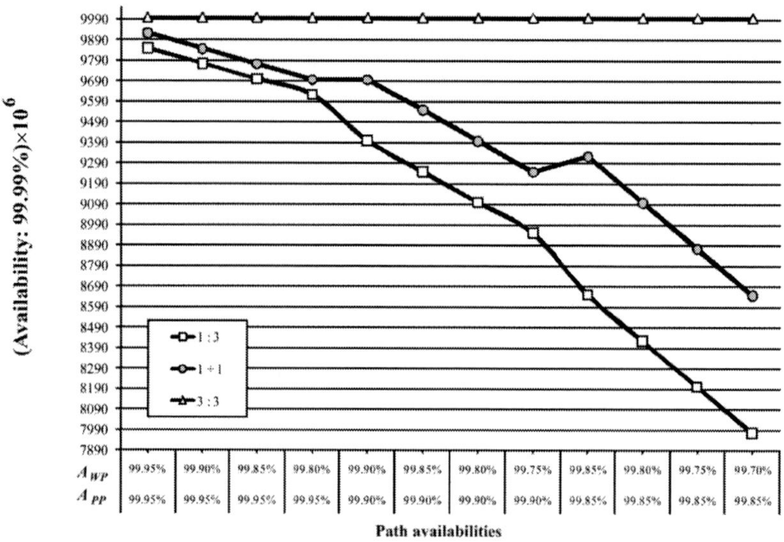

Figure 12. Comparison of three example protection schemes.

Although in the presented example the 3:3 connection seems to be the most promising from the reliability viewpoint, we should note that it is far more expensive than the 1:3 protection. This is the main reason why, generally, the 1:*N* protection is used much more often than the *M*:*N* protection. To show that the usage of the latter scheme is doubtful we can use a more clear presentation than that on the basis of the availability analysis. If all paths have the same exponential distribution of the failure function with failure rate λ (here we follow the presentation given in [8]) and if, additionally, the cost of each path is identical and equals θ, we can see that the Mean Time to Failure values of both schemes are very similar. For 1:*N* protection *MTTF* is given by the following equation:

$$MTTF_{1:N} = MTTF_{N|N+1} = \sum_{i=N}^{N+1} \frac{1}{i\lambda} = \frac{2N+1}{N(N+1)\lambda}$$

with the cost of recovery equal to $\theta_{1:N} = \theta$ while for 2:*N* protection *MTTF* can be calculated as:

$$MTTF_{2:N} = MTTF_{N|N+2} = \sum_{i=N}^{N+2} \frac{1}{i\lambda} = \frac{3N^2+7N+2}{N(N+1)(N+2)\lambda}$$

with the cost of redundancy at least twice as high as for 1:*N* case: $\theta_{2:N} \geq 2\theta$. Meanwhile, the ratio of *MTTF*s amounts to:

$$\rho(N) = \frac{MTTF_{2:N}}{MTTF_{1:N}} = \frac{3N+1}{2N+1}$$

We can see that in exchange for the doubled recovery cost: $\rho(1) = \frac{4}{3} \approx 1.33$, $\rho(2) = \frac{7}{5} = 1.4$, and for values of N large enough, it tends to: $\rho(\infty) = \frac{3}{2} = 1.5$. Practically, it should be remembered that the situation is more advantageous for the 1:N protection since the presented modeling describes only the case when failures are not repaired and, additionally, the cost of the next recovery path is usually higher because it is another path in a network, often longer than the paths chosen as a working and a first backup ones. On the other hand, the resources reserved in alternative paths can be used before a failure occurrence to convey some extra traffic which makes their usage cheaper.

3.5. Example 5: Bidirectional Protection Rings vs. *p*-Cycles

Since the preconfigured protection cycles (*p*-cycles) resilience technique was proposed quite recently, not much effort has been devoted to *p*-cycles reliability analysis. In [9] and in this chapter, a novel approach based on the *MTTF* analysis which is more precise than the reliability/availability studies performed earlier is presented. First, we derive formulas for the reliability function. It is the most generalized formula. Then, on this basis the availability is calculated. Subsequently, *Mean Time to Failure* models are applied. To present the influence of failures on network operation we will transform the availability values into so-called *Expected Loss of Traffic ELT*. It represents the average value of traffic which is lost during a year as a result of failures. It is expressed in units like OC-*n* (*Optical Carrier level n*) hours per year [10]. To simplify the formulas and calculations, we take some common assumptions, which is usually the case in any reliability assessment: failures of two links (even located between the same nodes, possibly in different conduits) are supposed to be statistically independent. This is not always the case, but it considerably simplifies the analysis and does not influence the generality of the results. We want to obtain closed-form formulas which can be used so as to draw practical conclusions concerning planning of *p*-cycles. In our model we assume that a span refers to a conduit in which many links, i.e., fibers with different lightpaths, can be laid. All lightpaths within a span are subject to common failures: if a span is faulty, all of them are simultaneously disconnected. 4-fiber versions of BLSR are resilient to transponder failures. However, to sustain the simplicity and clarity of the models we do not consider such failures here. Thus, we consider only total span and total node failures. Here, a pair of bidirectional fibers (or links of another type) is considered as a span. Therefore, from the reliability viewpoint, we do not distinguish *p*-cycles whose spans consist of two bidirectional fibers from these whose spans consist of one unidirectional fiber. For each span we determine the reliability function as: $\bigwedge_i r_{span\,i}(t) \equiv r_s(t)$. Where $r_s(t)$ is calculated as the mean value of all reliabilities resulting from lengths of the spans. Hence, a single average reliability function is used for all spans. Instead of the average value, we can also use the worst value: $\bigwedge_i r_{span\,i}(t) \equiv \min_i r_{span\,i}(t)$. Owing to it, we could calculate the lower bound. In the case of reliability/availability calculations we use the state enumeration method, i.e., all events fostering up states are listed and the sum of their probabilities is calculated. In the case of *MTTF* calculation, we model the behavior of a system as a continuous time Markov chain, where states are related to different failure situations. We assume that failure as well as repair processes are memoryless and we take into consideration failure/repair intensities in appropriate transitions. Thus, we use the homogeneous Markov chains. *p*-Cycles can be constructed on the basis of (optical) add-drop multiplexers (typically used in ring architectures) as well as of digital/optical cross-connects (on which mesh architectures are based); thus, in the reliability analysis of *p*-cycles, 'node' refers to (O)ADM as well as to DXC/OXC. We do not take into consideration the direction of the fibers in the pair of working fibers, i.e., we assume that both are located in a single cable/span. Therefore, both directions are fully correlated from the failure viewpoint.

The all-terminal reliability for a BLSR is related to the probability that every node can receive data from any of the others from the working path or in the case of a failure(s) from the protecting path. All nodes are connected when all nodes are up (factor indicated as (a)) and when one of the following statements is true:

- (b) all fibers are operational,
- (c) exactly one span is faulty, and all other spans are operational.

Therefore, we can derive the all-terminal reliability formula for BLSR as:

$$R_B(t) = \underbrace{r_n^N(t)}_{(a)} \times \left\{ \underbrace{r_s^N(t)}_{(b)} + \underbrace{N[1 - r_s(t)]r_s^{N-1}(t)}_{(c)} \right\}$$

where N stands for the number of nodes, and $r_n(t)$ for the node reliability.

In [11] different situations of how dual failures affect the *p*-cycle recovery were considered. Generally, if the maximum sharing is applied, all dual/triple, etc., failures are related to the loss of connectivity of some nodes i.e., some working capacity cannot be properly recovered. All nodes in a *p*-cycle are connected when all nodes are up (factor indicated as (a)) and one of the following statements is true:

- (b) all spans, i.e., on-cycle as well as straddling ones, are operational;
- (c) exactly one of the on-cycle spans is faulty and other on-cycle spans and all straddling spans are operational;
- (d) exactly one of the straddling spans is faulty and other straddling spans are operational and all on-cycle spans are operational.

The formula for the all-terminal reliability for a *p*-cycle is also dependent on the number of straddling spans L as follows:

$$R_P(k,t) = \underbrace{r_n^N(t)}_{(a)} \times \left\{ \underbrace{r_s^{N+L}(t)}_{(b)} + \underbrace{N \times [1 - r_s(t)]r_s^{N+L-1}(t)}_{(c)} + \underbrace{L \times [1 - r_s(t)]r_s^{N+L-1}(t)}_{(d)} \right\}$$

As was said above, to calculate *MTTF* we will need state space models instead of combinatorial ones used above. Here, we present the methodology of calculations and not the final formulas as they are, generally, very long. Instead, we present matrices related to the presented Markov models. On this basis, the final formulas can be obtained. The methodology will be shown by using an example of the simplest model, i.e., *MTTF* of a system which is here an all-terminal BLSR. To obtain the formula describing the *Mean Time to Failure* for a BLSR when repairs are taken into account, a Markov model of failure states, presented in Figure 13, will be used. In the Markov model we assume that it is impossible to have more than a double failure in a network. This allows us to have a relatively small state space. The influence of triple, quadruple, etc. failures is negligible. Therefore, we do not consider any transitions related to triple and higher order failures. The system behavior can be modeled as a homogeneous Markov chain, because the exponential time between failures is justified and the assumption of the exponential repair time is also a common practice. Let us denote the states in the model presented in Figure 13: s_0 is the state where all spans and nodes are operational. It is an initial state, i.e., the state in which the system starts to work (also, in all other cases discussed below, $s0$ refers to an initial state). s_1 is the state where only one of the spans is faulty and the others are operational, as well as all nodes are up. Other states are not shown, although transitions to these absorbing states are presented: one, from the non-failure state when a node goes down, and another, from the one span failure state when any other failure happens. There are also transitions between s_0 and s_1. The intensity of the transition from s_0 to s_1 equals $N\lambda_s$, where λ_s represents the failure intensity of a single span and it can be expressed as a reciprocal of its average $MTTF_{span}$ (i.e., *Mean Time to Failure* of a single span) value:

$$\lambda_s = \frac{1}{MTTF_{span}}$$

The intensity of transition from s_1 to s_0, μ_s, is the repair intensity of a single span. λ_n represents a node failure intensity.

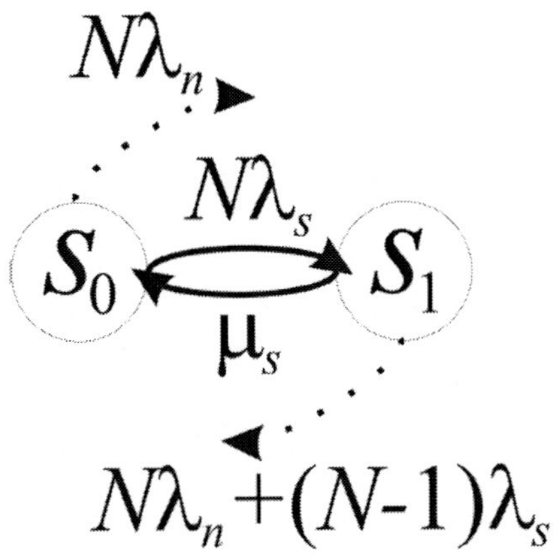

Figure 13. Markov reliability model related to the all-terminal reliability of a BLSR.

Similar models are also used to calculate the availability. The model presented here is simple, and can be used only to obtain *MTTF*. It non-explicitly treats the shown states as absorbing ones, because we would like to know when a BLSR fails for the first time, i.e., when for the first time it will not be able to recover the whole working capacity, that is it is treated as a non-repairable system. Finally, the value can be obtained:

$$MTTF_B = \frac{N\lambda_n + (2N-1)\lambda_s + \mu_s}{(N\lambda_n + N\lambda_s) \times [N\lambda_n + (N-1)\lambda_s + \mu_s] - N\lambda_s\mu_s}$$

Formulas for *MTTF* are generally very large and complex. For the next case, the all-terminal *MTTF* for a *p*-cycle ($MTTF_P$), we present only a simplified model (Figure 14) and the state descriptions: s_0 is the initial state where everything works properly, s_1 is the state where one on-cycle span is faulty, s_2 is the state where one straddling span is faulty. A more detailed model along with models for the two-terminal case can be found in [9].

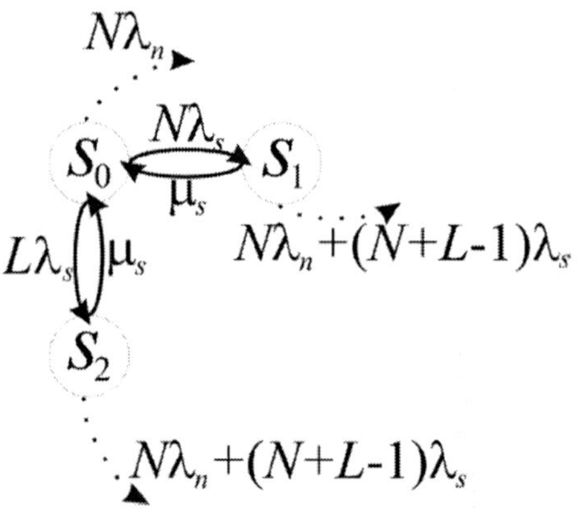

Figure 14. Markov reliability model related to the all-terminal reliability of a p-cycle.

Now, the derived formulas are used to present some values which can be used as an assessment of the recovery based on *p*-cycles. In the steady state, we have the relation:

$$MTBF = MTTF + MTTR$$

where: *MTTR* is the *Mean Time to Repair* and *MTBF* represents *Mean Time Between Failures*. It can be useful as an input in some studies, because its value can be obtained on the basis of statistical studies derived from the data collected by operators, i.e., the frequency of cable cuts. Let *CC* (cable cuts parameter, measured in kilometers) represents the average length of a fiber which is cut once a year. Provided it is known, the value of *MTBF* (in hours) of a fiber, which is *l* km long, can be calculated according to the following relation [10]:

$$MTBF = \frac{CC \times 365 \times 24}{l}$$

We apply the availability models to the reliability formulas derived above. We use the steady-state availability, *A*. If the availability of a cable substitutes function $r_s(t)$ in the formulas describing the reliability (a similar procedure is performed with the node availability), the formula for the steady-state availability will be obtained. To illustrate the influence of failures on the whole *p*-cycle operation, *Expected Loss of Traffic* (*ELT*) in OC-*n* hours per year will be calculated as follows (if the protected capacity equals the capacity of OC-*n*) [10]:

$$ELT = (1 - A) \times 365 \times 24$$

Here, we calculated $MTTF_P$ and ELT for different values of N, L, CC, l and $MTTR$. We took into account the following two cases:

1. where we have generally shorter span lengths, e.g., in MANs or/and in networks crossing areas with dense building development (smaller values of CC, l and $MTTR$), and
2. long-haul networks, where CC, l and $MTTR$ values are appropriately larger.

The values obtained by operators or suitable regulatory bodies can be found, e.g., in [4,10]. The description of the calculated values is given according to a pair (N, L). The values are shown in Figure 15.

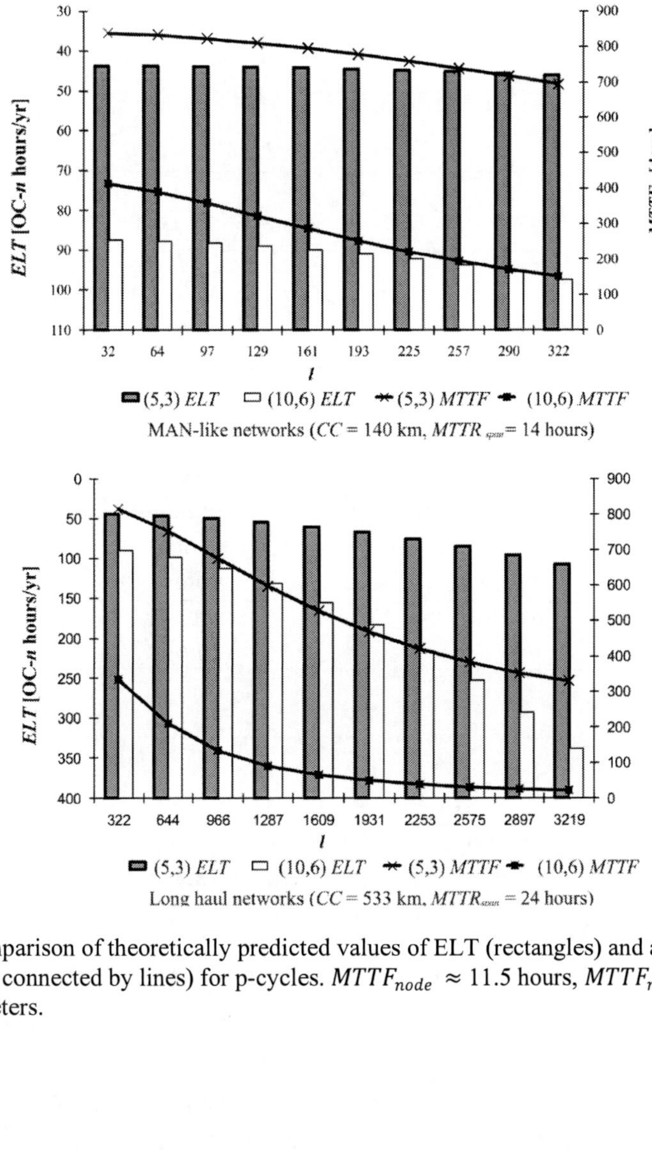

Figure 15. Comparison of theoretically predicted values of ELT (rectangles) and all-terminal $MTTF_P$ (points connected by lines) for p-cycles. $MTTF_{node}$ ≈ 11.5 hours, $MTTF_{node}$ ≈ = 6 hours. l is given in kilometers.

The comparison of all-terminal availabilities between BLSR and *p*-cycles is given in Figure 16 that *p*-cycles can be described by values worse than those characteristic of protection rings. It is apparent that a BLSR is related to the large resilience, while a *p*-cycle is much worse. Obviously, the availability decreases with the growing number of nodes and straddling spans. In Figure 17 we can see that although the large number of straddling spans is attractive, each next straddling span considerably decreases the all-terminal availability for a *p*-cycle.

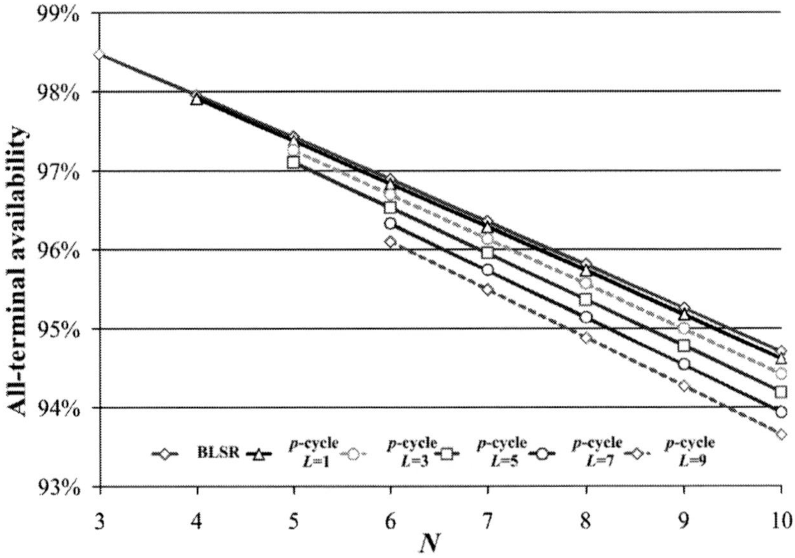

Figure 16. All-terminal availability of protection rings and p-cycles as a function of the number of nodes.

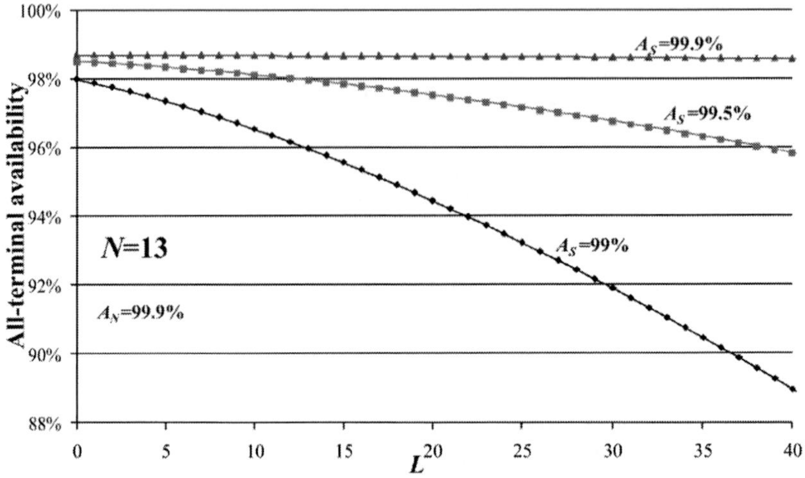

Figure 17. All-terminal availability of a p-cycle with 13 on-cycle spans as a function of the number of straddling spans.

4. Conclusion

In this chapter the introduction to the reliability theory is presented along with some methodologies to predict basic reliability measures in communications networks. Then, a few examples of modeling are given to show how this modeling works. The most comprehensive example concerns *p*-cycles, a recovery method suitable for mesh networks of the future.

5. Problems to Solve

1 Calculate the availability of the 2+1 structure Markov availability model (with known parameters λ, μ.

2 Find analytically the minimum of the availability of UPSR A_{UPSR} for identical span availabilities (treated as a variable).

3. Calculate the availability of the 1:N structure (Figure11) using its exact structure. Hint: use the enumeration method.
4. Use formulas for reliability functions for a selected network reported in the literature, and calculate values for the average case, where $\Lambda_i\, r_{span_i}(t) \equiv r_s(t)$ and for the pessimistic case, where $\Lambda_i\, r_{span_i}(t) \equiv \min_i r_{span_i}(t)$. Then, obtain also the upper bounds, using: $\Lambda_i\, r_{span_i}(t) \equiv \max_i r_{span_i}(t)$.

References

[1] *Terms and Definitions Related to Quality of Service and Network Performance Including Dependabilit*; ITU-T Recommendation E.800, 1994.

[2] R.E. Barlow, F. Proschan, L.C. Hunter, *Mathematical Theory of Reliability*, John Wiley and Sons, Inc.: New York, NY, 1965.

[3] K.S. Trivedi, *Probability and Statistics with Reliability, Queuing, and Computer Science Applications*, John Wiley and Sons, Inc.: New York, NY, 2001.

[4] W. Grover, *Mesh-Based Survivable Networks*, Prentice Hall PTR: Upper Saddle River, NJ, 2004.

[5] M.L. Shooman, *Reliability of Computer Systems and Networks*, John Wiley and Sons, Inc.: New York, NY, 2002.

[6] P. Cholda, A. Mykkeltveit, B.E. Helvik, O.J. Wittner, A. Jajszczyk, A Survey of Resilience Differentiation Frameworks in Communication Networks, *IEEE Comm. Surv. Tut.,* 2007, vol. 9, no. 4, 32-55.

[7] R. Ramasvami, K.N. Sivarajan, Optical Networks: *A Practical Perspective*, Morgan Kaufmann Publishers: San Francisco, CA, 2002.

[8] G. Bernstein, B. Rajagopalan, D. Saha, *Optical Network Control*, Addison-Wesley: Boston, MA, 2004.

[9] P. Cholda, A. Jajszczyk, Reliability Assessment of Optical p-Cycles, *IEEE/ACM Transactions on Networking*, 2007, vol. 15, no. 6, 1579-1592.

[10] J.P. Vasseur, M. Pickavet, P. Demeester, *Network Recovery*, Morgan Kaufmann Publishers: San Francisco, CA, 2004.

[11] D.A. Schupke, *The Tradeoff Between the Number of Deployed p-Cycles and the Survivability to Dual Fiber Duct Failures,* Proc. ICC 2003, IEEE: Anchorage, AK, 2003.

INDEX

A

B

C

D

E

F

G

H

I

J

L

M

N

O

P

Q

R

S

T

U

V

W

Y